Police Leadership

Rising to the Top

Police Leadership

Rising to the Top

Edited by

Jenny Fleming

OXFORD
UNIVERSITY PRESS

UNIVERSITY PRESS

Great Clarendon Street, Oxford, OX2 6DP,
United Kingdom

Oxford University Press is a department of the University of Oxford.
It furthers the University's objective of excellence in research, scholarship,
and education by publishing worldwide. Oxford is a registered trade mark of
Oxford University Press in the UK and in certain other countries

© Oxford University Press 2015

The moral rights of the authors have been asserted

First Edition published in 2015

Impression: 1

Published in the United States of America by Oxford University Press
198 Madison Avenue, New York, NY 10016, United States of America

British Library Cataloguing in Publication Data
Data available

Library of Congress Control Number: 2015934835

ISBN 978–0–19–872862–7

Printed and bound by
Lightning Source UK Ltd

Foreword

Throughout my career as a police officer and especially a chief officer, I have attended leadership courses and conferences to be told that there never had been a time of such change in policing. Well, I would contend that those periods were but minor squalls compared to the whirlwind that policing is going through as this timely work is published.

I joined the police in 1981 and then saw 30 years of almost constant growth in funding and, looking back, relative stability in the way the public and politicians regarded the role of the police and the certainty of the range of operational challenges we faced. General elections came and went, with politicians competing as to who could promise the greater growth in police officer numbers and all making crime and punishment one of the key election issues. There was little challenge to the orthodoxy of crime figures being the key measure of police effectiveness and the view that the dominant police task was bringing more offenders to justice.

In the ten years after the turn of the millennium there was a particular growth in spending and a conviction that more police officers were a guarantee of police effectiveness. There was also a move to greater central control of policing through national statistical targets and, crucially, comparison and competition. In the same period there was a growth in the range of police specialisms and a more functional approach was embraced. The doctrine of the public as customers was reinforced with customer charters and policing pledges. This was something which swept across the public sector as part of what was then termed 'New Public Management'.

The austerity budget in 2010 delivered a severe electric shock to policing. The almost unquestioning political view of more spending equalling better policing was demolished overnight. Long-term significant budget reductions which at the time of writing have seen a reduction of over 40,000 staff appeared on the horizon. Further reductions were assured. Many officers felt bereft, if not betrayed by what they regarded as a loss of appreciation and value for the policing role and the realities of life on front-line operations. They hoped it would just be 'a few bad years' but their sense of isolation was reinforced when policing and crime hardly featured at all as an issue in the 2015 General Election.

I certainly do not regard this as being 'a few bad years'. The most perfunctory examination of the state of the public finances, the impact of the ageing population, the hole in pension provision and the structural deficit say this is far more profound. In addition to those economic circumstances, however, I would argue there is a fundamental questioning of the effectiveness of the traditional law-enforcement model, a realisation that just feeding more and more into the prison population creates a huge social cost and that however you target police patrol, the public as a whole do not notice any significant difference.

The most fundamental challenge to the accepted orthodoxy was undoubtedly the continued reduction of crime across North America and Europe largely oblivious to either economic recession or growth or different policing strategies. The bluff of many police leaders over the years was well and truly called when crime continued to fall despite one of the most severe recessions in UK history and the sharpest reduction in police officer numbers. Broadly, the public has not noticed the difference and has no great appetite for increased taxes to fund more law enforcement.

This new paradigm has tested to the limit the abilities of police leaders and policymakers and the traditional police structures and processes of decision-making. Policing is facing the sort of fundamental challenge to its 'market', customer base and income stream that traditional manufacturing and service industries saw from foreign competition and new technology in the sixties and seventies. Many of the companies in those industries disappeared, unable to react with sufficient speed and innovation; incapable of changing their leadership and organisational cultures and the skill base of their workforce with the speed that the tide was coming in.

The range of challenges facing policing are too long to list but are characterized by their complexity, their interconnection, and their volatility. Change is so rapid that the very nature of how organisations design and manage change has itself to change. The constant turmoil and uncertainty is unnerving for staff, many of whom joined policing because of its certainty, stability, and security. This of itself creates new challenges for accepted notions of police leadership and the traditional hierarchical paternalistic models.

If members of the police service saw the constant reductions in budget as a form of betrayal they at least hoped for a degree of public lowering of expectations, some softening of accountability, and perhaps some increase in police powers to compensate for less financial resources. Again, the movement has been in the opposite direction. Politicians, the public, and media have shown an aversion to any greater erosion of privacy, and a range of police powers such as the retention of DNA and use of bail have been put under greater scrutiny and oversight. The holding of misconduct hearings in public, the prevention of officers retiring while under investigation, and the extension of liability to include retired officers are signs of exasperation with what many see as the lack of accountability in the police complaints system. At the same time, the greater use of social media and the capability of the public to record encounters with the police has brought many troubling incidents of police misconduct to the public gaze in the UK. What in the past may have been a turning of a blind eye to the methods officers used to keep the 'bad guys' under control has become a thirst for greater openness and visibility which is constantly moving ahead of the Service.

A change in social attitudes has also seen a fundamental public intolerance towards violence in relationships, child sexual exploitation, and abuse of the vulnerable. This has fundamentally impacted on the performance conversation in police forces, the range of skills staff need, and the make-up of the demand forces are experiencing. Leaders now look back in bewilderment, if not shame, at the focus given previously to more easy-to-measure matters such as vehicle crime where small percentage movements in recording were pored over in such great detail. A Service which now sees its focus as protecting vulnerable people rather than cutting crime starts to question the viability of the traditional law enforcement model and whether the skills required actually fit better with the training and expertise of other professions.

One of the reactions to constant funding reduction is a renewed focus on demand reduction and a shift from the speed and quality of reaction to incidents to problem solving and eliminating 'repeat business'. It starts to highlight the enormous cost and often ineffectiveness of what feels like an industry of referral processes, case conferences, and organisational silos. It puts into sharp focus the way that the Service has been drawn into responsibilities that its staff do not have the professional background to deal with. It questions why, when so many crises in people's lives happen at night and at weekends, many of the 'caring' and crisis-intervention services work office hours.

Research and our own experience has taught us time and time again that a large proportion of public service demand comes from a relatively small number of families and individuals who sadly often have their futures mapped out for them before birth. 'Attachment theory' has long shown the impact on brain development of babies growing up in the midst of domestic violence and lack of affection. Other research points to how the abused often become abusers themselves. Many children in the criminal justice system, it could be argued, are being punished for the impact of the very upbringing they had no control over. This need to get 'upstream', to use the jargon, is creating the momentum to challenge the way public services are designed and has many forces moving from structures and processes of partnership with other agencies to new models of integrated services, pooled budgets, and devolution to allow this local join-up.

If this was not enough, a further element of the whirlwind of change has been the change in the nature of governance. The introduction of police and crime commissioners and increasingly city mayors has brought a fundamental shift in the nature of governance, the influence of politicians, and the notion of operational independence. It is probably still too early to assess the full impact of this but again many in the police service have resented this greater political oversight and have failed to see it as part of a more general movement of politicians having more day-to-day control of the delivery of public services, as for instance is so evident in local government and, I would argue, the Civil Service. This challenge to traditional power bases and the degree of political acumen required is proving difficult to many police leaders but has a lot further to travel yet.

When you collect all of this together—without taking into consideration the growth of extremism, the impact of conflicts in other parts of the world, the tensions over immigration, and the growing inequality and lack of cohesion in UK society—there emerges a daunting challenge to those aspiring to rise to the top of policing. It even challenges the very notion of what the 'top' is, given that part of the debate is a challenge to the dominance of hierarchy and rank in traditional police organisations barely questioned since the dawn of modern policing. I will not go into wider changes we are seeing in the world of work such as portfolio careers, the ending of the notion of a job for life, and the impact of digitalisation but what is remarkable is how little they have affected policing up to now; but it has done our workforce few favours that it has been protected for so long.

The current senior leaders in policing came through the years of funding growth where, certainly in middle management, effectiveness was largely judged against the ability to deliver on statistical targets. Such a culture favoured trans-actional rather than transformational leadership styles and at its worst only encouraged innovation and challenge when that innovation and challenge improved the figures. There has not been the reform of the means of reward and recognition seen in other parts of the public services. Rather, we have what is seen as a slowing down of the pace with which talented people get to the 'top' and, as I have pointed out above, little change to the traditional structure and notions of command and control. There have not been the developments in internal 'democracy' seen in the most successful private-sector organisations and often communication is one-way.

The Service is encumbered with a rigid, over-bureaucratic complaints and misconduct system which means that police organisations deal with internal incidents and internal conflict as a police force, not as a modern employer. Recent developments have arguably strengthened the blame culture rather than creating one of 'lessons learned', and there has been little impact on public confidence in the system overall.

It is in this context that the struggle of the Police Service to embrace diversity and its difficult history on race issues has to be seen. When viewed in terms of representation and progression of ethnic minorities, current employment law combined with the continued reduction in workforce means the Service will continue to lag far behind where it needs to be. There are more fundamental issues for leadership, however, on how to create a culture and workforce model which values rather than restricts different approaches, personalities, and philosophies. In the past, staff have been seen in terms of their rank or grade and whether they are a warrant holder or not. Future leaders must see each member of staff as an individual whose skills and experience must be drawn out and utilized, and work-force structures and a system's reward and recognition must support that.

Increasing complexity and higher standards of accountability and public expectation, and sadly a number of notorious cases such as the Yorkshire Ripper, the Hillsborough disaster, and the murder of Stephen Lawrence, have moved the Service to adopt accredited standards of expertise, competence, and experience.

No longer does the attainment of a rank confer the ability to lead a serious investigation or firearms operation. Staff have been required to adopt the characteristics of other professionals without policing itself having the features expected of most professions such as a bedrock of evidence-based practice and an engrained professional ethic. The creation of the College of Policing in 2012 was a significant step on that journey, but, as the *Leadership Review*, its first significant publication, demonstrated, there is still a long way to go if the distinction between leadership development and professional expertise development is fully accepted and adopted.

All this may seem rather gloomy, but the Police Service has enormous strengths and recent years have seen some of the highest levels of public confidence in policing undented by more negative coverage in the mainstream media. At the start of my policing career, the dominant attitude I experienced was that the public were at best an inconvenience, at worst 'the enemy'. In the West Midlands Police of that time (now transformed) there was a siege mentality and in certain areas police activity felt like the incursions of an invading force that infiltrated, made its capture, and then quickly withdrew. The introduction of Police Community Support Officers in 2002 and the wholesale adoption of neighbourhood policing has led to engagement and involvement with the public and a sophisticated understanding of community dynamics. There is in my view a remarkable commitment to working with local people and community groups to address fundamental issues of deprivation and alienation most strongly evident in the most deprived and traditionally alienated areas.

The greatest strength the Service has is the remarkable dedication, compassion, and humanity of its workforce and its 'can do' attitude. It is easy to criticize the front-line police culture, but its ability to deal with such a complex range of operational incidents, traumas, social problems, and the very worst life can do to people is remarkable. We take the routinely unarmed status of UK policing as a given. It is only when you look at the situation in most other countries where those armed with bladed weapons or exhibiting irrational violent behaviour due to mental illness are shot dead by police officers on a daily basis, that the restraint, expertise, and courage of British police officers can be seen as quite extraordinary. In moving forward and adapting to this very changed situation it is crucial that we retain the ability of the Service to react quickly and decisively, to advance into danger when others are running away, and to continue to be that agency of last resort when others have given up.

So those aspiring to rise to the 'top' in the future have a daunting challenge ahead of them. There are lessons to be learnt from the past from leaders who have succeeded, but for much of the territory aspiring leaders are heading for there are no maps; no past practice to draw upon, for these are uncharted lands. On top of the core values, well accepted as the bedrock that all successful leaders must build upon, future police leaders must see themselves rather as public service leaders able to work with other professions to use the full range of disciplines to tackle entrenched social problems. It will be more likely that they will move in and out of policing to get the full range of experience and to broaden their vision. They will need to be highly skilled at handling political relationships and at mastering a constantly evolving world of new digital media. They will need the skills to master far higher standards of transparency and accountability and to mould organisations with an unquestioning commitment to professional ethics. They will need to be entrepreneurs and innovators, able to reimagine how policing is delivered and the way police organisations are structured and operate, and able to rethink the traditional power bases and hierarchy of police forces.

Future leaders will need to be secure on how far their own expertise can take them, and skilled at drawing together and making the best use of the expertise of others in their team and indeed outside the team. They will need to be coaches, mentors, coordinators, conductors, coxes, and much less commanders or parents. Above all, they will need to be self-aware and personally resilient and committed to living out through their own personal example the values and leadership behaviours they expect of others. The task of responding to these challenges will fall squarely on the shoulders of policing leaders, and they will need all the help they can get. Help is out there and this book is but one example. We can benefit from the advice of academics (provided they take the time to write for practitioners and not just for themselves). Here, much valuable research is synthesized in an accessible way. We can also draw on our experience. It is true that the lessons of the past will be an inexact guide. We cannot simply transplant yesterday into today. But we can look at the challenges that have confronted police leadership over the past decade and ask which bits of that experience we can use.

Remarkable people have contributed to this work; leaders who have made their own mark on policing and continue to do so. They have risen to the top more than anything because of the way they have inspired others and combined great intellectual strength with humanity and that commitment to ensuring that the future generation is better than the current one. This work is also a welcome strengthening of the bond between policing and academic research and learning, and demonstrates the potential productivity of such partnerships. This has to be one of the key features of the police profession of the future, able to master this new world of greater uncertainty and upheaval through the strength of its arguments and its commitment to evidence-based professional practice, but underpinned by a professional ethic infused with the best of the past.

Sir Peter Fahy
Chief Constable, Greater Manchester Police
June 2015

Acknowledgements

I incurred a number of debts while editing this book. The greatest debt is to the contributors both academic and practitioner who participated willingly, fully, and were always generous with their time and patience in the face of what one contributor politely called my 'hands-on editorship'. Without their significant contributions and cooperation there would be no book. Special thanks to Sara Thornton, Peter Fahy, and Denis O'Connor for the preliminary discussions that helped shape this collection. Many colleagues, contributors, and friends have assisted with the 'thinking' of this book—in particular, Rod Rhodes, Peter Daniell, and Mark Kilgallon—thank you. I am of course responsible for any errors of fact or judgement. Thanks to Lucy from Oxford University Press for her enthusiasm for the project and to Matthew in Production for his always polite forbearance.

To Rod for all these things and more.

Contents

Contents

Abbreviations

ACPO	Association of Chief Police Officers
ACPOS	Association of Chief Police Officers in Scotland
ASB	anti-social behaviour
BAWP	British Association for Women in Policing
BCS	British Crime Survey
BCU	borough command unit
CEO	chief executive officer
Centrex	Central Police Training and Development Authority
CEOP	Child Exploitation and On-line Protection Centre
CEPS	Centre of Excellence in Policing and Security
CIPD	Chartered Institute of Personnel and Development
CIPFA	Chartered Institute of Public Finance and Accountancy
CPD	continual professional development
CSEW	Crime Survey for England and Wales
CSR	comprehensive spending review
DCI	detective chief inspector
DCLG	Department for Communities and Local Government
DTS	Detective Training School
EHRC	Equality and Human Rights Commission
EI	emotional intelligence
FTE	full time equivalent
GDP	gross domestic product
GED	gender equality duty
HET	Historic Enquiries Team (Northern Ireland)
HMIC	Her Majesty's Inspectors of Constabulary
HPDS	High Potential Development Scheme
IED	improvised explosive device
IFS	Institute for Fiscal Studies
IOM	integrated offender management
IPCC	Independent Police Complaints Commission
IT	information technology
MASH	multi agency safeguarding hub
MPS	Metropolitan Police Service
NAO	National Audit Office
NAPAC	National Association for People Abused in Childhood
NCA	National Crime Agency
NIPB	Northern Ireland Policing Board
NMA	neighbourhood management area
NNDR	national non-domestic rates

NPIA	Central Police Training and Development Authority
NPRP	National Police Reform Programme
NPRT	National Police Reform Team
NPT	National Police Training
NSPCC	National Society for the Prevention of Cruelty to Children
NSY	New Scotland Yard
OFSCT	Office for Security and Counter Terrorism
OIC	officer in charge
ONS	Office for National Statistics
PACE	Police and Criminal Evidence Act 1984
PACT	Police and Community Together
PAF	police allocation formula
PCC	police and crime commissioner
PCSO	police community support officer
PITO	Police Information Technology Organisation
POP	problem-orientated policing
PRG	Police Research Group
PSC	Police Staff College
PSNI	Police Service of Northern Ireland
RCT	randomized control trials
RSG	revenue support grant
RUC	Royal Ulster Constabulary
SCC	Strategic Command Course
SIO	senior investigating officer
SIPR	Scottish Institute for Policing Research
SOPs	standard operating procedures
SSA	Standard Spending Assessment
UPSI	Universities' Police Science Institute (Cardiff University)
VPF	Victoria Police Force
WG	Welsh Government

List of Contributors

Professor Nic Beech is Vice-Principal for Academic Planning and Performance at the University of Dundee and Chair of the British Academy of Management. His research interests are in management practice, change, and the construction of identity, particularly in music and the creative industries and in health services. He is a fellow of the Royal Society of Arts, the British Academy of Management, the Chartered Institute of Personnel and Development, and the Academy of Social Sciences. His publications include: *Managing Creativity* (with B Townley, Cambridge University Press, 2010), *Managing Change* (with R MacIntosh, Cambridge University Press, 2012), and *Organising Music* (with C Gilmore, Cambridge University Press, 2014).

Dr Robin Bhairam joined the Metropolitan Police in 1985 and joined the Criminal Investigation Department in 1988, where he has spent all his service. He has conducted a number of leadership roles within the CID including specialist operations, serious crime, homicide command, and territorial policing; he is currently the Deputy National Coordinator for the National Domestic Extremism and Disorder Intelligence Unit. As a senior investigator and Intelligence specialist he has been involved in a number of high-profile investigations, including as the Senior Investigating Officer for the London Disorders in 2011. He has a BSc (Hons) in Policing and Police Studies, an MSc in Police Science and Management, and is a Doctor of Criminal Justice Studies, where his research examined the impact of serious youth violence through the narratives of young people.

Dr Timothy Brain OBE QPM is an Honorary Senior Research Fellow at Cardiff University and a Visiting Professor at the University of Gloucestershire. He studied history at Aberystwyth University, graduating BA in 1975 and PhD in 1982. He was Chief Constable of Gloucestershire from 2001 until his retirement in January 2010, having previously served in Avon and Somerset, Hampshire, and the West Midlands. He was ACPO's national lead on police finances and led several high-profile operations, notably Gloucestershire's response to the extensive flooding of 2007. He is a frequent writer and broadcaster on police matters. He is the author of two major studies of policing, *A History of Policing in England and Wales from 1974* (Oxford University Press, 2010) and *A Future for Policing* (Oxford University Press, 2013).

Professor Adam Crawford is Professor of Criminology and Criminal Justice and Pro-Dean for Research and Innovation in the Faculty of Education, Social Sciences and Law at the University of Leeds. His recent publications include *Legitimacy and Compliance in Criminal Justice* (edited with Anthea Hucklesby, Routledge, 2013), *Crime Prevention Policies in Comparative Perspective* (Willan, 2009), and

International and Comparative Criminal Justice and Urban Governance (Cambridge University Press, 2011). He is Director of the N8 Policing Research Partnership, which was awarded a Catalyst Fund grant by HEFCE in 2015 totalling over £7.2m to implement a five-year collaborative programme of research co-production and knowledge exchange between the N8 universities and 11 police forces across the north of England. He has held visiting positions at the Australian National University, Griffith University, Sydney University, and the Maison des Sciences de l'Hommes in Paris and Lyon. He has been studying policing and community safety partnerships of one kind or another for over 20 years.

Mike Cunningham QPM was appointed as Her Majesty's Inspector of Constabulary in September 2014, following five years as Chief Constable of Staffordshire Police. Prior to this he rose through the ranks in Lancashire Constabulary up to become Deputy Chief Constable. He is recognized as a passionate and committed advocate of integrated partnership working and collaboration. Nationally, he has led the police service in his role as lead for Professional Standards and National Policing Workforce Development Business Area. His achievements within policing have been recognized at the highest level, and he was awarded a Queens Police Medal in the New Year's Honours list for 2013. Most recently he was awarded an Honorary Degree of Doctor of Staffordshire University. Prior to joining the Police, he graduated from the University of Durham with a degree in Theology in 1984 and became a teacher.

Sir Peter Fahy joined the police in 1981. Before taking up the position of Chief Constable in the Greater Manchester Police in September 2008 he was the Chief Constable with Cheshire Constabulary, a post he had held since 2002. Prior to that he was Assistant Chief Constable at Surrey, and had positions with Hertfordshire and West Midlands forces. Peter Fahy was knighted in the 2012 Birthday Honours 'for services to policing'. Sir Peter announced his retirement in July 2015 and will be leaving policing to take up the position of chief executive of the children's charity Retrak.

Professor Jenny Fleming joined the University of Southampton as Professor of Criminology in 2012, where she is also the Director of the Institute of Criminal Justice Research. Professor Fleming's expertise lies in collaborative research with police practitioners covering such topics as police partnerships, knowledge exchange, and management. She has lectured, taught, and worked with police officers of all ranks in China, the Netherlands, the United Kingdom, Australia, and New Zealand. She is interested in organizational imperatives that impact on the way in which 'police do business' and police collaboration and has published widely in this area. She is the co-author of *Fighting Crime Together: The Challenges of Policing and Security Networks* (with Jennifer Wood, University of New South Wales Press, 2006) and *The Sage Dictionary of Policing* (with Alison Wakefield, Sage, 2009). Professor Fleming is the Editor-in-Chief of *Policing and Society, An International Journal of Research and Policy*, the leading policing peer-reviewed journal in the United Kingdom.

Professor Nick Fyfe is founding Director of the Scottish Institute for Policing Research, Professor in the School of the Environment at the University of

Dundee, and a Fellow of the Scottish Police College. He has been a Special Advisor to the Scottish Parliament's Justice Committee for its inquiries into the use of police resource and community policing and co-chairs the Policing Working Group of the European Society of Criminology. He is currently leading a four-year project to evaluate police and fire reform in Scotland.

Professor Emeritus John Grieve CBE, QPM served for over 37 years with the Metropolitan Police Service (MPS) from 1966 in uniform and CID. This latter included nearly every role, including undercover officer, Intelligence, Murder, Drugs, Robbery, Anti Terrorism, Race and Violent Crime investigator, and team leader. He was a uniform team Inspector, and a Divisional Commander as a Chief Superintendent in the East End of London. He was head of training as a Commander at Hendon. He managed the Intelligence Reform Programme as the first MPS Director of Intelligence in modern times, he was National Coordinator for Counter Terrorism, and he created and led the MPS team responding to the Stephen Lawrence Public Inquiry. In the past 12 years he has taught at the University of Portsmouth and London Metropolitan University, and all over the world. He has published extensively on policing issues in general and on complexity, ethics, leadership, community engagement, miscarriages of justice, terrorism, intelligence, crises, and critical incidents in particular, amongst others.

Professor Keith Grint is Professor of Public Leadership at Warwick University, where he is Academic Director of the High Potential Development Scheme for the police. He has held Chairs at Cranfield University and Lancaster University and was Director of the Lancaster Leadership Centre. He spent 12 years at Oxford University and was Director of Research at the Saïd Business School and Fellow in Organizational Behaviour, Templeton College. He is a Fellow of the British Academy of Social Sciences. He is also a Visiting Research Professor at Lancaster University, and at the Leiden University Leadership Centre, The Hague. His books include *Fuzzy Management* (Oxford University Press, 1997), *The Arts of Leadership* (Oxford University Press, 2000), *Organizational Leadership* (with John Bratton and Debra Nelson, South-Western College Publishing, 2004), *Leadership: Limits and Possibilities* (Palgrave Macmillan, 2005), *The Sociology of Work* (3rd edn, Polity Press, 2005), *Leadership, Management & Command: Rethinking D-Day* (Palgrave Macmillan, 2008), and *Leadership: A Very Short Introduction* (Oxford University Press, 2010).

Dr Elizabeth Gulledge is a research fellow at the University of St Andrews, United Kingdom. She received a BA in Political Science at Duke University and MLitt and PhD in Organizational Theory from the University of St Andrews. She is a faculty member of the School of Management at St Andrews and also served as Research Assistant at the Institute for Capitalizing on Creativity. Her work on creativity and innovation has been published in edited volumes such as the *Oxford Handbook of Creative Industries* and *Managing Creativity: Exploring the Paradox*.

Professor Martin Innes is a Professor in the School of Social Sciences at Cardiff University, where he leads the work of the Universities' Police Science Institute. He is recognized as one of the world's leading thinkers on policing and social control.

He is the author of *Investigating Murder: Detective Work and the Police Response to Criminal Homicide* (Oxford University Press, 2003), *Understanding Social Control* (Open University Press, 2003), and *Signal Crimes: Social Reactions to Crime, Disorder, and Control* (Oxford University Press, 2014), *Investigating Murder: Detective Work and the Police Response to Criminal Homicide*. From 2004 to 2014 he was Editor of the journal *Policing and Society*, and he has been a contributor to the *Guardian* and *Prospect Magazine*. His work on signal crimes was one of the key influences upon the development of Neighbourhood Policing in the United Kingdom, and has led to him being regularly asked to advise policing agencies and governments around the world, including in the United States, Australia, Canada, and the Netherlands.

Matt Jukes is Deputy Chief Constable of South Wales Police. Previously, he served with South Yorkshire Police for 15 years, principally in crime and intelligence posts, also working on the development of national counter-terrorism policing. Later he served as a divisional commander, before joining South Wales Police in 2010 as Assistant Chief Constable for Specialist Crime, responsible for major crime investigation, intelligence, public protection, and covert operations. With the Welsh government, he was co-Chair of the CONTEST (counter-terrorism) Board for Wales and became Deputy Chief Constable in 2013. He was programme director for the implementation of the National Police Chiefs' Council and leads its portfolio addressing property crime. Matt is a graduate of the police High Potential Development Scheme and holds a degree in mathematics from the University of Oxford. He researched the impact of police culture on partnership working for a Master's degree from the University of Leicester, where he was an External Marker for the Department of Criminology. He is a Friend of the Windsor Leadership Trust.

Dr Mark Kilgallon is the former academic director for the Strategic Command Course at Bramshill Police College, where he worked with policing executives from the United Kingdom and abroad. He was one of the founding members of the Police Ethics Committee (UK) and a former participant in the Leadership Forum for the Association of Chief Police Officers (ACPO). His many papers on leadership development have helped to shape the police leadership learning agenda for the past decade. He is an associate member of staff with the University of Derby. As a qualified coach and mentor, he works with policing leaders at national and international levels. He is the Managing Director of Policing Matters, an organization established to help leaders to bridge the gap between academic theory and policing practice.

Adrian Lee is Chief Constable of Northamptonshire Police. He joined Greater Manchester Police in 1985, where he was latterly Divisional Commander for South Manchester Division, which was the force's largest division, with unique challenges. Its geography includes the largest housing estate in Europe, and areas such as Moss Side and Longsight, generating tough inner-city policing issues such as gang violence and gun crime. He moved to Staffordshire Police as Assistant Chief Constable (Crime and Operations) in 2003 and was promoted to Deputy Chief Constable in 2006. He took up his current post as Chief Constable of Northamptonshire Police in 2009. On behalf of the Association of Chief Police Officers

(ACPO) he established and led the Professional Ethics portfolio from its inception in 2008 through to mid-2013. He also took up the role as ACPO Lead on Alcohol Licensing and Harm Reduction in 2012. He is a graduate of the Gregorian University in Rome and Manchester University, with a BPhil in Philosophy, an LLB (Hons), an MA in Management, and an MPhil in Police Ethics.

Professor Allyson MacVean is a research professor in policing and criminology at Bath Spa University. She was previously the Director of the John Grieve Centre for Policing and Community Safety and worked as a researcher within the Serious and Organised Crime Directorate at the Home Office. Professor MacVean is currently working with Avon and Somerset Constabulary, leading on a three-year project to evaluate the role of ethics committees in policing. She has written and co-authored a number of books on ethics and professional standards, including *Handbook of Policing, Ethics and Professional Standards* (with Peter Spindler, Routledge, 2012) and *Police Ethics and Values* (with Peter Neyroud, Sage, 2012).

Alex Marshall is the Chief Constable and CEO of the College of Policing. He was previously Chief Constable of Hampshire Constabulary (2008–13). He started his career in 1980 with the Metropolitan Police Service, transferring in 2000 to Cambridgeshire Constabulary. During this time he also worked as a consultant for the Home Office on bureaucracy in frontline policing. In 2004, he joined the Chief Constable's team in Thames Valley Police. He studied at Wolfson College and the Institute of Criminology, University of Cambridge, and became a Cropwood Fellow in 1999, and he obtained a Master's Degree in Criminology at the University of Cambridge in 2006.

Dr Aogán Mulcahy teaches in the School of Sociology at University College Dublin. Prior to that, he held research positions at Keele University and the University of Leeds. His main research interests concern the nature and dynamics of police legitimacy; policing and social division; and culture and social control. He has written extensively on policing in Northern Ireland, and the transition from the Royal Ulster Constabulary to the Police Service of Northern Ireland. Previous publications include *Policing and the Condition of England* (with Ian Loader, Oxford University Press, 2003) and *Policing Northern Ireland* (Routledge/Willan, 2006).

Sir Denis O'Connor QPM works on the Police Executive Programme at the Institute of Criminology, Cambridge University. He is an independent Director of the Board of the College of Policing. He was Her Majesty's Chief Inspector of Constabulary between 2008 and 2012. Prior to the Inspectorate, he was Chief Constable of Surrey between 2000 and 2004, and Assistant Commissioner in the Metropolitan Police, charged with developing a strategy to change the Force following the public inquiry into the death of Stephen Lawrence. Sir Denis was awarded the Queen's Police Medal in 1996 and a CBE in 2002 for services to policing. He was knighted in 2010 in the Queen's Birthday Honours. In 2011, he was awarded a place in George Mason University's 'Evidence-Based Policing Hall of Fame'. He received an Honorary Doctorate in Laws from Wolverhampton University in September 2012. He holds a BEd (Hons) and an MSc in social policy.

Sir Hugh Orde QPM is an international consultant on policing with a particular focus on police reform and endgames in terrorism. He joined the Metropolitan Police Service in 1977 and was promoted to Deputy Assistant Commissioner in October 1999. In September 2002 he was appointed Chief Constable of the Police Service of Northern Ireland (PSNI), a position he held for seven years. During his time in Northern Ireland he reformed the police force, increasing Catholic recruitment; established the HET—the Historical Enquiries Team; and made significant inroads into the developing peace process. He was appointed Vice-President of the Association of Chief Police Officers in 2006, becoming President in 2009, a position he held until retiring in 2015. Sir Hugh was awarded an OBE in 2001 for services to policing, and in 2005 was knighted for his work. In 2008, he was awarded the annual Leadership Award from the Police Executive Research Forum in the United States, recognizing his work in changing policing in Northern Ireland following the Good Friday Agreement in 1998. He is a graduate of the FBI National Executive Institute and holds a degree in Public Administration, an honorary Doctorate in Civil Law from the University of Kent, and an honorary Doctorate in Law from Ulster University, where he is a visiting professor.

Lynne Owens QPM is Chief Constable of Surrey Police. Previously, she was an Assistant Commissioner with the Metropolitan Police Service, operating as part of its Executive Board with responsibilities, including public order and event policing and specialist crime. She contributes to this book at the request of the Association of Chief Police Officers (ACPO) Finance Business Area. She leads the Operations Coordination Committee and contributes to the Criminal Justice Committee with responsibility for Charging and Out of Court Disposals. In 2013, she was appointed as a Member of Sentencing Council and later the Criminal Procedure Rule Committee. She holds a Master's degree in leadership studies from Exeter University and was awarded the Queen's Police Medal for distinguished service in the 2009 New Year's Honours.

Colette Paul QPM is Chief Constable of Bedfordshire Police. She spent a large part of her career as an operational detective with the Metropolitan Police Service (MPS), including work within the Vice Unit, Murder Squad, and the Race and Violent Crime Task Force. In 2000, she was appointed as the Detective Superintendent of the MPS Anti-Terrorist Branch and set up the MPS War Crimes Unit and the Counter Terrorist Intelligence Cell. She was promoted to Chief Superintendent in 2004, and served as Staff Officer to Lord Stevens, MPS Commissioner, before becoming Borough Commander for Ealing Borough, covering Ealing, Acton, and Southall, West London. She went on to hold responsibility for organizational strategy in the MPS, before joining South Wales Police as an Assistant Chief Constable in 2008, responsible for protective services, serious and organized crime, counter-terrorism, firearms, roads policing, and other operational policing specialisms. She was promoted to Deputy Chief Constable for South Wales, overseeing the Professional Standards, Corporate Communications and Performance, and Inspection departments; in addition to line managing the ACCs for Specialist Crime, Territorial Policing and Support, and the ACOs for Finance, HR, and

Corporate and Legal Services. She was also the strategic lead for corporate planning, organizational change, and collaboration. Colette is a graduate of the Home Office Special Course (accelerated promotion and the Cabinet Office Top Management Programme).

Professor Robert Reiner is Emeritus Professor of Criminology in the Law Department, London School of Economics. He has also worked at Bristol and Brunel Universities. His books include: *Law and Order: An Honest Citizen's Guide to Crime and Control* (Polity Press, 2007); *The Politics of the Police* (4th edn, Oxford University Press, 2010); *Policing, Popular Culture and Political Economy: Towards a Social Democratic Criminology* (Ashgate, 2011); and *The Oxford Handbook of Criminology* (edited with M Maguire and R Morgan, 5th edn, Oxford University Press, 2012).

Dr Marisa Silvestri is an Associate Professor at Kingston University, United Kingdom. Her research interests are focused on the broad area of gender, policing, and criminal justice. In particular, she is interested in women in police leadership and the impacts of a gendered criminal justice system. She has published widely on a range of related issues and is author of *Women in Charge: Gender: Policing and Leadership* (Willan Press, 2003), *Gender and Crime* (Sage, 2008), and the forthcoming *Gender and Policing* (Policy Press, 2015). She has acted as an academic adviser in a range of forums—most recently she contributed to the Independent Police Commission into the Future of Policing, led by Lord Stevens—and is a steering group member of the Policing Network (British Society of Criminology). She is also currently an editorial board member for *Policing and Society* journal and is a Series Editor for the *Key Issues in Policing Series* with Policy Press.

Peter Spindler joined the Metropolitan Police in 1985, after graduating from the University of Warwick. In 1998, he was seconded to the Regional Crime Squad and was promoted to Detective Superintendent in 2000, whilst on the National Crime Squad, where he took on the national lead for combating child abuse on the Internet. In 2002, he returned to the MPS to lead on pro-activity and major investigations for the Child Protection Command. As Detective Chief Superintendent, he took the lead for all child abuse investigations in London in 2004. Having completed the 2006 Strategic Command Course, he spent a year overseeing the MPS Counter Corruption Command and was promoted to Commander in 2008. He has had three postings as Commander at New Scotland Yard; Covert Policing, Director of Professional Standards and head of Specialist Crime Investigations, where he took the national lead for Operation Yewtree. He led for ACPO on technical surveillance and family liaison as well as being vice chair of the ACPO Homicide Working Group and chair of the Europol Homicide Working Group. He has been actively involved in Hostage and Crisis Negotiation since 1996 and was trained as an ACPO Counter Terrorism Commander in 2011. In April 2013, Peter transferred to Her Majesty's Inspectorate of Constabulary as Assistant Inspector of Constabulary, where he assisted in monitoring the efficiency and effectiveness of our police service and led on integrity issues. After completion of his secondment, Peter returned to the MPS in January 2015, where he now leads on specialist crime investigations, including murder, rape, and child abuse.

David Stewart spent 30 years with Strathclyde Police and then the Police Service of Scotland, retiring as a Chief Superintendent. During his police service he worked in both urban and rural environments, gaining varied experience across a range of specialist functions. As Chief Superintendent he was the Head of Safer Communities and Divisional Commander with Strathclyde Police, before working for the Association of Chief Police Officers (Scotland) as the Programme Manager for the National Police Reform Programme in Scotland. This was described as the largest public sector reform programme in the United Kingdom and saw the merger of the ten Scottish Policing organizations into the single entity of the Police Service of Scotland. After the successful merger, he became the Head of Business Change for the new Police Service. After leaving Police Scotland, he established his own company, Taynuilt Associates Ltd, which provides advice, guidance, and consultancy services in relation to change management, programme management, and policing services. Presently, he is also Police Advisor to the Foreign and Commonwealth Office for the Southern Oceans Overseas Territories. He is a Chartered Fellow of the Chartered Management Institute and was awarded 'Chartered Manager of the Year' in 2013. He is a Member of the Association for Project Management and is an Associate of the Scottish Institute for Policing Research.

Sara Thornton CBE QPM is Chair of the National Police Chiefs' Council (NPCC). The NPCC replaced the Association of Chief Police Officers (ACPO) as a new body bringing together the expertise of police leadership to coordinate operational policing and agree national approaches in the public interest. She was previously Chief Constable of Thames Valley Police from 2007 to 2015, as well as Vice President of ACPO, Vice Chair of ACPO Terrorism and Allied Matters since 2010, and Director of the Police National Assessment Centre. She served with the Metropolitan Police from 1986 and, over the next 15 years, her career alternated between operational postings in West London and strategic roles within New Scotland Yard. She joined Thames Valley Police as Assistant Chief Constable Specialist Operations in November 2000 and in August 2003 was appointed Deputy Chief Constable. In January 2006, she was appointed Acting Chief Constable of Thames Valley Police. She is a member of the Royal College of Defence Studies, a member of the Advisory Board for the Oxford University Centre for Criminology and an active alumnus of the Windsor Leadership Trust. In July 2011, she was awarded a Master of Studies degree (MSt) in Applied Criminology and Police Management from Cambridge University. In March 2012, she received a Career Achievement Award from the Police Training Authority Trustees. She has received honorary doctorates from Oxford Brookes and Buckinghamshire New Universities.

Dr Sarah Tucker is a Research Associate at the Universities' Police Science Institute (<http://www.upsi.org.uk>; accessed 21 April 2015) having previously served as a police officer for over a decade. She gained broad experience in policing, working as both a uniformed officer and a detective, principally specializing in child protection. She was a central figure in the Olympic Security Planning Team for Wales in 2012, and also formed part of the Project Team which led the transition of governance structures from the Police Authority to the Police and Crime Commissioner. Her research interests include public protection and vulnerable victims, operational policing, and rural crime. Current research is focused on the future role and function of neighbourhood policing in rural communities and the use of social media in policing, working directly with forces within the United Kingdom. She is also conducting research on the policing of honour-based violence and hidden victims of crime, as part of her doctorate.

Dr Martin Wright is the Academic Director of the Global Institute for Cyber, Intelligence and Security. He is a former police officer and previously led in the development of the uniformed services degrees at the University of Wolverhampton. He is currently the Managing Editor of *Policing: A Journal of Policy and Practice*, published by Oxford University Press. Recent publications include *Professional Police Practice* (with PAJ Waddington and John Kleinig, Oxford University Press, 2013).

Experience and Evidence
The Learning of Leadership

Jenny Fleming

Introduction

Leadership in policing is an attribute only partially defined by rank or position. Not everyone is a 'natural' leader. Leadership is required not just at the highest level of the structure, but at all levels of policing if they are to operate effectively in a complex environment and across the many demanding and multifaceted activities that make up the role of the 21st-century police officer or member of police staff. The problem of understanding leaders and leadership is compounded by the diverse and rapid changes confronting the police. Times have changed. Sophisticated technologies have created new social spaces; threats and acts of terrorism continue to dominate the security agenda; continuing austerity erodes services and morale; citizen and community expectations continue to rise. As Innes, Tucker, and Jukes (Chapter 8) point out, 'what the public thinks about the police *matters*'—with better access to knowledge, communities are aware and critical of how police allocate their resources.

Police officers hold a unique role in liberal democracies and their ability to lead is generally regarded as key to performance. Effective leadership is an important predictor of whether organizations are regarded by those inside, and indeed externally, as legitimate and able to function in an increasingly diverse and dynamic landscape. There is increased public demand for greater levels of accountability and scrutiny. Mechanisms are reviewed and multiplied; codes and standards are specified and refined as the need for unquestionable integrity and ethical behaviour become non-negotiable. The pursuit of effective leadership has become an integral part of any police reform agenda as policing leaders struggle to manage rapid change and adapt accordingly (Neyroud 2011: 43). So, we know that 'leadership' is important—but how do we go about accessing 'what works'? How does the aspiring leader think and learn about 'rising to the top'?

This chapter provides a brief overview of the leadership literature and where an interested individual may go to learn more. It suggests that the literature is useful in thinking about different styles, behaviours, competencies, and leadership development practice. In acknowledging the importance of learning, training, and education, and in considering the contributions of this book, the chapter demonstrates the relevance of narrative and experience in conjunction with 'what we know' about policing.

Leadership as Conundrum

The general leadership literature is a complex set of puzzles spanning several academic disciplines. It is context specific and in the non-partisan sense of the word, highly political. Police themselves cannot apparently agree on what constitutes 'a successful leader' (Caless 2011: 117). There are no 'comfortable' definitions of leadership and 'several contradictory perspectives without any clear consensus about any of them' (Rhodes and 't Hart 2014: 1). Do we, for example, talk about leaders as individuals, or leadership teams, or do we consider 'leadership' as a process? Should leadership be formal or informal (Pielstick 2000)? Are leaders born or can we make them? Can they be *born and made* (Haberfield 2013: 1)? Many definitions emphasize the importance of influence, the ability to mobilize and provide purpose, ie, 'bringing people together to make something different happen' (Cleveland 2002: xv).

While acknowledging the importance of leadership at every level, this chapter focuses on senior officers as leaders. The policing leader is an administrative leader, ranging from 'the front line supervisor...to the non-political head of the organization' (Van Wart 2003, cited in Rhodes 2014: 101). Leadership is 'a process of influence where a person or group influences others to work towards a common goal' (Morse and Buss 2007: 4).

Yet even when we have a 'working' definition, many questions arise. Is it possible to have leadership without having followers? Are followers active or passive and subordinate? Are the official policing leaders doing the leading or are they merely figureheads? How is 'good' leadership recognized? What does it look like? Is there anything unique about policing leadership? What mechanisms are available to improve on the 'ideal' and how can aspiring policing leaders learn the science of leadership (or is it a craft)? Speaking in the context of political leadership, Rhodes and 't Hart (2014: 3) cite the 'bewildering array of concepts, frameworks, propositions, stories, assessments, prescriptions and clichés about leadership across many academic disciplines and professional domains'. So, for example, social psychology considers leadership not just in the context of 'leaders' and not just 'leaders and followers', but as being 'about leaders and followers

2

in situated social groups' (Reicher, Haslam, and Platow 2014: 156). The feminist perspective contends that organizations need to look at 'the gendered configurations of recruitment, promotion and behaviour . . . as well as the gendered production of the concept of political leadership' (Sjoberg 2014: 83). The tendency to view leaders as a homogenous group in policing has been noted, if not explored in detail (Pearson-Goff and Herrington 2014: 21), although the likelihood of women displaying different leadership styles to men in policing has been canvassed by Silvestri (2006; 2007).

While the police literature cannot boast such a breadth of knowledge—the early 'leadership' literature, largely found under the rubric of management and/or organizational studies, is well known to police academies and colleges. For those officers enrolled on their courses, an understanding of this literature has become part of the everyday learning experience. They know that trait theory (ie the research that sought to identify specific intellectual, personality, and physical traits of successful leaders) and behavioural theory approaches (ie the diagnosis and development of people's style of working) have largely been discredited. Rather, situational theories and contingency models are in favour; although there still appears to be a role for transactional theory (Burns 2003; see also Campbell and Kodz 2011: 7, 4). They are aware that the most resilient theory in policing and leadership studies has been Burns' transformational thesis (1978), where 'the personality of the leader stimulates change by raising consciousness, motivation and morale' (Haberfield 2013: 50). Burns' theory and his extended model of full-range leadership (incorporating transformational leadership while acknowledging the importance of situational and adaptive theories) has been the basis of several influential police leadership studies (Campbell and Kodz 2011: 7).

Perhaps the greatest contribution to policing of these leadership theories is that they allow interested parties to examine police leaders through a variety of prisms as a way of analysing leaders' approaches, activity, and decision-making. The leadership development literature is largely situated in public sector organizations. There are few evaluation studies for the policing sector. Generally, the public sector literature is 'perceived to be effective', with some 'promising learning methods' available (Kodz and Campbell 2010: 3).

What Works in Leadership Development?

The importance of attracting, selecting, and developing senior policing leaders has been evident since the Desborough Committee Report of 1920 recognized the 'special nature of policing'. But it was not until 1947 that a post-war committee established the National Police College and set the parameters of police-led leadership programmes (Neyroud 2011: 31; see also Kilgallon, Wright, and Lee, Chapter 11 for a more extensive discussion). Almost 70 years on, despite the extensive array of literature 'out there', the available evidence base on 'what makes a great police leader', or indeed any leader, is limited. There are difficulties linking leadership with organizational outcomes (not least because of the complex environment in which police work) (Campbell and Kodz 2011: 8). There is much ambiguity in research results. Methodological issues blur the boundaries of 'what works' as impact. The methodological issues are largely concerned with the instruments used for measuring leadership styles, competencies, and behaviours, and the difficulty of finding more robust research methods to uncover 'what works in leadership studies'. Given the speed of change, even if one model worked at an identified point in time, it may not withstand the rapidity of contextual development.[1]

There are no leadership studies that would warrant a 'what works' stamp of approval. In their rapid evidence assessment of 'what works', Kodz and Campbell (2010: 11) conclude that there is no evidence relating to the 'value for money' of leadership development programmes and no studies that 'measure the impact of police leadership development programmes and other opportunities in terms of long-term impacts on behaviour and values of participants'. The authors (2010: 3) do, however, identify the potential effectiveness of participation selection; a variety of teaching methods and the salience of reflection in leadership development. Individual coaching, feedback mechanisms, and the importance of creating and embedding a police culture that welcomes and supports leadership. Education training is also deemed 'promising'.

Pearson-Goff and Herringtons' review of police leadership (2014) demonstrated that there was considerable agreement about the range of leadership competency frameworks that have developed in the public service generally, and in Australia and New Zealand in particular. Leadership competencies on such tasks as communication, influencing and negotiation skills, achieving results, and shaping strategic direction have been developed in Australasia by drawing on the leadership expectations of police officers in the middle and senior ranks. As the authors noted, in terms of guiding the development of senior police officers, these competencies largely reflect what we think we know about the development of leaders (based on the perceptions of subordinates), rather than objective measures of effective leadership. In other words, we are assuming that 'there is a shared understanding about what characterizes effective leadership', rather than reflecting that this may be 'a received wisdom based on flawed evidence focusing on perceptions' (2014: 8; on this point, see also Caless 2011: 84–5).

It is not all gloom and doom. While the studies under review, particularly in the rapid evidence assessments, draw the dispiriting conclusion that 'there is no reliable evidence of what impacts styles and behaviours make on the ground', there are 'indications of the potential effectiveness of different leadership styles, competencies, behaviours and where the "weight of evidence lies"' (Campbell and Kodz 2011: 3–4). We are aware, for example, that transformational

---

[1] I am grateful to Mark Kilgallon for this point.

leadership that provides vision, encouragement, a focus on values, and 'intellectual stimulation' is more positive and more likely to be appreciated by 'followers' than those leaders who do not exhibit such characteristics. Evidence suggests that in this context, 'followers' are more likely to follow, to be loyal, to exert more effort, and to be compliant. This approach is complemented by a participative approach that provides for inclusive decision-making and suggests stronger organizational commitment and job satisfaction, although there is some evidence to suggest that the transformative approach—with its emphasis on inspiration, motivation, and positive encouragement—may be less effective than leaders who motivate through active participation, 'leading by example', and employ role-modelling strategies (Campbell and Kodz 2011: 3–4).

Additionally, transactional leadership styles do resonate positively with some 'followers', while a 'mixed style' that combines transformational and transactional behaviours is more likely to be effective than one that relies solely on a transformational approach. Leaders that adapt themselves to particular situations and take into account the characteristics of those who are 'following' are also likely to be 'successful'. More recently, Goleman's emotional intelligence thesis (see 1998, for example) has become positively related to notions of effective police leadership (see Kilgallon, Wright, and Lee, Chapter 11), although as some studies have noted, this effectiveness may be undermined when coupled with 'high levels of narcissism' (Yokum 2007).

In summary, the leadership development literature provides some useful context for thinking about styles, competencies, and potential development. Many well-thumbed books testify to the value of such considerations. However, much more targeted research needs to be done on the impact and effectiveness of these programmes.

The 'evidence base'

The emphasis on 'evidence-based policy' and employing 'what works' as 'evidence-based practice' in policing has had greater momentum since the establishment of the College of Policing in 2012. A fundamental development in the College is the use of knowledge and research to develop an evidence-based approach to policing. Committed to the development of a standardized and evidence-based profession, the College sets standards for the police service on training, development, skills, and qualifications with a view to sharing knowledge and providing 'practical evidence-based insights' to inform decision-making. Much of this research, particularly that associated with the What Works in Crime Prevention Centre,[2] is being developed with academics through rigorous systematic reviews and stringent methodological practice. The favoured

---

[2] The What Works Centre is led by the College of Policing and supported by an eight-university consortium. It is jointly funded by the College and the Economic and Social Research Council.

approach is a robust quasi-experimental research design (using control groups and comparative sites and controlling for specific factors). The aim is to build up a professional knowledge base conducive to identifying, for example, interventions in crime prevention. Yet, there are no such studies meeting these methodological standards in leadership and one is inclined to agree with Campbell and Kodz (2011: 8), that 'such "what works" type evidence will be difficult to ever achieve'.

However, policing has a rich research tradition and there is much available to the police officer who aspires to lead and wishes to know more (see Fleming, Fyfe, and Marshall, Chapter 12; Reiner 2015). As Reiner and O'Connor note (in Chapter 3), the specific literature in the United Kingdom on senior policing leaders is largely concerned with the 'sociology *of* rather than *for* the police' (see Reiner 1991; Wall 1998; Savage et al 2000; Silvestri 2003; Caless 2011) and is not primarily concerned with the 'improvement' of an officer. While the College and its academic colleagues endeavour to broaden the 'what works' base to inform police policy and practice and to expand its professional body of knowledge, other ways of knowing can complement this learning and represent a key component of the 'learning organization'.

Storytelling

March (2010: 99) defines the learning organization as:

> . . . an organisation that uses mechanisms of learning to improve the return of actions. Some of the ideas come from research, some from experience, some from analysis, and some from various forms of personal imagination. They all seek to provide clues to improving organisational adaptiveness.

In the sense that we can 'know' anything about outcomes and impact, we 'know' that learning from one's colleagues, peers, and senior leaders is a 'preferred' method of informed learning for police officers. Kodz and Campbell (2010: 13) have noted that, 'amongst the most commonly cited benefits of attending police leadership development courses are the opportunities for self-reflection and interacting with peers; these are often said 'to have more learning impact than the formal course content. The value of learning from others (peers, superior officers and leaders from other sectors) appears in all of the evaluations on NCPL/ Bramshill courses.' Alex Marshall, CEO of the College of Policing, also acknowledges the power of 'oral history' in policing (Chapter 12).

My own experience of working with and talking to police officers in a variety of contexts is that the credibility of an idea or 'way of doing business' is always higher if a colleague has endorsed it. There is a lot of this first-hand 'evidence', knowledge, and information available to aspiring leaders. Storytelling is often a feature of leadership courses, where participants are encouraged under Chatham House rules to discuss the challenges and experiences of their role. None of this, however, is written down or systemized, unfortunately. Another way of accessing this knowledge/experience is to immerse oneself in biographies, conversations, and case studies of senior officers. Bryn Caless's (2011) *Policing at the Top* demonstrates the importance of senior officers' views and conceptions and the saliency of such accounts (2011: 3). Caless's chapter, 'The Challenge of Leadership', from the perspective of senior police officers is illuminating (2011: 81–118).

There are solid, informative biographical accounts by senior officers in the United Kingdom—Sir Robert Mark's autobiographical accounts of his time in the service provide a personal view of a Chief Constable's term of office (1977; Mark and Charlton: 1978). Additionally, Graef (1989), Stephens (2005), and Blair (2009) offer interesting insights. In the United States, Darren Gates (1992), Dorothy Schulz (2004), and Bratton and Knobler (2009) are representative of an extensive literature. In Australia, numerous biographical accounts testify to the storytelling tradition in that part of the world (see eg Avery 1989; Nixon and Chandler 2009). The role of Police Commissioner as leader is also prevalent in the literature, and not only in Mark Moore's (1990) perception of police leadership as an 'Impossible Dream'! (See eg Geller 1985; Reiner 1991; Adlam and Villiers 2002; Fleming 2004; 2008; Fleming and Hall 2008; Isenberg 2009; Haberfeld 2013).

Rising to the Top

This book looks at policing from the standpoints of both academics, who are expert in their respective fields, and senior practitioners, who provide practical organizational and operational experience. The subjects of the various sections were chosen in consultation with senior officers. They identified the several subject areas as the most complex issues influencing policing today. Obviously, the list is not exhaustive. The aim of this collection is to provide detailed theoretical insights and practical accounts of the role of senior police management and the process of leadership in an accessible format for a wide readership, in particular aspiring policing leaders. Academic contributors were asked to present key ideas, concepts, and debates in their area of expertise and identify leading contributions and research studies. One of the strengths of this book is that experienced academics provide concise reviews of some of the most important literature in policing scholarship. In response, senior practitioners provide their own 'local knowledge' and 'stories' and reflect on their leadership achievements and challenges.

As academics outline 'what we know' about specific problems and situations familiar to those involved in policing at a senior level, the practitioner reflects on their understanding of the literature, the relevance of that research to their own practice, and how they themselves have addressed the 'wicked issues' that invariably frame their everyday thinking and decision-making. As academics provide the theory and context of comprehensive bodies of literature, the senior practitioners provide what March calls their 'narratives of experience'. These narratives of 'good practices' equate to 'plausible conjectures' (Bourdon 1993). Thus in place of quasi-experimental research design, I substitute 'plausible conjectures', ie general statements which are plausible because they rest on good reasons, and the reasons are good because they are inferred from relevant information, in this case the experience of senior practitioners.

As storytellers, the practitioners create and share their stories 'as bases for describing and explaining' and 'transforming the ambiguities and complexities of experience into a form that is elaborate enough to elicit interest, simple enough to be understood and credible enough to be accepted' (March 2010: 44–5). The importance of 'shared meaning' to learning organizations has been noted elsewhere. In his book, *Imaginization*, Morgan (1993) uses 'images, metaphors, readings and storylines to cast situations in new perspective and open possibilities for creative action', arguing that 'organization always hinges on the creation of shared meaning and shared understandings' (Morgan 1993: 11). Readers can draw on those experiences. In this book, academics and practitioners come together in dialogue to provide 'shared reflections'. They consider, for example, the importance of theory to practice, the salience of academic–practitioner partnerships, the challenge of creating and embedding a research culture in police organizations, the perils of politics in policing, and the need to acknowledge significant legacies of the past.

Most of the areas discussed by practitioners in this book are provided against the backdrop of continuing austerity and the challenge of reducing expenditure and sustaining service delivery. Brain and Owens (Chapter 2) suggest that policing leaders 'require an understanding of how police finances work, how to maximize their benefit, how to account for their use, and how to do so in a highly political environment'. Lynne Owens notes the need for 'leaders with an expanded skill set' to deal with the puzzles of 'revenue streams', 'funding formulas', 'audit requirements and general Schemes of Governance'; but in the end if leadership is about dealing with such 'uncertainty' it will ultimately be about being 'present alongside . . . officers and staff to understand the impact of change, respond to suggestions, and talk honestly about concerns'.

The 'highly political environment' is highlighted in Reiner and O'Connor's narrative (Chapter 3) of the politics of policing. Their message to policing leaders stresses that it is crucial they 'recognize the significance of the politics of policing, eschewing partisan involvement without sheltering behind the myth of an impossible separation from politics'. O'Connor's narrative provides advice to aspiring leaders about rethinking 'the limits of independence', political accountability, consent, 'the value [you] place on public support in decision-making, and the case—the narrative—[you] make to political leaders'.

Crawford and Cunningham (Chapter 4) look to the 'collaborative advantages' in their dialogue on partnerships. The chapter underscores 'the importance of strong leadership and strategic direction' in facilitating collaboration and organizational commitment in pursuit of 'the goal of a genuinely joined-up, holistic, and coordinated response to crime and disorder'. Both authors consider the importance of collaboration between higher education institutions, practitioners, and knowledge exchange. The salience of fostering such relationships for building capacity and advancing the scope for high-quality research evidence to inform police decision-making is also discussed in Fleming, Fyfe, and Marshall's chapter on the connections between research and practice (Chapter 12).

Collaboration and decision-making are also the hallmarks of Grint and Thornton's section on leadership and command (Chapter 5), where leadership, management, and command are considered as separate decision-making modes, all associated with different kinds of problems. The distinctions, of course, reflect the 'essentially contested' nature of this area. Grint notes that the media and politicians often drive a leader down the command mode when leadership would have been more appropriate. Thornton challenges Grint's 'narrow definition of leadership' and reflects on the literature and her practice as a leader. The 'push and pull' of their debate comes together in their shared reflections on this 'wicked' issue.

The impact of ethical leadership is in the embryonic stages of research (see Tasdoven and Kaya 2014), reflecting perhaps the recent salience of ethical policing in discussions about professional practice and leadership. The College of Policing's Code of Ethics, introduced in 2014, provides the framework for the standard of professional behaviour expected of all officers, not just recognized leaders. In Chapter 6, MacVean and Spindler reflect on principled and ethical policing and remind us of the problems that arise when there is 'inconsistency between the behaviour of leaders and the expectations of their staff'. Research suggests that 'ethical leadership, as role models can promote ethical behaviour by encouraging employees to do the right thing and deal with ethical issues in their organisations' (Tasdoven and Kaya 2014: 530). Yet, as MacVean and Spindler observe, 'one of the greatest challenges for policing leaders will be how they manage to facilitate the duty of challenge' in an organization where 'the tradition of following orders is embedded within a hierarchical arrangement'.

The ABC of investigative leadership is canvassed by Grieve and Bhairam (Chapter 7). In exploring the historical and contemporary antecedents of police investigation, the authors urge aspiring leaders to 'open their minds to the rigours and potential of the theoretical and experimental application found in academic discovery' and encourage existing leaders to hand on 'the torch of rigorous academic and practical knowledge, sharing their experiences, good and bad, leaving a record, mentoring and nurturing the next generation of investigative leaders'.

In a context where 'reduced police funding is "the new normal"', Innes, Tucker, and Jukes (Chapter 8) provide a realistic account of what community engagement 'can and cannot do' and how new media ecology and 'the widespread uptake of social media platforms, affords new opportunities for more effective and cost-efficient police-community engagement'. Speaking specifically to the idea of frontline community engagement in the context of counter-terrorism activities, Jukes notes the absence of any 'academic reference or professional doctrine that can do more than guide or inform police leaders'. Community engagement of another kind is considered in Mulcahy and Orde's overview (Chapter 9) of police leadership and social division.

Earlier in this chapter, I noted that policing leadership was 'context specific and in the non-partisan sense of the word, highly political'. Mulcahy and Orde (Chapter 9) remind us of the multifaceted nature of police leadership and how the 'where', 'why', and 'when' is equally important as the 'how' and 'what'. The high-profile, heavily scrutinized role of the Chief Constable in Northern Ireland, and the highly political nature of the role, highlight the importance of 'building consent', 'resilience', listening and empowering others in the leadership process.

A transformational leadership style is often associated with women in police leadership. Silvestri (Chapter 10) notes that, 'our knowledge of how women *do* police leadership is limited' (although see Fleming 2008) and Colette Paul's account of her experience 'rising to the top' is an example of the kind of research that is lacking in the policing literature. In their reflective thoughts, Silvestri and Paul assert that women in policing 'make a difference', particularly at the senior level, although, as they both observe, 'the concept of "women" as leaders remains a key and controversial issue in discussions about organizational leadership'.

Kilgallon, Wright, and Lee (Chapter 11) extend the discussion begun earlier in this chapter about leadership development, and reflect on how training and education assists leaders in their roles. Developing policing leadership is here considered 'a political event . . . influenced by the political hue of the moment'. The authors argue that 'there is a direct correlation between the qualities of policing, educational and leadership development, and access to current and informed theoretical knowledge and data'. From a practitioner's perspective, Adrian Lee emphasizes the importance of personal responsibility to leadership and asserts that a leader's significant responsibilities begin with their 'preparation, training, and learning', and that all leaders need to make 'a commitment to continuous learning'.

In making the connections between research and practice, Fleming, Fyfe, and Marshall address 'the paradox of policing research' in Chapter 12. Kilgallon, Wright, and Lee (Chapter 11) observe that 'there is still some debate regarding the extent to which there is an expectation that policing leaders should be adequately informed by current literature about policing'. As Fleming and Fyfe suggest here, 'for those who wish to become leaders in their profession, an understanding of where the profession has come from, and where it might be going, can often be found in its research archives'. The chapter considers the history of policing research and the collaborative attempts of police and academics to create and exchange knowledge. In his 'narrative of experience', Marshall notes that he had been an officer for 15 years and a newly appointed inspector when he came to look on research as important to police practice and to consider the value of the academic–practitioner relationship. Alex Marshall has led the academic push in his own leadership roles since the 1990s. He now leads the professional body responsible for establishing an authoritative evidence base for the police service and encouraging the academic–practitioner relationship.

Most officers, and police staff, have at some level of their careers been involved and/or led in organizational change and appreciate the upheaval and uncertainty associated with such activity. As we have seen in the management and organizational literature around leadership, there is a significant body of work that addresses the theory of change leadership. Beech, Gulledge, and Stewart (Chapter 13) summarize three of the literature's key themes, noting the relevance of transformational theory to the practical example of organizational change in Scotland. As ex-Chief Superintendent David Stewart notes in the same chapter, most police constables have been ' "subject" to change' but 'you become a senior officer and are responsible for the change itself '. In bringing the notion of 'Police Scotland' to life, Stewart recounts his experience of leading change in a highly charged political environment.

Conclusion

This book is about drawing lessons from experience. It uses dialogues between academics and practitioners to stimulate reflections not just on theory, but on the 'real-life' accounts of those practitioners who have been, or are in, 'the field', capturing the meaning of their everyday activities through their 'narratives of experience'. What specific and more general insights can we draw from these several dialogues? Briefly, I identify three areas where these academic/practitioner accounts identify common ground and positive ways forward for 'the learning of leadership'.

Small 'p' politics

As Reiner and O'Connor remind us (Chapter 3), 'policing is of its nature intricately intertwined with politics'. The highly political environment of policing provides the backdrop to many of the chapters here. Mulcahy and Orde's chapter (Chapter 9) is perhaps the most obvious example where in policing 'fractured communities, different approaches need to be subject to different oversight and are vulnerable to naive interpretation and complex politics'. While Northern Ireland speaks to notions of big 'P' politics (along with the politics of austerity and the political nature of police governance), it is the small 'p' politics in policing that are increasingly important—the micro-politics of local communities and the politics of partnership. Strong and effective police leadership is increasingly about negotiating and managing the often unpredictable external environment—leaders have to be able to recognize the changing and dynamic nature of that environment, to identify the important actors, anticipate needs and wants, and successfully interact at the local level (Fleming and Hall 2008: 166). David Stewart's account of bringing together 'Police Scotland' (Chapter 13) demonstrates the usefulness of this. Community engagement of local communities, and the 'new politics' at the heart of a partnership approach to governing safety, are two other areas where 'small 'p' politics' are writ large.

Working together

In a bid to connect research and practice, there has been an abundance of literature in recent years on the potential of the collaborative relationship between the police practitioner and the researcher, (see Chapter 12). In this book, over the following chapters, academics and practitioners have developed a dialogue between themselves to identify key debates, share knowledge, and effectively sit down at the table and write together. As we read the various accounts, we note that practitioners and researchers alike have found perhaps unexpected points of contact—sharing commonalities and acknowledging points of departure. Many contributors have alluded to the value of bringing together the theory and practice. Others have identified the 'overly ethereal nature' of some of the research and the apparent gap between the model and the reality.

The challenges of working together have been well documented—the sharing of data; staff mobility and issues of trust, for example (see Fleming 2010); yet researchers and police practitioners have come a long way in the past two decades. While the journey is not always smooth, we are no longer necessarily 'professional strangers' (Agar 1996). We have more understanding of one another's organizational imperatives and cultural sensibilities and are more likely to employ 'the strategy of continuous negotiation and communication' to maximize collaborative success (Fleming 2010). Increased funding opportunities to 'work together' encourage this activity. The dialogues in this book confirm Cordner and White's (2010: 90) observation that 'the police research/police practice relationship is evolving quite positively' and bode well for forthcoming endeavours and cooperation.

The importance of the 'narrative experience'

Barbara Czarniawska (1997: 28, cited in March 2010: 44) tells us that most people would prefer to tell stories than answer questions—to interpret our experiences in a way that allows us to make sense of the complexities of our everyday lives (see also Weick 1995). The practitioners' stories in this book have allowed, albeit briefly, the reader the 'capacity to sit where the other person is sitting and to see the world through their eyes' (Fleming 2011: 23). As noted in the chapters of this book, there is a dearth of research that allows for the 'up close and personal' perspective and prioritizes the practitioner's view. If we are to add effectively to the knowledge base of policing scholarship we have to include the policing practitioner's voice.

Conger (1991: 31) has argued that 'there is an important link between language and leadership'. The 'language of leadership', is an important skill for leaders wanting to communicate with followers. As Tom Peter has stated, 'the best leaders . . . almost without exception and at every level, are master users of stories and symbols' (Peter 1988, cited in Macdonald 1995: 222). As O'Connor points out in Chapter 3: 'If police leaders do not tell the story of their role and their aims, who will?'

The claim here for the importance of the practitioner voice is not without its caveats. Broadly speaking, put a group of practitioners in a room and ask them about their job, and one notes quite quickly the propensity for chatting and the tendency to 'group whinge' (Fleming 2011: 23). This doesn't negate the 'experience' but in such a situation, considered reflection is not always a characteristic of the narrative. March (2010: 114) reminds us of the limits to experience, while at the same time being committed to the idea of the learning organization that garners information of many kinds to 'improv[e] organisational adaptiveness' (2010: 99):

> There is no question that individuals and organisations regularly and routinely learn from experience in the sense of modifying behaviour and understandings on the basis of experience ... organisations learn how to operate successfully in specific contexts in which they find themselves. That knowledge is likely to be limited in application and generality, but it represents the useful fruits of trial and error learning, imitation and selection in narrow domains. In almost every kind of specialised human activity, experience effects are positive (March 2010: 101–2).

I reiterate the point that the 'narrative of experience' is only one way of adding to the puzzle of 'learning leadership'. It stands amongst the search for evidence-based research to inform practice, it accompanies competency learning, and best of all it allows for the academic researcher and the practitioner to engage in an important 'dialogue of the listening'. March concludes that such research is 'messy' and 'constructed', 'contested' and 'ambiguous', but all research is a bit like that.

Where to next? No self-respecting academic ever fails to seize the opportunity to call for more research. Opinion collecting via surveys (see Schaefer 2010), the characterization of leadership that seeks to ascribe specific styles of leadership to theories (Haberfield 2013; Sarver and Miller 2014), leaders' views on how they perceive their role (Caless 2011; Gottschalk and Glomseth 2012), and the autobiographies of the 'how I achieved' variety (Blair 2009; Bratton and Knobler 2009) are all examples of existing literature on police leadership. Much of this work is useful and, indeed, represents a significant part of the knowledge base available to aspiring leaders. Yet as policing reform gathers apace we are at risk of moving past some of the significant opportunities for leadership research. What, for example, is the impact of new governance arrangements and the new role of the Police Crime Commissioner on police leadership activity? How will the first cohort of direct entry 'leaders' manage and lead their teams? What can we learn from looking at leadership within the ranks—the significant role of informal leadership particularly at operational level?

As Kodz and Campbell (2010: 15) demonstrate, there are a number of limitations in the existing 'evidence base' in the literature as it pertains to police leadership. In their review of the police development literature, the authors identified the need for evaluations of leadership development in the police sector, noting particularly the difficulty of appraising and measuring outcomes of specific programmes:

> ... this area of study could be best researched through a 'realist' approach and by building up a bank of more context specific but detailed case studies. Studies

that include direct observations and more sensitive qualitative methods, such as repertory grid, are likely to be useful, as well as ethnographic approaches.

In a similar vein, Pearson-Goff and Herrington (2014: 21) demonstrate that this literature provides little understanding of leadership 'beyond what others perceive to be effective'. Such research, say the authors, does not allow for 'clear and objective measures of what effective leadership is, with no research assessing the impact of leadership on organisational or operational outcomes'.

It is clear that there are many other ways to collate and systemize evidence than the 'what works' paradigm allows for. This is not to malign or marginalize such research but merely to note, as this book and others have suggested, that the 'narrative experience' and the reflection and sense-making that lies behind such narratives has much value and can add greatly to the growing mosaic of leadership studies. It is no longer the case, at least in the United Kingdom, that police data is inaccessible to researchers (Fleming 2010), and that there are problems gaining access to departments and police leaders (Pearson-Goff and Herrington (2014: 8). Indeed, as the College of Policing reaches out to the academy, encouraging collaborations and research networks, there is ample opportunity for academics and police organizations to work together to address the thorny issue of leadership studies.

References

Adlam, R and Villiers, P (eds) (2002), *Police Leadership in the Twenty-first Century: Philosophy, Doctrine and Developments* (Winchester: Waterside Press)

Agar, M (1996), *The Professional Stranger* (2nd edn, San Diego, CA: Academic Press)

Avery, J (1989), 'Issues in Police Leadership' in Chappell, D and Wilson, P (eds), *Australian Policing Contemporary Issues* (Sydney: Butterworths) 95

Blair, I (2009), *Policing Controversy* (London: Profile Books)

Bourdon, R (1993), 'Towards a Synthetic Theory of Rationality' 7(1) *International Studies in the Philosophy of Science* 5

Bratton, W and Knobler, P (2009), *The Turnaround: How America's Top Cop Reversed the Crime Epidemic* (New York: Random House)

Burns, JM (1978), *Leadership* (New York: Harper and Row)

Burns, JM (2003), *Transforming Leadership: A New Pursuit Of Happiness* (New York: Harper and Row)

Caless, B (2011), *Policing at the Top: The Roles, Values and Attitudes of Chief Police Officers* (Bristol: Policy Press)

Campbell, I and Kodz, J (2011), 'What Makes Great Police Leadership? What Research Can Tell Us About the Effectiveness of Different Leadership Styles, Competencies and Behaviours. A Rapid Evidence Review', National Policing Improvement Agency, London

Cleveland, H (2002), *Nobody in Charge: Essays on the Future of Leadership* (San Francisco, CA: Jossey-Bass)

Conger, JA (1991), 'The Language of Leadership' 5(1) *The Executive* 31

Cordner, G and White, S (2010), 'The Evolving Relationship between Police Research and Police Practice' 11(2) *Police Practice and Research* 90

Czarniawska, B (1997), *Narrating the Organization: Dramas of Institutional Identity* (Chicago, IL: University of Chicago Press)

Fleming, J (2004), '*Les Liaisons Dangereuses*: Relations between Police Commissioners and their Political Masters' 63(3) *Australian Journal of Public Administration* 60

Fleming, J (2008), '"Managing the Diary"—The Role of Police Commissioner' 86(3) *Public Administration (UK)* 679

Fleming, J (2010), 'Learning to Work Together: Police and Academics' 4(2) *Policing* 139

Fleming, J (2011), 'Qualitative Encounters in Policing Research', in Bartels, L and Richards, K (eds), *Qualitative Criminology: Stories from the Field* (Leichhardt, NSW: Federation Press), 13

Fleming, J and Hall, R (2008), 'Police Leadership' in 't Hart, P and Uhr, J (eds), *Understanding Public Leadership: Perspectives and Practices* (Canberra: ANU E Press), 165

Gates, D (1992), *Chief: My Life in the LAPD* (New York: Bantam Press)

Geller, WA (ed) (1985), *Police Leadership in America: Crisis and Opportunity* (New York: Praeger)

Goleman, D (1998), 'What Makes a Leader?' 76(6) *Harvard Business Review* 93

Gottschalk, P and Glomseth, R (2012), 'Attitudes of Police Managers to Different Leadership Roles in their Jobs: An Empirical Study in Norway' 6(1) *Journal of Leadership Studies* 23

Graef, R (1989), *Talking Blues: The Police in Their Own Words* (London: Collins Harvill)

Haberfield, MR (2013), *Police Leadership, Organisational and Managerial Decision-Making Process* (2nd edn, Upper Saddle River, NJ: Pearson Education)

Isenberg, J (2009), *Police Leadership in a Democracy: Conversations with America's Police Chiefs* (Boca Raton, FL: CRC Press)

Kodz, J and Campbell, I (2010), 'What Works in Leadership Development? A Rapid Evidence Review, National Policing Improvement Agency, London

MacDonald, R (1995), 'Skills and Qualities Required of Police Leaders' in Etter, B and Palmer, M (eds), *Police Leadership in Australia* (Annandale, NSW: Federation Press) 208

March, JG (2010), *The Ambiguities of Experience* (Ithaca, NY: Cornell University Press)

Mark, R (1977), *Policing a Perplexed Society* (London: Allen and Unwin)

Mark, R and Charlton, E (1978), *In the Office of Constable* (London: Collins)

Moore, MH (1990), 'Police Leadership: The Impossible Dream?' in Hargrove, EC and Glidewell, JC (eds), *Impossible Jobs in Public Management* (Lawrence, KS: University Press of Kansas) 72

Morese, R and Buss, TF (2007), 'Transformation of Public Leadership' in Morse, R, Buss, TF, and Kinghorn, CM (eds), *Transforming Public Leadership for the 21st Century* (NewYork: ME Sharpe) 3

Morgan, G (1993), *Imaginization* (London: Sage)

Neyroud, P (2011), 'Review of Police Leadership and Training', Home Office, London

Nixon, C (with Chandler, J) (2012), *Fair Cop* (Melbourne: Victory Books)

Pearson-Goff, M and Herrington, V (2014), 'Police Leadership: A Systematic Review of the Literature' 8(1) *Policing* 14

Pielstick, CD (2000), 'Formal vs. Informal Leading: A Comparative Analysis' 7(3) *Journal of Leadership and Organizational Studies* 99

Reicher, SD, Alexander Haslam, S, and Platow, MJ (2014), 'Social Psychology' in Rhodes, RAW and 't Hart, P (eds), *The Oxford Handbook of Political Leadership* (Oxford: OUP) 149

15

Reiner, R (1991), *Chief Constables—Bosses, Bobbies or Bureaucrats?* (Oxford: OUP)

Reiner, R (2015), 'Revisiting the Classics—Banton, Skolnick and Bittner' 25(3) *Policing and Society* 308

Rhodes, RAW (2014), 'Public Administration' in Rhodes, RAW and 't Hart, P (eds), *The Oxford Handbook of Political Leadership* (Oxford: OUP) 101

Rhodes, RAW and 't Hart, P (2014), 'Puzzles of Political Leadership' in Rhodes, RAW and 't Hart, P (eds), *The Oxford Handbook of Political Leadership* (Oxford: OUP) 1

Sarver, M and Miller, H (2014), 'Police Chief Leadership: Styles and Effectiveness 37(1) *Policing* 126

Savage, S, Charman, S, and Cope, S (2000), *Policing and the Power of Persuasion* (London: Blackstone)

Schafer, JA (2010), 'Effective Leaders and Leadership in Policing: Traits, Assessment, Development, and Expansion' 33(4) *Policing* 644

Schulz, DM (2004), *Breaking the Brass Ceiling: Women Police Chiefs and their Paths to the Top* (Westport, CT: Praeger)

Silvestri, M (2006), ' "Doing Time": Becoming a Police Leader' 8(4) *International Journal of Police Science and Management* 266

Silvestri, M (2007), ' "Doing" Police Leadership: Enter the "New Smart Macho" ' 17(1) *Policing and Society* 38

Sjoberg, L (2014), 'Feminism', in Rhodes, RAW and 't Hart, P (eds), *The Oxford Handbook of Political Leadership* (Oxford: OUP), 72

Stevens, J (2005), *Not for the Faint-hearted: My Life Fighting Crime* (London: Weidenfeld & Nicolson)

Tasdoven, H and Kaya, M (2014), 'The Impact of Ethical Leadership on Police Officers' Code of Silence and Integrity: Results from the Turkish National Police' 37(9) *International Journal of Public Administration* 529

Wall, DS (1998), *The Chief Constables of England And Wales: The Socio-Legal History of a Criminal Justice Elite* (Brookfield, VT: Ashgate)

Weick, KE (1995), *Sensemaking in Organizations* (Vol 3) (London: Sage)

Yocum, R (2007), 'The Moderating Effects of Narcissism on the Relationship between Emotional Intelligence and Leadership Effectiveness, Moral Reasoning and Managerial Trust', PhD, Seattle Pacific University

2

Leading in Austerity

Timothy Brain and Lynne Owens

Introduction

It is an obvious statement but the starting point of any study of police funding is to place it firmly in the context of public service. It is a service which, with minor exceptions, is free at the point of delivery to all members of society. As a consequence, again with minor exceptions, it receives its money from national or local government sources. Beyond that, however, all is complexity. Police funding is probably the most complex in the public sector, mixing the national with the local, and the highly centralized with the locally democratic, and as elected politicians ultimately make all the key decisions about levels of funding, police financing is a matter of national and local politics. The use of the funds is highly regulated, following the principles of local rather than central government, and the use of those resources is subject to general and specific public scrutiny. Despite its high degree of regulation, the system possesses numerous anomalies, of practical and political implication, which are difficult to redress. While the major decisions concerning the extent to which the police are funded are determined by politicians (the Home Secretary and, since 2012, police and crime commissioners (PCCs)), the use of those funds is largely devolved to chief constables (Home Office 2013a: 6).

Consequently, the professional leaders of the service require an understanding of how police finances work, how to maximize their benefit, how to account for their use, and how to do so in a highly political environment. They also have to do so with little evidence-based research and, at a time of unprecedented public spending austerity, with little corporate experience to draw upon. The challenge is that as the age of austerity is set to continue for an extended period, police leaders will have to rise to the highest levels of professionalism to maintain both internal morale and external confidence.

Overview

Policing in England and Wales is principally a devolved activity, undertaken by 43 individual forces, but supplemented by a small, if significant, number of national bodies. The forces range from the extremely large (the Metropolitan Police with over 45,000 personnel and a budget in 2013 of £2.6 billion) to the small (Warwickshire 1,550 personnel and annual budget of £80 million) (CIPFA Actuals 2012–13). All, however, conform to broadly the same financial operating principles.

In 2012–13, the gross revenue expenditure for the 43 forces amounted to £13.5 billion. There were three national sources of funding—Home Office Core and Specific Grants, National Non-Domestic Rates (NNDR), Revenue Support Grant (RSG), and council tax set, raised, and collected locally. Nationally, this was divided as 33% (£4.5 billion) Home Office Core Grant, 9% (£1.3 billion) Specific Grants, 25% NNDR and RSG (£3.4 billion), and 25% council tax (£3.3 billion) (Parliament UK, 2014). Approximately £1.5 billion was spent on national bodies—the College of Policing, the Independent Police Complaints Commission (IPCC), the National Crime Agency (NCA), the Office for Security and Counter Terrorism (OFSCT), and the Police ICT Company (College of Policing 2014a; IPCC 2012–13; Home Affairs Committee 2014; and Home Office 2013b). The net cost of police pensions was calculated to be £1.9 billion in 2009–10, although these costs are no longer funded out of annual revenue (Boyd 2014: 6). Even if pensions are included, the total police spend amounted to approximately 1% of gross domestic product (GDP) in 2012–13, or 2% of all public spending, compared to approximately 9 or 19%, respectively, for Health (ONS 2014a and ukpublicspending 2014).

The Home Office core grant is distributed to the 43 forces by means of the Police Allocation Formula (PAF). It does not allocate funds to each of the 43 forces according to a calculation of need:

> The police allocation formula (PAF) is essentially a calculation that uses various data sources (such as population density) to share money between police authorities in England and Wales. It is not a calculation of absolute needs, that is, it does not estimate how much each force needs independently of other forces. Instead it shares out the amount of money designated for police funding between forces based on their relative needs compared to each other. (Gov.uk, 'Guide to the Police Allocation Formula' 2013b).

The PAF broadly weights funding towards larger, urbanized forces. There is, however, an element of 'damping'. Every force is guaranteed an increase of 2.5% (known as 'the floor'). If the PAF calculation is less than 'the floor', then the grant is made up to that level. It means, however, that the remaining forces, while receiving an allocation above the 2.5% floor, will not receive the scale of allocation which the PAF would dictate without 'damping' ('the ceiling'). This mechanism dates from the formula's introduction in the mid-1990s, when it was realized that an unbridled implementation of the formula would produce such variation in funding that some forces would either lose significant resources or risk compensating with unacceptable rises in council tax. Neither were considered acceptable alternatives, so the damping mechanism was introduced. Intended as a temporary measure it has remained, because its removal, or even its greater application, would still produce volatile results (see Flanagan 2008: 29). It consequently remains a bone of contention and is subject to Home Office review, but the outcome is uncertain.

In addition to the 'core grant', there are specific grants. These include a separate calculation for Welsh forces, which are funded outside the Department for Communities and Local Government (DCLG) mechanisms, and five specific, 'Rule 2', grants, such as the 'Rural Policing Fund' and the 'Forensic and DNA' grant. Before 2010, these were allocated separately and for their specific purposes; since then they have been 'combined into one non-ring fenced grant to give police authorities more control over how they are used' (Gov.uk 2013b). Forces continue to receive a security grant of approximately £0.5 billion, but while distribution details are obscure, evidence suggests that this is predominantly allocated to the Metropolitan Police (Brain 2011–12: 8). From 2012–13, there has been a small (£90 million in 2012–13) Community Safety Grant element for allocation by PCCs to approved local partners (Gov.uk 2013a).

The third element of national grants are the combined Revenue Support Grant and the NNDR, distributed in England by the DCLG and in Wales by the Welsh government (WG). These are distributed by a different formula (the Standard Spending Assessment (SSA)), which takes into account both 'relative resources' and 'relative need' (Gov.uk 2013b).

The final component of police funding is the locally raised council tax. Until the Police and Magistrates' Courts Act 1994 came into force, only joint authorities, such as Avon and Somerset and Thames Valley, were constitutionally permitted to set their own council tax, while single-authority forces (the majority) operated as constituent committees of the principal authority (a county or metropolitan authority). This changed in 1994, with the Police and Magistrates' Courts Act enabling all police authorities (including after 1999, the Metropolitan Police, hitherto funded directly by the Home Office) to raise their own council tax.

However, this is another system that has never operated entirely as intended. Limits on annual increases ('capping') are often set by the responsible government department to prevent what central government considers excessive rises. In 2011, the requirements of the Localism Act 2011 substituted local referendums for increases deemed 'excessive' (for police 4% in 2013–14 and 2% in 2014–15). Since 2012, PCCs have replaced police authorities and have become responsible for setting the budget and precept (with minimal oversight from the nominated local Police and Crime Panel). Since inception only one PCC (Bedfordshire in 2015) has risked a referendum, but such was the scale of rejection and associated costs, future referenda are likely to prove rare. Neither council tax capping nor council tax referendums apply in Wales. It will be noted that the DCLG and the Welsh government therefore have significant influence on police funding, but with imprecise accountabilities.

As might be expected from such a complex system, there are significant differences between force areas. In 2012–13, Surrey raised 49% of its net revenue requirement by council tax, whereas Northumbria raised only 14%. The Metropolitan Police is the highest funded force per head of population at £313. In contrast, Northamptonshire is funded at the rate of £131 per head of population. In 2012–13, the average funding per head of population for English provincial metropolitan forces was £198, for English non-metropolitan forces £168, and for the four Welsh forces £195 (extrapolated from CIPFA Actuals 2012–13). While the levels of council tax for each force area will change incrementally over time, the idiosyncrasies of the PAF, with its damping mechanism, mean that the relative anomalies between levels of force funding will remain indefinitely, creating practical difficulties for local police leaders, both professional and political, in articulating why their area receives less grant or pays higher council tax than others.

Such a complicated system, with so many diverse sources of funds calculated by such diverse methods, has resulted in a system where accountability, much less responsibility, for police funding is massively obfuscated. Despite the post-2010 Coalition (Conservative–Liberal Democrat) government's enthusiasm for direct democracy, there seems to be no likelihood of clarification. Such are the risks of disruption involved in untangling the system, that it may even be beyond fundamental change. Consequently forces, and their democratic and professional leaders, will have to live with the inequalities of the PAF, and its practical implications for grants, council tax, and therefore available resources, for the foreseeable future.

Context Pre-2010

That such a complicated arrangement exists is a consequence of policing's historical development. The practical politics of the early nineteenth century demanded that policing developed incrementally in the British Isles. In England and Wales, policing was devolved to localities—first the Metropolitan Police (1829), then the boroughs (1835), and finally the counties (from 1839). At first responsibility for funding was wholly local, but a desire to raise standards in the mid-nineteenth century resulted in the institution of the Home Office grant, whereby a quarter of the annual funding requirement for a force was met by the Home Office consequent on a certificate of efficiency from the new body, Her Majesty's Inspectors of Constabulary (HMIC) (Tobias 1979: 101). It signalled the start of the detailed involvement of the Home Office in the affairs of local forces, and subsequent administrations have wrestled with the problem of striking the right balance between national standards and local responsibility.

The system of funding became increasingly complex as a consequence of local government itself, expanding in terms of responsibilities in the late nineteenth century and the extension of 'assigned grants' for specific purposes, notably health, education, and transport. This system eventually morphed into that of 'Rate Support Grant', and more latterly that of 'Revenue Support Grant'. Originally councils were able to levy their own business rates, but after radical changes in the late 1980s this abruptly changed into the NNDR, set nationally and then redistributed to local authorities. Because of its origins in devolved local government, and the set determination of successive governments, regardless of party, not to create a national police force in England and Wales (conspicuously the contrary with the devolved Scottish government), there the complexity has remained.

There was, however, a trend for more of the requirements of policing to be determined nationally and implemented locally, especially so after the advent of the Police Act 1964, which reduced the number of police forces from over 100 to eventually just 43, and commensurately increased the powers of Home Secretaries. Successive governments also pursued a policy of increasing police strength, both in relative and absolute terms. By 1979, there were approximately 110,000 officers and 42,600 civilian staff. However, in 1979, the Conservative Party under Margaret Thatcher made policing, and specifically police numbers and police pay, an election issue, which proved a highly successful strategy. From then until 2010 both main political parties vied with each other over the degree to which they would increase police resources. This was especially true of the revitalized Labour Party under Tony Blair, which increased police Full Time Equivalent (FTE) personnel (officers and civilian staff) by almost 60,000 posts. The extent of growth under Labour is illustrated in Tables 2.1 and 2.2, as is the increasing significance of specific and special grants.

This was part of a conscious political strategy to wrest the 'law and order' issue from the Conservatives, and for a while it was politically successful. In practical

Table 2.1 Police Funding Resources, 43 Forces, England and Wales 1998–99 to 2010–11

	1998–99	2010–11	Change	% Change
Council tax (£bn)	1.027	3.191	2.164	211
Consolidated DCLG/WG, NNDR, and RSG (£bn)	2.526	3.724	1.198	47
Home Office Core police grant (£bn)	3.656	4.625	0.969	26
Home Office Special and specific grants (£bn)	0	1.461	1.461	n/a
Other income (£bn)	0.241	0.872	0.631	262
Total grants (£bn)	6.182	9.810	3.628	59
Total funding (£bn)	7.450	13.873	6.423	86
Total funding per 1,000 population (£s)	142,099	251,138	109,038	77
Total grant funding per 1,000 population (£s)	117,914	177,587	59,673	51

Source: Parliament UK (2014) and CIPFA (1999 and 2011).

21

Table 2.2 Police Workforce, 43 Forces, England and Wales 1999 and 2010

	31.3.1999	31.3.2010	Change	% Change
Officers (FTE)	123,846	143,734	19,888	16
Civilians (headcount)	52,465	79,596	27,131	52
PCSOs (FTE)	0	16,918	16,918	n/a
Designated officers	0	3,840	3,840	n/a
Total police personnel (excl traffic wardens)	176,311	244,088	67,777	38

Source: CIPFA (2000) and Home Office (2010a).

terms it also enabled the simultaneous growth in local forces to adequately address a prescribed form of 'Neighbourhood Policing', as well as to implement a whole series of national initiatives and new national organizations, for example the Serious and Organised Crime Agency. However, the strategy also came with intense inspection regimes and increasing prescription as to how the money was to be spent, which in turn led to an increase in the number of specific 'ring-fenced' grants and more auditing and inspection. The most significant of these ring-fenced grants was the 'Crime Fighting Fund', which was specifically to increase police officer numbers. Police authorities were, however, required to 'match' central specific grants with a commensurate level of local finance, which, together with a brief period in the early 2000s of relaxing central controls, encouraged increases in council tax.

By 2009–10, council tax had almost doubled as a proportion of police funding, representing 27% of net police funding, compared to 14% in 1998–99. Labour had managed to pull off the political feat of increasing central controls while simultaneously increasing the amount of funding paid for locally. By its last year in office, Labour had certainly delivered in terms of increased police resources, but in the process the system had become massively centralized and prescriptive, while police funding had become even more complicated with the proliferation of special and specific grants, limiting discretion for chief constables and police authorities alike. This was a situation that David Cameron and his revitalized 'New Conservatives' could exploit by depicting themselves to the electorate as the restorers of local democracy and financial efficiency, and to professional police officers as the restorers of managerial discretion (Police Reform Taskforce 2007: 9–12 and Brain 2013: 12–25, and 55–65).

Context Post-2010

It was not expected that this level of funding would be sustained even in normal economic circumstances (Flanagan 2007: 6–7, and Brain 2010: 365); what ensured this was the severe economic recession of 2008–09, and the significant increase in government debt and concomitant pressure to rapidly reduce it once the worst of the recession was over. To this was added the Conservatives' philosophical commitment to reduced government expenditure (Brain 2013: 72–4), and although the 2010 general election produced a 'hung Parliament', it was this policy (specifically to eliminate the structural deficit by 2014–15) which prevailed in the Conservative–Liberal Democrat Coalition agreements (Conservative Liberal Democrats 2010: 1).

Rapid action followed these declarations of intent. An emergency budget took £6 billion out of public spending almost immediately, the police share of which was £125 million. The subsequent 2010 Comprehensive Spending Review (CSR) required 'real' (that is relative to GDP and inflation) cuts of up to 25% in departmental spending over the period 2011–12 to 2014–15. While health and overseas aid were exempt, and the defence share was smaller, conspicuously, the police force was not exempt, although at 20% it received a slightly smaller cut than the rest of the Home Office and it was calculated, somewhat speculatively, that council tax would increase to take up some of the shortfall. When all was balanced out there would be a net cash reduction of £0.8 billion in the funding of the 43 forces by 2014–15 (HM Treasury 2010: 10; Home Office 2010c: 10; and NAO 2011: 14).

However, there was more to it than that. Under the leadership of David Cameron, the Conservatives developed a new political philosophy based on the principles of 'civil society' and localism, with increased community self-reliance and individual volunteerism, smaller central and even local government, and an injection of more direct democracy. Less money would be spent by the state, a consequence of which was intended to be a revitalized economy. All was summed up in the term 'The Big Society' (Conservative Party, 2010). The police service would not simply be swept up by the new philosophy; it would, in David Cameron's vision, become an exemplar.

For David Cameron, the police was 'Britain's last great unreformed public service' (Elliott 2006) and in opposition a whole package of 'reforms' were developed by a 'Police Reform Taskforce'. Directly elected PCCs would replace unelected police authorities; Labour's regime of central targets and bureaucracy would be slashed; officers would be incentivized by radical changes to pay and conditions of service; 'flexible' pensions would be introduced (which in practice meant delayed and reduced benefits) (Police Reform Taskforce 2007). In government these ideas were quickly encapsulated in a policy document, *Policing in the 21st Century*, effectively the template for the Conservative–Liberal Democrat Coalition's policing programme (Home Office 2010b).

The amount of money available for policing fell rapidly, with cuts in all forms of central grants instituted from 2011–12 onwards. Many forces, however, had anticipated the change and already commenced recruiting freezes. To ensure that council tax was kept under control, the Coalition eschewed capping but instead introduced an incentive in the form of a 'Council Tax Freeze Grant' which, as its name suggested, was a grant given if a local authority did not increase its council tax. It was not, however, a like-for-like replacement, as it did not build into the base budget. Nevertheless, it was an incentive no police authority could resist in its first year, but because it did not build the base budget and there was no guarantee for how long it would continue. It became increasingly less attractive over time, and by 2014–15 only five PCCs took up the offer (DCLG 2014a, 2014b).

Budget cuts and increasing efficiencies were two of the principal strands of government policy designed to reduce police expenditure and meet the strictures of the 2010 Spending Review. The third was reducing in the short and long term, the demands of police pay. The short-term requirement was met, in common with the rest of the public sector, by a pay freeze and reductions in overtime. The longer term was addressed by root-and-branch changes to police pay and conditions consequent upon a review headed by future Chief Inspector of Constabulary, Tom Winsor. By a combination of lowering the starting salary, shortening pay scales, eliminating bonus payments, and rescheduling specialist payments, Winsor estimated that £741 million would be saved by 2017–18, although that assumed a full implementation date in 2012, always unlikely and in the event not achieved. At the time of writing, the full financial benefits of Winsor are still to be delivered, while the pressures of inflation on pay cannot be indefinitely delayed. Winsor also fitted into a broader review of pensions by Lord Hutton, and while in future officers would have to work longer for reduced pension benefits, this would have little impact on the short-term need to reduce general expenditure (Winsor 2012).

Effect

It is difficult to exaggerate the scale of the task which the collective police leadership (chief officers, staff associations, and those involved in governance) faced in 2010. The first government cuts were delivered in the December 2010 grant settlements (Home Department 2010), but there was an explicit expectation by ministers that service to the public should not be diminished, reflecting a belief that the police force was fundamentally inefficient and that cuts could be borne by 'the back office', while frontline officer time would be freed up by scrapping central bureaucracy and targets, with efficiencies delivered by increasing outsourcing and inter-force collaboration, which would all protect delivery to the public (eg Home Secretary 2011). It was always debatable whether these measures would be as effective as believed, but in any case, savings thus accrued could only be delivered incrementally, whereas government spending requirements meant that the cash savings had to be delivered within the lifetime of the 2010–15 Parliament. However, despite the scale of the challenge, by March 2014 the police service had collectively achieved the cuts required of it, as exemplified in Tables 2.3 and 2.4.

Table 2.3 Police Funding Resources, 43 Forces, England and Wales 2010–11 to 2013–14 (funding)

	2010–11	2013–14	Change	% Change
Council tax (£bn)	3.191	2.981	−0.143	−7
Consolidated DCLG/WG, NNDR, and RSG (£bn)	3.724	3.345	−0.379	−10
Home Office Core police grant (£bn)	4.625	4.768	+0.143	+3
Home Office Special and specific grants (£bn)	1.461	1.004	−0.457	−31
Other income (£bn)	0.872	0.790	−0.820	−9
Total grants (£bn)	9.810	9.117	−0.693	−7
Total police funding (£bn)	13.873	12.888	−0.985	−7
Total funding per 1,000 population (£s)	251,138	227,835	−23,303	−9
Total grant funding per 1,000 population (£s)	177,587	161,171	−16,416	−9

Source: Parliament UK (2014) and CIPFA (2011 and 2014).

Table 2.4 Police Workforce, 43 Forces, England and Wales 2010–11 to 2013–14

	31 Mar 2010	31 Mar 2014	Change	% Change
Officers (FTE)	143,734	127,909	−15,825	−11
Civilians (strength)	79,596	64,097	−15,499	−19
PCSOs (strength)	16,918	13,066	−3,852	−23
Designated officers	3,840	4,273	+433	+11
Total police personnel (excl traffic wardens)	244,088	209,345	−34,743	−14

Source: CIPFA (2011) and 2013–14, and Gov.uk (2014).

It should be noted, however, that the apparent increase in the core Home Office Police Grant shown in Table 2.3 is more a matter of presentation than genuine growth, as it has been Home Office policy under the Coalition, in contrast to Labour, to reduce the number and value of special and specific grants, and consolidate them within the core grant, amounting to an overall reduction in funding of 7%.

Given that over 80% of income, in common with most labour-intense service industries, is spent on personnel, a commensurate reduction in the workforce was inevitable, as is illustrated in Table 2.4. Effectively, half of the growth in the police workforce delivered between 1998–99 and 2010–11 had been eliminated by March 2014.

Between 31 March 2010 and 31 March 2014, nearly 35,000 posts were lost, equating to over half of the growth between 1998–99 and 2009–10. Police officer posts, however, took the brunt of the cuts, losing almost 16,000 FTE posts, or 77% of the growth in numbers between 1998–99 and 2009–10. Simply planning how to lose this number of posts in such a short space of time, while maintaining something of a balanced workforce and delivering a service to the public without serious dislocation, was in itself a significant leadership challenge, the achievement of which had to take place while absorbing fundamental constitutional change (the introduction of PCCs in 2012) and changes to pay and conditions of service (the Winsor Report recommendations), but without the comforting injection of cash which can often accompany radical structural change in the workplace (eg as with Labour's Health Service 'reforms' of 2003–08; see Butler 2003).

In its 'Valuing the Police' series of reports, HMIC has identified a range of standard responses by forces to 'austerity', including recruiting freezes; redundancy programmes; civilian staff regrading; structural reorganization (moving away from the near-ubiquitous Basic Command Unit model into various hybrids which HMIC has labelled the 'local planning model'); merging response and neighbourhood policing; outsourcing of functions to private sector providers (although no mention of the Serious Fraud Office investigations into G4S and Serco, see Independent 2013); station and other building closures (the former offset to an unquantifiable extent by use of other public access points); the increased use of volunteers; and the wider application of new, labour-saving technologies (eg the national single non-emergency number, mobile data, and demand forecasting). HMIC also emphasized reductions in 'back office' staff with an ostensible refocus on the 'frontline' (although even it has accepted that the latter has only been 'protected' and not 'preserved'), and despite its enthusiasm for collaboration (adopting a wide definition) it has recognized that it encompasses no more than 14% of force budgets and is subject to wide variation between forces. Of significance was the absence of clear evidence of beneficial outcomes arising from cuts in bureaucracy (HMIC 2013 and 2014b:), suggesting either that not much has been achieved or that what has been achieved is not easily quantifiable as material benefits. HMIC also recognized that opportunities for genuine 'income generation' were limited, although by mid-2014 an increasing number of PCCs were applying the 'Late Night Levy' on businesses which stay open in their area, thereby weakening the 'free-at-point-of-delivery' ethos of the police service (Weinfass 2014).

Nevertheless, in its 2014 assessment, HMIC concluded that the 43 forces had 'risen to the challenge of austerity', balancing their books and finding almost £2.53 billion of savings. It recognized that the response of forces to the challenge of austerity had been 'impressive', and that there had been 'strong leadership across the service', with many chief officers taking their 'workforces with them during this period of unprecedented change', although it was perhaps disappointing to wait until we got to page 71, *Meeting the Challenge*, before finding this assessment (HMIC 2014a: 71).

Cuts on this scale, however, could not be delivered painlessly. The cuts were undiscriminating, with those forces which had been the more efficient before

2010 and with lower costs, being subjected to the same degree of cuts as the more costly and inefficient. As has been noted, given that personnel accounted for over 80% of revenue expenditure, it was clear from the start that there would have to be substantial reductions in police numbers, and these would have to be delivered by the blunt instruments of freezing both officer and civilian recruiting and civilian staff redundancies. While some forces were, by HMIC's assessment, coping with the cuts, three (Bedfordshire, Gwent, and Staffordshire) needed 'improvement' (HMICb 2014: 120).

By the end of the CSR 2010 period there was growing evidence that neighbourhood policing was diminishing (HMIC 2014b: 33) and that internal morale was suffering (Hoggett et al 2013: 5 and Sky News 2013). Furthermore, after initially holding up well, by 2014 there were indications that performance and public perceptions were beginning to suffer. Despite a continuing long-term reduction in Police Recorded Crime Figures, in 2014 for the first time in several years the Crime Survey for England and Wales (CSEW) recorded slight drops in the percentages of those surveyed who thought the police were doing a good or excellent job, and who had confidence in the police (ONS 2014b: 4–7). The CSEW assessed the drops to be statistically insignificant, but uncertainty remains as to whether they are the first signs that the public were beginning to notice that there were fewer police around and that after several years of attrition quality was not quite as good as it had been.

However, arguably the greatest problem facing police leaders, both of the professional and political varieties, is that the era of austerity is set to continue for most of the Parliament commencing in May 2015, following the election of a majority Conservative government. In their manifesto, the Conservatives made it clear that further spending cuts of £27.5 billion would be required from most government departments, the Home Office share of which, by extrapolation, would be in excess of £1 billion (Conservative Party, 2015, 8). By mid-2014, some forces were already recognizing that they would have to save as much as they had already saved in the next CSR period (HMIC 2014b: 33 and 120), with the clear risk that future personnel losses, at least as far ahead as the midpoint of the next Parliament, might be as great as those sustained between 2010 and 2015 (Brain 2013: 168), while a 2015 National Audit Office (NAO) report warned that the Home Office possessed 'insufficient information to determine how much further it can reduce funding without degrading services' (NAO, 2015: 8).

Furthermore, despite enthusiasm for forces to appoint more volunteer special constables, by March 2014 there were indications that numbers were at best stagnating, and possibly declining (Gov.uk 2014). Such were the prospects that in August 2014 one PCC was quoted as fearing his force would 'go bust' in the future, although such are the rules governing local authorities that this is not an option; forces simply have to take whatever steps are necessary to balance budgets and carry on (BBC News 2014a).

The leadership requirement

In this scenario of continuing decline in resources, what are the options for police leaders? In its 2014 report, HMIC saw further opportunities to work in partnerships with other organizations, use of predictive technologies leading to early intervention problem-solving, and reducing further the 'target culture' and thereby its associated bureaucracy (although this last observation ignored the imposition of force level targets by PCCs in their Police and Crime Plans). It also placed great faith in improved technology, although even it was forced to admit that the new Police IT Company, the successor body to the Police Information Technology Organisation (PITO), had as yet failed to make 'any appreciable impact'. It might also have added that, at best, the beneficial impacts of improved technology would be in the medium to long term, and would require upfront financial investment in a period of continuing austerity while competing with the costs of maintenance, upgrades, and replacing obsolescent equipment.

In such circumstances, with the prospect of some forces potentially reaching the limits of financial stability, even viability, it was inevitable that HMIC would, if only by implication, raise again the prospect of amalgamations, notwithstanding the inadequacies of the business case for the mergers proposed in 2005–6 (which stressed the supposed benefits and underplayed the costs) and, more recently, the uncertain benefits of the creation of the single Scottish force in 2013 (Auditor General 2013: 8 and 21–8; HMIC 2014a: 36–40), together with the decided lack of enthusiasm shown by Theresa May in autumn 2014, who instead has preferred closer, if unspecified, collaboration between police, fire, and ambulance services (BBC News 2014b). If mergers were to be seriously pursued then the ability to lead forces through a prolonged period of fundamental change would be added to the leadership requirement list.

The reality is that police leaders will have to consider all of the options available and assess their relevancy to their own situation. Some options, if correctly implemented, may serve to mitigate the very worst of the organizational consequences of prolonged austerity, but it is simply improbable that further personnel losses, probably on the same scale as in the CSR 2010 period, can be avoided. The evidence is that by 2014–15 many PCCs were prepared to stretch the council tax increases to the limit of what was politically practical, but even this only reduces (but does not avoid) cuts in workforce numbers. The possible future election of a Labour government, or at least a Labour-dominated coalition, might offer the prospect of some long-term relief, but in opposition Labour policy-makers have signalled their initial intention to maintain the Conservative–Liberal Democrat Coalition's spending plans. So police leaders are not yet able to signal to their workforces that the end of austerity is in sight.

Even in the era of austerity, to a great extent the leadership requirements are the standard ones for any period: the ability to create, articulate, and implement a strategic vision; to manage ambiguity; and to convince potentially sceptical audiences, both internal and external, that the destination is attainable and the journey worthwhile; in short, the ability to motivate the workforce and maintain the confidence of the community. However, the age of austerity demands heightened qualities of financial acumen, budget control, and change leadership. There will have to be the fundamental desire and ability to drive out inefficiencies using tools such as 'Lean Management' and techniques developed by the European Foundation for Quality Management. Also required will be the ability to forge and then work within new, imaginative partnerships between forces and between local organizations. Political acumen and negotiating skills will be essential components of the relationship with the PCC. Whatever techniques are used, and solutions identified, leaders must conduct full cost/benefit analyses before adoption. Finally, in the long list is the ability to drive through change management, managing large-scale projects while maintaining the balance between the imperative of the outcome and the ability to maintain the confidence and morale of the workforce. For this the leader must be visible, dynamic, communicative, and accessible. Ultimately, the police leader in the age of austerity must convey a sense that despite all of the current vicissitudes something better will emerge for the future.

There is, however, a further problem to consider. During the continuing period of austerity police leadership itself is set to undergo a fundamental change, with the introduction of direct entrants at junior, middle, and chief officer ranks. At least some senior leaders will have little strategic experience of the organizational environments in which they will operate and, consequently, have to learn 'on the job'. All this amounts to a significant leadership challenge, for which, in the current political climate, even those who are very successful are unlikely to receive much appreciation. Virtue, therefore, must be its own reward.

Practitioner's Perspective

This section reflects the writer's own experiences based on present practice across two forces, the Metropolitan Police Service where I was an Assistant Commissioner, and Surrey, where I have been Chief Constable since February 2012. It also reflects my role as an active party to discussions within the College of Policing and Chief Constables' Council (the national operational decision-making forum attended by the chiefs of the 43 forces). A chief constable is charged in law with running an efficient and effective police force.[1] As a constable, like all others, chief constables have sworn on oath[2] to serve the public to the best of their skill, keep the peace, and prevent crime. It follows, therefore, that their primary focus is keeping people safe and protecting the vulnerable whilst

---

[1] Police Reform and Social Responsibility Act 2011, s 35, Value for money.
[2] Form of wording for the attestation of a constable. Police Act 1996, s 29 and Sch 4.

adhering to the standards of behaviour, more recently and helpfully articulated within the College of Policing Code of Ethics (College of Policing 2014b).

It is tempting to focus on policing structures alone, as the complexities of funding formulas, and the governance processes Dr Brain explores, lead to a labyrinthine web which adds to the tortuous decision-making faced by operational leaders. In managing change, however, there are other equally important issues also worthy of consideration.

Changing demand

The police service is immensely and rightly proud of its contribution to the greatest reduction in crime ever seen in this country. Whether you accept the crime recording statistics or place more relevance on the Crime Survey for England and Wales (ONS 2014c), there can be no room for doubt that crime in many categories is falling. However, what is also evident is that there are some significant areas of under-reporting (eg domestic abuse, hate crime), crimes occurring in a less visible manner than the more traditional offences such as burglary or street robbery (eg fraud, online child sexual exploitation), and growth in complex historic case examination (the post-Savile experience). These changes mean that chief constables must make risk-based investment decisions at the same time as down-sizing.

Technological advances over the past ten years have led to significant new crime phenomena that have impacted on how the public experience crime and the ability of police forces and national policing agencies to respond promptly and effectively to them. Offences of fraud are now often committed by offenders operating worldwide but from within their own homes. The sharing of indecent images and its associated abuse at the touch of a button, reaches every corner of the globe. The supply of controlled drugs and non-criminalized, but highly damaging psychoactive substances, requires an international and joint police and governmental response. The risks faced in terms of domestic and international terrorism are increasingly diverse in nature. Crime of volume and high severity or financial impact is now very often part of a national or international problem. This contrasts with the traditional patterns of offending and risk to the individual communities we police, where crime and anti-social behaviour concerns and expectation occur within the boundaries of the 43 police forces of England and Wales and their jurisdiction. The reality of crime now and in the future is difficult for many to comprehend, which may explain why a survey in 2014 showed that public concern about law and order was surveyed to be at a 20-year low (IPSOS MORI 2014). Crime without borders is now commonplace, yet the funding provision remains localized.

It simply should not be a publically accepted proposition that policing can remain the same, yet smaller. The philosophy of 'policing by consent',[3] the

---

[3] Formed from the nine Peelian Principles of Policing, Metropolitan Police General Instructions to new officers, 1829. See <https://www.gov.uk/government/publications/policing-by-consent> (accessed 20 April 2015).

world-renowned hallmark of British policing, requires that the public accept current and future policing models as having legitimacy. To ignore such changing crime patterns will, in time, undermine public support.

Growing smaller apart

Chief constables and their teams are finding it necessary to articulate more effectively to the public, partners, and politicians the demands on the police service. Early findings from across the country show that the number of incidents previously dealt with by other public services, now dealt with by the police, has increased, as has the number of mental health-related incidents (College of Policing 2015). In Surrey, over 500,000 calls are received per year,[4] approximately 135,000 of which result in an incident report being generated and subsequent officer/staff deployment, yet fewer than 50,000 of which lead to a crime being recorded.[5] A less well-resourced present and future require that we understand this picture better than our predecessors did. Indeed I would contend that as resources grew historically (as spelled out by Dr Brain), the police service may have, wittingly, subsumed work that is the primary, or at least partial, responsibility of other agencies. Of course, this is a double conundrum in that most of these same public and voluntary bodies have been subject to similar budget reductions and it is clear, locally at least, that reductions have occurred in an isolationist manner, meaning that the public sector has shrunk apart rather than together.

As chief constables gain a better understanding of the demand for policing services, they need to ensure that other bodies, such as health trusts and local authorities, take responsibility for their areas of core demand. This is not a simple task, as the vulnerable often touch every part of the public sector. Telephone calls from these bodies on Friday evenings passing over responsibility for risky cases are not unusual and, with the spectre of IPCC scrutiny, the police service is reticent to resist. Equally, frontline officers are understandably nervous of their accidental mishandling of a situation that such scrutiny might bring. The leaders of the service, at every level, must be bold in their negotiation with partners and auditors/regulators (whether the IPCC or HMIC) who must participate in this process. Failure to do so leaves the frontline decision-makers vulnerable to the hindsight judgements of others—for example, the media—which is unacceptable. The work led by the Association of Chief Police Officers (ACPO) on the Mental Health Concordat is an example of such necessary and appropriate pre-emptive leadership (Department of Health and Home Office 2014). With their wider remit (beyond policing), PCCs have an opportunity to support chief constables in this renegotiation with the public, partners, and regulatory bodies alike.

---

[4] Surrey Police Telephony statistics, 2013/14. Total number of phone calls received was 566,460, comprising 123,863 emergency (999) calls and 442,597 non-emergency (101) calls.

[5] Surrey Police, Total incident reports generated for 2013–14: 135,249. Total notifiable offences recorded for 2013–14: 48,486.

Meanwhile, chief constables have a responsibility to explore and propose alternative models of delivery. Co-locating neighbourhood resources and understanding the gaps/overlaps of provision between the 999 emergency services are good starting points. We are seeing a patchwork of such developments nationwide. Work on response to mental health and the troubled families' agenda (DCLG 2011) across the country has also yielded gains and there is an important role for the newly formed College of Policing in establishing 'what works'.[6]

A new addition to the budget complexity expounded by Tim Brain is the ability to bid for various 'funds' (for policing an 'innovation fund'). With each of these funds apparently operating in isolation from within a variety of central government departments that exist in this space (the DCLG, Home Office, and Department of Health) there is a risk that public money is being wasted if genuine best practice remains undiscovered. Significant resources, diverted from elsewhere, are engaged in compiling the bids and reporting against them, rather than focusing on delivery. Equally, if monitored effectively this could provide a real opportunity to identify best practice, but it will rely on a shift in approaches to the definitions of success rather than monitoring process. Policing culture (influenced, to a greater degree than they may realize, by those who inspect and oversee, such as PCCs, HMIC, the IPCC, and auditors) will need to be mature and confident enough to test new ideas, accepting that models of delivery may not succeed, and, equally importantly, be prepared to import best practice from others. The race to innovate may lead to fragmentation and poor public value. As an example, I have decided that in Surrey we will not be in the vanguard of the body-worn video pilots. This was a conscious decision, as it would seem unhelpful to start an alternative exploration when best practice will be identified, and a procurement framework set, built on real experiences from elsewhere in the country, evaluated by the College of Policing. As chief constable I have, however, heard positive comments being made about forces at the forefront of the developments.

Resisting such pressures for the reasons articulated requires leadership confidence.

It is an unassailable fact that the police service is also only one small, but vitally important, part of the British criminal justice system. The courts, Crown Prosecution Service, and defence system have been subject to considerable budget reductions too. The move to a more digital process of case transference and early indicators of transforming justice schemes being proposed by senior judges are welcome, but processes within the system must be focused on victims and witnesses to a degree that is not currently tangible. If administrative efficiency is the only goal, the existing shortcomings in service to the witness may remain, and public confidence may suffer.

---

[6] The government has selected the College of Policing to host the What Works Centre for Crime Reduction—part of a world-leading network of centres providing robust, comprehensive evidence to guide public spending decisions, see <http://whatworks.college.police.uk/About/Pages/default.aspx> (accessed 20 April 2015).

Structures and impact upon leadership

Dr Brain is absolutely right to assert that collaborative relationships are an important feature of present/future policy. Most forces have developed innovative partnerships, some with the private sector, others with local public sector bodies, some with other forces, and many a combination of all three. I am not aware of any academic or other independent assessment of the real impact of changes on the totality of policing delivery. Do the public recognize these changes and do they impair policing legitimacy?

This amalgam of solutions to the issue of austerity does pose some leadership challenges both locally and nationally. First, the British policing model (of 43 forces) requires that in times of crisis (such as the riots of 2011) British policing operates as one body, sharing resources in response to the threats. Whilst individually identified solutions—whether exposed by PCCs or chief constables—often have evident efficiency gains, there is an absolute responsibility to ensure that this core national policing capacity is maintained.

Furthermore, such a mismatch of solutions seems, in great part, reliant on local relationships. It requires a different skill set to the command and control approach and relies on a chief constable's ability to influence through evidence-based, public-focused proposals rather than simply asserting their own personal view. Negotiating skills are the order of the day. The converse argument to this, of course, is that the individual chief constable does have liability in law to ensure effectiveness and efficiency in *their* policing area which can encourage protectionism. For example, in the South East region the funding solution for the regional, and shared, assets has been tricky to negotiate. When one Force, Surrey, receives such a significantly higher proportion of its' monies from the local council tax payer (as explored by Tim Brain and further expanded later), any cost-sharing agreement becomes complex. A share based on the totality of budget sees the local tax payer disadvantaged (the Surrey position). Alternatively, other forces (taking Hampshire as the example) would, understandably, argue that their force (and therefore community) is already penalized by the dampening mechanism established at a national level because of the vagaries of the current funding formula. The negotiated solution, recommended to PCCs, sees a move towards a percentage share of the total budget but achieved over a number of years, so as not to create abrupt financial loss for any force in one financial period.

As Dr Brain indicated, Surrey Police receives the second lowest grant from the government of all police forces in England and Wales and, subsequently, approximately half of its funding is generated from precept through the council tax. Currently, this precept can be set up to the value of the 'Council Tax Lock' of 2% set by the government without the legal requirement for a costly public referendum. Surrey Police benefits from the bold decision-making of previous chief constables and police authorities, as historic rises are now embedded within our revenue base. However, such increases are now an understandably sensitive local issue for residents and actively discouraged by central government, which will award a Council Tax Freeze Grant to the value of 1% for those PCCs who desist.

This mix of devolved and central funding approaches has led to the significant differences that Dr Brain highlights. As Surrey and Sussex Police deliver their collaborative working, it would be ethically wrong to ignore the fact that the Surrey taxpayer contributes considerably more than their Sussex equivalent. The chief constables and PCCs are left resorting to different financial models for different areas of policing business, potentially increasing the costs in the finance function in the process. Other forces in a similar position in terms of collaboration (Warwickshire and West Mercia, for example) have more similar tax bases, so this particular complexity does not occur.

For all of the aforementioned practical and operational reasons a structural solution, ie considering the merger of forces, appears a more cost-effective approach. It would reduce management overheads, benefit from economies of scale, provide operational resilience that is already diminishing in the smallest forces, and enjoy the support of chief police officers. Political and funding structures are more intractable problems in achieving this solution but would provide significantly better value for money in policing in this continuing world of austerity.

Knowledge

This new reality requires financial astuteness to be raised to unprecedented levels. As Tim Brain says, there is limited research in this area and few studies for the police leader to draw upon. Many of the political commentaries are now dated and I have drawn benefit from HMIC's 'Valuing the Police Inspection'. This is now in its fourth year, providing a helpful analysis of the 43 forces, enabling me to identify where the Sussex Force's resourcing levels are different or look expensive or underinvested.

Whichever way you look at it, the current austerity drive requires leaders with an expanded skill set. This may not be a natural acquisition for every chief officer who has been otherwise, rightly, immersed in the provision of operational services to their public. There is a need for reliance upon accredited finance professionals to provide advice and guidance ensuring decisions are made appropriately, in accordance with the law, for best value, and ethically. Chief constables must appoint a person responsible for the proper administration of the police forces' financial affairs—the chief finance officer.[7] However, the ability to provide effective scrutiny is not wholly assuaged by such appointments, and the need for formal fiscal training for chief police officers has been recognized. There is a clear requirement for all chief officers to understand the nature and impact of funding formulas, other revenue 'streams', capital budget, procurement rules, audit requirements, and general Schemes of Governance. The Strategic Command Course, the prerequisite leadership development programme for any officers wishing to attain

---

[7] Police Reform and Social Responsibility Act 2011, s 4(1) and Sch 2.

chief police officer rank within the United Kingdom, was significantly revised by the College of Policing in 2013–14. An online self-assessment and pre-entry learning requirement was set, followed by both business and partnership modules including specific sessions on financial awareness, change, and leadership provided by proven private sector organizations.

Impact on staff

No discursive document would be complete, however, without recognizing the impact on officers and staff. The pay, conditions, and pensions of all have been downgraded and many staff have been, and continue to be, exposed to the spectre of redundancy. These phenomena, whilst not new in the private sector, have rarely been seen in policing before (and certainly not in my tenure). Uncertainty has become the new normality and the requirement for leaders, at all levels, to be present alongside their officers and staff to understand the impact of change, respond to suggestions, and talk honestly about concerns is underestimated at their peril.

Despite this unsettling environment, the men and women of the police service remain focused on their role of keeping people safe and protecting the vulnerable. This dedication to duty is fragile, however, as reflected through staff surveys, and sickness and staff leaver rates.

Conclusion

The leadership challenge in responding to the requirements of an austerity programme, for all the reasons articulated, is significant. The ultimate goal is to provide a professional public service that operates in the public interest to keep people safe, at reduced costs providing the best value for money, whilst retaining the goodwill of staff on which policing depends.

Shared Reflections

What can be concluded from these contributions? The common themes are that the financial situation for police forces is serious but not yet critical. It is, however, at the very least, likely to become much more serious in the next few years. The financial problems will be exacerbated by the changing nature of demands upon the police, with greater emphasis upon crimes of a personal and secretive nature, requiring intensive investigative resources. This suggests the utility of a fundamental review of the nature and delivery of policing in the 21st century, but none seems likely.

While levels of police funding will create enormous challenges for the police and its leadership, whether professional or political, they will not prove fatal. Taking relative levels of funding back to those of the late 1980s will not spell the end of the service; it will simply mean that the process of returning to those levels will create enormous difficulties, and once those levels have been attained the level of service will be much reduced. The level of service at the end of the 1980s was essentially response policing and investigation, in other words a core service. It may not have been ideal, but response plus investigation is a survivable model until something better comes along. The problem is that public and professional expectations have increased exponentially since the late 1980s. Put simply, the public expect problem-solving neighbourhood policing, with investigative techniques that are extensive and which deal with a wider range of crimes, not the least of which are personal and historical.

The way in which the police service is funded does not help leaders to deal with the problems. Police funding is, by any standards, highly complex, with responsibility diffused or obfuscated. This enables funders, principally central government and PCCs, to each blame the other for a situation, and leaves the public with no effective accountability. Equally, the new constitutional arrangements, with powerful PCCs, make it difficult for chief constables to criticize local funding settlements, even should they choose to do so. The prospects for change to these arrangements which would more effectively balance appropriate democratic oversight with professional independence are remote, with a future Conservative government likely to persist with PCCs, while Labour promises to replace PCCs with boards formed of councillors nominated from local constituent councils, thereby removing direct democratic accountability and subordinating police funding to other local authority priorities, as was the case before the streamlined police authorities were created in the mid-1990s.

The future for police funding therefore appears to be depressing for both professionals and the public, but allowing depression to take a collective hold simply allows internal morale and external confidence to implode, and leaders cannot allow this. It is the job of leaders to inspire confidence, but the public and police personnel are now too sophisticated to be convinced by unrealistic promises or expectations. Police leaders must therefore devise rational plans for the service which at the very least give the people they lead confidence that the leadership is being realistic. It will require an equally realistic debate with the public, not the amorphous 'general public' but the specific local public of a force area. It will require an honesty which may be difficult to reconcile with the political aspirations of the local PCC, and there may, as a consequence, be professional casualties, but that is the price of leadership.

The alternative is simply that both national and local political leaders will allow the state of policing to deteriorate to such a level that a crisis is engendered and new, realistic funding and means of democratic governance are instituted. Unfortunately, that is the historical pattern, as demonstrated by the situation reached in the late 1950s and 1970s. It would be pleasant to end on a more upbeat note, but that would be unrealistic. Fortunately, both political leaders and the public can rely on the sense of duty inherent in police personnel. It is to be hoped that politicians do not take that asset too much for granted.

Recommended Reading

Considering that finance is such a vital activity for policing, there are regrettably few studies available to the police leader. Essential reading includes my own study *A Future for Policing in England and Wales* (Oxford: OUP, 2013), the 2007 Police Reform Taskforce report, 'Policing for the People' (Conservative Party, London), and the Home Affairs Committee (2011), 'Accountability and Cost Reduction in the Police Service', at (<http://www.nao.org.uk/wp-content/uploads/2011/06/1012-policing-landscape-briefing.pdf> (accessed 20 April 2015), while for a greater understanding of the mysteries of the Police Allocation Formula there is Home Office (2013c), 'Guide to the Police Allocation Formula', at <https://www.gov.uk/guide-to-the-police-allocation-formula> (accessed 20 April 2015). HMIC's various reports, commencing with 'Adapting to Austerity' (2011), continuing with 'Policing in Austerity: Rising to the Challenge' (2013), and concluding with 'Policing in Austerity: Meeting the Challenges' (2014), together with 'Policing in Austerity: Rising to the Challenge Compendium' (2014) serve to chart the service's response to the spending cuts. HMIC is not a neutral source, and it is therefore necessary to read past some of the comments, but its 'Policing in Austerity' is, nevertheless, evidence-based and unrivalled for its comprehensiveness. The NAO's 2015 report 'Financial Sustainability of Police Forces in England and Wales' is also required reading. For detailed statistics, there is the estimable 'Police Actuals' and 'Estimates' provided by the Chartered Institute for Public Finance and Accounting (CIPFA), although the first-time user would probably benefit from force financial staff guidance.

For those seeking introductions to business process re-engineering, there is a legion of literature on 'lean methodology', but the classic study is JT Womack and DT Jones (2003), *Lean Thinking* (New York: Simon and Schuster). The British Quality Foundation website provides an introduction to EFQM, although the 2011 study by J Gomez, M Costa, and A Lorente ('A Critical Evaluation of the EFQM Model' 28(5) *The International Journal of Quality and Reliability Management* 484) emphasizes the model's limitations. The derivative 'QUEST' programme, continues to have the Home Secretary's official sanction (Gov.uk, 'Police Reform: Home Secretary's Speech to the Reform and KPMG Summit on the Value for Money In Policing' (<https://www.gov.uk/government/speeches/police-reform-home-secretarys-speech-to-the-reform-and-kpmg-summit-on-the-value-for-money-in-policing> (accessed 20 August 2014)). The Harvard Business School's compendium 'On Change Management' is an excellent introduction, but S Keller and C Aiken's (2009) 'The Inconvenient Truth about Change Management' (<http://www.mckinsey.com/app_media/reports/financial_services/the_inconvenient_truth_about_change_management.pdf> (accessed 20 August 2014)), and JP Kotter's 'Leading Change: Why Transformation Efforts Fail' (January 2007) *Harvard Business Review* (at <http://hbr.org/2007/01/leading-change-why-transformation-efforts-fail/ar/1> (accessed 20 August 2014)), which remind us that 30% of change management programmes fail, are essential corollaries.

S Brookes and K Grant (2010) provide an extensive study of what they consider to be the requirements of public service in *The New Public Leadership Challenge* (Basingstoke: Palgrave Macmillan). It is up to the reader, however, to approach all these sources with a degree of detachment and to test them against their own circumstances, experience, and requirements.

References

Auditor General (2013), 'Police Reform Progress Update 2013', Audit Scotland, Edinburgh

BBC News (2014), 'Devon and Cornwall Police May go Bust, Commissioner Says', 26 August, at <http://www.bbc.co.uk/news/uk-england-28926988> (accessed 26 August 2014)

BBC News (2014), 'Police, Ambulance and Fire Services "Need Integrating"', 3 September, at <http://www.bbc.co.uk/news/uk-29048661> (accessed 22 September 2014)

Boyd, E (2014), 'Police Officer Pensions: Affordability of Current Schemes', at <http://www.policyexchange.org.uk/publications/category/item/police-officer-pensions-affordability-of-current-schemes> (accessed 15 August 2014)

Brain, T (2010), *A History of Policing in England and Wales from 1974: A Turbulent Journey* (Oxford: OUP)

Brain, T (2011–12), 'Police Funding (England & Wales) 2011–12', Universities' Police Science Institute (UPSI), Police Briefing Paper No 1, at <http://www.openeyecommunications.com/wp-content/uploads/2011/09/UPSI-Police-Briefing-Paper-No-1-12-Aug-11.pdf> (accessed 20 April 2015)

Brain, T (2013), *A Future for Policing in England and Wales* (Oxford: OUP)

Butler, P (2003), 'NHS Reform: The Issue Explained', *The Guardian*, 7 May, at <http://www.theguardian.com/society/2003/may/07/health.theissuesexplained> (accessed 21 April 2015)

CIPFA (1999), Police Actuals 1998–99, at <http://www.cipfastats.net> (accessed 21 April 2015)

CIPFA (2000), Police Actuals 1999–2000, at <http://www.cipfastats.net> (accessed 21 April 2015)

CIPFA (2011), Police Actuals 2010–11, at <http://www.cipfastats,net> (accessed 21 April 2015)

CIPFA (2013), Police Actuals 2012–13, at <http://www.cipfastats.net> (accessed 21 April 2015)

CIPFA (2014), Police Actuals 2013–14, at <http:/www.cipfastats.net> (accessed 21 April 2015)

College of Policing (2015), College of Policing Analysis: Estimating Demand on the Police Service, at http://www.college.police.uk/Documents/Demand_Report_21_1_15.pdf (Accessed 5 July 2015)

College of Policing (2014a), Business Plan December 2012 to March 2013, at <http://www.college.police.uk/en/docs/College_Business_Plan_12-13.pdf (accessed 7 April 2014)

College of Policing (2014b), Code of Ethics: Principles and Standards of Professional Behaviour for the Policing Profession of England and Wales, at http://www.college.police.uk/What-we-do/Ethics/Pages/Code-of-Ethics.aspx (Accessed 5 July 2015)

Conservative Liberal Democrats (2010), 'Conservative Liberal Democrat Coalition Negotiations: Agreements Reached 11 May 2010', at <http://www.ucl.ac.uk/constitution-unit/research/coalition-government/initial-agreement-11-may-2010.pdf> (accessed 16 August 2014)

Conservative Party (2010), 'The Big Society not Big Government', at <http://www.conservatives.com/~/media/Files/Downloadable%20Files/Building-a-Big-Society.ashx> (accessed 16 August 2014)

Conservative Party (2015), 'Conservative Party Manifesto', at <https://www.conservatives.com/Manifesto> (accessed 4 June 2015)

DCLG (2011), 'Helping Troubled Families Turn their Lives Around', Policy 2011, at <https://www.gov.uk/government/policies/helping-troubled-families-turn-their-lives-around> (accessed 20 April 2015)

DCLG (2014a), 'Council Tax Freeze 2014 to 2015 Scheme', at <https://www.gov.uk/government/policies/making-sure-council-tax-payers-get-good-value-for-money/supporting-pages/council-tax-freeze> (accessed 21 April 2015)

DCLG (2014b), 'Council Tax Levels Set by Local Authorities in England 2014–2015 (revised)', at <https://www.gov.uk/government/publications/council-tax-levels-set-by-local-authorities-in-england-2014-to-2015> (accessed 21 April 2015)

Department for Communities and Local Government (2011), 'Helping Troubled Families Turn their Lives Around', Policy 2011, at <http://www.gov.uk/government/policies/helping-troubled-families-turn-their-lives-around> (accessed 20 April 2015)

Department of Health and Home Office (2014), Mental Health Crisis Care Concordat—Improving Outcomes for People Experiencing Mental Health Crisis, Department of Health and Home Office, 18 February 2014.

Elliott, F (2006), 'Cameron Says Police Service must be Radically Reformed', *The Independent*, 1 January, at <http://www.independent.co.uk/news/uk/politics/cameron-says-police-service-must-be-radically-reformed-521288.html> (accessed 21 April 2015)

Flanagan, R (2007), 'The Review of Policing: Interim Report', Home Office, London

Flanagan, R (2008), 'The Review of Policing: Final Report', Home Office, London,

Gov.uk (2013a), 'Community Safety Fund Communication', at <https://www.gov.uk/government/publications/community-safety-fund-whats-available-for-pccs> (accessed 21 April 2015)

Gov.uk (2013b), 'Guide to the Police Allocation Formula', March, at <https://www.gov.uk/guide-to-the-police-allocation-formula> (accessed 15 August 2014)

Gov.uk (2014), Police Workforce England and Wales, 31 March, at <https://www.gov.uk/government/publications/police-workforce-england-and-wales-31-march-2014/police-workforce-england-and-wales-31-march-2014> (accessed 21 April 2015)

Gov.uk (2015), 'Budget 2015', HM Treasury, at <https://www.gov.uk/government/publications/budget-2015-documents> (accessed 21 April 2015)

HM Treasury (2010), 'Spending Review', TSO, London, at <https://www.gov.uk/government/publications/spending-review-2010> (accessed 21 April 2015)

HMIC (2013), 'Policing in Austerity: Rising to the Challenge', at <http://www.justiceinspectorates.gov.uk/hmic/publication/policing-in-austerity-rising-to-the-challenge> (accessed 21 April 2015)

HMIC (2014a), 'Policing in Austerity: Meeting the Challenges', at <http://www.justiceinspectorates.gov.uk/hmic/publication/policing-in-austerity-meeting-the-challenge> (accessed 21 April 2015)

HMIC (2014b), 'Valuing the Police Data', at <https://www.justiceinspectorates.gov.uk/hmic/data/valuing-the-police-data> (accessed 21 April 2015)

Hoggett, J, Redford, P, Toher, D, and White, P (2013), 'Police Identity in a Time of Rapid Organizational, Social and Political Change: A Pilot Report, Avon and Somerset Constabulary', University of the West of England, Bristol

Home Affairs Committee (2014), 'Written Evidence: The Work of the National Crime Agency' (as at 1 April 2014), at <http://www.parliament.uk/documents/commons-committees/home-affairs/NCA-written-evidence.pdf> (accessed 21 April 2015)

Home Department (2010), 'Police Authority Grants (England and Wales)', 13 December, at <http://www.theyworkforyou.com/wms/?id=2010-12-13a.72WS.4> (accessed 21 April 2015)

Home Office (2010a), 'Police Service Strength, England and Wales', 31 March, at <https://www.gov.uk/government/publications/police-service-strength-england-and-wales-31-march-2010> (accessed 21 April 2015)

Home Office (2010b), *Policing in the 21st Century: Reconnecting Police and the People* (CM 7925)

Home Office (2010c), 'Proposals for Revised Funding Allocations for Police Authorities in England and Wales 2010/11', at <https://www.gov.uk/government/uploads/system/uploads/attachment_data/file/115669/justice-home-affairs-wms.pdf> (accessed 21 April 2015)

Home Office (2011), 'Have You Got What it Takes? The Police ICT Company', at <https://www.gov.uk/government/uploads/system/uploads/attachment_data/file/117420/police-ict-company.pdf> (accessed 21 April 2015)

Home Office (2013a), 'Financial Management Code of Practice for the Police Forces of England and Wales', October 2013, at <https://www.gov.uk/government/uploads/system/uploads/attachment_data/file/252720/fm_code_of_practice.pdf> (accessed 2 April 2013)

Home Office (2013b), 'Annual Report and Accounts 2012–13', at <https://www.gov.uk/government/uploads/system/uploads/attachment_data/file/210660/Annual_Report_and_Accounts_FINAL_updated_logo.pdf> (accessed 21 April 2015)

Home Office (2013c), 'Guide to the Police Allocation Formula', at <https://www.gov.uk/guide-to-the-police-allocation-formula> (accessed 21 April 2015)

Home Secretary (2011), 'The Home Secretary's Speech on Police Bureaucracy', May, at <https://www.gov.uk/government/speeches/home-secretarys-speech-on-police-bureaucracy> (accessed 20 April 2015)

Independent (2013), 'G4S and Serco Face £50 million Fraud Inquiry', *The Independent*, 12 July 2013, at <http://www.independent.co.uk/news/uk/politics/g4s-and-serco-face-50-million-fraud-inquiry-8703245.html> (accessed 21 April 2015)

Independent Police Complaints Commission (2012–13), Annual Report and Statement of Accounts 2012/13, at <http://www.ipcc.gov.uk/sites/default/files/Documents/publications/annual_report_IPCC_2013_web.pdf> (accessed 21 April 2015)

IPSOS MORI (2014), 'Long Term Concern about Crime 1974–2013', at <https://www.ipsos-mori.com/researchspecialisms/socialresearch/specareas/politics/trends.aspx> (accessed 4 July 2015)

NAO (2011), 'Accountability and Cost Reduction in the New Policing Landscape', briefing prepared for the Home Affairs Select Committee, at <http://www.nao.org.

uk/wp-content/uploads/2011/06/1012-policing-landscape-briefing.pdf> (accessed 21 April 2015)

NAO (2015), 'Financial Sustainability of Police Forces in England and Wales', at <http://www.nao.org.uk/report/financial-sustainability-of-police-forces-in-england-and-wales/> (accessed 4 June 2015)

ONS (2014a), 'Second Estimate of GDP—Time Series Dataset Q2 2014', at <http://www.ons.gov.uk/ons/rel/naa2/second-estimate-of-gdp/q2-2014/tsd-gdp-second-estimate--q2--2014.html> (accessed 5 July 2015)

ONS (2014b), 'Public Perceptions of the Police and Police Visibility, 2012/13', at <http://www.ons.gov.uk/ons/rel/crime-stats/crime-statistics/focus-on-victimisation-and-public-perceptions–2012-13/rpt—chapter-1.html> (accessed 21 April 2015)

ONS (2014c), 'Crime in England and Wales, Year Ending December 2013', at <http://www.ons.gov.uk/ons/rel/crime-stats/crime-statistics/period-ending-december-2013/stb-crime-stats-dec-2013.html> (accessed 5 July 2015)

Parliament UK (2014), 'Topics: Police Page—Police Funding: Social Indicators', SN/SG/2616, at <http://www.parliament.uk/business/publications/research/briefing-papers/SN02616/police-funding-social-indicators-page> (accessed 21 April 2015)

Police Reform Taskforce (2007), 'Policing for the People', Conservative Party, London, at <http://conservativehome.blogs.com/torydiary/files/policing_for_the_people.pdf> (accessed 21 April 2015)

Sky News (2013), 'Police Facing "Serious Drag" On Morale', 7 July, at <http://news.sky.com/story/1112504/police-facing-serious-drag-on-morale> (21 April 2015)

Tobias, J (1979), *Crime and Police in England 1700–1900* (Dublin: Gill and Macmillan)

ukpublicspending.co.uk (2014), 'Public Spending Breakdown', at <http://www.ukpublicspending.co.uk/breakdown> (accessed 21 April 2015)

Weinfass, I (2014), 'Business Police Tax "Makes Us Safer"', *Police Oracle*, 26 August, at <http://www.policeoracle.com/news/Business-police-tax-'makes-us-safer'_84937.html> (accessed 26 August 2014)

Winsor, T (2012), *Independent Review of Police Officer and Staff Remuneration and Conditions, Final Report* (Cm 8325–1) vols 1 and 2, at <https://www.gov.uk/government/uploads/system/uploads/attachment_data/file/229006/8024.pdf and https://www.gov.uk/government/uploads/system/uploads/attachment_data/file/250816/8325_ii.pdf> (accessed 5 July 2015)

3

Politics and Policing

The Terrible Twins

Robert Reiner and Denis O'Connor

Totem and Taboo: The Terror of Political Policing

Debates about the modern British police have always been haunted by the spectre of 'political' policing. This was a major theme of those who opposed the creation of a state-funded and organized police force, before Sir Robert Peel finally succeeded in piloting the 1829 Metropolitan Police Act through Parliament. Representing the police as quite separate from politics was a core element in the construction of legitimacy and public consent during the 19th and 20th centuries (Reiner 2010: ch 3). The independence of the police from government and politics has been a totemic trope of the characterization of 'policing by consent', constantly re-articulated as the key to what makes the British model supposedly 'the best police in the world'.

The other side of the 'policing by consent' totem is a taboo about contaminating policing with the taint of the 'political'. Accusing opponents of this remains a refrain of politicians and press today. Some examples from the past decade indicate the constancy of that refrain:

- *'The row over the resignation of Sir Ian Blair, the Metropolitan Police Commissioner, has intensified after Jacqui Smith, the Home Secretary, accused Boris Johnson, the Mayor of London, of forcing him out for political reasons.* Miss Smith suggested that the Mayor had indulged in "party politics" over the issue', *Daily Telegraph*, 3 October 2008.

- *'Proposals for direct elections to police authorities have been scrapped after the Home Secretary caved in to growing concerns about the politicisation of the police.* The plan was to be contained in the new *Policing and Crime Bill*... Ms Smith... accused the Conservatives of fuelling worries over politicisation... Shadow Home Secretary Dominic Grieve said: "The danger of politicisation of the police comes from the micro-management that has been the hallmark of the Labour government over the last ten years."' *Daily Telegraph*, 18 December 2008.

- *'Policing and politics have never mixed and until fairly recently they have never had to'* (Johnson and Clarke 2014).

- *'The Tories have politicised policing*... They are looking for political control of policing.'... Williams (Police Federation Chair) says... "Police officers are not and must not be answerable to politicians."' Nick Hopkins and Sandra Laville, 'Police Federation, the Coppers' Union, Falls Foul of the Conservative party', *The Guardian*, 14 February 2014.

Over the past decade, this Punch and Judy show of political parties accusing each other of politicizing policing has raged ever more fiercely. But politicization of policing can be traced back to the late 1960s, and became overt during the run-up to the watershed 1979 General Election. There can be no doubt that the prime mover was the Conservative Party under Margaret Thatcher, who used 'law and order' as a key weapon in their campaign against the Labour government, in conjunction with the police staff associations.

This chapter argues that the shibboleth of a Berlin Wall between policing and politics is a classic case of the narcissism of small differences, to borrow another Freudian metaphor. Policing is, of its nature, intricately intertwined with politics. The dangers flowing from this are best tackled by frank recognition rather than by repression. It is crucial that chief constables today recognize the significance of the politics of policing, eschewing partisan involvement but without sheltering behind the myth of an impossible separation from politics.

The following section considers the issue in terms of first principles. After that, the history of the politicization of policing is analysed. The final section probes a mysterious recent development. How can we understand the 2010 Coalition government's radical reform programme, which amounts to a reversal of previous Conservative positions, and an assault on the totemic traditions of British policing that they have done so much to establish as objects of veneration? It will be argued that profound changes in the political economy of Britain have weakened the power of the police to resist major changes.

Policing and Politics: Definitions and First Principles

The group of words, police, policy, polity, politics, politic, political, politician is a good example of delicate distinctions.

Maitland 1885: 105

This quotation from an eminent Victorian jurist points to the common etymological roots of police and politics, indicating their close relationship, but also noting the 'delicate distinctions'. Politics and policing are Janus-faced, reflecting the dual aspects of power, the defining feature of both. As theorists as diverse as Talcott Parsons, Louis Althusser, and Michel Foucault have shown, power has two intertwined aspects: power may be (a) *enabling*—the power *to* do things of collective benefit; or (b) constraining—power *over* others for particularistic advantage and domination (Lukes 2005). And power is also intimately bound up with 'knowledge' and ideology, which (in Max Weber's language) can legitimate and stabilize power, constituting it as authority.

Both politics and policing have a dual character. 'Politics' connotes 'the activities associated with governing a country or area', the *Oxford English Dictionary* tells us. But this involves *both* the pursuit of the common good *and* conflicts over policy: 'who gets what, when, and how?', in Harold Lasswell's celebrated definition.[1]

Functional definitions of policing, which attempt to specify the supposed social effects of policing—whether law enforcement, order maintenance, crime control, peace-keeping, or safeguarding security—are misleadingly consensual. They gloss over the perennial and inevitable conflicts about *whose* law and *what* order is enforced and maintained.

Like its etymological sibling, politics, policing has a dual face. Police are responsible both for 'parking tickets' *and* 'class repression' (Marenin 1983). They simultaneously reproduce *general* and *specific* order: the conditions of existence for organized social life in general (in the collective universal interest), *and* specific distributions of advantage and power (benefiting particular partisan interests over others).

The amorphous terms of functionalist definitions also conceal the huge heterogeneity of concrete policing jobs, as stressed by the most influential analysis of the concept of policing, Egon Bittner's 'Florence Nightingale in Pursuit of Willie Sutton' (Bittner 1974; for recent discussions see Brodeur 2010; Reiner 2010: ch 1; Brown 2014: Pt I). Police perform a bewildering miscellany of tasks, from controlling traffic to combatting terrorism, but all involve 'something that ought not to be happening and about which someone had better do something now!' (Bittner 1974: 30). These fall to the police because they are the specialist repositories for legitimate force. 'The policeman, and the policeman alone, is equipped, entitled and required to deal with every exigency in which force may have to be used' (Bittner 1974: 35).

Bittner's analysis of police echoes Max Weber's seminal account of politics and the state: 'A state ... cannot be defined sociologically by enumerating its activities ... the modern state can be defined only sociologically by the specific *means* that are peculiar to it ... namely, physical violence' (Weber 2004 [1919]: 33). Weber's (or any) conceptualization of the state raises the central analytic and normative issues in classical as well as contemporary political theory. The

---

[1] H Lasswell, *Politics: Who Gets What, When and How?* (New York: Whittlesey House, 1936).

isomorphism of Bittner's analysis of police and Weber's of the state indicates that this *should* also be true of the police.

Policing (unlike punishment) has seldom attracted the attention of political theorists. But policing is (at least implicitly) pivotal in philosophical theories of justice. For example, Rawls' analysis of justice, the most influential of the twentieth century, seeks to derive and defend principles that, because they would be reciprocally consented to in circumstances of unbiased choice, involve the least 'strain of commitment' (Rawls 1971: 176–83). In a just society there is the least necessity to resort to coercion against those recalcitrant to or resentful of it. In other words, forceful policing and punishment may be minimized by justice.

Legitimacy is crucial to stabilize rule, as Weber's analysis of the state argued. 'The state represents a relationship in which people *rule over* other people... based on the legitimate use of force (that is to say, force that is perceived as legitimate). If the state is to survive, those who are ruled over must always *acquiesce* in the authority that is claimed by the rulers of the day' (emphases in original) (Weber 2004 [1919]: 34). As with the state, legitimation is crucial to policing. This is widely recognized, and important current work develops Tyler's finding that procedurally just treatment of people by police can achieve legitimacy, even if people feel that the substantive outcome of encounters is unjust (Tyler 2004; Smith 2007; Jackson et al 2012; Tankebe and Liebling 2013; Bradford, Jackson, and Hough 2014). Or in the proverbial lingo of the old English villain being arrested, 'It's a fair cop, guv'. However, there are also wider conditions for the existence of police legitimacy, beyond the behaviour of the police themselves.

A particular style of policing, intended to legitimate the police in the face of the widespread hostility to their creation, was deliberately constructed by Peel and the Commissioners he appointed to command the Met, Rowan and Mayne (Reiner 2010: chs 2, 3). One crucial aspect was how to gain acceptance for police legal powers. British police power was legitimated originally by denial, the myth of the constable as 'citizen in uniform', who lacks any special powers but is paid to do what all citizens have a moral and social obligation to do.

In reality, constables always had greater powers than ordinary citizens, but the myth had some plausibility until the late 1960s. After that, a steady accumulation of statutory and common law powers rendered it increasingly untenable. A new myth was coined by the Royal Commission on Criminal Procedure Report of 1981 to confer legitimacy on the considerable extension of statutory powers in the ensuing Police and Criminal Evidence Act 1984 (PACE). This was the notion of a 'fair balance' between powers and safeguards, a strategy to 'authorise and regulate' special police powers (Dixon 2008). There is a vast empirical literature assessing whether this regulatory strategy did achieve the purported fundamental balance, with results suggesting that the glass could be described as either half-full or half-empty from different political perspectives (Reiner 2010: 205–19).

Extensions of police power have accelerated since the early 1990s, without even any pretence that there are corresponding safeguards, and indeed some watering-down of those in PACE (Reiner 2010: 219–23). 'Fundamental balance' has been eclipsed as a legitimatory strategy by a new narrative, more congruent with the 'law and order' consensus that has prevailed since the early 1990s (Reiner 2007: ch 5; Downes and Morgan 2012). This is the tragic legitimation of greater powers as 'necessary evils' in an era of insecurity, perpetual emergency, and apocalyptic threats, the 'Dirty Harry' rationale (Reiner 2010: 96–111).

It is important to recognize, however, that the success of the Peelian 'citizen in uniform' legitimatory strategy, in the 19th and first three-quarters of the 20th centuries, had essential non-police conditions of existence. It required the spread of 'citizenship' in the sense used by TH Marshall: the incorporation of the mass of the population into a fundamentally common status of citizens with civil, political, and socio-economic rights (Marshall 1950). This was the essential precondition for policing not to be seen as 'class repression' but as 'parking tickets', administering sometimes unpleasant medicine for the common good of orderly, cooperative coexistence (Marenin 1983). Social justice and cohesion did the heavy lifting of social ordering, and were the prerequisite of police effectiveness and legitimacy.

When politicians or police chiefs declare that politics should play no part in policing, they probably accept that policing is the sharp end of governmental power, the routine deployment of surveillance and patrol to regulate conflicts and troubles, potentially using coercive force. What they claim is that in the British tradition police policies and practices are insulated from politicians, primarily by the legal doctrine of 'operational independence'. As two former Labour Home Secretaries put it recently: 'Sir Robert Peel's 1830s doctrine of "operational independence" was rightly sustained by all political parties' (Johnson and Clarke 2014).

'Operational independence' has been the most sacrosanct of all sacred cows in discussions of British policing, ritualistically recited by Home Secretaries even as they whittle away at it. The introduction of directly elected police and crime commissioners (PCCs) by the Police Reform and Social Responsibility Act 2011 has been accompanied by fierce debate on this issue, but Home Secretary Teresa May was at pains to deny any departure from operational independence: 'let me make it absolutely clear—elected individuals will in no way undermine your operational independence' (May 2010).

The operational independence doctrine is not of Peelian origin, *pace* the comments by Alan Johnson and Charles Clarke. Most historians argue that in the 19th century no fundamental distinction was made between the accountability of the police and other local services, and borough forces in particular were often directed on operational matters by their Watch Committees (Reiner 1991: 11–14; Emsley 2014: 18–19).

Until the 1920s, the doctrine of 'constabulary independence', that police should be insulated from political control in 'operational' matters, functioned as a shield for Home Secretaries to dodge sharp Parliamentary questions (although Home Secretaries frequently intervened in operational matters, especially during strikes or other conflicts with a political dimension) (Morgan 1987; Weinberger 1991). The strong constabulary independence doctrine developed in the late 1920s, crystallized by the 1930 judgment in *Fisher v Oldham*.[2] The case held that constables exercised an original authority under the Crown, so did not stand in a master–servant relationship with police authorities of any kind. The emergence of the doctrine, probably not accidentally, followed in the wake of the universal franchise and the election of radical Labour local authorities (Lustgarten 1986: 55–61; Jones et al 1994: 12–13; Walker 2000: 44–53; Turner 2014: 18–20).

The survival of the broader doctrine of constabulary independence after the Police Act 1964 (which made police authorities vicariously liable for constables' torts) was confirmed by a subsequent series of cases cementing it as law (for all their flaws in legal logic or constitutional principle, as devastatingly deconstructed by Lustgarten 1986; Walker 2000). In any event, whatever the legal niceties, and despite official denials, ministers have intervened behind the scenes in policing during the most controversial politically charged disorders of recent times, just as they did in the 19th and early 20th centuries (Reiner 1991: 190–2, 274–5).

The politically charged character of policing creates a perennial problem of legitimation. Procedurally just use of powers and other strategies may help to achieve legitimacy, but only if there is a wider background sense of fair citizenship, that 'we're all in it together', to borrow a phrase. This is undermined if the use of power is seen as partisan, bearing down on some more than others. Disproportionate deployment of stop-and-search powers, suggesting extensive discrimination, is a long-standing example. Such apparent injustice always threatens to make policing issues enter the arena of open political contestation and partisan conflict.

Although policing is inherently political, it is not necessarily *politicized*. However, since the late 1960s the successful legitimation launched by Peel and his associates has been challenged, and policing has become re-politicized as an issue of partisan conflict.

Police Politicization: Phases and Stages

Police politicization has two dimensions: (a) policing issues becoming politically controversial; (b) police themselves becoming active in politics.

During the early 1970s, police representative associations, and some prominent chief officers, began intervening in public and political debate in unprecedented ways. This 'bobby lobby' emerged together with the rise of a broader politicization of 'law and order' (Reiner 2007: ch 5). It was spearheaded by the Marksist revolution at Scotland Yard, symbolized by Sir Robert Mark's celebrated 1973

---

[2] *Fisher v Oldham* (1930) 2 KB 364.

Dimbleby lecture, and given a more openly partisan edge by the Federation 'law and order' campaign launched in 1975 (Reiner 1978: 46). Police support for the Conservative law and order platform was crucial to the 1979 Thatcher victory.

The polarization of Conservative and Labour positions on policing, crime, and criminal justice became ever sharper in the 1980s, climaxing during the 1984–85 Miners' Strike. The partisan conflict embodied principled differences in social, political, and legal philosophy, and in criminological analysis. Whilst the Tories promised tougher policing and punishment in the 'war against crime', Labour remained committed to an essentially social democratic criminology, which had been the tacit cross-party consensus during the decades of the post-World War II Keynesian-welfarist-mixed economy settlement (Reiner 2007, 2011: Pts 1 and 3). During the late 1970s this became electoral poison, condemning Labour to successive defeats. Labour's traditional commitments in criminal justice—concern for civil liberties and trade union rights; a social democratic analysis of crime as primarily shaped by 'root causes' including inequality and social exclusion, rendering policing and penal policy marginal to crime control—all became 'hostages to fortune' (Downes and Morgan 2012). Labour was condemned as 'soft on crime' in the increasingly febrile rhetoric of the Tories and their police fellow-travellers.

The root cause of the politicization of law and order was the resurgence of neoliberal political economy and culture, sweeping aside the post-War Keynesian consensus (Harvey 2005; Mirowski 2013). This was associated with economic, social, and cultural changes that generated rising crime, disorder, and public anxiety (Reiner 2007; Hall et al 2008), at any rate until the mid-1990s when recorded crime began to fall. These same factors underlie the delegitimation and re-politicization of the police since the 1970s, mediated by an unintentional reversal of the Peelian police tactics that had initially constructed legitimacy (Reiner 2010: ch 3). This can be encapsulated in a formula I call the 'calculus of consent': deepening divisions (inequality, diversity) + declining deference = delegitimation (Reiner 1992a).

The advent of 'New' Labour in the early 1990s transformed the politicization of law and order, encapsulated by the legendary sound bite 'tough on crime, tough on the causes of crime'. A 'second order' consensus on the fundamentals of law and order developed, as New Labour tried to out-tough the Tories. Paradoxically, however, this underlying consensus was masked by shrill partisan competitive conflict over toughness and delivery. Since 1992, there has been a shared acceptance of core crime control priorities and 'businesslike' policy models, disguised by the parties insisting: 'Anything you can do, I can do tougher (and smarter).' This generated an unbalanced, accelerating expansion of police powers. Accountability was reconfigured as accountancy. The 'constabulary independence' doctrine remains a sacred mantra to which lip-service is regularly paid. But it has been hollowed out, as priorities and policy decisions are 'steered' 'at a distance' by 'calculative and contractual' governance, aka new public management (Reiner 2010: ch 7).

The politicization of policing has continued over the past ten years, but with a bewildering admixture of partisan cross-dressing. The Conservatives began riffing with old Labour themes after 2005 when David Cameron and Teresa May were concerned to decontaminate their brand as 'the nasty party'. They flirted with civil liberties (eg opposing Labour's attempt to increase the detention time limit for terrorism suspects to 90 days), and even a quasi-social democratic probing of the root causes of crime.[3] They agonized over the lack of local democratic accountability of police, and in their revolutionary police reforms since 2010 made chief officers subordinate to elected Commissioners, albeit in an idiosyncratic way inviting all the criticisms they levelled at Labour in the 1980s (Jones et al 2012).

'New' Labour began playing old Tory law and order tunes back in the early 1990s. For example, two former Labour Home Secretaries recently used terms that might have been lifted from their Tory opposite numbers in the 1980s, claiming the latter's 'conventional law-and-order stance was sacrificed to the civil libertarians' (Johnson and Clarke 2014). This political cross-dressing is a culmination of the two decades of deep consensus on law and order following New Labour's acceptance of the terms of debate framed by the Conservatives in the 1970s, coupled with fierce fighting for the mantle of law and order champions.

The Coalition and the Constabulary

The Conservative-led Coalition government's policing policies since 2010 embody a profound rupture in the politics of policing. Paradoxically, the Conservatives have been tougher on the police in the name of 'austerity' than any 'old' Labour government would ever have dared to be. Relations with the police, the Tories' erstwhile pet institution, are at an all-time low (Stevens 2013: 27).

Launching the reforms, Home Secretary Teresa May declared them 'the most radical change to policing in 50 years' (Home Office 2010: 3). For once the government's claim is too modest. The 50 years presumably refers to the Police Act 1964. But the 1964 Act, important as it was, primarily consolidated existing arrangements for police governance. The Coalition programme, for good or bad, mounts a revolutionary assault on the traditions developed since the early 19th century.

The package has several core elements. Policing has been amongst the hardest hit of all public services in the Coalition's spending cuts. 'In the October 2010 spending review, the Government announced that central funding to the police service in England and Wales would be reduced in real terms by 20% in the four years between March 2011 and March 2015 ... Forces plan to achieve ... 73% of the savings by cutting the total police workforce ... by 31,600' (HMIC 2013: 14–16).

---

[3] cf G Hinslif, 'Cameron Softens Crime Image in "Hug-a-Hoodie" Call', *The Observer*, 9 July 2006.

The government claims that the cuts will not threaten police performance and public safety because they are accompanied by fundamental reforms of pay, conditions of service, management, and governance that eliminate inefficiencies and will incentivize the police to produce more from less (embodied largely in the Winsor Report 2012).

Although much of this had roots in new public management and other initiatives (notably the 1993 Sheehy Report) since the late 1980s, Winsor is Sheehy on steroids. Unsurprisingly, this has provoked fierce criticism from many police quarters.[4]

Even more profound than the dramatic cuts and transformation of police conditions of service and management is the revolution in governance. The Coalition accountability model, enshrined in the Police Reform and Social Responsibility Act 2011, at first glance appears to achieve the old Labour ambition of subjecting police to elected control, defying the erstwhile Conservative apprehensions about politicization. But first impressions can deceive.

A central pillar of the Coalition government rhetoric presenting the reforms is that they achieve democratic policing. Theresa May referred to them as 'the most significant democratic reform of policing in our lifetime' (May 2012). The claim rests, of course, on the election of the PCCs, who are placed in pole position in the new governance structure. The other elements are the Home Secretary, the Chief Constables, and the Police and Crime Panels (a concession to the Liberal Democrats). The latter are selected in a similar way to the old police authorities, but with an explicitly advisory, not even nominally powerful, role. 'Constabulary independence' is formally preserved,[5] although many have underlined the threats to the doctrine, given the PCCs' powers to hire and fire chief constables.[6]

Unsurprisingly, the government has sought to present the reforms as a success. So too has HMIC, now headed by Tom Winsor, who is not only the author of many of the reforms but also personally embodies the changes, being the first civilian to become HM Chief Inspector of Constabulary in the century-and-a-half of the Inspectorate's history. Although sounding some cautionary notes, the HMIC evaluation of the impact of the cuts echoes the government's assessment. Its presentation of the findings accentuates the positive nuggets of good news, downplaying the bad. For example, the planned increase in the proportion of the workforce on the 'frontline' is highlighted over the fact that this nonetheless means an absolute reduction (HMIC 2013: 16). The 'frontline' is defined simply as 'crime-fighting' in the same paragraph, even though many, probably most, calls for service and police operations concern emergencies not reducible to crime-fighting (Reiner 2013). The whole report is framed as a response to

---

[4] 'Coalition's Cuts to Police Budgets "Risking Public Safety" ', *Daily Telegraph*, 2 December 2012; 'Police Federation, the Coppers' Union, Falls Foul of the Conservative Party', *The Guardian*, 14 February 2014.

[5] Policing Protocol Order 2011, SI 2011/2744.

[6] House of Commons Home Affairs Committee, *Police and Crime Commissioners: Power to Remove Chief Constables* (HC 487, 2013).

'austerity', which is treated as an inevitable act of God rather than a contentious policy choice (Blyth 2013; Stuckler and Basu 2013; Seymour 2014), to which there are cogent alternatives (Krugman 2012; Stiglitz 2013).

There is a rapidly growing critical literature on the Coalition's policing project (eg Jones et al 2012; Lister 2013, 2014; Reiner 2013; Turner 2014). A judicious critique, accepting the validity of some measures, but questioning others, is provided by the Report of the Independent Police Commission chaired by former Met Commissioner Lord Stevens, established but not controlled by the Labour Party (Stevens 2013), and the wide-ranging volume of essays prepared as evidence for it (Brown 2014).

The Coalition's package amounts to a dramatic weakening of police power, autonomy, pay, and conditions of service. The purpose of this section is not to add to the burgeoning literature, indicated previously, assessing the virtues and vices of the reforms, but to probe why this has happened at the hands of the Tory Party, formerly the avid paramour of the police, and why now.

The programme, self-billed as 'the most radical change to policing in 50 years', is not proposed because of a law and order crisis. Crime has been falling for two decades, and there isn't even a hint in the government's statements of any special emergency or failing on the part of the police. The argument is only that things could always be improved. The main justification offered is principled rather than pragmatic: to reverse the shift in power over policing from central government to 'the people', an aspect of the more general localism agenda (Home Office 2010: 1–4).

So revolutionary a package arguably could only happen under the Tories. If a Labour government had attempted anything as radical, it would have been vulnerable to attack as soft on crime but tough on the police, charges that would have been electorally damaging and probably fatally so, as with their 'hostages to fortune' of the 1980s (Downes and Morgan 2012). For all the efforts of Tony Blair and his successors, Labour has never managed to supplant the Tories as the party of 'law and order' in popular sentiment. But this still leaves some questions. Why do the Tories want this programme? And how is there the political space for them to get away with it? What has happened to the cultural capital of the police? Why do the cries of police spokespersons that cutting cops is Christmas for crooks no longer carry the clout they used to?

At one level the cutbacks on police are congruent with a larger libertarian agenda, dating back to the Thatcher government, of cutting back the state as much as possible. This only received lip-service in the Thatcher era, because the police were treated as a special case, exempt from the pressures of achieving efficiency, effectiveness, and economy that were being applied to the rest of the public sector. In small part this may have been for sentimental reasons. The main factor was the pivotal role played by the police in bringing to heel trade union-ism, especially during the 1984–85 Miners' Strike. Police powers, resources, and morale were also crucial in handling the urban disorders resulting from the unemployment and deprivation generated by monetarist economic policies.

During the 1990s, politically edged public disorder receded, and the focus of law and order switched to ordinary crime. Here the special case treatment given to the police had not paid off. Recorded crime (and BCS-measured victimization) rose to historical highs, as noted by several ministers in John Major's Cabinet. This was the context for the application of ever more stringent financial accountability and New Public Management techniques, which continued under New Labour from 1997 to 2010. Throughout this period, however, increasing police expenditure and numbers remained totemic proof of Labour's commitment to be tough on crime.

For reasons that remain debated, from the mid-1990s recorded crime fell consistently, throughout the Western world. The most convincing explanation is the 'security hypothesis': the adoption of much more effective physical and situational crime prevention (Farrell et al 2011), which was a universal trend, whilst policing and penal policy varied between different jurisdictions. The part played in the crime drop by policing is questionable, but it certainly helped to satisfy performance targets and took pressure off the remorseless demand for more police.

The decline in crime and political/industrial disorder reduced the demand for policing—the police may have done their job too well. Although opinion surveys suggest most people believe crime continues to rise, denying the contrary statistical evidence, they do not feel this about their own neighbourhoods or through personal experience, as most did in the 1980s and early 1990s. At the same time, anxiety about crime and disorder remains, albeit less acute, because of a widespread recognition that the fundamental drivers of criminality have been suppressed, not removed, by better crime prevention.

Beneath the trends in crime an even deeper change in the political economy and culture of British society underlies the transformation of policing. This is the rise of neoliberal hegemony since the 1970s, remorselessly eliminating any space for alternatives to free market economics and a culture of narcissistic individualism (Harvey 2005; Gamble 2014), which has been strengthened rather than weakened by such apparent shocks as the post-2008 economic crisis (Mirowski 2013). The consequences for crime, criminal justice, and policing are profound (Reiner 2007; Hall et al 2008; Brogden and Ellison 2012; Turner 2014).

The key link between neoliberal political economy and policing is the growth of massively greater inequality. The Gini coefficient, the most common measure of overall income inequality, fell to an all-time low of just under 27 in 1979, but shot up during the Thatcher government to a high of 37 in 1990. It fell again to 33 in the Major and early Blair years, before shooting back to 37 at the turn of the millennium, and has fluctuated around 33 ever since. Even more striking is the trend for the very richest to greatly increase their share of income and wealth, moving them qualitatively away from the rest of society. The share of income going to the top 10% of the population fell over the first 40 years following World War II, from 34.6% in 1938 to 21% in 1979, while the share going to the bottom 10% rose slightly. Since the embedding of neo-liberalism the share of the top 10% has returned to nearly 32%, almost touching pre-war levels (Equality Trust 2014).

The growth of inequality generates problems of order that the police must deal with. Econometric studies show that increasing inequality is directly linked to a growth of expenditure on policing overall (Jayadev and Bowles 2006; Rikagos and Ergul 2011, 2013; Bowles and Jayadev 2014), and within that a shift from public police to private security. Although all sections of society have benefited from the crime reduction, it has disproportionately advantaged the better-off, who can pay for more and better security (Tilley et al 2011).

In terms of the analysis of the police function at the start of this chapter, the balance between general and particular order is shifting. The rise of the publicly provided police in the early 19th century was part of a modern project of constructing a broadly universal order based on a common status of citizenship in which all shared, albeit unequally. Given the survival of some inequality, the order reproduced was simultaneously general and particular, but over time the former became more significant (until the late 1970s). Overt inequality in the delivery of policing services was seen as illegitimate, although it has always survived.

It is significant that the creation of the modern police was opposed not only by the working class, who were not yet incorporated into citizenship, but also by the elite. The aristocracy and gentry saw state policing as an unnecessary expense. The ruling class was protected from the 'dangerous classes' by physical segregation and private staff (Silver 1967). Analysts of the growth of private security have long seen this as threatening a return to pre-modern policing forms, a 'new feudalism' (Shearing and Stenning 1983; Zedner 2006), suggesting a dystopian vision in which the privileged float free, cocooned from the masses in security bubbles.

These *Blade Runner* nightmares are not here yet, but the massive increases in inequality and the cutbacks in public provision of all services, including policing, point in that direction. The bottom line politically permitting the Conservative police reforms is that the powerful are simply less dependent on public police protection, benefiting from bespoke services that are cheaper than extending universal guardianship to all citizens. Conservative theorists have long argued that only a 'night watchman' state can be justified as a call on taxation that would receive universal assent (Nozick 1974). But this overlooks the degree of redistributive benefit in publically financed policing. In the present conjuncture the police are being rolled back with the rest of the state, and privatization, with no mandate for the public good, flourishes. At present there seems little tangible prospect of reversing the trajectory towards extreme social and economic polarization. In the words of Arundhati Roy, 'while the elite pursue their voyages to their imaginary destination, some place at the top of the world, the poor have been caught in a spiral of crime and chaos' (cited in Bauman 2005: 2).

The prospects for political change to counteract the baleful effects of growing socio-economic polarization are considerably worsened by the growing influence of affluence, charted devastatingly by Martin Gilens (Gilens 2014). Nonetheless, against all the odds there remains support in public opinion polls for broadly egalitarian values, and some politicians clearly recognize the problems outlined here, even if they are currently circumscribed in their ability to act against them (Kenworthy 2014). The enthusiasm expressed, on both sides of the Atlantic, by leading centre-left politicians like Obama and Ed Miliband for Thomas Piketty's recent magisterial analysis of the sources and consequences of galloping inequality is one positive straw in the gale (Piketty 2014).

The current dystopian path cannot continue forever without generating a reaction by the vast majority of the population who are endangered by it. At present the stirrings of such reaction are taking forms disturbingly reminiscent of the 1930s, when popular fear and anger engendered by the Depression were all-too-successfully diverted against ethnic minority and other vulnerable scapegoats.

But if the lessons of history are considered, it is possible that political leadership can reinvigorate the more benign march of justice and inclusive citizenship. As argued earlier, this underlay the successful legitimation of the British police in their first 150 years, so it is a precedent that today's chief officers should ponder. 'Policing by consent' is not an impossible dream. It flourished as an ideal for much of the twentieth century, and still has considerable vigour, for all the tensions that have always bubbled beneath the 'public tranquillity' the police are charged with trying to preserve. The legitimation of British policing in the 19th century was achieved in the face of massive social and political divisions and conflicts. It is to be hoped that today's police and political leaders can safeguard that precious heritage.

Practitioner's Perspective

Experience

My experience of police and political relations began as a freshly minted Constable with the Grosvenor Square riots in October 1968, and progressed via exposure to public inquiries (eg Scarman 1982; the McPherson Inquiry into the death of Stephen Lawrence 1999, and more recently the Leveson Inquiry in 2012) and encompassed dealing with politicians as a Chief Constable, while leading a national trial of the impact of dedicated officers in neighborhoods. My policing career finished as Chief Inspector of Constabulary, overseeing aspects of security assurance for the 2012 Olympics.

Reflections

Ambitions for policing between police leaders and politicians in England and Wales have been a source of tension and difficulty over the past 30 years, contrasting with the unanimity of Peel and the first Commissioners in their desire to win public confidence in policing. There are many plausible reasons and explanations for this, but the absence of a commonly agreed view of what is required from British policing has been a particular source of difficulty. Reiner's sober assessment in 1992 that policing could not be restored to its former status as a 'beloved symbol' and would come to be seen like other European police forces as another 'mundane' institution of government, illustrates this (Reiner 1992b: 269–70). Reiner's analysis was that larger structural forces were at play. Since then there has been much change but not enough reform in policing. While some good things have happened, the effects of dysfunctional police/political relationships have been evident on the airways and on the ground. If police and political leaders want to improve the distinctive capability of the British police in a rapidly changing society, they would be wise to rebalance their efforts on reform for *consent*, rather than reform for *control*. For police and political leaders this will require vision, as it did in Peel's time.

Throughout my career, three issues recurred: control, competence, and consent. I begin with a case study from my time as HMIC. I refer not only to my experience but also to recent interviews with a small study of leaders of policing (including police officers, officials, and politicians).[7]

Case study: why discretion is as essential as it is inescapable

On a warm Friday evening in July 2012, officers in the inner city attended calls without the benefit of mobile data (malfunctioning), IT support (50% of computers were down), and vans (one out of four was available). Officers attended a call to a beleaguered tower block where their radio system (Airwave) didn't work—it could have been the 1970s. A manager of a 21-year-old woman had raised the alarm after her unexplained absence from work for over 2 weeks. Entry was gained to her home by threatening to use force after early police efforts were met with silence. The migrant family within were separated and questioned. The officers established that she had been ordered by her absent 17-year-old brother to remain at home because he (as head of the family) feared (correctly) that she had an unapproved boyfriend. This wasn't revealed to the family. Her brother had confiscated her phone and she had been warned of the consequences of leaving the house. The officers showed remarkable sensitivity in finding a way through this without resorting to arrest, avoiding exposing the young woman to repercussions by her brother or the family. When we left I assumed that they would go to the next call, but the senior constable said that they would have go to the police station to document everything and show an audit trail informing a range of agencies. I said, 'Most people would applaud your efforts here and understand what you have done.' He said, 'I may have to satisfy the Coroner, and I don't have the right to be wrong!'

---

[7] I have been interviewing a small sample of leading 'entrepreneurs' on policing-police/politicians/criminologists/officials at the Home Office on the anatomy of implementation of police reform. That work is not completed. The comments in this chapter emerged during the course of 18 open-ended interviews conducted between September 2013 and March 2014.

They exercised discretion here without intelligence from other agencies and/or reliable risk assessment tools, despite being acutely aware of the potential difficulties. They exercised discretion to make a good decision despite the poor development of police infrastructure and knowledge to support their judgment. This was one of many incidents that features in an HMIC report which concluded that in six forces studied: 'Out of the 19 basic technology operating systems now required by a constable to carry out frontline roles away from police stations, only one was consistently available and was not always effectual' (HMIC 2012: 2).

Local and national politicians and police leaders could hardly be entirely satisfied with this audit of support to the frontline. But they should be proud of the overlooked skills of the frontline itself as shown here. But these skills show discretion in action. The relationship between police and politicians has been riven with problems because of the exercise of discretion by frontline and chief constables alike. The problem revolves around the competition for control of discretion in policing.

Control

The police thinking around independence from politics amongst police leaders during the 1970s was set out by the then Commissioner Sir Robert Mark, in reminding us of the celebrated *Blackburn* case: 'every constable in the land should be and is independent of the Executive'(Mark and Charlton 1978: 283).[8] The case in point applied to enforcing the law in a particular set of circumstances but expanded into a doctrine that was uncomfortable with 'interference' in a wide range of circumstances, including the resourcing of policing.

Robert Mark's pride in independence was nuanced by an acknowledgement of the consent issue, in his now famous maxim for police engaged in public order to, 'win by appearing to lose' (Mark and Charlton 1978). As one who was a constable at those demonstrations, this was a little too subtle for many involved at the time!

The dominance of concern with the 'independence' element, above other aspects of the British model (restrained use of force, accountability to the rule of law, consent) led some Chiefs to rail inexplicably against modest efforts to improve accountability, framing them as political control. Of course, they found common cause with some politicians at the time. Consent did not feature in these officers' arguments (Simey 1988).

The 2012 reforms introduced local political governance of policing through a directly elected individual PCC, responsible for 'the totality of policing in their area', replacing the so-called tripartite system of distributed responsibilities between the Home Office (HO) the local police authority, and the Chief Constable with a bipartite system (HO-PCCs).[9] Whilst many police officers had seen

---

[8] See also *R v Commissioner of Police of the Metropolis, ex p Blackburn* [1968] 2 QB 118.

[9] See <https://www.gov.uk/government/collections/police-and-crime-commissioners-publica tions> (accessed 24 April 2015).

it as a virtue that they were separate from politics and accountable to the law, the government's view was that '[police] have become disconnected from the public they serve' (Home Office 2010). The truth was that a drive for efficiency and 'results' via targets had eroded the wider independence that chiefs had exercised or sought to exercise in the 1970s.

The radical proposals were challenged by the Association of Chief Police Officers (ACPO) and a variety of politicians and commentators with concern about the independence of the police. Discretion and impartiality were centre stage in the reforms.[10]

It remains to be seen how individual locally elected politicians will connect with a diverse public between elections,[11] hold the police to account for the exercise of discretion, and improve the police infrastructure overall.

Amidst this turmoil several influential academics provided me with different spectacles to view the changes. Policing can be an insular vocation. The work of Robert Reiner (1992b) and Egon Bittner (1974) pointed up the 'inherently political' nature of policing in providing civil order, and the tensions that forced crime fighters on the frontline to deal with the social fallout of crime. Their insights may not have moved the political debate, but they helped me to make sense of political comments from the left and right. However, in setting out the constraints and contradictions in which policing is nested, their conclusions struck a pessimistic note; these writers suggested that those committed to and dependent on the policing mission were destined to be disappointed. It is a conclusion I struggled with then but understand all too well now. I accept that it is part of the academic's task to throw down such gauntlets to the practitioner.

Consent

As a young inspector I was more optimistic. Leaders have to be the bearers of hope or they fail to motivate others. In seeking change, I didn't give enough weight to the broader coalition of political, social, and economic interests that came together to change policing.

Luckily I was engaged in the 1981 response of the Metropolitan Police (Met) to Scarman's report (1981) on urban disorders. The Scarman Report penetrated even the Met's thick skin, requiring the organization to attach a practical programme of actions to his recommendations. Of course, the recommendations extended to action beyond the Met itself, but the expectation of police officers was explicit and unavoidable.

---

[10] 'Sir Hugh Orde Threatens Resignation over Tory Plans for Directly-elected Commissioners', *The Telegraph*, 22 November 2009, at <http://www.telegraph.co.uk/news/uknews/law-and-order/6631249/Sir-Hugh-Orde-threatens-resignation-over-Tory-plans-for-directly-elected-commissioners.html> (accessed 21 April 2015)

[11] Only 11% of voters are able to name the elected police and crime commissioner in their area, see <http://ukpollingreport.co.uk/blog/archives/category/crime> (accessed 24 April 2015).

The rationale for much police action lies in the independence of constables and their accountability to the law. I had my doubts about this rationale when I saw the thin nature of the initial 'analysis' from the Met's *Operation Swamp Stop and Search* programme, that had arguably figured prominently in the initiation of the riots in the first place. The intelligence behind, and costs of, those particular tactics, and the perception of those at the receiving end, were not considered. A crime spike had occurred and police had reacted 'independently' without consultation. Such 'independence' seemed distant from the emphasis in my training as a constable that 'much depends on the approval and cooperation of the public'.[12]

By contrast, the Scarman Report set out a working framework of four 'principles' of 'consent and balance' and 'independence and accountability'. It attempted to provide a principled and prudent reference point for balanced judgments not only about 'what' police objectives might be pursued but also, crucially, about 'how' that should be done (Scarman 1981: 62–3). In the context of the Brixton disorders, the Scarman Report developed the Peelian rationale by explicitly embracing the trade-offs between the law, and social and political realities. It was the exercise of discretion in its social and political context.

However, as Reiner points out, there are 'conceptual ambiguities' in the notion of consent. One cannot be absolutist about how consensual a police service can be, given that it deals with conflict arising from human and social or policy failure (Reiner 1992b: 59). It cannot imply a policy of retreat. Conflict requires calculation (Bottoms and Tankebe 2012: 140). Any guiding principle taken to extremes generates difficulties; police have to be permanent 'tightrope' walkers.

Before returning to the Metropolitan Police in 1997 to develop a strategy to address the issues arising from the Lawrence Inquiry, I spoke to Lord Scarman about consent. He was more assertive about the significance of consent: 'By "Consent" I refer to the basic *objective* [his emphasis] of policing, namely to secure the assent of the community which they police to their policing operations.'[13]

Consent matters because it is, as others have described it, 'foundational' and, 'If consent be withdrawn, that is the sign of lack of political legitimacy' (Bottoms and Tankebe 2012: 134).

> Importantly, we know more about the building blocks of consent now. The evidence mounts that public cooperation hinges on the fairness and effectiveness of the police. Even the most skeptical reformers should find it compelling that 'perceptions of legitimacy are stronger predictors of compliance with the law than perceptions of deterrent risk. (Jackson et al 2012: 8–10)

---

[12] *Metropolitan Police Instruction Book*, (1969). Printed by the Receiver for the Metropolitan Police District, New Scotland Yard, Broadway, SW1. Introduction, Para 3 (author's copy).

[13] Letter to the author dated 13 May 1997. He blamed himself in his letter for being, 'too concise in paragraphs 4.55. and 4.56 [in his 1981 report] that many have not grasped my meaning'(the paragraphs dealing with his framework). Those who regard his work as less compelling should be aware of this more radical approach to policing.

Perceptions of legitimacy are contextual in time and place but the key point for police is awareness of their significance for their operations.

Competence

From the 1960s, as political parties became increasingly vocal about police effectiveness and efficiency in controlling crime, the expertise, judgments, and persuasiveness of senior police leaders came under increasing scrutiny. All of this provided a backdrop punctuated by Irish Republican Army terrorism activities, industrial disputes, riots, and emergencies (fuel disputes, foot-and-mouth outbreak, floods, etc.). It was evident that as each of these individual pressures came to the fore, police leaders were listened to, if not courted, by government, even when police were believed to have 'failed' (Reiner 1992b: ch 2).

It is no longer the case. The tone began to change in the 1990s with increasing political agreement on the need for reforming control of police (Home Office: 1993; 2001). Even though recorded crime fell in the late 1990s, fear of crime spilled over into the 2000s and Al Qaeda terrorism took on a new and worrying form. Both issues and crime spikes (e.g. street crime) generated successful if uneasy collaborative relationships between government and police.

Part of the police surprise over the latest reforms arose from their pride in crime reduction achieved over 15 years and some improvement in public satisfaction. As the threat of crime receded, with the economy, less regard was paid to police advice (Atkinson 2013). Concerns over consent receded as 'new public management', and 'deliverology' (Barber 2007) took hold from the mid-1990s. Older concerns surfaced from time to time; for example terrorism, the issue of public confidence, and police integrity, and a more recent surge connected to scandals and perceived failings.

Change and advice to aspiring leaders

There is no shortage of issues for aspiring leaders to address. They include some old favourites—consent, independence, scandal, and failure—as well as old favourites in new clothes—political accountability.

Frontline officers and consent

The anecdote presented previously illustrates the dilemmas confronting the police. It is a cautionary tale of what police and leaders have achieved in supporting frontline officers in dealing with a changing world. This is particularly telling, given the officer's view of the intolerance of error. But it is an exemplar of the constables' understanding that they need to win consent, as well as exercise independence in exercising discretion about applying the law. Scarman would have been proud.

There are many controls and formal accountability mechanisms that increasingly reveal police wrongdoing. But we need to recognize their limitations. They may deter some bad behaviour but are less successful in promoting the best in British policing. There is a real possibility that unless we get the balance of reform right we could encourage a reduction in the sense of self-legitimacy of officers and produce a 'safer' response for them but also an unfortunate legalistic response for the public (Bradford and Quinton 2014: 2).

Independence

Independence is important in British law, but applies to the narrow ground of particular events and operations. Over-reliance upon constabulary independence has been part of the political relationship problem. Aspiring leaders need to understand constitutional *realpolitik* and the tightrope associated with it. In strategic decision-making, there will always be an 'unequal dialogue' between public service leaders and politicians, especially national politicians (Cohen 2002: ch 7).

Scandal and failure

Aspiring leaders need not be pessimistic about the police recovering their status; even now, when some disquieting police failings are in constant public view. Policing can recover. Of course, police standing will not return to levels attributed to the 1950s, but then it never could. Poll ratings which fell precipitously between the 1980s and 2003 stabilized and have, if anything, recovered since the commencement of the Neighbourhood Policing in 2005. This followed the professionally led National Reassurance Policing Programme in eight forces, trialling ideas to re-invent local police and public relationships. Leaders (police and political) need to remember that then as now, there was evidence that the public did not accept crime statistics or police and government assertions about crime control, and are most strongly influenced about the value of policing by local interactions like those in the case study described earlier (Tuffin et al 2006).

Political accountability

In the latest reforms, politicians are explicitly involved in the governance of the police. Police officers are cast in an executive role. Politicians bring a mandate to their role. Aspiring police leaders must bring not just experience but also recognized expertise. This is part of the rationale associated with the introduction of direct entry Superintendents in 2014.

There is some evidence that accommodations are being made at a local level since the advent of PCCs, albeit individualized in nature. As one PCC said to me: 'It's taken months to get a real sense of agreement, I have folded [the Chief Constable]'s words into my priorities.' A local politician explained it succinctly:

'Analysis of risks between us became quite close.' Individual adaptation, locally by chiefs, to the new political environment, is a necessary but not sufficient development, given that policing crosses boundaries. The small 'p' political skills of negotiation are at a premium.

Building expertise

At the national level, matters are more difficult. As a senior civil servant explained in a personal communication with the author:

> The biggest problem around police leadership influencing this or another set of ministers, [is that] when you compare them to any of those other professional cadres that deal with national security matters... there is still at the top end of policing something about the projection of police knowledge and expertise that is not quite as intellectually sharp in the communication as there is in other high risk services.

Building expertise that will be valued in the 21st century requires aspiring police leaders to have ideas and options that they can articulate, based upon current evidence of 'what works' in controlling crime (Sherman 2013) *and* fostering consent (Hough et al 2010).

The chief officers I have interviewed acknowledge an absence of an agreed 'bedrock of knowledge', as one put it, on 'crime control and crime tactics'. This gap, and the inconsistencies it fosters, make it harder to project competence in crime control confidently. Those interviewed see this as a symptom of the need for more professionalization and hope the College of Policing will fill this gap.

Back to consent

Surprisingly, perhaps, and despite the never-ending debate over the future of the police, few address the thorny issue of 'policing by consent'; for example, it does not directly feature in the ACPO National Decision Model (2012). Yet both politicians and police need consent, the former to win elections, the latter to deal with the logistics of the 1:500 ratio of constables to members of the public. It also requires politicians to understand the dynamics of the institution they govern. Reform cannot only be about controlling scandal and crisis. Reform must also, 'enable consent' (Reiner 1992b: 251). After all, 'there is little evidence that the *structures* of external police governance make much difference in how police do their job, how much controversy they generate, or how well they secure public safety and human rights' (Sherman 2011: 590).

Properly developed, a doctrine of consent is arguably more relevant today than it was at the foundation of modern policing. Advanced and aspiring democracies that prize freedom question those in authority, especially the police. Focusing on consent in decision-making develops an 'outside in view' as decision-makers take into account the several publics of the police. It has the potential to deal with political demands, trends, and fashions (Smith 2005).[14] Combined with impartiality and restraint, it helps to provide a balanced response at both a local and national level. Such a response is essential when police leaders eschew narratives—so vital in politics—believing that the value of the police is self-evident. It is not. Reiner suggests, in the earlier section of this chapter, that the decline in demand for policing has helped to pave the way for reform and, I would suggest, the narrative accompanying it. In fact, 'the decline' masked a growing demand for better policing of vulnerability and online crime. Some narrative or rationale is central when engaging with new ideas and reforms. If police leaders do not tell their story of their role and their aims, who will? The narrative must prompt questions not just about what is to be done. Above all it requires police leaders and politicians alike to answer questions on how the proposal will command the consent of the public.

Operationalizing consent

So how do we build consent? Whether one sees 'what' the police do as crime fighting or peacekeeping with a social purpose (Stevens 2013), the distinguishing British feature was, and remains, the independent constable and 'how' they do their job. Their discretion is inescapable but it must be exercised with consent. Yet, overly vague references to 'policing by consent' will not work either; nor can consent be an issue only considered in discussions about the benign face of the police, such as neighborhood policing. It is not just a question of technical professional expertise and competence, important those these skills are. Rather, consent needs to be central to any dialogue with the public, and all decisions and actions. It requires consideration in any intervention or policy as to whether sufficient thought has been given to fairness, effectiveness (Bottoms and Tankebe 2012), and attention to public support. Has there been an application of engagement, explanation, and justification?

Consent should certainly feature in the more difficult areas of policing because it sharply focuses on what matters most; for example, triage activity and solving cases. The screening out of crime is a vexed issue regularly aired in the media. The justifications for more, or less, police action, require police officers to explain to victims what does, and what does not constitute the best strategies when trying to solve a crime. Such explanations may defuse misgivings about how the police respond to particular calls. In dealing with public disorder the test is, as I found myself explaining to a senior officer at the G20 protests, not whether an officer can apply restraint techniques he/she has learnt in training, including striking 'non-compliant' demonstrators with a police baton, the question is 'should' they do so (HMIC 2012). The same consideration applies in stop and search. In contemplating the use of highly intrusive undercover operations, taking public

---

[14] As military services step back from large-scale wars to undertake constabulary roles, they are thinking in their own way about the consent issue.

consent into account means that officers must go beyond making a justification based on 'proportionality and necessity'. And such cases can be made. The issue is whether authorizing officers think there is 'sufficient cause' to pursue a case, given how we in the United Kingdom value freedom of speech and the right to protest; at its simplest, is the proposed game worth the candle? (HMIC 2012: 36).

Conclusion

In short, during my time in policing there has been a lot of change, an understandable focus on control, but insufficient reform to support officers exercising their inescapable discretion in dealing with the demanding issues of competence and consent in changing times. That is still the case and it won't be resolved by reform relying heavily on more regulation and accountability. It will require those that lead the police to rethink the limits of independence, the value they place on public support in decision-making, and the case—the narrative—they make to political leaders.

However, it will also require from politicians a degree of reflection on how to develop policy that shapes the kind of policing they admire and wish to foster, as well as the kind they wish to firmly deter. Reiner's observation that despite reducing demand for policing, '"Policing by consent" is not an impossible dream' is heartening. Arguably, the inequality and vulnerability that he points towards can only be legitimately served by such an approach. The recent set of scandals (stemming from the continuing fallout from the Stephen Lawrence murder above all, but many other causes célèbres too) may command headlines, but the urgent reform is to build consent and give a degree of urgency to this, which has not been evident for some time.

Indeed, true effective reform is much more likely to succeed when there is a shared evidenced-based approach between politicians and police, with both seeking to build and to sustain consent in and around policy and operations in order to control crime well. A local politician of some weight recently reminded me of where Peel began: 'You live and die together on something as vital as crime and security, you can't stand back . . . It's our [politicians'] job to build trust just as much as theirs [the police].'

Shared Reflections

First let me say that it has been a pleasure and an honour to exchange views on policing and politics with Sir Denis O'Connor in this collaborative venture. Sir Denis is a shining star amongst recent police leaders, with an outstanding, thoroughly merited reputation for integrity, intelligence, insight, and innovation. These have been amply demonstrated many times over during his career, culminating in his service as a chief officer and HM Chief Inspector of Constabulary.

From the outset I thought this topic could not really be fitted into the template envisaged for most chapters in this work. The fundamental reason is that it is obviously and inherently *political*, ie it is fundamentally about and characterized by conflicts of viewpoint and principled controversies that cannot be resolved by empirical evidence. Reflecting this, there is little empirical research on the topic. The few works on senior officers in this country (Reiner 1991; Wall 1998; Savage et al 2000; Silvestri 2003; Caless 2011) are studies of their background, careers, perspectives, and organization, with some material on their interactions with politicians in local and central government. They yield little if anything about how they could improve their performance in this regard, or even what that would mean. In this they are prime examples of sociology *of* rather than *for* the police.

My argument draws heavily on my book *The Politics of the Police*, as far as I know the only work that contains these two key terms in its title (Reiner 2010). It considers the common roots of both terms and their parallels. Above all it emphasizes that both have twin sides to their joint concern with order: preserving the conditions of the universal good, but given the inequalities of almost all known societies, but necessarily benefitting some more than others. Thus even if overt bias and discrimination are absent there is an inherently partisan dimension to both politics and policing.

However, whilst this means that policing is always political it is not necessarily politicized, ie an object of overt partisan conflict. The achievement of the first century-and-a-half of modern British policing was to de-politicize an institution born in deep conflict, creating a tradition widely known as 'policing by consent'. It is important to note that policing by consent was *not* a result of social and political consensus. On the contrary, it was the result of strategies aimed precisely at defusing the bitter conflicts surrounding it. But it is vital to realize that these strategies succeeded only because they were rolled out in a supportive political, economic, social, and cultural context. This was the long (albeit always contested and uneven) march of citizenship, the inclusion of the whole population in basic civil, political, and socio-economic rights.

The roots of the re-politicization of policing lie in the reversal of this inclusive citizenship project. It has been ousted by the rise of neo-liberalism, the resurgent dominance of free-market economics since the 1970s. A key consequence of this is the growth of ever more economic and political inequality, with baleful consequences for crime, order, and all public services, including criminal justice and policing.

The realization of this in the case of the police was delayed by the vital role they played in the establishment of neo-liberal hegemony, especially during the 1980s. But for reasons that I explore in the final part of the chapter, this has become tenuous with the embedding of neo-liberalism across parties, and the qualitatively greater socio-economic divide as the mega-rich have soared away from the rest of society. The present trajectory appears highly dystopian, but it should be remembered that the original creation of policing by consent was in circumstances that appeared at least as unpropitious.

The determination of key police leaders like Sir Denis to preserve the virtues of traditional British policing is inspiring. There is extensive debate in the literature about whether there is a 'police personality'. I doubt it (although there is, I believe, a characteristic police culture shaped by the structural exigencies of policing). But one quality of the police officers I have met since starting police research in the late 1960s is what in my discussion of police culture I called 'pragmatism'. This is a determination to do what can be done even in the most dangerous and difficult circumstances. What Gramsci called 'pessimism of the intellect' is warranted, I believe, by an examination of current trajectories in political economy and culture. But reading the 'optimism of the will' to safeguard policing by consent that shines through Sir Denis's writing and experience is an inspiration to me, and hopefully to all academic analysts, politicians, and police.

Sharing reflections

Robert, I admire you for shining some light for me and others in the difficult world of policing, where big ideas are too often in short supply.

If I had been half as good as the fellow you are writing about I would have done more to turn the tide and made fewer mistakes along the way. British policing would better than it is today—I have to take some responsibility for that. I could have done more on policing by consent as a serving chief police officer beyond my efforts on neighbourhood policing. I could have been less pragmatic and more assertive in print about why the consent principle was vital, fragile, and endangered. I did more on it as Chief Inspector of Constabulary, where I endeavoured to reflect on what needed to be done from the outside in. But that was a bit late in the day.

You see you are right in many ways about pragmatism—we want our police leaders, like frontline officers, to deal with problems that present themselves in a reasonable and logical way. And we surely don't need over-opinionated police leaders. However, pragmatism is both a real strength in dealing compassionately with human failing and socially inept interventions by government and also a weakness in relation to the ideal of policing by consent.

Unlike pragmatists, as a young professor you developed a perspective on what the world should hear about your area of expertise in our society. It took me too long to do that publically and I should have articulated it better in writing at an earlier stage in my career.

Policing by consent needs less uncertain or absent trumpets amongst its leaders, in their prime, for as we are reminded in 1 Corinthians 14:8:

> Yet even lifeless things, either flute or harp, in producing a sound, if they do not produce a distinction in the tones, how will it be known what is played on the flute or on the harp? For if the bugle produces an indistinct sound, who will prepare himself for battle? So also you, unless you utter by the tongue speech that is clear, how will it be known what is spoken? For you will be speaking into the air.

Now I do acknowledge that it can be awkward to reflect in writing, as a serving police leader, in a democracy where politicians make policy. Yet as I reflect now, they (politicians),would surely not deny or have denied the value of thinking and rethinking how we should aim to provide policing by consent, in an increasingly sceptical democracy.

Recommended Reading

Bittner, E (1974), 'Florence Nightingale in Pursuit of Willie Sutton: A Theory of the Police' in Jacob, H (ed), *The Potential for Reform of Criminal Justice* (Los Angeles, CA: Sage)

Marenin, O (1983), 'Parking Tickets and Class Repression: The Concept of Policing in Critical Theories of Criminal Justice' 6(2) *Contemporary Crises* 241

Reiner, R (2007), *Law and Order: An Honest Citizen's Guide to Crime and Control* (Cambridge: Polity)

Reiner, R (2010), *The Politics of the Police* (4th edn, Oxford: OUP)

Reiner, R (2011), *Policing, Popular Culture and Political Economy: Towards a Social Democratic Criminology* (Farnham: Ashgate)

Silver, A (1967), 'The Demand for Order in Civil Society' in Bordua, D (ed), *The Police* (New York: Wiley)

References

ACPO (2012), National Decision Model, at <http://www.acpo.police.uk/documents/president/201201PBANDM.pdf> (accessed 18 September 2014)

Atkinson, C (2013), 'Beyond Cop Culture: The Cultural Challenge of Civilian Intelligence Analysis in Scottish Policing', PhD, University of Glasgow

Barber, M (2007), *An Instruction to Deliver: Tony Blair, the Public Services and the Challenge of Delivery* (London, Politico's Publishing)

Bauman, Z (2005), 'The Demons of an Open Society', Ralph Miliband Lecture, 20 November, London School of Economics, London

Bittner, E (1974), 'Florence Nightingale in Pursuit of Willie Sutton: A Theory of the Police' in Jacob, H (ed), *The Potential for Reform of Criminal Justice* (Los Angeles, CA: Sage

Blyth, M (2013), *Austerity: The History of a Dangerous Idea* (New York: OUP)

Bottoms, A and Tankebe, J (2012), 'Beyond Procedural Justice: A Dialogic Approach to Legitimacy in Criminal Justice' 102 *Journal of Criminal Law and Criminology* 119

Bowles, S and Jayadev, A (2014), 'One Nation Under Guard', *New York Times*, 15 February

Bradford, B and Quinton, P (2014), 'Self-legitimacy, Police Culture and Support for Democratic Policing in an English Constabulary' 54(6) *British Journal of Criminology* 1023

Bradford, B, Jackson, J, and Hough, M (2014), 'Police Futures and Legitimacy: Redefining "Good Policing"' in Brown, J (ed), *The Future of Policing* (Abingdon: Routledge) 79

Brodeur, J-P (2010), *The Policing Web* (New York: OUP)

Brogden, M and Ellison, G (2012), *Policing in an Age of Austerity: A Postcolonial Perspective* (London: Routledge)

Brown, J (2014) (ed), *The Future of Policing* (Abingdon: Routledge)

Caless, B (2011), *Policing at the Top: The Roles, Values and Attitudes of Chief Police Officers* (Bristol: Policy Press)

Cohen, E (2002), *Supreme Command: Soldiers, Statesmen, and Leadership in Wartime* (New York: Free Press)

Dixon, D (2008), 'Authorise and Regulate: A Comparative Perspective on the Rise and Fall of a Regulatory Strategy' in Cape, E and Young, R (eds), *Regulating Policing* (Oxford: Hart)

Downes, D and Morgan, R (2012), 'Overtaking on the Left? The Politics of Law and Order in the "Big Society"' in Maguire, M, Morgan, R, and Reiner, R (eds), *The Oxford Handbook of Criminology* (Oxford: OUP) 182

Emsley, C (2014), 'Peel's Principles, Police Principles' in Brown, J (ed), *The Future of Policing* (Abingdon: Routledge) 11

Equality Trust (2014), 'About Equality', at <http://www.equalitytrust.org.uk/about-inequality/scale-and-trends> (accessed 27 February 2014)

Farrell, G, Tilley, N, Tseloni, A, and Mailley, J (2011), 'The Crime Drop and the Security Hypothesis' 48(2) *Journal of Research in Crime and Delinquency* 147

Gamble, A (2014), *Crisis Without End* (London: Macmillan)

Gilens, M (2014), *Affluence and Influence* (Princeton, NJ: Princeton University Press)

Hall, S, Winlow, S, and Ancrum, C (2008), *Criminal Identities and Consumer Culture* (Cullompton: Willan)

Harvey, D (2005), *A Brief History of Neoliberalism* (Oxford: OUP)

Hinslof, G (2006), 'Cameron Softens Crime Image in "Hug-a-Hoodie" Call', *The Observer*, 9 July

Home Office (1993), *Police Reform: A Police Service for the Twenty-First Century* (Cm 2281)

Home Office (2001), *Policing and a New Century: A Blueprint for Reform* (Cm 5236)

Home Office (2010), *Policing in the 21st Century: Reconnecting Police and People* (Cm 7925), at <http://www.homeoffice.gov.uk/publications/consultations/policing-21st-century> (accessed 27 February 2014)

HMIC (2012), 'A Review of National Police Units which Provide Intelligence on Criminality Associated with Protest', at <http://www.justiceinspectorates.gov.uk/hmic/media/review-of-national-police-units-which-provide-intelligence-on-criminality-associated-with-protest-20120202.pdf> (accessed 18 September 2014)

HMIC (2013), 'Policing in Austerity: Rising to the Challenge', at <http://www.justiceinspectorates.gov.uk/hmic/media/policing-in-austerity-rising-to-the-challenge.pdf> (accessed 12 April 2015)

Hough, M, Jackson, J, Bradford, B, Myhill, A, and Quinton, P (2010), 'Procedural Justice, Trust and Institutional Legitimacy' (2010) 4(3) *Policing* 203

House of Commons Home Affairs Committee (2013), *Police and Crime Commissioners: Power to Remove Chief Constables*, HC 487

Jackson, J, Bradford, B, Stanko, EA, and Hohl, K (2012), *Just Authority? Trust in the Police in England and Wales* (Abingdon: Routledge)

Jayadev, A and Bowles, S (2006), 'Guard Labor' 79 *Journal of Development Economics* 328

Johnson, J and Clarke, C (2014), 'Labour Can Take the Politics Out of Policing', *The Guardian*, 13 February

Jones, T, Newburn, T, and Smith, D (1994), *Democracy and Policing* (London: Policy Studies Institute)

Jones, T, Newburn, T, and Smith, D (2012), 'Democracy, Police and Crime Commissioners' in Newburn, T and Peay, J (eds), *Policing: Politics, Culture and Control* (Oxford: Hart) 219

Kenworthy, L (2014), *Social Democratic America* (Oxford: OUP)

Krugman, P (2012), *End This Depression Now* (New York: Norton)

Lasswell, H (1936), *Who Gets What, When and How?* (New York: Whittlesey House)

Leveson, Lord Justice (2012), 'An Inquiry into the Culture, Practices and Ethics of the Press: Executive Summary and Recommendations' (the Leveson Report), TSO, London

Lister, S (2013), 'The New Politics of the Police: Police and Crime Commissioners and the "Operational Independence" of the Police' 7(3) *Policing* 239

Lister, S (2014), 'Scrutinising the Role of the Police and Crime Panel in the New Era of Police Governance in England and Wales' 13(1) *Safer Communities* 22

Lukes, S (2005), *Power* (2nd edn, London: Macmillan)

Lustgarten, L (1986), *The Governance of the Police* (London: Sweet & Maxwell)

Macpherson, SW (1999), *The Stephen Lawrence Inquiry: Report of an Inquiry* (Cm 4262–I)

Maitland, F (1885), *Justice and Police* (London: Macmillan)

Marenin, O (1983), 'Parking Tickets and Class Repression: The Concept of Policing in Critical Theories of Criminal Justice' 6(2) *Contemporary Crises* 241

Mark, R and Charlton, E (1978), *In the Office of Constable* (London: Collins)

Marshall, TH (1950), *Citizenship and Social Class* (Cambridge: Cambridge University Press)

May, T (2010), Police Reform: Theresa May's speech to the Police Federation, at <http://www.gov.uk/government/speeches/police-reform-theresa-mays-speech-to-the-police-federation> (accessed 21 February 2014)

May, T (2012), 'Police Reform', speech to ACPO conference, 22 May, at <http://www.gov.uk/government/speeches/police-reform-home-secretarys-speech-to-acpo-conference> (accessed 3 October 2013)

Mirowski, P (2013), *Never Let A Good Crisis Go to Waste: How Neoliberalism Survived the Financial Breakdown* (London: Verso)

Morgan, J (1987), *Conflict and Order: The Police and Labour Disputes in England and Wales 1900–1939* (Oxford: OUP)

Nozick, R (1974), *Anarchy, State and Utopia* (New York: Basic Books).

Piketty, T (2014), *Capital in the Twenty-first Century* (Cambridge, MA: Harvard University Press)

Rawls, J (1971), *A Theory of Justice* (Cambridge, MA: Harvard University Press)

Reiner, R (1978), *The Blue-coated Worker* (Cambridge: Cambridge University Press)

Reiner, R (1991), *Chief Constables* (Oxford: OUP)

Reiner, R (1992a), 'Policing a Postmodern Society' 55(6) *Modern Law Review* 761

Reiner, R (1992b), *The Politics of the Police* (2nd edn, Oxford: OUP)

Reiner, R (2007), *Law and Order: An Honest Citizen's Guide to Crime and Control* (Cambridge: Polity)

Reiner, R (2010), *The Politics of the Police* (4th edn, Oxford: OUP)

Reiner, R (2011), *Policing, Popular Culture and Political Economy: Towards a Social Democratic Criminology* (Farnham: Ashgate)

Reiner, R (2013), 'Who Governs?: Democracy, Plutocracy, Science and Prophecy in Policing' 13(2) *Criminology and Criminal Justice* 161

Rikagos, G and Ergul, A (2011), 'Policing the Industrial Reserve Army: An International Study' 56(4) *Crime, Law and Social Change* 329

Rikagos, G and Ergul, A (2013), 'The Pacification of the American Working Class' 9(2) *Socialist Studies* 167

Savage, S, Charman, S, and Cope, S (2000), *Policing and the Power of Persuasion* (London: Blackstone)

Scarman, L (1981), *The Brixton Disorders* (Cm 8427)

Scarman, L (1982), *The Scarman Report: The Brixton Disorders 10–12 April 1981* (Harmondsworth: Pelican)

Seymour, R (2014), *Against Austerity* (London: Pluto)

Shearing, C and Stenning, P (1983), 'Private Security: Implications for Social Control' 30(5) *Social Problems* 493.

Sherman, LW (2011), 'Democratic Policing on the Evidence' in Wilson, JQ and Petersilla, J (eds), *Crime and Public Policy* (New York: OUP) 589

Sherman, LW (2013), 'The Rise of Evidence-based Policing: Targeting, Testing, and Tracking' 42(1) *Crime and Justice* 377

Silver, A (1967), 'The Demand for Order in Civil Society' in Bordua, D (ed), *The Police* (New York: Wiley)

Silvestri, M (2003), ' "Doing" ' Police Leadership: Enter the ' "New Smart Macho" ' 17(1) *Policing and Society* 38

Simey, M (1988), *Democracy Rediscovered: A Study of Police Accountability* (London: Pluto Press)

Smith, D (2007), 'New Challenges to Police Legitimacy' in Henry, A and Smith, D (eds), *Transformations of Policing* (Aldershot: Ashgate) 273

Smith, R (2005), *The Utility of Force: The Art of War in the Modern World* (London: Allen Lane)

Stevens, Lord (2013), 'Policing for a Better Britain: Report of the Independent Police Commission' , at <http://independentpolicecommission.org.uk/uploads/37d80308-be23-9684-054d-e4958bb9d518.pdf> (accessed 18 September 2014).

Stiglitz, J (2013), *The Price of Inequality: How Today's Divided Society Endangers Our Future* (London: Penguin)

Stuckler, D and Basu, S (2013), *The Body Economic: Why Austerity Kills* (London: Allen Lane)

Tankebe, J and Liebling, A (2013) (eds), *Legitimacy and Criminal Justice* (Oxford: OUP)

Tilley, N, Tseloni, A, and Farrell, G (2011), 'Income Disparities of Burglary Risk and Security Availability during the Crime Drop' 51(2) *British Journal of Criminology* 296

Tuffin, R, Morris, J, and Poole, A (2006), 'An Evaluation of the Impact of the National Reassurance Policing Programme', Home Office Research, Development and Statistics Directorate, London

Turner, L (2014), 'PCCs, Neo-liberal Hegemony and Democratic Policing' 13(1) *Safer Communities* 13

Tyler, T (2004), 'Enhancing Police Legitimacy' 593 *The Annals* 84

Walker, N (2000), *Policing in a Changing Constitutional Order* (London: Sweet & Maxwell)

Wall, D (1998), *The Chief Constables of England and Wales: The Socio-legal History of a Criminal Justice Elite* (Aldershot: Ashgate)

Weber, M (2004 [1919]), 'Politics as a Vocation' in *The Vocation Lectures* (Indianapolis, IN: Hackett)

Weinberger, B (1991), *Keeping the Peace? Policing Strikes in Britain 1906–1926* (Oxford: Berg)

Winsor, T (2012), *Independent Review of Police Officer and Staff Renumeration and Conditions: Final Report* (Cm 8325–1)

Zedner, L (2006), 'Policing Before the Police' 46(1) *British Journal of Criminology* 78

4

Working in Partnership

The Challenges of Working across Organizational Boundaries, Cultures, and Practices

Adam Crawford and Mike Cunningham

Introduction

The appeal to partnerships as the effective means of delivering policing and community safety has been an established mantra in crime control and crime prevention policy for nearly three decades now. Yet, whilst much has changed in the intervening years to facilitate and embed partnership working, the goal of a genuinely joined-up, holistic, and coordinated response to crime and disorder seems as stubbornly elusive as ever. Having spent some considerable time during the early 1990s researching the emerging shift to partnerships in community safety, it strikes me that many of the obstacles apparent then remain prevalent today (Crawford 1994; 1997; 1998; Crawford and Jones 1995). This was brought home recently whilst conducting research commissioned by the Nuffield Foundation into anti-social behaviour (ASB) interventions with young people (Crawford et al 2012). Anti-social behaviour by its very nature straddles the concerns of a variety of organizations and demands a collaborative approach (Crawford 2009). Hence, the ASB partnership arrangements studied saw police working with local authorities, social housing providers, and youth justice workers. The research found that effective partnership working was vital for identifying local problems, delivering preventive solutions, and ensuring an accurate understanding of the needs of young people and their families. It noted that where coordination is well-organized through effective partnerships, there are significant benefits to community safety and crime prevention. A coherent and consistent area-wide policy that combined the efforts of different partner agencies was held out as desirable by many managers not only because it provided the basis for more effective solutions but because it accords with principles of fairness, equity, and transparency with positive implications for engagement with parents and compliance on the part of young people. However, the research found evidence of 'a lack of joined-up working and insufficient coordination of local service delivery, such that the same individuals or families were often the subjects of disjointed interventions by diverse local agencies' (Crawford et al 2012: 2). It concluded that: 'Delivering [partnerships] on the ground was demanding and often not accomplished' (Crawford et al 2012: 3). The conundrum, therefore, is that whilst partnerships have become a dominant feature in the local governance landscape, their realization remains precarious, and considerable debates persist about what makes for good partnership working.

This chapter sets out to identify and revisit some of the fundamental challenges associated with working in partnerships across organizational boundaries, cultures, and established practices, and to consider some of the vexed issues that often stymie good intentions as well as their implications for police leadership. This critical starting point is deliberately chosen to prompt consideration of how best to manage inter-organizational relations. It also underscores the importance of strong leadership and strategic direction in providing organizational commitment and coordination of effort, as well as facilitating engagement with and buy-in from multiple partners. The intention of this chapter is not to undermine the rationale for a partnership approach but, rather, to highlight often ignored problems and structural conflicts, so as to inform contemporary thinking and good practice and to help enlighten leadership strategies for negotiating these. For it is only by recognizing the barriers and the working assumptions that inform organizational hurdles that we can begin to surmount them. The implication is that successful inter-organizational partnerships don't just happen; they need to be fashioned, crafted, nurtured, and supported. They need both strategic leadership and the appropriately skilled people to deliver them on the ground. I shall leave it to Chief Constable Mike Cunningham (later in this chapter), to reflect on his experience in the context of what we know from research about partnerships and to highlight some of the ways in which police leaders and their partners are attempting to realize the potential benefits that undoubtedly accrue to working in partnerships.

A Short History

Nearly 50 years ago, influenced by the management modelling trend of the time, the United State's Report of the President's Commission (1967), entitled 'The Challenge of Crime in a Free Society', sought to apply a 'systems analysis' to criminal justice. This systemic mode of thinking—most iconically captured some years later in the image of the criminal justice 'funnel' advocated by Blumstein (1986)—emphasized the inter-dependence and 'system quality' of the diverse institutions and processes that had grown up around the modern criminal justice enterprise. Similarly informed modelling of criminal justice was conducted in the United Kingdom some years later (Morgan 1985; Moxon 1985). The idea that the police, courts, lawyers (both prosecution and defence), parole, probation, and penal institutions had something in common, reciprocal interests, shared modes of exchange and communication, similar ways of thinking, and mutual regard as part of a coherent system was certainly innovative. It was, however, an ahistorical reading of criminal justice which, since the late 19th century had witnessed the slow growth of an elaborate and complex division of labour in relation to the tasks of crime control, in which specialized organizations and professional groups organized themselves around and appropriated aspects of criminological work (Garland 1985). It was also counter-intuitive, since the premise of common law was that conflict and mediation were necessary to produce 'case-by-case' justice. However, one of the by-products of this 'systems thinking' was a growing recognition that in practice criminal justice represented, and was experienced as, a 'non-system' (Cohn 1978). Following this line of thinking, commentators identified 'system failures' and 'institutionalized gaps' which engender problems of coordination and responsiveness. In relation to neighbourhood services, Mudd evocatively described the problem as follows:

> If a rat is found in an apartment, it is a housing inspection responsibility; if it runs into a restaurant, the health department has jurisdiction; if it goes outside and dies in an alley, public works takes over. More complex undertakings compound the confusion (Mudd 1984: 8).

Wilson and Kelling, building on Mudd's analogy in the policing context, added: 'a police officer who takes public complaints about rats seriously will go crazy trying to figure out what agency in the city has responsibility for rat control and then inducing it to kill the rats' (1989: 52). Subsequent gurus of organizational cultural change and management have likewise emphasized problem-oriented approaches to enterprising government through forms of preventive partnership (Osborne and Gaebler 1992).

Consequently, the past 30 years or so have seen the emergence and institutionalization of a new politics and landscape at the heart of which is a partnership approach to governing safety problems, broadly conceived. Writing a decade and a half ago, Garland noted how:

> ...a whole new infrastructure has been assembled at the local level that addresses crime and disorder in a quite different manner... The new infrastructure is strongly oriented towards a set of objectives and priorities—prevention, security, harm-reduction, loss-reduction, fear-reduction—that are quite different from the traditional goals of prosecution, punishment and 'criminal justice' (2001: 16–17).

This new politics has been marked by:

- a focus upon pro-active *prevention* rather than reactive detection;
- an emphasis upon *wider social problems*, including broadly defined harms, quality of life, anti-social behaviour, and disorder;
- a focus upon modes of *informal social control* and local normative orders, as well as the manner in which they relate to, and connect with, formal systems of control;
- implementation through decentralized, *local* arrangements for the delivery of this politics—'local problems require local solutions';
- delivery through a *partnership* approach, drawing together a variety of organizations and stakeholders, in horizontal networks;
- producing *holistic solutions* that are 'problem-oriented' rather than defined according to the means or organizations most readily available to solve them.

Key policy landmarks in the United Kingdom have included: the inter-departmental Circular 8/1984, which recognized that 'since some of the factors affecting crime lie outside the control or direct influence of the police, crime prevention can not be left to them alone' and urged various organizations (such as the probation service) to join the new coordinated approach; the Report into the Cleveland child abuse cases of 1987 (Butler-Sloss 1988), which recommended improved inter-agency coordination; the Morgan Report (1991), which advocated a partnership approach to community safety; and the Crime and Disorder Act 1998, which placed a statutory duty on the police to work with partners in delivering local community safety strategies. Importantly, the 1998 Act also provides a legal basis (in section.115) for sharing information between community safety partner agencies where this is necessary for fulfilling the duties contained in the Act. More recently, partnership practice has been extended through the national roll-out of neighbourhood policing in England and Wales in 2008. As a result, partnerships can now be found in diverse areas of policing, from domestic violence, child abuse, mental health, public protection, and road traffic to counter-terrorism—notably those partnerships promoted under the *Prevent Strategy*[1] (HM Government 2011).

The Theory and Practice

It is in the light of this growing recognition that a fundamental rupture in thinking has transpired at the heart of which has been a partnership approach to diverse aspects of prevention, policing, and criminal justice processing. This

---

[1] Prevent is part of the Government's counter-terrorism strategy, CONTEST. Its aim is to stop people becoming terrorists or supporting terrorism—see 'Prevent Strategy, at <https://www.gov.uk/government/uploads/system/uploads/attachment_data/file/97976/prevent-strategy-review.pdf> (accessed 26 January 2015).

shift in emphasis and concomitant transformation in governing structures has had significant implications for contemporary policing. In many senses, the police organization is required to work in partnership with other agencies due to the interdependent nature of the problems that they are called upon to deal with. These cooperative relationships extend from health, housing, social, and youth services to education, probation, penal institutions, voluntary sector organizations, commercial businesses, and community groups. As a result of the breadth of the police mandate and the fact that the police are a '24-hour' service shaped in response to citizen demands, crime fighting and law enforcement (in any straightforward way) are only a relatively small part of police work (Bittner 1970). Many crime and policing issues are by their very nature 'wicked problems' that demand the engagement of multiple actors and agencies. Policy problems are referred to as 'wicked' where they have multiple causes and many of them are interdependent (Rittel and Webber 1973).[2] Solutions are similarly interconnected and, in some cases, contradictory. The challenge when addressing such 'wicked' issues is how to combine effectively the contributions of diverse knowledgeable and competent actors and organizations towards a clear understanding and confidence in how to proceed (Conklin 2006). Yet, the hierarchical nature of the police organization and its culture, with its strong internal sense of occupational identification and suspicion of 'outsiders' (Reiner 2010), serve to render partnership working particularly problematic.

Partnership approaches to policing are largely built on the premise that no single agency can deal with, or be responsible for dealing with, complex community safety and crime problems. Partnerships are a product of fragmentation of resources, knowledge, and capabilities. As such they are a product of social complexity and an intricate division of labour. The fragmented pieces are, in essence, the perspectives, understandings, and intentions of the different partners. Fragmentation exists where the diverse actors involved view, understand, and define a problem through the organizational lens in which they work, in which information is constructed and across which knowledge is scattered. Different agents have differing, and sometimes incompatible, tacit assumptions about the problem, and often each believes that their understandings are complete and shared by all. Whilst the vertical chains within and between departments and agencies in any one field and in professional groups such as the police, teachers, doctors, and nurses are strong, the horizontal links tend to be weak or non-existent. Partnerships, therefore, require a movement away from working in and through hierarchies—the traditional structure of bureaucracies (most evidently command-and-control type organizations like the police)—to working through networks. These networks are characterized by diplomacy, trust, and reciprocity rather than the hierarchical authority and rules of bureaucracies (Fleming and Rhodes 2005). However, as a framework of governance, they are

---

[2] Wicked problems contrast with 'tame problems', which are ones for which the traditional linear process is sufficient to produce a workable solution in an acceptable time frame.

also different in essence from the contracts that structure and regulate relations between the police and private sector in most so-called 'public–private partnerships'. Price and competition structure the organized contractual relations of outsourcing, sponsorship, and sub-contracting, where mutual obligations are spelled out in relations of exchange (Crawford forthcoming).

The potential of this radical shift in governance through partnerships is significant in that it:

- recognizes that the levers and causes of crime lie far from the traditional reach of criminal justice;
- acknowledges that there is no 'single agency solution' to crime—it is multifaceted in both its causes and effects;
- recognizes the need for social responses which reflect crime's multiple aetiology;
- enables a shift to 'up-stream', early intervention—causes not symptoms;
- allows for an holistic approach which is 'problem-focused' rather than 'bureaucracy-premised' (ie existing service provision);
- affords the potential coordination and pooling of expertise, information, and resources, enabling the targeting of scarce resources.

Thus partnership working challenges many assumptions about professional expertise, specialization, state paternalism, and monopoly. In theory, if not in practice, it offers a de-differentiated response that is not segmented but a generalized, non-specialist activity. As such, it challenges introspective organizational cultures and the often cosy working assumptions of specialized agencies. In so doing, it potentially facilitates a re-articulation of powers within and between the state (public sector), community, voluntary, and commercial sectors. Furthermore, it questions taken-for-granted conventions about who should provide which services and their legitimacy and competency for so doing. It also challenges the fundamental premise of services which provide responses to problems—so evident in policing and criminal justice—rather than seeking to anticipate or prevent problems from occurring (upstream) in the first place. Hence, Detective Chief Superintendent John Carnochan of Strathclyde Violence Reduction Unit, reflecting on his partnership work and the importance of early intervention, is quoted as stating that, 'If I had the choice between a thousand extra health visitors and a thousand extra police officers I'd choose a thousand health visitors every time' (cited in Allen 2011: 23). Whilst the observation may be hypothetical, it nevertheless raises vexed questions about the appropriate balance of resource allocation between public sector services in relation to particular social problems and thus prompts some challenging issues about the rationale for the existing distribution of resources—particularly in times of austerity.

The research literature (Crawford 1998; Rosenbaum 2002; Bullock et al 2006; Fleming 2006; Turley et al 2012; O'Neil and McCarthy 2014) highlights significant benefits that derive from partnership working. These include:

- enabling the development of creative and targeted interventions by combining different approaches;
- delivering efficiencies through better coordination of resources and opportunities to reduce duplication;
- providing for multiple interventions that may be more effective than single-agency interventions and maximize the impact on any particular target audience;
- helping to transform insular police occupational culture;
- enabling more effective problem-solving;
- facilitating the development of collaborative skills and collective intelligence;
- increasing staff job satisfaction.

A recent Home Office-commissioned rapid evidence assessment of partnership working sought to address two questions: first, whether partnerships are more effective and efficient in achieving crime-related outcomes than alternatives; and second, the factors that have been identified as making partnerships work effectively and efficiently in delivering crime-related outcomes (Berry et al 2011). Given the framing of its questions, the report drew largely on the evidence from the United States. In relation to the first question, it noted that 'isolating the contribution that particular components of an intervention make to crime reduction can be difficult' (Berry et al 2011: 23). Partnerships, after all, are an approach to working relations rather than a strategic intervention or mechanism of change with a theory of causation; albeit, that processes can significantly determine outcomes (Pawson 2006). Nevertheless, despite a 'mixed' picture, the report concluded that 'on balance, the evidence suggests that the principle of applying partnership working as a component of initiatives to tackle complex crime and disorder problems is effective' (Berry et al 2011: 20). It found the catalyst that brought most partnerships into existence to be either a response to the identification of a particular problem or the provision of funding to address an identified problem. In relation to the second question, the report highlighted a variety of specific mechanisms and strategies associated with effective partnerships (see Table 4.1). Many of these are consistent with earlier findings. However, they need to be understood in the context of the wider and deeper barriers to implementation of partnerships as well as the structural, cultural, and organizational challenges that they imply.

The Barriers

In many senses, community safety partnerships, given their legislative footing, have been at the forefront of much debate, policy innovation, and research. However, such has been the political disappointment with community safety partnerships—despite the steady decline of aggregate crime rates since the mid-1990s—that in late 2004, the government announced a major review of their activities, governance, and accountability, acknowledging that: 'a significant

Table 4.1 Mechanisms Associated with Better Partnership Working

Leadership	• Shared vision, values, and norms of partners involved to establish collaborative advantage • Strong leadership and strategic direction (focused on proving a central coordination effort, getting buy-in from partners and managing the project) • Full integration of project aims into partner organizations' aims • Clear project brief, roles, and responsibilities • Core groups to oversee problem-solving approach
Data sharing and problem focus	• Clarity regarding the problem(s) being tackled through focused analysis to ensure a properly problem focused intervention • Regular exchange of relevant information • Having focused interventions in each area • Including researchers within partnership • Continual evaluation to review and inform activity of group
Communication and co-location	• Regular face-to-face contact and communication between partners • Co-location of agencies, partners, and staff • Presence of partners at local level
Structures	• Flexibility of structures and processes • Having a research partner as an active member of the taskforce • Clear monitoring, accountability, and integrity mechanisms • Having operational groups to implement strategies • Involvement of most appropriate agencies
Experience	• Prior experience in working together in partnership (ie established relationships) • Secondment of skilled officers into joint team • Careful selection of appropriate partners • Joint training of team members

Source: Berry et al (2011: iii)

number of partnerships struggle to maintain a full contribution from key agencies and even successful ones are not sufficiently visible, nor we think accountable, to the public as they should be' (Home Office 2004: 123). The question then is why have the high hopes been so severely curtailed? And what has happened to derail such aspirations? One response might be that the initial claims of a rupture with the past were exaggerated. Another is that the obstacles—structural, organizational, and cultural—that stand in the way of realizing a genuine partnership approach are more substantial, entrenched, and ingrained than otherwise acknowledged. Furthermore, the absence of genuinely critical debate about the processes involved in delivering multi-agency partnerships may serve to impede practice. The development of good practice conversely requires the recognition and exploration of the many unspoken problems that both practitioners face and that are implied by practice.

The main barriers to successful partnerships include a reluctance of some agencies to participate (especially health, education, and social services); the dominance of a policing agenda; unwillingness to share information; conflicting interests, priorities, and cultural assumptions on the part of different agencies; local political differences; lack of inter-organizational trust; desire to protect budgets; lack of capacity and expertise; and over-reliance on informal contacts and networks which lapsed if key individuals moved on. The involvement of the private sector has often been patchy and the role of the voluntary sector frequently marginalized. In practice, partnerships experience considerable problems in reaching agreements or protocols about what data they could legitimately share and on what basis. As a result, concerns over confidentiality often hinder partnership working and problematize inter-organizational trust relations.

Information sharing

Data sharing remains one of the most intractable and contentious aspects of policing and community safety practice: technological and cultural barriers to data exchange often undermine effective partnership work. Recent research into ASB partnerships found that:

> Misunderstandings of data protection legislation are widespread and reluctance on the part of some partner agencies to share information remains a significant obstacle to effective work. Practitioners were uncertain about the circumstances and purposes for which data can and should be exchanged. Some formed arbitrary distinctions between what they were willing to exchange in face-to-face interactions and what they were prepared to share electronically (Crawford et al 2012: iii).

In many, but not all, areas of policing, there exists a pervasive and deeply ingrained reluctance to share information between agencies. This is sometimes based on an over-interpretation (and occasionally a misinterpretation) of the current data protection legislation. There also remains substantial ignorance about and misunderstanding of the implications of data protection legislation for data sharing. In risk-averse organizational cultures, data protection is commonly cited as a reason not to release data, often in circumstances in which it may be perfectly legitimate to do so (Thomas and Walport 2008: 37).

Yet for partnerships, good quality data collection, management, and use matters because they:

- allow for joined-up provision and continuity of service over time and between different service providers;
- afford opportunities for joint analysis and coordinated working between relevant agencies;
- provide the capacity to track individuals and families through service provision and diverse interventions, and assess their trajectories and pathways;

- enable interventions provided by different service providers to be used in a more strategic manner in which consideration is given to the relations between them and how they interact;
- provide an evidence base from which to assess effectiveness and to evaluate what works, for whom, and in which contexts;
- ensure the best use of resources and facilitate best practice;
- afford opportunities to monitor performance and render services accountable and reviewable.

Managerial obstacles

In many ways, the dominant managerial reforms of the past 20 years or so have worked counter to the demands of partnerships by focusing attention on hierarchical control and on the clear distribution of authority and responsibility in the name of efficiency, economy, and value for money. Perversely, managerialist reforms (notably since the 1983 Home Office Circular 114) have served to increase the introspection of many criminal justice, policing, and other public sector organizations. They encouraged an *intra*-organizational focus that pays scant attention to the task of managing *inter*-organizational relations. Less regard is afforded to the more complex process of negotiating shared purposes, particularly where there is no hierarchy of control. Managerialism may suit hierarchical line management structures but is largely inappropriate for managing horizontal inter-organizational networks. As such, there have been fundamental tensions between a partnership approach and aspects of the *intra*-organizational focus of much recent managerialist reform. Furthermore, the intra-organizational focus on outputs and performance measurement has often encouraged partner organizations to concentrate their energies upon their core tasks and activities at the expense of peripheral ones. This has frequently served to frustrate those working on cross-cutting, horizontal accountabilities, and responsibilities in multi-organizational networks.

Structural dynamics

As implied earlier, policing partnerships by their very nature embody a number of key structural dynamics. The first is the existence of often fundamental *conflicts* over ideology, purpose, and interests. Criminal justice agencies have very different priorities and interests, as do other public sector organizations, voluntary bodies, the commercial sector, and local community groups. The second dynamic is the existence of *differential power relations* between the partners. Third, partnerships intrinsically *blur the boundaries* between the roles and functions, as well as accountabilities of the partner organizations. This can present difficulties for accountability and for the appropriate distribution of responsibilities. Together, these dynamics can prompt or generate a number of unhelpful strategies within partnership work (Crawford 1997; Crawford et al 2012).

The first is *conflict avoidance*, whereby the parties seek to avoid conflict to such a degree that real issues are not confronted or addressed. This may be an understandable strategy in certain contexts (particularly in the earliest stages of an initiative's life) but leaves power differences unaddressed. Furthermore, real conflicts are often dispersed into other arenas, rather than being negotiated or resolved.

Second is a *strategy of multiple aims*, whereby increasingly disparate aims or objectives are accorded to a particular partnership project. This is what I earlier described as the 'Smögasbord approach' (Crawford 1998), in which something for everyone is placed upon the menu. In the process, projects can find themselves signing up to such broad and sometimes confused sets of aims, as to be almost meaningless. The danger is that in the attempt to appease all interests, fundamental aims are not prioritized. This may lead to 'lowest common denominator' solutions and a lack of clarity and coherency. This also presents significant problems for subsequent evaluations as it is unclear which criteria should be prioritized in assessing success.

The third strategy is where decisions are taken outside the frame of formal partnership arrangements 'behind the scenes' and in private settings, often in part to avoid conflict. Often, important decisions are taken elsewhere. Such 'shadow' relations are hard to monitor and present problems for accountability. This can be, and often is, justified in terms of 'getting things done'. However, it runs counter to the spirit of transparency and often reinforces the power of the more dominant partners and, at the same time, undermines the role of weaker partners.

Trust and difference

By contrast, there is a need to maintain the clarity of the divergent inputs and their collaborative objectives—with significant implications for leadership. Hence, one of the key aspects of successful partnerships involves establishing and sustaining trust relations across agency boundaries. This is not easy, particularly where there is a history of mistrust or misunderstanding. Trust is a central coordinating mechanism of networks and is essential for cooperative behaviour (Tyler 2010). A crucial element in establishing trust relations is making partners aware of the limitations of their own and other organizations' contribution, so that they neither try to 'do it all' (something that the police are particularly prone to do), nor do they have unrealistic expectations of what others can deliver. There is a need for mutual respect for different types of contributions. In this regard, there is an important role for training in multi-agency relations and working dynamics which needs to be recognized, particularly in relation to designated staff performing link functions within partnership networks. Tensions between organizations with very different ideologies and working practices are often mediated by long-term (primarily inter-personal) working relationships (Crawford et al 2012). Tensions are frequently most strained during periods of personnel change, when bridges between different working cultures and practices have to be rebuilt and new interpersonal and inter-institutional trust relations forged.

One of the negative inferences of employing 'systems logic' to an understanding of responses to crime and criminal justice is to accord to the partners a unity of purpose where this may not exist. This does not mean that the basis of a consensus cannot be constructed, but rather that to do so necessitates the acceptance of difference and the active negotiation of commonalities, as opposed to an assumed 'ideology of unity' (Crawford 1997: 137). The danger of such an ideology is that it assumes a homogeneity of interests without ever really questioning the interests served, the tensions over purpose and working ethos, and where conflicts, as well as common purpose, may exist. 'Independence' and 'partnership' stand in a highly ambiguous relation to each other. For, as Paul Rock noted, it is the 'independent interdependence' between organizations which constitutes 'the weak force which binds the criminal justice system together' (1990: 39). Criminal justice, after all, is concerned with balancing sometimes competing individual and group rights and interests and embodies finely balanced tensions between the independence and interdependence of criminal justice agencies. The goal of unity can serve to efface rather than manage and negotiate conflict and exclude or side-line difficult issues or 'awkward partners'. In this light, conflict and difference are perceived to be the enemies of effective partnerships, despite the fact that they structure the material and ideological relations which exist between organizations involved in much policing partnership work.

Shared understanding

By contrast, the basis for effective partnerships lies in creating shared understanding about the problem and shared commitment to the possible solutions. However, shared understanding does not mean that all the partners necessarily agree on the problem or hold the same view of it. Shared understanding demands that the partners understand each other's positions well enough to have meaningful dialogue about the different interpretations of the problem, and to exercise collective intelligence about how best to seek to resolve it. Fleming and Rhodes (2005: 195) note: 'Shared values and norms and an appreciation of divergent organisational cultures are the glue which holds the complex set of relationships together.'

Finally, partnerships exhibit significant problems with regard to accountability; given the very nature of partnerships, their multiple layers of authority and complex interdependency. Joint and negotiated decisions tie the various parties into corporate policy and outcomes but often fail to identify lines of responsibility. Institutional complexity further obscures who is accountable to whom and for what. This gives rise to what Rhodes (1996: 663) identified as, ' "the problem of many hands", where so many people contribute that no one contribution can be identified; and if no one person can be held accountable after the event, then no one needs to behave responsibly beforehand'. As authority is 'shared', it becomes difficult to disentangle, and can become almost intangible. Clarifying lines of responsibility in this context is crucial; so too, are mechanisms of shared accountability, monitoring, and oversight. Developing methods to encourage shared ownership throughout the partnership and building evaluation into the project can also assist in this regard. In summary, all the foregoing point to the importance of effective leadership and strategic direction in creating the inter- and intra-organizational infrastructures that support partnerships and the organizational culture conducive to their implementation.

Conclusion

As noted earlier, many partnerships have been brought into being facilitated by the incentives of accessing resources and new funding streams. Hence, the current period of austerity in public sector funding, which has resulted in unprecedented reductions in police budgets and police officer numbers, presents critical challenges for the future. On the one hand, austerity has added a powerful dynamic to the receptiveness of governments and police managers to the involvement of the private sector in searching for solutions to budget cuts and how to do 'more with less' (HMIC 2012). Fiscal restraint, combined with an ideological commitment by the current government to greater private-sector involvement in the delivery of public services—including policing—as *the* 'rational response' to conditions of austerity (Letwin, cited in Mason 2012), is certainly likely to prompt and energize novel experiments in public–private partnerships. However, across Europe there appears less of an appetite for analogous responses to similar fiscal and crime-related policing problems. Some jurisdictions (notably Scotland and the Netherlands) have responded by way of very different reform strategies of internal organizational restructuring and centralization (Fyfe et al. 2013).

Nevertheless, in England and Wales as the HMIC 'Policing in Austerity' reports (HMIC 2012) suggest, thus far, the main form of post-austerity police partnerships has been 'collaborations' between police forces. And yet, the HMIC recently concluded that: 'The extent to which forces are collaborating in order to save money and transform efficiency is deeply disappointing' (2013: 18). This acknowledgement of the barriers to collaboration appears to have prompted the Home Office to provide incentives to collaborate via the Police Innovation Fund.[3] Regardless, these collaborations do not seem to be delivering the savings expected of them. Hence, the prospects of the greater recourse to outsourcing and sub-contracting in the provision of policing remain firmly on the agenda and have far-reaching implications. They raise fundamental questions about the role, function, and legitimacy of police authority within society, as well as the cultural

---

[3] The outcome of the £50m Police Innovation Fund for 2014/15 is available via a Home Office Press Release, at <https://www.gov.uk/government/news/home-office-rewards-police-innovation-with-50-million> (accessed 4 November 2014).

place of the police institution as a 'sacred symbol' of national identity (Reiner 1995). Thus far, there has been little systematic academic, practitioner, or policy debate that has reflected on the benefits, disadvantages, and limits of private-sector involvement in policing. The Independent Police Commission warned: 'the service, constrained by the lack of finances available to it, risks outsourcing key aspects of policing to the private sector in an ad-hoc and unprincipled manner' (Stevens 2013: 13). Likewise, the National Audit Office (2013) identified a distinct lack of transparency and scrutiny with regard to major contractors in delivering public services, as well as a growing crisis of confidence in contracting out processes.

On the other hand, how the public and voluntary sectors respond to austerity is also uncertain. A number of possible scenarios might be envisaged unfolding in the face of sustained fiscal pressures. First, organizations (including the police) might retreat into their 'silos'; retracting from inter-organizational collaborations, redrawing their boundaries to focus on core objectives, and seeking to off-load responsibilities to others, wherever possible. Short-term cost savings may arise at the expense of partnership commitments, particularly where key individuals or posts are lost to early retirements or workforce reorganizations. A second scenario might prompt more fundamental questions about purpose, expertise, responsiveness, and effective service delivery. This might look for collaborative advantages through partnerships as a means of finding longer-term cost efficiencies. Such prompting might also see investments in 'upstream' preventive solutions to crime problems and away from reactive fire-fighting. However, as decades of policing research has demonstrated, such far-reaching thinking would necessitate significantly bold shifts in police organizational culture and working practices. The extent to which either, or a combination of both, of these scenarios prevails; only time will tell. However, the manner in which police leaders respond to austerity will undoubtedly shape the next phase in the development and institutionalization of policing partnerships.

Ultimately, partnership working is a means to an end, not an end in itself. However, means are outcome determinative. As well as enhancing a specific crime-related strategy, through pooled knowledge, collective intelligence, collaborative skills, and multi-level interventions, partnerships also afford benefits for organizations—notably the police—in terms of cultural change and openness to external engagement and critical reflection. In many ways, specific local partnerships must work with the grain of local cultures, tailor the constellation of partners, and reflect the nature of the problems to be addressed, but they can also serve to transform these in constructive ways. Partnerships based on trust, mutual understanding, and regard for difference can facilitate approaches that are 'problem-oriented' rather than defined according to the means or organizations most readily available to solve them. Whilst a philosophy of partnership is strongly embedded within the policy frame there is still much to do and to learn in fashioning and nurturing partnerships that meet their lofty ambitions through a combination of strategic leadership and the appropriately skilled people to deliver partnerships on the ground. As I have sought to highlight, the challenges associated with working across organizational boundaries, cultures, and established practices are significant but not insurmountable, while the benefits are many and varied.

Practitioner's Perspective

It is difficult to bring to mind any sustainable and effective community safety intervention that is delivered by a single agency. Adam Crawford correctly identifies that the reason for this is that community safety problems are multi-faceted ('wicked problems'), requiring multifaceted solutions. Partnership working was once the province of small, specialist police departments who were regarded by some as peripheral to operational policing and who I once heard referred to as 'the trumpets and pamphlets department'. There was also a distinct impression that the role of partners was to help the police to do our job, the 'cultural dominance' described by Adam Crawford.

There is a recognizable shift in emphasis that is increasingly apparent across the public sector: a shift from reacting to preventing and early intervention. It is apparent in the Health Service where the cost of prevention appears to be dwarfed by the cost of acute care. It is apparent in centrally driven initiatives such as 'Troubled Families'. It is apparent across those agencies charged with protecting communities from fire prevention to crime prevention. This change in emphasis is brought into sharper relief by the current climate of austerity; prevention is cheaper than cure.

It is now widely recognized by police officers and staff at all levels that effective preventive interventions which stand a chance of having a lasting impact are reliant upon two or more (usually more) agencies working together to achieve joint outcomes. It is also widely recognized that partnership working can be extraordinarily difficult to achieve. Police leaders, in particular chief officers and those who lead departments and local policing areas, are thinking more carefully about how best to enable partnership working. When I reflect on the successes and travails of leading partnership working, a number of hallmarks emerge, the characteristics of effective joint working. In this section, I set out, based on my experience, what I consider to be the characteristics of effective partnerships and how the leadership challenges of working across organizational boundaries can be best confronted.

Focus on the problem

The first hallmark of effective partnerships is a clear focus on the problem. The late 1990s into early 2000s saw the emergence of some police forces explicitly adopting a 'problem-solving philosophy', 'problem-oriented policing' (see Goldstein 1990). The Tilley Award in the United Kingdom saw forces competing to demonstrate the initiative which best demonstrated a problem solved and United Kingdom forces were well represented at the international Goldstein Awards for problem-solving. The police appetite for activity can lead partners to accurately describe the Service as 'getting things done' or, equally accurately, describe the Police as 'bulls in china shops'. To solve a problem requires understanding the problem and analysing before responding. Problem-solving exposed the requirement for new analytical skills, and in some exemplars, joint analysis of the problem between agencies. Take the issue of alcohol misuse, which presents community safety problems, health problems, and education problems, for example. Joint analysis of the problem is the only way to identify the most appropriate action it also helps to decide who should be around the table. Under the Crime and Disorder Act 1998 that established 'Community Safety Partnerships', some sterling work was done. However, the limitation of that approach was that it meant in some places the emphasis was on which partners should be at the table before the specific problems were identified. The nature of the problem should determine the contributors and each of the contributors should be clear about what they can offer to the joint solution.

Focusing on the problem assists in the identification of shared desired outcomes. In the early 2000s, I had leadership responsibility for the police in Blackpool when we developed the 'Tower Project'. This project was an offender management programme primarily delivered by the police, the probation service, and the health service. Chaotic drug users presented many problems which were the responsibility of a number of different public agencies. The problem for the police and the probation services was that there were a number of chaotic and prolific offenders who were motivated to commit crime to feed their drug habits. For the health service the problem was to reduce the waiting times for drug-dependent people to receive treatment and to reduce the number of drug-related deaths. The challenge for the leaders of each of these agencies was how to coalesce resources to have the best opportunity for problem-solving. The reason that Tower gained the traction that it did was the synergy of outcomes resulting from addressing the problems of drug-dependent individuals. When the partners focused on the problem, it simply made sense to work together; drug-related criminality reduced, treatment waiting times shortened. To use Adam Crawford's terms, the approach was 'problem-focused' rather than 'bureaucracy-premised'.

Trust

Developing trust across organizational and cultural boundaries is hugely difficult. Some of the barriers to partnership working identified in the previous section—such as the dominance of the policing agenda, conflicting interests and priorities, and the protection of budgets—can result in a lack of trust. My reflection on the most effective partnership working is that trust has developed between key individuals, often in spite of the identified barriers. Leaders can ensure that the following four steps are taken to enhance mutual trust:

- *Early engagement of all parties in the design and build of the interventions.* It is essential that all contributors feel some ownership and stake in the planned activity.

- *Co-location.* It is said that co-location is not essential for effective partnership working, and that is surely true. However, when I think of the most effective partnerships I have seen they have all involved staff being co-located and jointly managed. There is often an initial reluctance to this arrangement on the part of the affected staff which time and again I have seen replaced by a new partnership dynamic which makes the whole greater than the sum of the parts.

- *Sharing success.* The words most often quoted in this regard are ascribed to Harry S Truman: 'It's amazing what you can achieve if you do not care who gets the credit.' Governance arrangements, discussed more in the next section, need to be developed in such a way that successes are jointly claimed. This can also lead to mutual advocacy, partners recognizing and praising the contributions of each other.

- *Retaining professional identity.* The power of partnerships has to lie in the unique professional contribution of each of the agencies, described by Adam Crawford as 'independent interdependence'. I have observed occasions when the police officers who have been working in partnership have lost or diluted their professional identity. The police should be there to make a policing contribution, health to make a health contribution, for example.

One of the barriers identified in the previous section is 'the over reliance on informal contacts and networks which lapse if key individuals move on'. This is a double-edged sword. Brilliant and committed individuals from different agencies working on solutions to common problems can often establish relationships of trust which greatly accelerate the effectiveness of the partnership.

Leadership

Demonstrable and clearly stated commitment from leaders is essential. Specifically, I refer here to chief officers and to those who lead local policing areas or departments. These are the people who set the tone and bring great influence to bear on the environment in which people are working. Ultimately, it is these people who will enable or prevent effective partnership working. In order to best protect vulnerable people, many areas have recently developed a Multi Agency Safeguarding Hub (MASH). Within the MASH safeguarding experts from the police, local authorities, and health trusts are co-located and jointly managed. The intention is to facilitate the better sharing of information and risk assessing across agencies to ensure the best possible protection of vulnerable people. My experience of the MASH in Staffordshire is that it required the most senior leaders in the respective organizations to sign up to the concept. That sign up involved a commitment to the delivery of joint outcomes (focusing on the problem) and shared clarity as to what success would look like. The leaders had to be sufficiently senior to commit resources both in terms of people and money. Other tiers of strong leadership were required to ensure the delivery of the concept and the alignment of the different organizational business processes. Yet other tiers of leadership were required to ensure that teams worked together and that cultural differences were overcome. Leadership is required well beyond start-up into the ongoing daily business, long after the gleam of the new initiative has worn off. Senior leaders also have to identify the managerial permafrost which blocks and stymies progress. It is relatively straightforward to deal with those who openly object to any particular initiative. It is less straightforward to identify and deal with those who seek to block with indifference.

The establishment of shared governance ensures a commitment that goes beyond informal contacts. If properly established, the governance should also ensure that the desirable individual organizational objectives are achieved whilst remaining focused on joint outcomes. In the MASH scenario, the desired joint outcome is that vulnerable people are safer, the organizational objective for the police is that there are fewer crimes (fewer victims) as a result of better information sharing and earlier interventions. This is what Adam Crawford refers to as the radical shift in governance enabling a 'problem-focused' response. The governance should be established in such a way as to allow all of the contributing partners to hold each other to account. This relies on clearly expressed success indicators and openly available management information. Most importantly, it relies on strong leadership because holding others to account and being held to account is not for the faint hearted.

Leaders set the tone for the organizations they lead. If the tone is not conducive to partnership working then joint work will falter. Tone is set by explicit and implicit actions on the part of the leader and is often exhibited by those who thrive. Traditionally, police commendation ceremonies were a celebration of those who are the bravest or those who are best at detecting large numbers of crimes or bringing villains to justice for the most serious offences. It sends a clear message to an organization as to what is valued. It is true that bravery and skilful detections are causes for celebration, but so too are the ingenious preventive partnerships which have often been delivered in the face of serious obstacles.

If partnership working is central to core policing, then it follows that those who aspire to leadership positions at all levels in the Service are able to demonstrate that they have the skills and attributes to foster such working. This is likely to require skills which have to date not been high priorities in training curricula: negotiation skills; analytical skills; and problem-solving skills. It is reassuring to see that increasingly a multi-agency approach is being taken to leadership development. Development opportunities for leaders across public sector agencies which allow them to come together and to consider how they can work better together for the public good has to be a positive step in ensuring more effective and efficient public services.

Leading partnerships also requires an appetite for risk. The best partnerships I have seen usually involve trying something for the first time, not something that comes naturally to the risk averse. For example, it can often involve giving up direct management control of your resources or committing resources to something which is likely to accrue results in a timescale which is longer than immediately. A traditional police culture has been risk averse, but there are signs (and in some places clear evidence) that this culture is changing.

Information sharing

Adam Crawford correctly identifies the 'unwillingness to share information' as a barrier to partnerships. When things go wrong in the protection of vulnerable people, public sector agencies have been correctly castigated for their inability or reluctance to share information. Professionals can hide behind a restrictive interpretation of legislation to 'protect' information. If the hallmarks identified earlier are evident in any partnership initiative, then information sharing can be easier. Many parts of the country have Integrated Offender Management (IOM) programmes. Partners in Staffordshire, quite properly, take great pride in their joint IOM work. There is a clear focus on the problem, how to assist offenders to reform, and a clear joint outcome of safer communities. There is tangible trust between the public sector and voluntary agencies who work together in one team. There is strong leadership at all levels, creating a sense of purpose. IOM is also reliant on lawfully audacious information sharing across agencies to gain an accurate picture of offending behaviour, a careful analysis of the motivating factors for the offending, and an assessment of the most appropriate interventions. Across the spectrum of partnership working, this is still work in progress. Different agencies use incompatible systems which are still overly reliant on manual transactions and there are still too many examples of organizational preciousness.

The list of hallmarks of effective partnership identified previously is not intended to be exhaustive; rather, the product of my reflections on effective partnerships I have been involved in and the observations of Adam Crawford earlier in this chapter. What has changed relatively recently is the context within which partnerships are operating: austerity.

The potential shift in governance, according to Adam Crawford, 'affords the potential coordination and pooling of expertise, information, and resources, enabling the targeting of scarce resources'. I believe this to be the case, but like much else in this area it easier said than done. If there are efficiencies and economies to be had from joint working, then collaborative and integrated approaches ought to be more easily achieved. Whilst I am witnessing some evidence of a new urgency to some partnership discussions, I am also seeing evidence of organizations becoming more protective of their diminishing resources. The positive impact has been a discernable shift in discussions with much more cross-agency emphasis on prevention, 'upstream' is the word of the moment. This makes sense, as money spent in prevention appears to provide a greater return than money spent on consequences. It is also the right thing to do.

In the world of community safety there is a recent potential catalyst for encouraging participation from partners in a time of austerity. Police and crime commissioners (PCCs) have a democratic mandate to bring partners to the table; they also have control over a number of budgets, ie they have (potential) influence and they have money. It is too early to say whether this opportunity is being fully, or even partially, exploited, but nevertheless I believe it exists.

Community safety practitioners deal with wicked problems. Problems which are multifaceted cannot be resolved by one-dimensional responses. Solutions at times have to be complex and multi-layered and, if they are to be sustainable, will have to be delivered by more than one agency or organization. Partnership working is not an optional extra; it sits at the very heart of community safety. The earlier part of this chapter has carefully analysed the challenges to such working and the potential opportunities it can provide. As leaders and practitioners in policing we have a responsibility to understand these challenges and to craft solutions; there is no alternative.

Shared Reflections

It is becoming increasingly apparent that austerity measures are requiring police leaders to think very differently about how policing services are delivered and by whom. It appears that more than ever innovative thinking is a desirable—and possibly a necessary—trait in the leadership of the police service. Partnership service delivery with an emphasis on early intervention and prevention is at the heart of these new approaches. Shifting resource and effort from responding to incidents after the event to prevention is seen not just as delivering better community safety but also providing better value for money; it is more affordable. Hence, rising to the challenge of budget cuts has prompted police leaders to ask fundamental questions about purpose, expertise, responsiveness, and effective service delivery and, in doing so, to look for collaborative advantages as a means of finding efficiencies. It has also placed the question of investment in 'upstream' preventive solutions to crime problems firmly on the agenda. Partnership working and inter-organizational collaborations are undoubtedly pivotal in delivering the necessary organizational change that will underpin any sustained shift in resources, priorities, and commitment to prevention and early intervention to address the causes of crime and anti-social behaviour.

There is much discussion in policing about structural reform, including mergers of police forces (where there are passionate voices on both sides of the debate) and inter-force collaboration. Undoubtedly, there is more to be said about both issues, and there will certainly be continuing structural reform going forward. However, police leaders are likely to devote as least as much, and very often more, time and energy to consideration of the redesign of collaborative public service delivery within their force borders. This is currently manifested in pioneering initiatives, such as those dealing with 'troubled families', safeguarding the vulnerable, and managing prolific offenders. There are signs in some areas that this thinking is moving beyond specific initiatives to a reflection on a much broader approach to mainstream collaborative delivery of services. This is most developed in areas where leaders across relevant agencies are sharing priorities, sharing resources, and looking for joint outcomes in the public interest.

One domain that remains ripe for the greater development of collaboration and partnership working is in relations between the police and higher education institutions. This book is itself testimony to the undoubted benefits that derive from greater mutual understanding and knowledge exchange between research and practice in the field of policing. Moreover, the shift to prevention will need to be premised upon a firm evidence base to justify the allied reallocation of resources and targeting of interventions. Here, research has a key role to play. The development of new approaches with less money has also given a new emphasis to the requirement for evaluation. It is increasingly important to know what works, where, and for whom. The advent of the College of Policing has brought a renewed focus on the requirement to build a solid evidence base and rigorous evaluation of practices. Yet, as Peter Neyroud recognized in his 'Review of Police Leadership and Training' for the Home Office, achieving the translation of research into policing practices requires a 'transformation of the culture of learning in the police service' (2011: 2). He went on to note: 'the relationship between police education and practice and higher education has not reached the level of embedded partnership that it has done in medicine or education' (2011: 81). It follows that there is a new imperative for greater collaboration between policing and universities. Academic scrutiny must be sought and welcomed in building a more open and reflective police culture. Whilst policing has traditionally been about getting on and doing things, the 'can-do' culture of policing is regularly highlighted by partners, usually as a strength; the need for what is being done to be evaluated has never been more pressing.

A new partnership between police and higher education institutions to facilitate research impact, support police innovation, enhance training and learning opportunities, and promote an evidence-based profession is both timely and prescient. In their joint foreword to the College of Policing's 'Strategic Intent' document, Dame Shirley Pearce and Chief Constable Alex Marshall state:

> ... the police should be able to easily access the most recent and credible evidence about what works best and equip themselves with the skills to use that evidence ... They should have access to ongoing professional development and education to support the skills, attitudes and behaviours needed in modern policing (College of Policing 2013: 5).

No doubt there is still a long journey to be made before this ambition can be realized. Nevertheless, there are signs that new regional collaborations are emerging that will complement the work of the College of Policing and foster greater police–academic partnerships to build capacity and foster knowledge generation, translation, and application. It is hoped that this collection of essays can help along the way.

Finally, talk of partnerships in policing is frequently in danger of sounding like 'apple pie'—an inevitably good thing that radiates a warm, 'fuzzy' glow—yet remains vague, all-encompassing, and imprecise. In thinking about the benefits and evaluating the impact of different types of policing partnerships, we need to be more unambiguous about the extent to which particular models of inter-organizational relationships fulfill specific purposes. What form, norms, and ethos best suit which strategic purpose? Does a given partnership arrangement constitute a legal contractual form, a formal agreement, or an informal collaboration? Whilst both partnerships and contractual relations are concerned with the distribution of responsibilities and obligations, as modes of organizing and constructing social relations they are fundamentally different in values and processes. The legal formality of a partnership will have implications for conflict processing and the nature of mutual obligations as well as the extent to which these are premised on relations of exchange, trust, or collaborative advantages by 'drawing synergy from the differences between organisations, different resources and different expertises' (Huxham and Vangen 2005: 82). Here, both context and people matter; they constitute the stuff of partnership working. Furthermore, it cannot be assumed that the same models of partnerships work at the different scales of analysis or levels within the police (and partner) organizations. What works well among senior commanders will not necessarily be as applicable among frontline officers and workers. Hence, we need to know more about what works, where, for which purposes, and for whom. In the preceding pages, we hope to have contributed, in small part, to this discussion and debate.

Recommended Reading

College of Policing (2013), 'Strategic Intent', College of Policing, Coventry

Huxham, C and Vangen, S (2005), *Managing to Collaborate: The Theory and Practice of Collaborative Advantage* (London: Routledge)

Neyroud, P (2011), 'Review of Police Leadership and Training', Home Office, London

References

Allen, G (2011), 'Early Intervention: The Next Steps', Cabinet Office, London

Berry, G, Briggs, P, Erol, R, and van Staden, L (2011), 'The Effectiveness of Partnership Working in a Crime and Disorder Context: A Rapid Evidence Assessment', Research Report 52, Home Office, London

Bittner, E (1970), *The Functions of Police in Modern Society* (Washington, DC: NIMH)

Blumstein, A (1986), 'Coherence, Coordination and Integration in the Administration of Criminal Justice' in van Dijk, J, Haffmans, C, Ruter, F, and Schutte, J (eds), *Criminal Law in Action: An Overview of Current Issues in Western Societies* (Arnhem: Gouda Quint) 247

Bullock, K, Erol, R, and Tilley, N (2006), *Problem-oriented Policing and Partnerships* (Cullompton: Willan)

Butler-Sloss, E (1988), 'Report of the Inquiry into Child Abuse in Cleveland 1987', HMSO, London

Cohn, AW (1978), 'Criminal Justice Non System' in Inciardi, JA and Haas, KC (eds), *Crime and the Criminal Justice Process* (Dubuque, IA: Kendall/Hunt)

College of Policing (2013), 'Strategic Intent', College of Policing, Coventry

Conklin, J (2006), *Dialogue Mapping: Building Shared Understanding of Wicked Problems* (Chichester: Wiley)

Crawford, A (1994), 'The Partnership Approach: Corporatism at the Local Level?' 3(4) *Social and Legal Studies* 497

Crawford, A (1997), *The Local Governance of Crime: Appeals to Community and Partnerships* (Oxford: OUP)

Crawford, A (1998), 'Delivering Multi-agency Partnerships in Community Safety' in Marlow, A and Pitts, J (eds), *Planning Safer Communities* (Lyme Regis: Russell House) 213

Crawford, A (2009), *Situating Anti-social Behaviour and Respect* (Leeds: CCJS Press), at <http://eprints.whiterose.ac.uk/43591/> (accessed 26 April 2015)

Crawford, A (forthcoming), 'The Appetite for and Limits to Markets in Policing' in Hucklesby, A and Lister, S (eds), *Private Sector Involvement in Criminal Justice* (Abingdon: Routledge)

Crawford, A and Jones, M (1995), 'Inter-agency Co-operation and Community-based Crime Prevention' 35(1) *British Journal of Criminology* 17

Crawford, A, Lewis, S, and Taynor, P (2012), *Anti-social Behaviour Interventions with Young People: Research Findings* (Leeds: CCJS Press), at <http://www.law.leeds.ac.uk/assets/files/research/ccjs/research-findings.pdf> (accessed 24 April 2015)

Fleming, J (2006), 'Working Through Networks: The Challenge of Partnership Policing' in Fleming, J and Wood, J (eds), *Fighting Crime Together: The Challenges of Policing and Security Network Policy* (Sydney: University of New South Wales Press) 87

Fleming, J and Rhodes, RAW (2005), 'Bureaucracy, Contracts and Networks: The Unholy Trinity and the Police' 38(2) *Australian and New Zealand Journal of Criminology* 192

Fyfe, N, Terpstra, J, and Tops, P (eds) (2013), *Centralizing Forces? Police Reform in Northern and Western Europe in Comparative Perspective* (The Hague: Boom)

Garland, D (1985), *Punishment and Welfare* (Aldershot: Gower)

Garland, D (2001), *The Culture of Control* (Oxford: OUP)

Goldstein, H (1990), *Excellence in Problem-oriented Policing* (New York: McGraw-Hill)

HMIC (2012), 'Policing in Austerity: One Year On', Home Office, London

HMIC (2013), 'Policing in Austerity: Rising to the Challenge', Home Office, London

HM Government (2011), *Prevent Strategy* (Cm 8092)

Home Office (1983), 'Manpower Effectiveness and Efficiency in the Police Service', Circular 114/83, Home Office, London

Home Office (2004), *Building Communities, Beating Crime* (Cm 6360)

Huxham, C and Vangen, S (2005), *Managing to Collaborate: The Theory and Practice of Collaborative Advantage* (London: Routledge)

Mason, R (2012), 'Private Companies in Hospitals, Police and Schools are Here to Stay, says Oliver Letwin', *The Telegraph*, 1 March

Morgan, J (1991), 'Safer Communities: The Local Delivery of Crime Prevention Through the Partnership Approach', Home Office, London

Morgan, P (1985), 'Modelling the Criminal Justice System', Home Office Planning Unit Paper No 35, Home Office, London

Moxon, D (1985) (ed), 'Managing Criminal Justice: A Collection of Papers', HMSO, London

Mudd, J (1984), *Neighbourhood Services* (New Haven, CT: Yale University Press)

National Audit Office (2013), 'The Role of Major Contractors in the Delivery of Public Services', TSO, London

Neyroud, P (2011), 'Review of Police Leadership and Training', Home Office, London

O'Neil, M and McCarthy, D (2014), '(Re)Negotiating Police Culture through Partnership Working' 14(2) *Criminology and Criminal Justice* 143

Osborne, D and Gaebler, T (1992), *Reinventing Government: How the Entrepreneurial Spirit is Transforming the Public Sector* (Reading, MA: Addison-Wesley)

Pawson, R (2006), *Evidence-based Policy: A Realist Perspective* (London: Sage)

Reiner, R (1995), 'From Sacred to Profane: The Thirty Years' War of the British Police' 5(2) *Policing and Society* 121

Reiner, R (2010), *The Politics of the Police* (4th edn, Oxford: OUP)

Report of the President's Crime Commission (1967), 'The Challenge of Crime in a Free Society', A Report by the President's Commission on Law Enforcement and Administration of Justice, Washington, DC

Rhodes, RAW (1996), 'The New Governance: Governing without Government' 44 *Political Studies* 652

Rittel, H and Webber, M (1973), 'Dilemmas in a General Theory of Planning' 4 *Policy Sciences* 155

Rock, P (1990), *Helping Victims of Crime: The Home Office and the Rise of Victim Support in England and Wales* (Oxford: OUP)

Rosenbaum, DP (2002), 'Evaluating Multi-Agency Anti-Crime Partnerships: Theory, Design, and Measurement Issues' in *Crime Prevention Studies: Vol 14* (Cullompton: Willan)

Stevens, J (2013), 'Policing for a Better Britain', Report of the Independent Police Commission, London

Thomas, R and Walport, M (2008), 'Data Sharing Review Report', Independent Review, Ministry of Justice, London, at <http://www.connectingforhealth.nhs.uk/systemsandservices/infogov/links/datasharingreview.pdf> (accessed 24 April 2015)

Turley, C, Ranns, H, Callanan, M, Blackwell, A, and Newburn, T (2012), 'Delivering Neighbourhood Policing in Partnership', Research Report 61, Home Office, London

Tyler, T (2010), *Why People Cooperate: The Role of Social Motivations* (Princeton, NJ: Princeton University Press)

Wilson, JQ and Kelling, G (1989), 'Making Neighbourhoods Safe', *The Atlantic Monthly*, February, 46

5

Leadership, Management, and Command in the Police

Keith Grint and Sara Thornton

Introduction

The Police, like many uniformed organizations, are often associated with images of mechanical hierarchies where strict discipline and the unquestioned execution of superordinate orders are the prevalent cultural norms. In an organization where no conventional trade union exists, and the 'right' to strike is illegal, it might seem apparent that 'leadership' in the police is primarily composed of issuing and obeying orders, but this is only one aspect of a much more complicated system of decision-making. In reality the police also operate with extraordinary levels of personal discretion and responsibility: each officer has the right to use legitimate force in the pursuit of his or her duty to uphold the law and there are many occasions when officers cannot refer to their line manager for advice or permission to act. Their duties range over a wide variety of tasks, from maintaining the peace to protecting vulnerable people and arresting people suspected of committing crimes. By definition, then, it would seem obvious that a singular authoritarian decision mode is unlikely to cover all the eventualities that are likely to occur. So how might we capture this complexity in a model of 'leadership' that is markedly different from models that differentiate between transactional and transformational 'leadership'—both of which assume that the 'leader' has the answer to the problem?

I want to suggest that we might usefully begin by differentiating between leadership, management, and command as three related but different decision modes that might usefully be associated with different kinds of problems facing the police. We can begin by considering the work of Rittel and Webber (1973), who suggested that public planners faced two different kinds of problems: tame and wicked. While tame problems were those that occurred on a recurring basis and had an existing solution, wicked problems were either novel (and therefore without a pre-existing solution) or recalcitrant (ie beyond traditional forms of resolution). Tame problems are associated with management as a decision style (what Heifetz (1998) calls 'Technical Leadership') and are addressed by unilinear solutions such as Standard Operating Procedures (SOPs) because the cause and effect are known and predictable. Arresting a suspect or cordoning off a crime scene or dealing with an inquiry might well be examples of tame problems and most police officers will view these kinds of activities as regular, and to some extent, mundane. Most of their activities will be undertaken within this frame of decision-making and little superordinate control is necessary because the procedures are known. That is not to say that the procedures or the problems are not complicated—like organizing a shift roster—but at least the procedures will work if followed correctly.

In contrast, wicked problems are complex, rather than complicated—you cannot take them out of their context, fix them, and put them back into the context without changing the context. Moreover, they tend not to have simple solutions, if any solutions, and might just offer better or worse alternatives. There might not, for example, be a 'solution' to Afghanistan's problems—there might just be better or worse alternatives. Wicked problems seldom have simple causes and usually sit across, and between different organizations or stake-holders to the point where not only is the cause and solution frequently disputed, but each apparent 'solution' often generates a further problem. So, for example, the building of the Jubilee River in 2002 was an attempt to protect Windsor and Eton from flooding—but the inhabitants of the area around Wraysbury—just to the east of Windsor and Eton—blamed their floods on the same change. Sometimes wicked problems are so obscure in causation that the solution pre-dates the problem analysis in the sense that you might have to try and 'solve' the problem before you have completely understood it, because only in that way can the main elements of the problem become clear. For instance, attempting to solve a community disorder problem by arresting some very visible individuals might unearth a much deeper issue about the use of stop-and-search policies. Indeed, it may be that the community disorder is itself a symptom of 'contradictory certitudes' where people hold completely contra-dictory understandings of both the problem and the solution and there may be a no 'stopping rule': a point at which such problems are actually resolved, so we may just have to accept their permanent presence and begin how to worry about how to manage them better, rather than pretend to fix them. One could argue that crime is precisely this kind of problem and the consequence is that whereas we would normally seek clarity on the problem and certainly about the solution, neither is likely. The consequence is what John Keats called 'negative capability'—the ability not to make a decision but to stand back and reflect on the issue. This is a crucial aspect of the skill of 'leadership' as defined here, for there is no prescribed management solution to fall back on or to reduce anxiety. As a consequence, 'leaders' need to be able to ask questions rather than pretend to have access to ready answers because they cannot know the answer (if they do, it is not a wicked problem). This also suggests that leadership is something that is present across all ranks in the police: a constable is just as likely as a chief constable to be faced with a wicked problem at some point in his or her career, though the latter will probably face more of them and they are more likely to be strategic in focus.

Since these problems are 'essentially contested'—people simply do not agree on the cause or effect—we might consider them as subjective not objective, and the consequence of this is that while the formal leader may not know the answer and configure the problem as wicked, someone else in the room may have been here before and may know the answer because to them the problem is tame, not wicked. If this is the case, the formal leader need only swap places with whoever considers it as a tame problem and allow that person to try to persuade the group of his or her approach to the answer.

This also highlights the importance of considering the framework as a language game, for in the absence of a collective language the group cannot agree on the problem or solution. In other words, while it is virtually impossible to conceive of a formal leader simply admitting to his or her followers that they have no idea what to do, a common language would allow the leader to ask the group whether anyone disagrees with his or her assumption that the issue before them is a wicked problem that behoves them all to engage in a collective response and not to rely upon either the formal leader or an SOP to fix the problem. The common language also facilitates challenge from subordinates because, by definition, the formal leader will not know the answer to the problem and requires subordinates to engage in collective decision-making.

A further aspect of wicked problems is that they can only be addressed if those facing them are actually engaged in their resolution. So whether the problem is obesity, alcoholism, or anti-social behaviour, then those 'with' the problem need to be engaged in attempting to address it. In other words, you cannot solve people's wicked problems for them; the role of the leadership here is not to solve people's wicked problems, but to get them engaged—to make them take responsibility. Of course, this does not make leadership a popular decision style, because leaders have to admit they are uncertain of the answer and to give the problem back to the people with the problem—which is unlikely to result in a rise in popularity. However, the role of 'leadership'—as defined here—is not to be popular but to make the population face and address its own wicked problems. Or, following Heifetz (1998), (adaptive) leadership is about disappointing people at a rate they can manage.

In sharp contrast, the decision-making model with which we began this chapter—the hierarchical authoritarian model—is totally inappropriate for these kinds of problems and might well compound them. This does not mean that there is no space for 'command' as a decision mode, but this is restricted to self-evident crises, or critical problems, where the prevailing uncertainty, the absence of management SOPs, and the time pressure, necessitates the decision-maker adopting a much more authoritarian response that embodies both the 'answer' to the problem and a willingness to use coercion—provided the action is undertaken for the collective good, not the private gain of the commander (Grint 2008). Thus while the police response to a terrorist incident might involve such coercive decision-making to move the public from harm's way, quite often such an event would also highlight a further point about problems: that they tend to combine all three elements and decision modes, and what counts as a critical problem for some might be a tame problem for others. Take a crash on the motorway: for those involved in the collision it is probably a crisis, possibly a life-threatening one; for the traffic police who are trained to deal with such incidents and probably attend them every day, it is a tame problem because they know the SOPs to divert the traffic and protect the injured. But for the Roads Agency this might be the third time a crash has occurred at this junction and it bears all the hallmarks of a wicked problem: it is not clear why it keeps recurring, nor how to solve it. Similarly, a bomb threat will also draw upon the SOPs for setting out cordons and alerting other services (appropriate for the management of tame problems) as well as coercing the public at the scene (command of critical problems) in the short term; in the longer term the wicked problem of understanding the radicalization of individuals will require the decision style appropriate for leadership.

The difficulty for many organizations, including uniformed ones like the police, is that the ability to act as a commander is a prerequisite for large elements of policing and tends to be crucial for assessing promotion. Furthermore, their hierarchical culture and the dangers inherent in the job generate a propensity to consider leadership, as defined here—the admittance of ignorance and the request for a collective response—as indecisiveness and weakness, not just a different form of decision-making appropriate for a different kind of problem. The opposite of this cultural mode can be seen in some organizations closer to the care of children where a more egalitarian culture prevails to generate maximum participation in decision-making, but also to protect individuals from responsibility by distributing it amongst the group where possible.

Etzioni (1964), in his work on compliance, suggested that there were probably three reasons why people would follow someone. His typology fits nicely with this one in the sense that 'coercive compliance' (what Nye (2004) calls 'hard power')—where followers could be forced to follow—fits with the command of critical problems, while calculative compliance existed where followers would comply because it was their job to do so, hence it was logical and rational for them—the framework for tame problems and management. Finally, Etzioni suggested that 'normative compliance' (what Nye (2004) calls 'soft power') occurred where followers wanted to follow, and this supports the implication of wicked problems and leadership, for unless followers want to engage in the resolution of their collective problems then little will be achieved.

The three problem formats and their associated decision-making are represented in Figure 5.1.

So far this might appear to be a relatively intuitive and rational model, but that does not mean that individuals are likely to adopt it as a way of addressing differentiated problems. In the first instance, and the irony of this model, is that in the region where we are most likely to require 'leadership' as a way of addressing wicked problems, we are more than likely to get command. This is for all kinds of reasons, but amongst them is a recognition that we tend to recruit and promote people on the basis of being effective commanders and efficient managers, not reflective leaders. In effect, leadership—defined here as the process by which formal 'leaders' get their followers, employees, or subordinates to accept responsibility for addressing their own wicked problems—is the most counter-cultural, especially in uniformed hierarchies, where those 'in charge' are supposed to *know* the answer, be decisive, and take personal control. In this sense it may be that some such organizations are addicted to command and allergic to leadership (Grint 2010). The pressure from political leaders and from the media often drives decision-makers down towards the command style and almost never towards leadership. There are, after all, no votes or newspaper sales in admitting that some problems are beyond us, are the responsibility of all of us, and require *us* to do something other than search for a scapegoat when things go wrong.

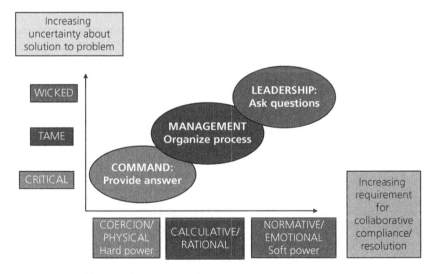

Figure 5.1 Problems and Decision Styles
Source: Grint 2008.

Thus neither the political leader, nor the newspaper, nor the general public, like to be told that we cannot stop parents killing their own children, we can only mitigate the dangers. Nor do we want to hear that flooding might be our responsibility when it is so much easier to blame the Environment Agency or the government, or even the moral corruption of some 'deviants'. For example, in January 2014, UKIP councillor David Silvester blamed the flooding in England on gay marriage.[1]

Even the scale of wicked problems often works to undermine a rational debate about them. For example, in the past few years we have lost perhaps a few thousand people globally to incidents of terrorism but we regularly lose 1.75 million to diarrhoea, yet while we have a war of terror there appears to be no war on diarrhoea. Even the so-called 'evidence base' for policy cannot rescue us from this: the investment in security at airports is extraordinary—and the absence of incidents can be taken as evidence that either it has worked or is totally irrelevant. Erich Fromm (1942) suggested that our collective 'fear of freedom'—our antipathy towards taking responsibility—might provide another reason for our compulsive submission to authority, or command. Or, as one of the covers of his book suggests, even when an individual has the ability to escape a dependency relationship they often choose not to do so since this demands that they take responsibility for their decisions; something that Baumann (1993) calls, 'the unbearable silence of responsibility'.

This also suggests that the avoidance of responsibility is a fundamental aspect of blame culture, in which the penalties for making a mistake far outweigh the rewards for taking a risk—and making a mistake. Better then, to bury the mistake or divert responsibility elsewhere than to take responsibility, admit the error, and ensure the organization as a whole learns from the error. The consequence of this is that little or no learning from errors and mistakes occurs and, in the absence of collective learning, there is likely to be what Dekker (2011) calls a 'drift into failure'. The other side of blame culture usually involves what Collinson (2012) calls 'prozac leadership'. Since most organizations operate on the basis of blame culture, little learning occurs and the senior group seldom knows what is actually going on in the rest of the organization because it is so good at burying errors, mistakes, and bad news. Thus the unremittingly positive spin from the top is often associated with perplexity when it becomes apparent that despite all the 'good news' something is actually radically wrong with the organization. We do not need to understand the bizarre conversations about the movements of non-existent armies and rescue plans between Hitler and his subordinates in the bunker at the end of World War II to realize that since superordinates are dependent upon subordinates for the information on which to base decisions, in the presence of blame culture and its associated prozac leadership, the more

---

[1] See <http://www.theguardian.com/science/brain-flapping/2014/jan/21/how-same-sex-marriage-causes-floods> (accessed 18 January 2014).

powerful you are the more likely you are to make less accurate decisions (Morrison et al 2011).

What are the Implications of this Model for Current Policing?

Several implications are worth highlighting. First, the model's dependence on a collective and common language implies that 'leadership' development approaches need to be rooted in the development of teams rather than just senior leaders. Only if teams have a common understanding of the world can the formal leader move into the leadership decision style described here without appearing indecisive, and only under the same circumstance can subordinates legitimately challenge their superordinates without appearing to be insubordinate.

Second, models of promotion based only on seniority or the ability to either command or manage are inadequate to address the most complex or wicked problems facing the police. The most successful are more likely to be proficient at all three decision modes rather than just one or perhaps two of them, but unless this mode is understood, recognized, and supported, senior decision-makers may well appear more comfortable with command than with leadership. If there are no wicked problems coming their way then this is insignificant, but if they are unable to act as leaders and encourage a collective response to a wicked problem they are likely to compound the problem rather than solve it.

Third, the ability to learn, rather than the ability to execute, might be a better way of recruiting and promoting police officers because being good at one decision style (probably command) might be sufficient for the first level of seniority, but as people proceed up the hierarchy the proportion of wicked problems is likely to increase and the proportion of tame problems is likely to decrease. It is also worth considering the internal hierarchies of cultures and their effects upon the organization. If departments traditionally associated with the command of critical problems—firearms, counter-terrorism, and serious organized crime, for instance—are prioritized over domestic violence and the protection of vulnerable children and adults, then it would be likely that command becomes the preferred decision mode, which has implications for the overall organization. Or, taking Archilochus' line, 'the fox knows many things but the hedgehog knows only one' (Grint 2014). This implies that being a command hedgehog is not sufficient to be a successful senior police leader; that requires the skills of a fox—to be proficient across the board.

Fourth, it is clear that permission-giving is an important aspect of leadership in the sense that leaders throw a long shadow over their organizations and are carefully watched by followers in what Mathiesen (1997) calls synopticism; in a reversal of Bentham's panopticon model, the many are watching the few. Thus it is incumbent on leaders at all ranks not just to require their subordinates to act in particular ways but to do it themselves; in effect, not to insist on a command mode as the default but to legitimate the acknowledgement of uncertainty when facing wicked problems.

Fifth, the ability to be Janus-faced might be a good indicator of a successful leader; by that I mean the skill with which the contradictory tensions that leak out of the political and media agenda can be handled successfully at the same time as coping with the organizational agenda that might require a different decision mode. In other words, since political leaders usually control access to resources—but may have the same demands that the media embodies, which force decision-makers to veer towards the command mode—police leaders need to be able to respond 'appropriately' to such agendas while simultaneously operating with a very different agenda that might require a different decision style. For example, when the riots broke out in London in 2011, the political agenda and the media frenzy that accompanied it insisted that the police responded instantly and with maximum force, despite the fact that the problem did not lend itself to the use of lethal force nor was this likely to have 'solved' the problem. However, ignoring that agenda would have damaged the reputation of the police significantly, so huge numbers were deployed onto the streets—but as much to satisfy the political and media agendas as to coerce the rioters.

Sixth, acknowledging that ambiguity and uncertainty are inevitable, this might encourage leaders, including those in the police, to accept that seeking instant, and ready-made, answers to all problems might not always be appropriate. When facing critical problems, then positive capability—the decisive actions of a commander—is appropriate. However, wicked problems do not offer themselves up for easy answers so the difficult issue is working out not what the answer is (because you cannot know) but what the question might be that you are trying to answer. Traditionally, organizations reward people who are quick with answers but not slow with questions. Take the use of chemical weapons in Syria in 2013; the instant 'answer' was to deploy cruise missiles to destroy the chemical weapons—but since it was not clear where these were, nor whether the regime was solely responsible for their use nor, most importantly, whether the missiles would have achieved the strategic goal of eliminating the weapons and encouraging a ceasefire, the quick 'answer' was probably wrong. What we needed to do was to work out what the question was that this answer was trying to address: destroy the weapons, weaken the government, protect the civilians, keep the Russians out of the conflict, force the UN to intervene, or what? The same might be said of police and crime commissioners (PCCs): what question is this the answer to? Is the question: how do we return the police to democratic control? Or how do we reinvigorate local interest in and support for the police? Or how do we make the police more accountable? Or how do we constrain the independence of the chief constables given their responsibility to the law, rather than to the government?

To conclude this section, let me draw out and reiterate the main points: default decision-making is often locked into a historical legacy and a contemporary practice that seems inevitable but is not. While it is possible to differentiate leadership, management, and command, it appears that we often confuse command with leadership. Command is about being decisive, being right, and not making a mistake, but leadership, as defined here, is about recognizing the limits of our understanding and expertise and taking a collaborative approach to the problem. For some organizations, and particularly uniformed ones, the preference for command is deep-rooted and has both beneficial and pernicious effects. On the one hand, it enables us to be secure when a crisis occurs because the police will almost certainly have the skills, knowledge, and wisdom to act appropriately and solve the crisis. But command as a decision style is both counter-productive and positively dangerous when facing wicked problems. The ability to deploy this decision style cannot be reduced to individual leaders because they appear indecisive and ineffective in a culture rooted in command. Hence only a collective understanding rooted in a common language and practice can shift the culture sufficiently to make a difference to these kinds of complex areas.

Practitioner's Perspective

I have been the Chief Constable of Thames Valley Police for seven years. It is a large force with over 9,000 staff and a revenue budget of nearly £400 million. There is tremendous professional satisfaction in being a police leader—the mission to protect the public matters and good policing can make a substantial difference to the quality of life for individuals and communities. There is also great personal pride in being at the top of my profession—Thames Valley Police is a force with a great reputation and I am following in the footsteps of outstanding leaders such as Lord Imbert. But it is also a very challenging role and above all unrelenting in its demands upon my time and energy. Policing is a risky business and accountability for Thames Valley Police rests with me—I feel this accountability and take it seriously.

Most people have a view about law and order and debate about the merits of policing has characterized its development since Sir Robert Peel founded the Metropolitan Police Service in 1829. Police forces are important institutions of the state and for many they promise much in terms of protection from harm but also are regarded with wariness by others. As in every part of the public sector, people's relationships with all institutions are changing—we are all more wary, more critical, require more scrutiny and openness, and do not trust professionals in the way we did 20 years ago. As a police leader I operate in the public eye, spending public money on public trust in public service!

I did not set out with the ambition of being a chief constable but I did work hard at every stage of my career. I have always tried to focus on growing the organization rather than my career—or to borrow Jim Collin's concept, 'level 5 leadership' (Collins 2001). Many leaders talk about leadership for good, and I hope that is what I practice. As a chief constable I want my officers and staff to use their formidable powers to protect the public and to cut crime and so earn the confidence and trust of the people who live in the Thames Valley.

For the past 20 years, I have regarded myself as a reflective practitioner—someone who seeks to think about their practice in order to learn and in particular to think about the relationship between theory and practice. I take a thoughtful approach to my work, trying to see it within a broader context, endlessly curious about new insights, and in the past ten years I have committed to a better understanding of evidence-based practice. Keith's section (which opens this chapter) focuses on literature with which I am reasonably familiar. Indeed, I heard Ronnie Heifetz lecture in the United States about ten years ago and I have often used his theory on adaptive leadership when thinking about change within the organization. I have quoted him in presentations and have sometimes asked myself: 'Am I on the dance floor or the balcony?'

However, most of my study has not been part of formal police training but additional external opportunities that I have pursued. I have taken both a post-graduate diploma and a Masters at Cambridge University, attended and organized many lectures at Oxford University, and generally networked with higher education institutions. It is important that we do not travel lightly through our careers—we need to cultivate a deeper understanding. I have found that there is nothing as worrying as a senior officer who does not know what they do not know!

Keith's section begins with a common perception of policing as a 'mechanical hierarchy' where leadership is about 'issuing and obeying orders'. As ever, it is good to see ourselves as others see us. This enables us to be more effective in our interactions with others because we are sensitive to the way in which we are perceived. I would never place such emphasis on command when reflecting upon my practice. And while Keith explains that decision-making is much more complicated in the police and that the wide discretion of officers demands a more sophisticated model, I still think that he is overly convinced that a command approach dominates policing—'to act as a Commander is a prerequisite for large elements of policing', and we 'are addicted to command and allergic to leadership'.

Keith differentiates between leadership, management, and command. I completely agree with the emphasis upon a separation between leadership and management, but I am less convinced that command is a separate approach to decision-making. I have found that viewing leadership as transformational and management as transactional is helpful. I therefore would see command as management or transactional activity that is appropriate in acute operational situations. I cannot recall when I last gave an order, nor do I recall when I was last given an order to obey. I might wear a uniform and badges of rank but I do not think that I exercise command in the military sense.

However, I suspect that some of my colleagues regard my requests as orders and it is important to keep an open mind about the power of the culture. Keith suggests that command is deep-rooted and both 'beneficial and pernicious'. In a hierarchical organization it is easy to become detached, to have a fan base rather than a management team, and unintentionally to silence debate. Creating a team that will give the leader the awkward feedback and bad news and argue with you is essential. I sometimes talk about the importance of humility in leadership and I always try to ensure that I see the issue from the perspective of the other. Most of the meetings I chair involve my own staff, but recently I chaired a meeting of 40 chief constables who were not in agreement. To reach consensus was vital but a great challenge—chief constables are used to getting their own way, But in some ways it is easier to have debate and negotiate agreement because no one is silenced, everyone is equal, and all are willing to listen with respect to colleagues. While I would never see my management meetings in the force as a case of 'issuing and obeying orders', I do appreciate that I don't have to try as hard for my views to be accepted as in a meeting of chief constables.

Leadership and management are concepts that are sometimes discussed as if they were opposites, as if they were alternatives for an organization. I strongly believe that to lead a police force effectively, both are necessary. As a leader I need to set a clear vision, to establish the right values and a healthy culture, and to encourage engagement, but I also need to manage the plan, align the budget, and ensure that systems are working. My job requires me to lead and manage, to be both transformational and transactional. I try to ensure that I do both simultaneously—for example, I might chair a budget discussion but I am ensuring that my values of service to the public and integrity are shot through the discussion. Similarly, in 2014 we are reducing the size and numbers of our buildings, with desk sharing and open plan offices for senior staff who have long enjoyed their own space. I also took the opportunity to work in an open plan office with my chief officer team—so I am walking the talk but also demonstrating an open, accessible, and modern culture.

Rittel and Webber's (1973) observations about wicked and tame problems are a useful way of thinking about the challenges I face. In particular, I will often talk about the need for senior leaders to deal with ambiguity. We need to accept that problems cannot always be fixed—that they are wicked. This morning I spoke with a chief constable colleague about his approach to tackling serious organized crime across force borders. Before I spoke with him I could not understand how he thought that his approach was right, neither could I understand how he could be, in my mind, oblivious to the negative impact on my force and others. Of course, he had a 'completely contradictory understanding' of both the problem and the solution. We are dealing with a wicked problem.

However, I am not sure that it is as straightforward as allowing the person in the meeting who views your wicked problem as a tame one to point the way forward. I find that some of my colleagues see simple solutions to systems problems which are endlessly complex and who don't know what they don't know. They can be quite frightening! But I do think that it can help if you declare a problem as wicked and therefore give permission for a more collective form of decision-making. While I would not use those words, I might say that no option under consideration solves the problem and we are looking for the least worse option. Of course, the temptation is to ride in on your white charger and rescue your colleagues—give them the answer. Many, many years ago I went on an Outward Bound course with a group of sergeants and learned about the danger of not allowing people the opportunity to solve their own problems and therefore denying them the opportunity to learn and to grow.

I found myself questioning Keith's narrow definition of leadership as 'the admittance of ignorance and the request for a collective response'. While I do think that Heifetz is right about the need to give the work back and orchestrate the conflict, he also talked about getting on the balcony and holding steady. We do need to involve our staff and live with a level of discomfort through the change process but we also need to provide the vision and nurture the right culture. Keith's definition of leadership sounds like a session on a beanbag, but I believe that leadership is more purposeful than that.

However, he is absolutely spot on when he says that some problems are beyond us all and that we should not just seek the scapegoat when things go wrong. Last year some of my best detectives brought seven men to justice for a terrible case of child sexual exploitation in Oxford. The case dominated the news and the force was criticized, and so was I, for having taken so long to stop the abusive harm to six young women. In such a situation, accountability to the media is immediate and they either demand your resignation or want you to promise that it will never happen again. But child sexual exploitation is a wicked problem in every sense of the word—it is about vulnerability, trust, threats, and violence. Of course we can, and must, do more to safeguard children but there is not an SOP to be followed. There are layers of difficult issues that cannot be explained in a 30-second interview, but nobody wants to hear those.

Procedural justice theories are currently very fashionable in policing—the importance of understanding why people obey the law rather than deviate from it (see Tyler 1990; Sunshine and Tyler 2003; Murphy et al 2008). In Thames Valley we also talk about organizational justice and by that we mean that the organization needs to be seen to be impartial, to treat people fairly, and to respect the individual. This is similar to Etzioni's description of normative compliance rather than coercive or calculative compliance as the reason why someone would follow a leader. We don't want followers who are forced to follow or even those who follow because it is logical to do so, we want followers to *want to follow*. I have seen this played out so many times in Thames Valley when we have wanted to improve performance against a target or improve service levels. I have often said that we can push in the short term and we will get short-term results, but if we want sustainable results then we need to pull. It is about the power of attraction, of taking people with you. A leader is more likely to take people with them if they are the good king—wise and making decisions in the interests of everyone, not just their own self-interest. I have found recent work by the University of Bath, School of Management on trustworthy leaders to be helpful

(CIPD/University of Bath 2014); we need to be competent in our role, concerned for others, fair and honest in our dealings, and predictable in our response.

Shared Reflections

The first issue is to recognize that there are different styles of decision-making that cannot be reduced to 'leadership' and that what counts as an appropriate decision style relates to both the culture of the organization and the preferences of the decision-maker. The reduction of command to a managerial activity, rather than a separate decision-making category, for instance, is a reflection of the 'essentially contested' nature of this area. Just because the chief constable issues a (managerial) request rather than an order (command), does not mean that the subordinates perceive it that way, and one of the consequences of a hierarchy is that compliance is usually such that an overt command is unnecessary. We know from Stanley Milgram's experiments in 1963 that most of us have the strongest desire to comply with those in authority.

The second issue concerns the responsibility of formal leaders in a wicked problem. In principle, some members of the group may believe it to be a tame problem and have the apparent solution, but these are always contested issues so simply declaring an issue to be a tame problem and claiming to have the answer does not negate the role of the formal leader in orchestrating the debate and retaining formal responsibility for the final decision. In effect, the leader's role is usually to facilitate a consultation, not to orchestrate a democratic vote or engage in a negotiation. Such engagement and involvement is exactly what those growing up in a digital age demand—they want to be co-producers, they expect to have a voice and their desire for self-actualization is much greater than that of their parents.

This brings us neatly to the push/pull, short-term/long-term role of leaders. If you tie a brick to the ceiling with a piece of string through a hole at the top end, and tie a similar piece of string to the bottom end and then yank the bottom string down as hard as you can, then the bottom string attaching the brick to your hand will probably snap, leaving the brick attached to the ceiling, because the inertia of the brick is greater than the strength of the string. However, if you pull *slowly* on the bottom string then the top string will probably break because the tension in the top string is greater than the tension in the bottom string. In metaphorical terms the ceiling is the past and the brick is the organization; the leader's forceful snatch or gentle pull represents the likelihood of moving the organization from the past (ceiling) to the future (hand). Followers are like cooked spaghetti—they are really hard to push and you're more likely to succeed if you pull them (Bratton et al 2005: 115).

The 'pull' of leadership is clearly visible in the current problem of public confidence in the integrity of policing, which has been potentially undermined by a series of events reported extensively in the media. Some, such as Hillsborough, are many years ago; others, such as 'Plebgate', much more recent. However, both have the potential to cast doubt on the honesty of all police officers. There has never been a greater need to clarify the professional standards expected of all those who work in policing. Therefore the first Code of Ethics for the police service, published by the College of Policing in April 2014, is timely and welcome. The challenge for all is to embed the Code in the culture and decision-making of the police service. We suggest that to push the Code will be ineffective—an action plan replete with SOPs and milestones will not address really difficult ethical issues.

Similarly, the police service continues to struggle to recruit officers from black and minority ethnic backgrounds and consequently does not look like the community it seeks to protect. While part of the answer might lie in holding recruitment events, ensuring fair application processes, and mentoring potential recruits, there is also a need for leaders to consider the operating culture of policing. For example, the disproportionate impact of stop and search on young men from black and minority ethnic backgrounds and the unconscious bias which so easily and sub-consciously affects our judgment must be addressed. Leaders will need to pull, not push. They will need to create space for conversations about how we treat each other, how we make decisions, the pressure to conform, the wilful blindness of organizations, and the unintended biases which shape our thinking.

Recommended Reading

Collinson, D (2012), 'Prozac Leadership and the Limits of Positive Thinking' 8(2) *Leadership* 7

Grint, K (2010), 'The Cuckoo Clock Syndrome: Addicted to Command, Allergic to Leadership' 28(4) *European Management Journal* 306

Heifetz, R (1998), *Leadership Without Easy Answers* (Cambridge, MA: Harvard University Press)

Morrison, KE, Rothman, NB, and Soll, JB (2011), 'The Detrimental Effects of Power on Confidence, Advice Taking, and Accuracy' 116(2) *Organizational Behaviour and Human Decision Processes* 272

Rittel, H and Webber, M (1973), 'Dilemmas in a General Theory of Planning' 4 *Policy Sciences* 155

References

Barnett, D (2014), 'How Same-sex Marriage Causes Floods', *The Guardian*, 21 January, at <http://www.theguardian.com/science/brain-flapping/2014/jan/21/how-same-sex-marriage-causes-floods> (accessed 18 January 2015)

Baumann, Z (1993), *Postmodern Ethics* (Oxford: Blackwell)

Bratton, J, Grint, K, and Nelson, D (2005), *Organizational Leadership* (Mason, OH: Thomson/Southwestern)

CIPD/University of Bath (2014), 'Cultivating Trustworthy Leaders', at <http://www.cipd.co.uk/hr-resources/research/cultivating-trustworthy-leaders.aspx> (accessed 26 January 2014)

Collins, J (2001), 'The Misguided Mix-up of Celebrity and Leadership', Board Annual Report, Annual Feature Essay, at <http://www.jimcollins.com/article_topics/articles/the-misguided-mixup.html> (accessed 26 January 2015)

Collinson, D (2012), 'Prozac Leadership and the Limits of Positive Thinking' 8(2) *Leadership* 7

Dekker, S (2011), *Drift into Failure* (Farnham: Ashgate)

Etzioni, A (1964), *Modern Organizations* (London: Prentice Hall)

Fromm, E (1942), *The Fear of Freedom* (London: Routledge)

Grint, K (2008), 'Problems, Problems, Problems: The Social Construction of "Leadership"' 58(11) *Human Relations* 1467

Grint, K (2010), 'The Cuckoo Clock Syndrome: Addicted to Command, Allergic to Leadership' 28(4) *European Management Journal* 306

Grint, K (2014), 'The Hedgehog and the Fox: Leadership Lessons from D-Day' 10(2) *Leadership* 240

Heifetz, R (1998), *Leadership Without Easy Answers* (Cambridge, MA: Harvard University Press)

Mathiesen, T (1997), 'The Viewer Society: Michel Foucault's "Panopticon" Revisited' 1 *Theoretical Criminology* 215

Milgram, S (1963), 'Behavioral Study of Obedience' 67 *Journal of Abnormal and Social Psychology* 371

Morrison, KE, Rothman, NB, and Soll, JB (2011), 'The Detrimental Effects of Power on Confidence, Advice Taking, and Accuracy' 116(2) *Organizational Behaviour and Human Decision Processes* 272

Murphy, K, Hinds, L, and Fleming, J (2008), 'Encouraging Public Cooperation and Support for Police' 18(2) *Policing and Society* 136

Nye, JS (2004), *Power in the Global Information Age: From Realism to Globalization* (London: Routledge)

Rittel, H and Webber, M (1973), 'Dilemmas in a General Theory of Planning' 4 *Policy Sciences* 155

Sunshine, J and Tyler, TR (2003), 'The Role of Procedural Justice and Legitimacy in Shaping Public Support for Policing' 37(3) *Law and Society Review* 513

Tyler, TR (1990), *Why People Obey the Law* (New Haven, CT: Yale University Press)

Walters, S (2014), 'The Wrath of Wraysbury: "We Drowned so the Gin and Jag Set in Windsor and Eton Could Keep Dry" Say Residents', *The Mail on Sunday*, 15 February, at <http://www.dailymail.co.uk/news/article-2560311/The-wrath-Wraysbury-We-drowned-Gin-Jag-set-Windsor-Eton-drg.html?> (accessed 15 February 2014)

6

Principled and Ethical Policing

Some Considerations for Police Leaders

Allyson MacVean and Peter Spindler

Introduction

In January 2013, the Committee on Standards in Public Life released a report, 'Standards Matter: A Review of Best Practice in Promoting Good Behaviour in Public Life'. This report stated that, along with MPs, the public perceived police officers to have the worst ethical standards in public life. The report indicated that public concerns related to both the police as an institution of the state and of individual officers working within it. The public perception of the police as being unethical and corrupt concurred with a review commissioned by Her Majesty's Inspector of Constabulary (HMIC) published two years earlier. This review, 'Without Fear or Favour—A Review of Police Relationships', asserted that at least one-third of the public believed 'that there is some problem with corruption' by police officers (2011: 4).

Concerns about unethical and deviant behaviour are significant challenges for police leaders, not least because of the unique powers vested in the police on behalf of the state and that policing in England and Wales is undertaken with the consent of the public (Reiner 2010). The fact that police have a wide latitude of discretion and autonomy, and make decisions that can bring significant benefit or harm to individuals, families, and communities, makes policing an immensely ethical matter (Hughes 2013). The extraordinary degree of professional discretion and autonomy, which is not afforded to many other professions, brings with it the challenge of ethical dilemmas for police officers seeking to resolve the issues and problems by which they are confronted. The complexities and context sensitivity of policing rarely allows for prescriptive responses; rather, as Kleinig notes, the service provided by officers is 'not dictated by a rigid and closely defined set of rules but by judgement and skill anchored in a thorough grasp of the principles governing the service' (1996: 38).

Public and media focus on police misbehaviour and corruption has waxed and waned since the inception of modern policing. Recently, however, this focus has intensified and highlighted police malfeasance, which has been particularly corrosive and damaging: scandals have involved the most senior of police leaders as well as rank and file officers. The Report of the Hillsborough Independent Panel (2012) identified wilful abuse of power by police leaders in concealing and obscuring the truth of what occurred at the time of the event. In 2012, the Chief Constable of Cleveland Police was sacked for gross misconduct, and in the past two years there have been investigations into more than ten senior police officers for acts of alleged misconduct and corruption. On 6 March 2014, the front page of *The Times* heralded the stark message 'You Can't Trust Police', which was the response of Doreen Lawrence on hearing the revelations of a secret undercover police unit which used covert surveillance against the family of Stephen Lawrence in the months leading up to the Macpherson hearings (O'Neill 2014). The Lord Justice Leveson report (2012) also reminds us that the public *perception* of police corruption and misbehaviour can be just as damaging. The report criticized the police not only for its errors in the way it failed to investigate the phone hacking scandal effectively but also for fostering a 'perception' that some senior police officers were too close to News International.

This public view of the declining standards of the police—whether real or perceived—was captured by the senior conservative MP David Davis following the 'Plebgate' scandal, who opportunely described it as a 'crisis of ethics in the police'. Davies called for police officers to be equipped with microphone cameras to record their behaviour in an attempt to redress the decline in public trust (Mason 2013). Whether the use of recording devices as the mechanism to enforce trust between the public and police will be enough to restore public confidence or if, on the contrary, such a move will produce a more impersonal and bureaucratic style of policing, which may create greater mistrust, remains to be seen. But as difficult as policing may be, and while most police officers carry out their role with integrity, currently a significant proportion of the public appear to have little trust in the police service as an institution.

What is not in question, however, are the implications of this public crisis for police leaders and the need for them to develop greater appreciation of how a code of ethics and policing with integrity will be crucial to restoring the trust between the police organization and public. Unlike the media, police leaders no longer have the luxury of having an intermittent interest in professional standards and ethics: this has to be an area of incessant focus and compassionate leadership from the very top. The recent media attention on unethical and corrupt policing brings into sharp focus the need for police leaders to fully engage and understand what is meant by professional ethics and how the newly introduced Code of Ethics (College of Policing 2014) for the police service may provide the instrument to restore public confidence.

In part, it could be argued that police officers are required to uphold and enforce the law regardless of moral consideration or content; for example, the Criminal Procedure and Investigations Act 1996 sets out that the role of the police is to investigate and present all relevant evidence, both inculpatory and exculpatory, and not just to present the evidence that a police officer has deemed relevant on the basis of what they consider morally right or wrong. If police officers were to enforce the law equally and without discretion, and apply the law according to the law, there would be no need for consideration of ethics (MacVean and Neyroud 2012). But policing comprises more than law enforcement; it includes protecting the rights of members of the community as well as being the gatekeepers of citizenship and respectability (Pollock 1998).

Harfield argues persuasively that while 'policing is an institutional activity essential to peaceful society', paradoxically it is facilitated by a range of practices which are considered morally harmful. He specifically identifies coercion, deception, and surveillance as three harmful methods utilized by the police in achieving their function (2012: 3). The deployment of legitimate deceptive and dishonest practices is articulated by Miller and Blackler as the moral theory of policing: 'Harmful and normally immoral methods are on occasion necessary in order to realise the fundamental end of policing, namely the protection of moral rights' (2005: 26). This theory asserts that if the police are to maintain law and order as well as social justice, then the police must have in its arsenal of tactics, immoral methodologies to fulfil its function. But for policing to maintain both its effectiveness and legitimacy, these practices have to be deployed and managed with organizational integrity, otherwise the fallout can be catastrophic. This is nowhere more clearly demonstrated than in what Keith Vaz[1] described as the 'gruesome practice' of the Metropolitan Police Services' Special Demonstration Squad stealing over 80 names of dead babies for the personal use of covert officers (Lewis and Evans 2013). But the use of legitimate deceitful and dishonest tactics is not in question in this chapter; it is the integrity with which these are governed, deployed, managed, and justified that is open to scrutiny, and more specifically, how these tactics may conflict with the personal values of police officers. Notwithstanding the use of sanctioned, morally harmful processes, if policing is to maintain its integrity, then police officers have to be subject to professional codes of practice. Trust and confidence in the police is essential for the functioning of modern democracies but, as demonstrated, if the public become mistrustful of the basic integrity of an organization, then the institution lacks legitimacy (Committee of Standards in Public Life 2013). The absence of trust weakens the ability of the police to police effectively and dealings with individuals become more difficult to the extent that social cohesion may become threatened (eg the shooting of Mark Duggan and the ensuing riots across England in the summer of 2011).

---

[1] Chair of the Home Affairs Select Committee.

If professional standards and ethical behaviour are an integral part of policing, then, as Mansfield notes: 'Essentially the errors and failures in professional standards start at the top. A culture is condoned, a blind eye turned, and a misdemeanour is overlooked or goes unpunished' (2013: 215). Lord Justice Leveson made much the same point, only this time the emphasis is not on what behaviour leaders may choose to overlook but on their own personal conduct: 'In a hierarchical organisation such as the police, the tone is set from the top, and how leaders behave will have an obvious filtering effect right through the force' (2012: 61). But as Punch (2009) observes, the very nature of policing presents impossible dilemmas and this would be true for both the new officer on their first day of patrol and the most senior of police leaders. Police officers are expected to uphold the law in dealing with an array of situations (from actions that can be defined as social ills to serious criminal activity), within a framework of legislation, with increasingly limited resources and intricate rules that restrict how the organization and officers can respond (Punch 2009). Manning (1977) refers to this as the impossible mandate, and one that encourages a diverse range of 'deviant' behaviours and practices in order to achieve solutions. While these explanations postulate that it is the function of the police itself that fosters unethical practice, Waddington, Kleinig, and Wright (2013: 5) assert that it is the reality of the role of policing that 'discourages officers from confronting the dilemmas and difficulties that their work imposes'. The reality of police work is very different from the one constructed and embodied in the police imagination:

> Policing is erected on a lie and buttressed by elaborate rhetorical support. The 'lie' is that policing is fundamentally about law enforcement, which protects the wholly innocent from the depredations of depraved criminals who are clearly and unambiguously guilty of crimes of which they are accused, even if the perversity of the criminal justice system obstructs their conviction (Waddington et al 2013: 5)

Whether, as the academic literature suggests, it is the role, function, or reality of policing that creates these dilemmas and ethical complexities, it is not unreasonable to establish a set of principles and values to define acceptable police conduct and decision-making.

The Police Code of Ethics

The concept of codes of conduct for policing is not new; the police have been bound by a range of codes and principles since the inception of the modern police force in 1829 through Peel's Principles, which were set out in the *General Instructions* issued to every new police officer. These principles have since been reinforced in a number of statements and oaths intended to establish standards and values for professional behaviour. For example, all officers on joining the service swear an oath of office that provides for a set of standards and expectations of behaviour and conduct. The values of behaviour expressed in the oath of office were further strengthened in 1993, when the Association of Chief Police Officers (ACPO) issued the Statement of Common Purpose and Values to which all police forces signed up.

In 1996, the Police Act introduced the Code of Conduct, which became operational in 1999. This Code established new misconduct procedures to replace the then existing police regulations. It presented a framework that authorized punishment for poor behaviour and performance but was a significant philosophical shift from the previous militaristic 'discipline code' (MacVean and Neyroud 2012). In 1999, HMIC published a seminal report, 'Police Integrity'. This report, for the first time sought to define the characteristics of 'integrity and principles' for policing and moved beyond the narrow dimension of corruption, describing qualities such as fairness, probity, and equal treatment, thus providing the context for the consideration of a code of ethics for the police.

The Taylor Review in 2005 was an attempt to consider whether the current codes and statements regulating police behaviour were fit for purpose and to deliberate on the development and incorporation of a code of ethics. The Review asserted that the police service, and police officers by virtue of their role and function, presented a number of distinctive factors that separated them from other agencies; not least, police officers were servants of the Crown, which gave them a range of obligations and responsibilities over and above those expected from employees in other organizations. However, a code of ethics did not feature in the Review implementations; rather, the Code of Conduct was replaced with the introduction of the Code of Professional Standards, shifting the professional standards regulations from a quasi-judicial focus on blame and punishment to one on a learning and improving model (Taylor 2013: 23). This was a marked change from the previous militaristic and legalistic approach that had represented policing since its inception, towards a system that focused on the concepts of equality, accountability, and professionalism.

Neyroud and Beckley (2001) have argued that despite the motivations for the introduction of these various codes and statements, they lacked the value and positive influence that a specific code of ethics could bring to engender good professional standards. Black (2003) went further, to contend that a code of ethics would more explicitly assist and direct ethical decision-making and behaviour. So while a substantial shift occurred at this time, the shift would have significant implications for future police leaders. The militaristic framework of policing had provided a legacy that located any association with bad, poor, or challenging behaviour—including behaviour which did not conform to the cultural norms—within the more general categorization of 'professional standards'. In the absence of a more refined understanding or the development of a code of ethics, terms such as 'ethics', 'integrity', 'conduct', 'principles', and 'fairness' became located in, and associated with, professional standards rather than becoming embedded in policy, practice, and professional development. In addition, while terms associated both with professional standards and codes of ethics are also used interchangeably, there are important and significant differences between definitions. It is imperative that an appreciation of these meanings is recognized if a code of ethics for policing is to be meaningful.

If, as described previously, police ethics are associated with 'professional standards', and therefore by default, with unacceptable or bad behaviour, this fails to appreciate the ethical dilemmas that police officers and staff encounter in their day-to-day work, and the potential consequences of not recognizing these dilemmas. Ethical dilemmas are decisions in which there is no 'right or wrong' answer, but whatever choice of action the officer decides upon will have consequences or ramifications; potentially some positive and some negative for different individuals and groups. Thus officers need to be able to reflect on these possible consequences and the impact upon various parties.

These consequences may be referred to as 'ethical hazards' (eg see Waddington et al 2013 for detailed case scenarios and discussions of ethical hazards). Thus an ethical dilemma is a situation where a decision is required that is beyond any legal constraints or demands, but nevertheless will have a positive or negative impact on one or more parties. As Kleinig (1996) notes, ethical dilemmas are frequently raised before legal limits are reached. As mentioned earlier, often an ethical dilemma occurs at the point where police officers have to exercise their discretion. Working through the ethical dilemma will provide an understanding of both the potential positive and negative hazards and how these will impact on different groups. This will enable the hazards to be considered and actions to mitigate them if required. In this context, recognizing an ethical dilemma and considering the potential responses and associated negative and positive hazards enables the officer to choose the actions that are most appropriate; the link between making the decision and the consequences become meaningful, enabling the officer to grasp the complex peculiarities of the situation.

Kelly (2010) argues that in determining what constitutes an ethical dilemma, it is necessary to make a distinction between ethics, values, morals, and laws and to have an understanding of the complex interaction between these principles at both the organizational and individual level. Congress (1999) defines ethics as a set of statements defined and exercised within a professional setting to guide or determine the right course of action in a given situation. Therefore, ethics relies on logical and rational criteria to reach a decision—a process referred to as making an ethical decision. Allen and Friedman (2010) describe values as the beliefs or standards that are held and cherished by the individual or organization. Values have a special and esteemed worth to a person and therefore are often associated with something that is to be cherished and valued. Allen and Friedman (2010) further assert that values are a set of ideals that individuals or organizations aspire to achieve, like equality or social justice. If values are aspirations, then according to Dolgoff et al (2009), morals are the constituent within a code of conduct that enables an individual or organization to negotiate, support, and strengthen relationships with others.

In recognizing the differences between these terms, notwithstanding the role of the police as upholders and enforcers of the law, whatever personal ethics, values, and morals police officers may hold, these have to be recognized within their professional role and function. It is therefore important that a distinction is made between professional and personal ethics, values, and morals. Kelly (2013) argues that conflicts between personal and professional values should not be considered ethical dilemmas, as values are personal; the rational and logical criteria required in resolving an ethical dilemma within a professional setting cannot be applied to value conflicts. When an officer signs up to a professional code of ethics, they are agreeing to comply with the organizational standards and values at the expense of relinquishing their own. Yet conflicts between personal and professional values may create a number of tensions, possibly even more so in policing, and it remains to be seen how officers will be able to recognize and manage personal values in a way that will allow professional values to guide police practice.

In July 2014, the College of Policing introduced the Code of Ethics for the police service. This became a code of practice under section 39A of the Police Act 1996 (amended by section 124 of the Anti-Social Behaviour, Crime and Policing Act 2014). This Code provides a set of statements that represent the collective moral values, beliefs, behaviours, and aspirations of the police service and expectations of police officers and staff. In short, it provides a framework for professional behaviour, responsibility, accountability, and compliance, allowing officers to consider their conduct, behaviour, and decision-making in fulfilling their duties. The Code of Ethics articulates the standard of professional behaviour expected from officers together with practical examples embodying the nine principles and ten standards of professional conduct. The Code further asserts that chief constables must have due regard to the Code in carrying out their duties as leaders of the service. However, this is not the first code of ethics for the UK police service; in 1992, ACPO issued a statement on the principles of policing which contained a code of ethics. Although this statement was widely circulated, it was not taken up or introduced as standard police practice at the time (MacVean and Neyroud 2012). More recently, the Police Service of Northern Ireland defined a Code of Ethics in the Police (Northern Ireland) Act 2000. The Northern Ireland Code was entrenched within a disciplinary framework that was binding for the behaviour of police officers both on and off duty. In 2004, the Association of Police Officers for Scotland also published a statement of ethical principles for police officers to observe and support (ACPOS 2004) and this was followed by ACPO issuing a Code of Ethics based on the Nolan Principles (ACPO 2004).

The Code of Ethics of England and Wales encapsulates the key features of previous codes of conduct and statements in that it articulates the 'highest-level declaration of the principles and standards of professional behaviour expected' by those who work for the police service. The consultation document states:

> In the complex environment that is policing, it is impossible to tell people what to do in every given situation. Ethical decision making is at the heart of police professionalism. The Code will guide decision making and help the police operate ethically (College of Policing 2013: 5).

The Code of Ethics was referenced in the House of Commons Home Affairs Select Committee Report, 'Leadership and Standards in the Police' (2014). It was recommended that not only police officers or staff should be bound by the Code, but also those who are contracted by police forces to carry out work on their behalf. Nonetheless, while the development of a code of ethics is laudable in itself in providing a statement of organizational ideals, aspirations, principles, and requirements for officers, this alone is not enough. Research by the Committee on Standards in Public Life has demonstrated that in professions that are empowered with great autonomy, good people may do bad things if they are placed in an environment that does not value morals and ethical practice (Kelly 2013; Bew 2014). Whatever the merits and demerits of the Code of Ethics, compared to other professions, police ethics are significantly undeveloped.

Kleinig, in his seminal book, *The Ethics of Policing*, notes that police ethics have largely been disregarded by academics; compared to the 'scholarly attention given to legal ethics, medical ethics, business ethics, ethics in government, and so on, police ethics comes off very poorly' (1996: vii). As previously discussed, unethical behaviour by individual police officers or as an organization has a significant and disproportional impact on public trust and confidence in a way that does not ordinarily affect other professions. Kleinig (1996) notes that not only is there disagreement about the nature of unethical behaviour, but there is also disagreement about the 'corruptness' of particular police practices. What one officer considers unethical, another sees as morally legitimate. Therefore, while it is tempting to contemplate a code of ethics as a prescriptive set of statements that will assist police officers to make better and considered ethical decisions when faced with an ethical dilemma, ethical issues are not simple transactions. Kleinig argues that the relationship between ethical theory and ethical decision-making is 'very complex, certainly not linear . . . involving judgement, not simple deductive inference' (1996: 2).

In his report (2013), Sir Christopher Kelly suggests that public sector organizations do not require any more codes of ethics or regulators to ensure compliance with such codes. He stated that there had been a proliferation of codes over the past decades, yet these had not redressed poor behaviour. Rather, what is required is for senior leaders and managers to constantly espouse and embody ethical values within the organization, thereby developing a culture where staff can discuss ethical issues and identify problems in an open and unthreatening manner. Kelly's view is that ethics in public service should be a set of applied principles rather than a set of philosophical concepts abstractly embodied within a set of dictums. He argues that ethical issues need to be a key feature on board agendas and that risks associated with poor standards should be part of risk assessments, with appropriate mitigating strategies (Kelly 2013). Thus, codes of ethics do not have an impact by simply existing; they require effective motivational leadership to create high standards. This leadership has to be understood and communicated throughout the organization. Fleming and O'Reilly (2013) helpfully identify the importance of the interplay of leadership, knowledge, and communication within an organization to enable strong ethical and integrity frameworks to develop.

It is not enough for leaders to espouse ethical values, they have to set an example and be seen to set an example; in a hierarchical organization, staff need to be aware at every level which behaviours are acceptable and which are not. But for an ethical culture to exist, it needs to go further than that—it requires an environment in which ethical issues and behaviours can be openly discussed and one in which the leaders set the standards by their own personal behaviour. The Filkin Report (2012) articulates the consequences when inconsistency exists between the behaviour of leaders and the expectations of staff:

> I am concerned by the extent to which police officers . . . and staff feel that some of their senior leaders abide by a different set of rules. There have been no clear standards set by the senior team for police officers and staff to use as a guide for their own behaviour and in some instances the standards set have been poor and have led to consequent damage (Filkin 2012: 39).

So while many of the requirements for high standards require action at the organizational level, these standards are defined and determined by leaders taking personal responsibility for observing and demonstrating high standards to others through their own behaviour. Mindlessly following rules and processes is not enough if people do not also engage their judgment about what is important. An individual who has internalized sound ethical principles and the reasons they are important is better able to make appropriate decisions than someone simply following a set of rules (Committee of Standards in Public Life, 2013: 64). Neyroud and Beckley (2001) contend that no matter what the indicative characteristics of professional standards or a code of ethics are, it is difficult to recognize what a principled police service looks like. As Taylor (2013) points out, this may be due, in part, to the historical, militaristic framework of policing, or it may be that the vocabulary associated with the term 'ethics' has been located within the professional standards framework and therefore by default associated with bad or unacceptable behaviour. The absence of any deliberations on what a principled police service looks like has ramifications for police leaders. If police leaders do not have a definitive end point, how do they know what they are doing will fulfil the requirements for a principled service? This becomes important for police leaders as they interpret and articulate the Code of Ethics in practice. Notwithstanding the way in which ethics is perceived within the context of policing and the factors which influenced these perceptions, it is likely that there will be as many different models of ethics in practice as there are police forces. These models will be located on a continuum from a philosophical model in which ethical dilemmas can be situated and which will support ethical decision-making in relation to ethical dilemmas, to a model in which ethics are firmly embedded within a professional standards structure, thus making it part of bad and unacceptable behaviour. This potentially has a consequence that what may be ethical practice in one force may be deemed unethical in another.

Practitioner's Perspective

'Leadership is a contact sport' and 'every contact leaves a trace'; of all the quotes from all the promotion and development courses I have attended over the years, these two from Marshall Goldsmith (the leadership guru with an extensive online library) and Dr Edmond Locard[2] are ingrained in my psyche and have informed my approach as a police leader over the past 29 years in policing. The text that follows introduces my particular style of ethical leadership and reflects the learning in some of the challenges and opportunities I have encountered. I have provided two specific case studies to illustrate how ethical leadership in action needs careful consideration and how ethical decision-making is central to all aspects of police activity. I have also listed some of the maxims and mantras that have assisted me and which I now routinely share with those I develop and mentor. Let me first give you some context to my career.

My early years in policing can be best typified as chasing credibility, trying to prove that the graduate entrant was as practical and effective as the mainstream cohort of officers. Entering the service on the Home Office scheme came with a label and attracted preconceived reactions from colleagues at the time of the so-called 'butterfly syndrome' or 'lighthouse in the desert effect' (bright but useless). Desperate to break these stereotypes, I always sought out fresh challenges and found myself drawn to specialist roles, seeking depth rather than breadth of experience. One of my role models advised, 'Don't try and play every instrument in the orchestra'. At every stage of my career I extended my time in the substantive rank, deferring promotion to maximize the learning and reflect on the ethical issues and dilemmas I was confronted with.

When I look back I realize that the models of ethical leadership I have followed have been role models rather than theoretical paradigms. Those role models were, however, people with immense integrity and although the concept of ethical policing was seldom discussed, they were principled people, trying to do the right thing for the public they served. As Macvean has articulated, there has been little academic literature on the ethics of policing, which meant there was a lack of any debate at both academic and practitioner level. The absence of academic paradigms enabling police officers to articulate these debates led one colleague to comment light-heartedly, when the subject first came to the fore in 2008: 'Ethics, that's the other side of London where proper villains live.'

I met the first of my role models as a young sergeant on the tennis court of the Police Staff College, Bramshill when I lent him a tennis racquet, only to find three months later he was my new Chief Superintendent back at a tough inner London division. He was an impressive, hard-working, and charismatic individual who took his duties and responsibilities seriously. I have tried to emulate his behaviour over the years, remaining in close contact long into his retirement and

---

[2] Dr Locard (13 December 1877–4 May 1966) was a pioneer in forensic science known as the 'Sherlock Holmes of France'.

realizing that I have continued many of his traditions and practices to this day. He was a man of great integrity and commitment, with a passion for policing.

Whilst I am a firm believer that you are responsible for the decisions you make as a police officer, there are certain individuals you will meet along the way who will support and create opportunities for you to develop your decision-making to enable better policing for the community. These people will be looking for talent and if you are seen to work hard and deliver they will bring you with them. Success comes to those who recognize those opportunities and grab them with both hands, even if it means diverting from a previously conceived career pathway.

Exposure to role models and ethical heroes has helped to shape the leader I am today. The group of distinguished senior Scotland Yard detectives I had the privilege to work for provided me with decades of knowledge and experience to learn from. I have ensured that I have continued their tradition of helping others by mentoring and developing aspiring senior detectives so that their legacy continues to benefit others from the generations that follow. Although I have attended many leadership and personal development courses delivering theories and case studies, the greatest impact on shaping my behaviour has been through observation of leaders in action and selecting their best attributes to add to my toolkit of ethical leadership. I employ the following tactics and techniques on a daily basis as part of my leadership style. These have been developed over the years through observing leaders in action:

- *Walk the floor.* Taking time at the beginning of the shift, day, or week to wander, speak, and engage with staff to identify issues at an early stage and address them appropriately. Taking an interest in their welfare and that of their families is vital.

- *Open door policy.* Being available 24/7 to your staff and making yourself approachable and accessible to deal with problems and concerns will ensure you have grip and exercise good governance.

- *Lead by example.* Both on and off duty, in your private as well as public life, ensure that you do not compromise the high standards you set for yourself and others. It won't be easy, but others will pounce upon the inconsistency if you say one thing and do another. It must also be remembered that integrity is demonstrated by what happens when no one is watching!

- *Be inclusive.* There is no 'I' in team. As a leader it is incumbent upon you to ensure that the teams who support you include a diversity of talent and experience; every individual has a unique value and something to offer.

- *Never miss the opportunity in a crisis.* A positive disposition is essential to successful leadership, maximizing each moment to improve the service provided to the public whilst ensuring you take the workforce with you.

- *Carry a strong moral compass.* Apply what is sometimes called the 'mum and dad' or 'Daily Mail' test to decision-making. Ask yourself, 'What will this look like on the front cover of the Daily Mail?' or 'What would your mum say if she knew what you had done?' An open and transparent approach will ensure high standards.

- *Recognize and reward.* Create opportunities to give thanks and appreciate those who deliver a high quality service for you.

- *Challenge and confront.* When dealing with those who behave inappropriately and perform poorly, do it in a constructive and supportive way whenever possible, adopting the approach 'Have you thought about doing X?' Likewise, creating a culture of challenge around you is essential to ensure that your own behaviour and decisions are the very best they can be. None of us is perfect and we all make mistakes.

This is by no means an exhaustive list of attributes for effective leadership; however, they have stood me in good stead when going about my day-to-day business. These considerations reflect the interaction between leadership, communication, and knowledge, which Fleming and O'Reilly (2013) articulate, although at the time there was no academic paradigm for me to consider. I will turn now to two specific case studies to illustrate how I used these techniques in practice as part of my leadership style.

Commander covert policing

My first posting as a chief officer was to lead Scotland Yard's covert capabilities in 2008, a post I held for over three years. This is a high-risk area of policing and thankfully I was a round peg in a round hole; the years of chasing credibility through specialist postings ensured that I already had the requisite knowledge and experience to take on this role. Transferring on promotion from the Directorate of Professional Standards, where I had been leading the Counter-Corruption Command, meant I had a strong reputation for integrity. A sound understanding of my role and good governance were concepts ingrained in me by my mentors and I quickly set about building the systems and processes that would ensure that I could manage risk and deliver the high-end capabilities that the specialist operational teams needed to achieve their aims. The management of risk also included the ethical risks and risks associated with poor standards to which Kelly (2013) alluded in his report. That said, I was also very fortunate to be supported by a number of small, dedicated teams of officers and staff who acted as gatekeepers for the various disciplines for which I was responsible, such as undercover deployments; covert source management; operational security; and witness protection. My own experience rising through the ranks had taught me that colleagues need clear boundaries and ethical expectations set for them by their leaders and are quick to identify inconsistent messages or behaviour.

Much of what we were involved in is regulated by the Human Rights Act 1998 and the primary legislation governing our activity is the Regulation of Investigatory Powers Act 2000, underpinned by specific codes of practice. My role as the senior authorizing officer for the deployment of undercover officers, participating informants, and juvenile informants was to ensure that the activity was proportionate, necessary, and legal, and also that there was accountability for our actions. The assessment and management of risk was a significant factor in the decision-making and in an overwhelmingly human rights context, ethics at that particular time was rarely mentioned. The very nature of covert policing and the threat of harm to the assets from the serious and organized criminals they were deployed against meant that good tradecraft and the need for secrecy were essential. We did, however, recognize that there could be great benefit from involving a wider community of knowledge than just the Office of Surveillance Commissioners who inspected our work.

In 2009, one of my more visionary detective superintendents established an ethics committee for covert policing. We invited representatives from Liberty, the legal profession, academia, and our own independent advisory group on race to come together and consider ethical dilemmas for us. This was a bold step in a covert environment where the risk of compromise was always great, and there-fore we did not share specific operational details but presented tactical options in a more general context. For example, we shared with the group some of the activities and behaviours a covert internet investigator might exhibit when interacting online with predatory paedophiles. We were operating within our own self-imposed boundaries where legislation had not kept pace with the evolution of the internet. What was interesting for us was that on presenting our proposed tactics, the group was surprised that we did not undertake such activity already and challenged our own ethical boundaries to act more in the public interest and safety of our children than in rigid adherence to the existing police policies and guidelines.

When I reflect on why we did not undertake such activity earlier, I surmise that it has been our focus on the legal rather than the ethical nature of our work and the fact that in covert policing our main consideration has been on issues of risk. The police service has developed models for the management of risk over many years, the one most often used in the covert world, although not necessarily used by mainstream policing, known by the mnemonic 3P-LEM (police and commu-nity. physical, psychological, legal, economic, moral) (Harfield and Harfield 2008). It is worth noting here that my considerations in relation to the 'moral' are as follows. What are the moral risks to the organization; its staff; the subject; and third parties? Can the operation be justified morally as well as legally? Is there a danger that the very essence of the ECHR[3] will be breached as well as the Article 8 rights in question? What are the risks of not doing anything? A second model for managing risk, known as PLAICE (physical, legal, assets, information and technology, compromise, and environment), had even less of a focus on the concept of ethics and morality.

---

[3] The Convention for the Protection of Human Rights and Fundamental Freedoms, generally shortened to 'European Convention on Human Rights'.

Juvenile informant application

Most of the time the gatekeepers ensured that applications had properly considered all the issues, and if they were unsure of what my tolerance level of risk was likely to be they would informally run a scenario past me to establish my view. On one occasion an application for a juvenile informant came before me where the individual concerned had about eight significant risk factors attached. Ordinarily this would have been rejected by the gatekeepers in the Covert Source Management Unit prior to formal application, however, since it had reached me and it had caused me to question my risk tolerance thresholds, I decided to allow a formal presentation from the applicants to see if what they were seeking to achieve was both proportionate and necessary. I remember their enthusiasm to use the troubled teenager to gather intelligence on serious crime committed on his estate and I mentioned my consideration of the leadership technique I made reference to earlier of the 'mum and dad test' in situations like this. The team eagerly and passionately responded, 'Don't worry we've met with his mother and she is fully supportive of his use, she thinks we'll be good role models for him.' They had misunderstood my application of the test; I had not meant his former-prostitute mother, who now wanted to live off his earnings, it was their own mothers' views I needed them to consider as part of the process. Needless to say, their application was unsuccessful.

The second case example involves a different set of challenges, when I was the strategic lead for Operation Yewtree in 2012. The Metropolitan Police Service (MPS) was still dealing with the consequences of the revelations about the relationship of the police service with News International and the Filkin (2012) and Leveson (2012) reports, leading to a strained relationship with the news media.

Operation Yewtree

As ITV's 'Exposure' documentary broke the story about the allegations of sexual abuse by the late Jimmy Savile, I was part of a senior group of colleagues charged with deciding on how best to respond to the groundswell of public concern that was emerging. The CEO of the Child Exploitation and On-line Protection (CEOP) Centre had already taken the wise decision to engage with the National Society for the Prevention of Cruelty to Children (NSPCC) to provide a helpline facility for victims. Surrey Police, one of our smallest forces, had already carried out an investigation into some of the allegations, and although MPS staff were providing analytical support to CEOP who had the national lead on policy, there was no overall national investigative response.

In the days after the ITV programme, there were an ever-increasing number of victims coming forward to both the NSPCC and police. As some of their allegations focused on BBC Television Centre there were only really two options: re-activate the Surrey inquiry or open a new MPS-led review using our wider resources. The needs of the victims were paramount, although the reputational risks to the police service were also evident in a subject area beset by challenges in recent years over our response to the investigation of serious sexual offences, which had significantly undermined public confidence in reporting such crimes. My instincts told me the right thing to do was to take on the inquiry as the lead force and to invite the NSPCC to join us in a joint investigation to ensure we met the needs of the victims, undoubtedly the best decision of my six months leading this incredibly high-profile inquiry. The NSPCC's presence ensured transparency and challenge to our decision-making throughout, it demonstrated our victim focus as they addressed the perspectives of victims directly through the media to complement our operational updates and practically through access to their 24-hour helpline.

Our activity dominated the news headlines for 14 consecutive days, making this the second biggest news story of 2012, after the London Olympics. Coverage continued well into 2014, with the prosecution of other prominent individuals as a direct result of the high profile of the police/NSPCC response. We maintained the culture of challenge and transparency with the addition of the CEO of the National Association for People Abused in Childhood (NAPAC) to our gold group. The parallel investigations by the media were a cause for concern and we had to develop an inclusion strategy to protect our sensitive information whilst managing the media's insatiable appetite for facts and information. Balancing transparency with confidentiality whilst under intense scrutiny was never going to be easy, and having a strong group of critical friends, coordinated through a separate stakeholder forum, was key to the success of Operation Yewtree. This latter group grew to include a number of lawyers representing the different interests and reviews that were underway at a national level. This led at times to some interesting debates on their legal perspectives of our approach which needed to be balanced with the ethically based victim focus of the joint police/NSPCC response. Backed by senior figures from NSPCC/NAPAC, I made sure that the victims' voice was always the loudest.

Throughout this time I needed to ensure an impartial and neutral stance as we faced demands for information from across government, the BBC, reviewing lawyers, health trusts, and the media. My team needed to maintain high standards of professionalism and operational security to maintain the integrity of the investigation and thereby ensure victim confidence. The results of this ethical approach speak for themselves, with reporting of sexual abuse to police increasing by 17%. The NSPCC found the Operation Yewtree effect to be enduring, having to recruit 20 extra full-time staff for their helpline in 2014. Many more victims have now received the recognition and support they deserve as a direct result of our approach. Most significantly, the annual crime figures released by the Office for National Statistics in October 2014 have shown a 21% increase nationally in the recording of sexual offences, and the NSPCC has seen a similar rise in reporting of child abuse, primarily about abuse that is occurring today rather than the historical abuse being investigated by Operation Yewtree.

My reflections and considerations to ensure that my police leadership style and actions were ethical were taken at a time when there was little by way of academic writing or theories that could assist me as a police leader. Although I drew upon the police Code of Conduct and reports from HMIC to inform my ethical considerations, it would have been useful to have had a defined structure to support my decision-making process. Hopefully, this is about to change. In July 2014, the College of Policing issued a new Code of Ethics for policing, which was mentioned earlier in this chapter, and sets out the principles and standards of behaviour that officers and staff should adhere to. These are now being communicated across forces and will be embedded in the service over the coming years. Many forces are considering ethics committees as a forum to support decision-making in relation to the ethical dilemmas that police leaders have to consider, either as part of operations or for the organization itself, as I have illustrated in my two case studies. The benefits of an ethics committee enabled me, as a leader, to consider aspects of ethical dilemmas and the consequences of decisions that I would not have contemplated by myself. We developed an ethics committee in one of the most morally contentious areas of policing, covert operations, where it could be argued that due to their secretive nature this could not possibly be implemented. We proved that argument wrong, and the benefit to the organization and community was immeasurable. The Code of Ethics is unequivocal in stating that those in leadership roles are critical role models: 'The right leadership will encourage ethical behaviour. Those who are valued, listened to and well led are likely to feel a greater sense of belonging, and so be more likely to take pride in their work and act with integrity.'[4] I sincerely hope those who follow in my footsteps bring the Code to life and live by the principles it promotes, ensuring we maintain the public's confidence and continue to police by consent.

Shared Reflections

Standards and principles of behaviour expected from police officers have been embedded in a range of oaths and codes since the inception of the modern police service, but it is only recently that the police organization has articulated these into a specific code of ethics. Whether this newly introduced Code of Ethics has the capacity to enhance the integrity and ethical consciousness of those that work within the police organization is yet to be seen. A cynic would ask: how can a written code of instructions affect the behaviour of those who would otherwise engage in wrongdoing? Or put another way, can the principles and standards of behaviour defined in the Code of Ethics foster ethical sensibilities? Most officers who join the police service do so because they want to make a positive contribution to society and make it a safer place. Thus, the Code of Ethics provides a basis for

---

[4] Code of Ethics 2014, para 1.3.4.

these officers to think about how they apply the principles in practice and reflect on how the standards can have a positive effect upon their behaviour.

Yet, policing is a profession under immense scrutiny for unethical and corrupt behaviour. The Code of Ethics in and of itself cannot redress this matter. What is also required is compelling leadership, together with the development of an organizational knowledge of ethics and ethical issues within an effective communication system. An ethical culture can only occur if staff are comprehensively informed about how the essence of the Code plays out in practice in their day-to-day functions, and is clearly demonstrated in the behaviours and actions of the organization's leaders.

While the Code is beneficial in providing a definition of ethics for the purposes of policing, how the spirit of the Code is applied within operational practice will also be significant. Unlike many other organizations with codes of ethics, the complexities and challenges of police work are far more intricate and involved. After all, a lawyer or medic can refuse to provide their services to members of the public who threaten them with violence or wield a weapon; a police officer does not have the luxury of walking away from these challenging and often threatening situations. While the principles of the Code provide the framework for the behaviours of officers tending to these incidents, it will require leadership to effectively confront the ethical dilemmas and challenges these situations present for both the organization and for individual officers (see Waddington et al 2013). Thus there is a duty on police leaders to ensure that professional ethics are intricately woven into the very heart of not only what they do, but what they are ultimately responsible for as leaders of the organization.

As the Filkin Report (2012) identified, when the behaviour of leaders does not match the standards expected of their staff, the consequences are harmful and destructive to both individuals and the organization and the community. Moreover, Operation Yewtree demonstrated that where leadership was innovative in addressing ethical dilemmas (the creation of an ethically focused group involving partner agencies and community members to assist officers in their decision-making process had substantial benefits), it improved public confidence sufficiently to enable victims of crime to come forward and report incidents to the police. The setting up of such a forum for stakeholders to act as a reference group also developed knowledge of potential ethical dilemmas in relation to the operation. By extending the range of expertise to include partners and community members, the deliberation of ethical issues enabled considered reflection on the potential positive and negative consequences for various parties to which the operation might give rise, and how these consequences could be mitigated, or effectively managed.

Leadership is also about taking ethical risks; risks that may challenge current wisdom or policy on an issue. But what one person views as ethical, another will see as unethical. Others may wish to adhere to tried and tested policy, even though ethical reflection on the issue may indicate other suitable approaches. The paucity of academic research in this area cannot assist police officers who seek theories and paradigms to explore their thinking. This will be a case of continuing practice guiding academic theories, rather than research-based theories directing practice.

One of the greatest challenges for policing leaders will be how they manage to facilitate the duty of challenge, where staff are confronted by those whose behaviour falls short of the expectations set out in the Code of Ethics. In a rank-and-file organization, where the tradition of following orders is embedded within a hierarchical arrangement, officers at the lower part of the structure may be reticent to challenge those in more senior positions. What constitutes a suitable challenge and when it is appropriate for that challenge to take place has yet to be explored in practice.

Recommended Reading

Bew, Lord Paul (2014), 'Ethics in Practice: Promoting Ethical Standards in Public Life', Committee on Standards in Public Life, London

Filkin, E (2012), 'The Ethical Issues Arising from the Relationship between the Police and Media', Report commissioned by the Commissioner, Metropolitican Police Service, London

Kleinig, J (1996), *The Ethics of Policing* (Cambridge: Cambridge University Press)

MacVean, A, Spindler, P, and Solf, C (eds) (2013), *Handbook of Policing, Ethics and Professional Standards* (London: Routledge)

References

Allen, K and Friedman, B (2010), 'Affective Learning: A Taxonomy for Teaching Social Work Values' 7(2) *Journal of Social Work Values and Ethics*, at <http://www.jswvearchives.com/fall2010/f10neuman.pdf> (accessed 6 July 2015)

Association of Chief Police Officers Scotland (2004), 'Statement of Ethical Principles', ACPOS, Edinburgh

Bew, Lord Paul (2014), 'Ethics in Practice: Promoting Ethical Standards in Public Life', Committee on Standards in Public Life, London

Black, J (2003), 'Media Ethics: Between Iraq and a Hard Place', Honors Excellence Occasional Papers Series, Vol II, No 2, Florida International University, Miami

College of Policing (2013), 'Public Consultation, Draft Code of Ethics: Principles and Standards of Professional Behaviour for the Police Forces of England and Wales', College of Policing, Coventry

College of Policing (2014), 'Code of Ethics: A Code of Practice for the Principles and Standards of Professional Behaviour for the Policing Profession of England and Wales', College of Policing, Coventry

Committee on Standards in Public Life (2013), 'Standards Matter: A Review of Best Practice in Promoting Good Behaviour in Public Life', Committee on Standards in Public Life, The Stationery Office, London

Congress, E, (1999), *Social Work Values and Ethics: Identifying and Resolving Professional Dilemmas* (Belmont, CA: Wadsworth Group)

Dolgoff, R, Lowenberg, FM, and Harrington, D (2009), *Ethical Decisions for Social Work Practice* (8th edn, Belmont, CA: Brooks and Cole)

Filkin, E (2012), 'The Ethical Issues Arising from the Relationship between the Police and Media', Report commissioned by the Commissioner, Metropolitan Police Service, London

Fleming, J and O'Reilly, J (2013), 'Addressing the Scenario: Integrity, Insights and Dangerous Liaisons' in Waddington, P, Kleinig, J, and Wright, M (eds), *Professional Police Practice: Scenarios and Dilemmas* (Oxford: OUP) 48

Harfield, C (2012), 'Police Informers and Professional Ethics' 31(2) *Criminal Justice Ethics* 73

Harfield, C and Harfield, K (2008), *Covert Investigation* (2nd edn, Oxford: OUP)

HMIC (1999), 'Police Integrity: Securing and Maintaining Public Confidence', TSO, London

HMIC (2011), 'Without Fear or Favour—A Review of Police Relationships', TSO, London

House of Commons Home Affairs Select Committee Report (2014), 'Leadership and Standards in the Police. Third Report of Session 2013–14', HC 67–21, TSO, London

Hughes, J (2013), 'Theories of Ethical Standards and Professional Policing' in MacVean, A, Spindler, P, and Solf, C (eds), *Handbook of Policing, Ethics and Professional Standards* (London: Routledge) 7

Kelly, Sir Christopher (2013), *Standards Matter: A Review of Best Practice in Promoting Good Behaviour in Public Life* (Cm 8519), Fourteenth Report, Committee on Standards in Public Life, London

Kelly, P (2010), *Essentials of Nursing Leadership and Management* (2nd edn, US: Delmar Cengage Learning, 2010)

Kleinig, J (1996), *The Ethics of Policing* (Cambridge: Cambridge University Press)

Leveson, LJ (2012), 'The Leveson Inquiry: An Inquiry into the Culture, Practices and Ethics of the Press: Executive Summary and Recommendations', TSO, London

Lewis, P and Evans, R (2013), 'Police Spies Stole Identities of Dead Children' *The Guardian*, 3 February, 1

Macvean, A and Neyroud, P (2012), *Police Ethics and Values* (London: Sage)

Manning, P (1977), *The Social Organisation of Policing* (Cambridge MA: MIT Press)

Mansfield, M (2013), 'Unethical Policing on Trial' in MacVean, A, Spindler, P, and Solf, C (eds), *Handbook of Policing, Ethics and Professional Standards* (London: Routledge) 214

Mason, R (2013), 'Plebgate: David Davies Calls for Royal Commission into Police Ethics', *The Guardian*, 23 October, 1

Miller, S and Blackler, J (2005), *Ethical Issues in Policing* (Aldershot: Ashgate)

Neyroud, P and Beckley, A (2001), *Policing, Ethics and Human Rights* (Cullompton: Willan)

O'Neill, S (2014), 'You Can't Trust Police', *The Times*, 6 March, 1

Pollock, J (1998), *Ethics in Crime and Justice* (Belmont, CA: Wadsworth)

Punch, M (2009), *Police Corruption: Deviance, Accountability and Reform in Policing* (Cullompton: Willan)

Reiner, R (2010), *The Politics of the Police* (4th edn, Oxford: OUP)

Report of the Hillsborough Independent Panel (2012), HC581, TSO, London

Taylor, W (2005), 'The Review of Police Disciplinary Arrangements Report', HMSO, London

Taylor, W (2013), 'The Taylor Review' in MacVean, A, Spindler, P, and Solf, C (eds), *Handbook of Policing, Ethics and Professional Standards* (London: Routledge) 17

Waddington, P, Kleinig, J, and Wright, M (2013) (eds), *Professional Police Practice: Scenarios and Dilemmas* (Oxford: OUP)

7

'Say it Loud Without a Frown; Good Investigators Write it Down'

Theories of Leading Ethical Investigations

John GD Grieve and Robin Bhairam

> *All too often police officers appear defensive, limited, robotic and pun intended, a little plodding. The physical courage of the thin blue line is not in doubt. However its intellectual calibre and* leadership *are.*
>
> *Anonymous Editorial,* The Times, *26 March 2011, 2 (emphasis added)*

Introduction

This chapter considers some useful theories of investigation leadership, such as there are, written by academics and practitioners, set in the complex, ever-shifting, politically contentious, and risky contemporary moral landscape of policing. The single most important recent publication on this topic is by Newburn, Williamson, and Wright (2007), who note that there has been relatively little systematic research into how investigations are conducted and hence led. This is not strictly true and is modestly disproved by a case study of one of the editors—Williamson (see later). The 2007 volume includes Innes' rigorous account of investigative processes. Publication milestones which pick up the access and impact issues for practitioners are the series from Oxford University Press, and Blackstone's Practical Policing (eg Harfield and Harfield 2012). Volumes were also published by Routledge (MacVean et al 2013; Brown 2014), Wiley

(Carson et al 2007), Sage (Grieve et al 2007), and notably Willan (eg Hall et al 2009).

Two early developments in the academic theory of investigations are in the fields of psychology (see Carson et al 2007; Alison and Crego 2008 for examples and a summary and chronology) and in intelligence-led policing (see eg James 2013) for an up-to-date overview). However, it is agued here that these are all direct descendants of Hans Gross's work on investigation, theory practice, and leadership (originally published in 1893, translated in 1904, and with a third edition in 1934 introduced by the senior detective at New Scotland Yard), whose account of leading investigations is very similar to that eventually derived by Summerscale (2008) and Schpayer-Makov (2011). Moreover, they all parallel the teaching at the Detective Training School (DTS) set up in London in 1902, with now over a century of the application of Gross's theory.

As the founding fathers of the new police, Rowan and Mayne concluded that there were two policing imperatives. The primary imperative was the prevention of crime, the second was the task of investigation and detection. This latter is where Gross applied his thinking. These two imperatives emerged during the introduction of the 'new' police, and derived from Peel and Bentham. They remain relevant in the 21st century (see also Grieve 2014). The two imperatives are linked in that a proactive investigation (eg intelligence-led) could prevent crime. The primacy of prevention does not preclude a paradigm, indeed an imperative, of investigation (Ascoli 1979; Critchley 1967).

Significant Milestones in Investigative Leadership

The history of ethical investigations is complex and it is not the task of this chapter to provide a comprehensive literature review. For those interested in the influence of United States literature, you may wish to consult Vollmer (1936) and Wilson (1950). Savage (2007) has a helpful account of the trade winds of police thinking across the Atlantic; he also covers areas such as new police management thinking about mentoring and monitoring those investigating volume crime that are not dealt with here.

The core task for the senior investigating officer (SIO), or officer in overall command (OIC), or national coordinator is to set the strategic direction of the investigation, including its philosophy. Investigative reform milestones that emphasized the paradigms were realized under Howard Vincent in the 1880s (eg Vincent 1881: 104); the detail was picked up by Sir Edward Henry (Ascoli 1979; Morris 2007), and re-emerged in the reforms of Sir Robert Mark in the 1970s (Mark 1978), then in the Peter Sutcliffe Investigation (the Yorkshire Ripper) in the late 1970s and Sir Peter Imbert's Plus Program in the 1990s, which sought cultural changes, not least in investigative ethics. Most recently there are those reforms that followed the Stephen Lawrence Public Inquiry and its aftermath (Hall et al 2009; Ellison 2014) and other contemporary causes célèbres (Brain 2010; Savage 2007; May 2013). In summary, these milestones in reform reflect theory and application programmes responding not just to unethical investigative leadership but other kinds of reform, some driven from within the service (see Brain 2010; Grieve 2007; Savage 2007 for chronology and typology). The role of leadership in investigation was most clearly articulated as applied theory and practice in Lord Laming's Victoria Climbie Inquiry (Laming 2003) and quickly followed by the Association of Chief Police Officers (2003; 2005).

So what is the link? The impact of theory on practice Inspector Whicher and his mid-19th century investigative suspicions are thoughtfully described by Kate Summerscale (2008: 157–9 especially), who explores the investigative imperative and the ingredient investigative task of detection. She explains that the word 'detection' comes from 'de tegere', Latin for 'uncover', hence 'un-roof '. Lifting the domestic roof off is an unpleasant and, considered by some an un-English, task. Despite the statistical likelihood of being murdered by someone you know, the investigator has to ask how likely that connection—specifically in the case under investigation—was. And can you justify and explain that investigative thread, morally and objectively (ie in a way that is open to third-party examination, eg at an inquest, to the satisfaction of a coroner and jury or to some other form of public inquiry)? In Whicher's case, he could not provide that justification at an inquest, although he was proved right in time, although too late for his own reputation (Summerscale 2008). This is the investigator's dilemma to this day.

In the days when an SIO's tasks involved training the bulk of the team assigned to them, it is sometimes argued that there was no privacy in murder investigations. It had to be explained to murder squads that people lied for lots of reasons which were nothing to do with the murder they were investigating. The witnesses even told the truth in ways that were less than convincing. For example, sometimes witnesses looked as if they were lying, the analysed time line of their activities was all askew, and their statement to police investigators was wrong, all because they were concealing an affair with a neighbour (Beveridge 1959; Du Rose 1971; Herridge 1993). Sometimes, then, the application of the theory of the investigative imperative is an unhappy and unpleasant duty. The ethical leadership role is to consider whether to follow a particular line of inquiry, when and how to terminate it, and how to do this with the least unreasonable, unnecessary, unjustifiable pain to the subjects.

This was sometimes better explored in fiction. By coincidence Inspector Field's (the real life model for Charles Dickens' deeply ambiguous Inspector Bucket and an ancestor of Peter Falk's Colombo), mentor in Bleak House was Inspector Whicher, illustrating the crossover between fiction and practice. As late as 1969, a BBC drama from 1959 'Who, me?' (see Sydney-Smith 2002: 118–38) was being used as training material at the DTS in London and Devon and Cornwall). Barnett (1978), a retired SIO and novelist, is another neat example where the investigative process is explored in some procedural detail.

Some later investigative developments and a possible 'golden age'

The ambiguity identified so early by Dickens in the form of fiction and confirmed by Summerscale (2008) and Schpayer-Markov (2011) turned into provable corruption and led to the appointment of Howard Vincent (1881), who was called in to oversee reforms in investigation in the late 19th century following a series of corruption allegations against senior investigative leaders (Ascoli 1979; Critchley 1967). Later, the Czech Austrian investigator Hans Gross (later with Norman Kendall) (1893 and 1934) wrote a handbook of investigation which included theory. It was translated into English and ran to many editions. There were also many manuals and instruction books which emphasized the importance of first steps (literally and figuratively) at the scene of a crime and the primacy of the criminal justice system. Gross identified the concept of orientation, ie the physical identification of the crime scene, its context, and environment and all that implies for forensic science work. He identified not only the conceptual environment of the law but also of community and comparative case analysis. This formed the foundation of the disciplines of fingerprints, forensic science, community impact, and intelligence-led policing, and resulted in the establishment of the course supplied by the DTS. Orientation is achieved not just by leaders visiting a crime scene but by exploring the wider social, political, demographic, and conceptual environment (Chesshyre 1989; 2001; NPIA 2005).

Gross was translated into English in 1906 and reprinted up to 1962. The foreword to the 1934 edition is by the New Scotland Yard (NSY) Assistant Commissioner Crime, Norman Kendall. It was a text book for many years. The DTS was created by Sir Edward Henry in 1902 and the curriculum was upgraded in 1913 (Morris 2007). Investigative skills were taught from that time until the present by learning the law and what was needed by investigators as evidence to show where evidence and law had been woven together using lectures on forensic science, identification, and case studies by the leaders of successful inquiries, detailing their evolving tactics (Beveridge 1959; Du Rose 1971). An advanced course on how to manage investigations was augmented by the Police Staff College (PSC), covering series and cross-border crimes, the requirements of an OIC following the debacle of a series of Yorkshire murders in the late 1970s and early 1980s (Savage 2007; Brain 2010). These latter evolving tactics increasingly included academic theory and research, in particular psychology (see eg Carson 2007: 407–25; Grieve 2007: 39–64).

A golden age? It is sometimes argued that the golden age of 'who dun it' fiction is paralleled by a golden age of equally fictitious autobiographies of ex-detectives; who were aided and abetted by newspaper crime reporters (see eg Mark 1978; Chibnall 1977: 172). This chapter takes a different view of these autobiographies; at the very least they disclose an ideal ethical investigative leadership, albeit in different environments and contexts. They should not be taken at face value or by themselves be cited as evidence, but be subject to the ABC rule (*Accept nothing at face value, Believe no one without Confirmation or Corroboration*).

However, they are a form of evidence and the writers were engaged in teaching at the DTS and hence handed on these ideals. Contemporary cases are included in the DTS's syllabus (see eg Divall 1929 or Barnett 1978; Beveridge 1959).

Other milestones of some investigative leadership theories

There are causes célèbres, public inquiries, and some scandals which throw a light on theories of investigative ethical (and in some cases unethical) leadership. Space does not allow either detailed accounts of all of these or an examination of their impact, which has been explored elsewhere. One example may help. Sir Robert Mark (1978) led the shift in investigative leadership through a major anti-corruption programme, which in turn led to the rise of internal investigation departments. Departments in time led to complaints systems, independent oversight, and eventually completely independent/external investigation (Savage 2007; Brain 2010). The importance of this to the arguments presented here is that this produced a system of quality control on investigations which constantly revisited the ideals. The independent inquiries into alleged malpractice still had to either franchise leading investigators from other locations, serving in professional standards departments, or ex police officers, because they needed their expertise (Savage 2007).

Lord Scarman wrote, 'the police are the law's frontline. If they falter the law suffers', and 'The more complicated police work becomes the more necessary it is to ensure that the principles of policing are not lost in the complexity of the action' (Scarman, letter to the author 1993). In the post-Stephen Lawrence world, inquiries use independent advice from Gold or Diamond or even Platinum groups, which take a strategic leadership role, with the SIO, in considering ethical investigative perspectives of the moral landscape of policing, as part of Scarman's complexity of action (Hall et al 2009).

Lord Laming and his adviser, the experienced and thoughtful Detective Superintendent (now Dr) John Fox, articulated the leadership applied theory as an open mind, a healthy scepticism, and an investigative approach (Laming 2003: para 14.78). This is a recent manifestation of the traditional ABC theory, which can be traced back through Gross to Whicher and can be used by a leader in determining how to keep everyone on the team with an open mind, how to keep the scepticism reasonable and healthy as opposed to cynical, and how to ensure that the complex investigative systems that were sometimes called 'the machine' (Beveridge 1959: 9) are functioning to quality control the investigative actions and the evidence that is derived from them.

How does this fit with some other more general academic theories of leadership for investigation?

In 2003, Rob Adlam and Peter Villiers (formerly of the PSC, Bramshill—Rob a psychologist and Peter a philosopher) analysed 150 accounts and theories of (policing) leadership, some of which are backed by rigorous academic theory. They came up with six principles, of which two are particularly pertinent:

- *Principle of professional excellence.* This can be incredibly complex, on the one hand keeping up with changes in legal interpretation, academic research, and theory, and on the other keeping track of the impact of community concerns, and how these two threads interact.

- *Principle of endurance with integrity.* This relates to resilience and ethics despite many pressures, complexities, and ambiguities in personal and public lives. This second principle is the basis of long-term endurance—lifetime accountability—for the decisions taken by an ethical investigative leader (Adlam and Villiers 2003).

In the Adlam and Villiers volume, philosopher Roger Scruton wrote about the constabulary duty of 'doing the right thing' based on Kantian principles (Scruton 2003). Scruton balances duty with respect for the rights of others, not least that of 'due process' (Scruton 2003: 78), since without due process all other rights are ineffective. Another frequently used account is learning from military leadership models, which influenced policing from the earliest days. This, too, is covered by Adlam and Villiers. Another military leadership theory example used by the PSC and by the DTS London was that of Adair (1983), whose emphasis on the team, the task, and the individual was influential in the 1980s and 1990s.

McConville et al's work (1991) is another important milestone with considerable influence on DTSs and the PSC. The authors critically describe criteria in the risks—mistakes (at best)—police investigations might produce. They argue that a series of investigative steps form a model: first, that social factors define a suspect population for a crime for the police—the investigation is not a search by leaders for truth but rather confirmation of a view they have formed; second, that police detention places a suspect in a hostile environment and interviews take place on investigators' terms; third, that police manipulate 'paper reality' and case files dominate the criminal justice system. This is sometimes called case management or building, where the intention is to implicate the suspect. Fourth, they argue that the Crown Prosecution Service was judged (at that time) to be subordinate and not independent of police; and fifth and finally, that informal rules are maintained by investigators and that due process, or rather a search for the truth within a framework of law and human rights, does not dominate the investigative process. The result can be miscarriages of justice and calamity. Although there was, unsurprisingly, little agreement from investigators about that theoretical model of investigations, it did have an impact on thinking. Handling and preventing those steps or perceptions becoming a reality, and hence a possible calamity, became a risk leadership task for the SIO.

By 2005, this prevention of calamity had become a long-term project to professionalize investigations and strand three of that project was concerned with investigative leaders' skills. Amongst the many elements covered for SIOs and OICs were investigative strategy, evidential opportunities, hypothesis building and testing, immediate priorities and long-term direction, linking and series crimes, use of technology, house-to-house inquiries, search-and-arrest strategies, media and communication, community impact, critical incidents, governance, and reporting upwards (ACPO 2003: 5; NPIA 2005; Stelfox 2007).

In his excellent observations on homicide investigations, Innes (2003; 2007) explores the role of SIOs and their tasks in identifying strategic directions and evidential opportunities for their inquiries. He categorizes murders as self-solvers (called, in this author's experience, 'where's he [sic] gone'), whodunits, unsolved, and in extremis. They all require variations in investigative strategy, in extremis, having a very high profile in the media (Innes 2003: 247), being amongst the most difficult. Innes looks at the theory of the construction of a narrative by investigators which in some ways includes the more benign elements of McConville et al (1991) (which he cites) and considers ethical variations. Innes also develops the concept of 'concatenation', pathways through chaos, or perhaps the bewildering complexity faced by the SIO as he/she develops what Innes sees as three stages or movements of the investigation: first, identifying and acquiring information or evidence, the evidential opportunities; second, interpreting and understanding; and finally ordering, representing the evidence in such a way that it can be used by, and survive the tests of the Criminal Justice System (Innes 2007: 255). The practical implications for the SIO were spelled out in a handbook for defence lawyers (Ede and Shepherd 2000) and a response is set out in Hall et al (2009) and Crego and Alison (2008).

Conclusion

An example of an ethical investigative leader will help to pull this section together. Tom Williamson was a police officer, investigative team leader, academic, researcher, theologian, entrepreneur, and ethical leader as reformer. A man with true values, concerned with a search for the truth and due process of law and duty. This chapter began with Tom Williamson in his role with Newburn and Wright in their seminal work (2007). Tom bestrode many identities, not least (though very different in style, access, and impact from the 'golden age' autobiographies) explaining and understanding the investigator's task. David Rose's (2007) obituary of Tom reads:

> Building from the analysis of mishandled interrogations and miscarriages of justice contained in his 1990 Kent University PhD, Williamson was at the forefront of a radical shift in police interview techniques and training, determined that the one-time emphasis on 'getting a cough' at any cost should be replaced by a neutral search for reliable and durable evidence ... the drive towards what Williamson called 'ethical policing' dominated his working life.

This is the exact opposite of McConville et al's (1991) description of the factors at play in the police investigations they observed. It also gives the lie to the *Times* editorial with which this chapter started. Williamson provided access to theory concerning the most basic investigator's task, that of asking questions, which impacted in practical terms on others who follow in his wake. This was true, strategic ethical investigative leadership with considerable operational and tactical implications for all kinds of crime investigations.

Practitioner's Perspective

'Oh, uh, just one more thing'—this was the immortal catch phrase that often resonated from the scruffy, absent-minded, but ironically inspirational fictitious detective, Lieutenant Columbo.[1] Fumbling through his bits of scrap paper as he drew closer to snaring his quarry, this phrase was a subtle reminder to the viewer that behind the apparent chaotic, clumsy 'flat foot', there often sits a deep thinking, logical, systematic, and thoroughly professional practitioner. In fact, so effective was this phrase in raising expectation and suspense, that it was shamelessly embraced by none other than Steve Jobs at the launch of every new Apple product (Isaacson 2011).

People are fascinated by the apparent 'magical' skills, courage, and tenacity portrayed in police fiction (Reiner 2000: 148–9), and as John has stated, the public's attraction to the 'whodunit', as we see with the likes of Dickens or Wittgenstein, is quite compelling, particularly in relation to the tenacious, forensic, or behavioural practitioner. Of course, the reality is often very different, even with the significant recent developments in technology, detection rates in the United Kingdom still sit at under 30% of recorded crime (Home Office 2013), and whilst the technology is there to support SIOs, in reality, quite often it is essential to go back to the first principles that emanate from the founding imperatives that John describes.

Developing the 'senior leader'

In policing, the term 'senior leader' can often refer to the most senior officer present at the time, whether that be a sergeant or a chief inspector; however, for the benefit of this discussion, senior leader will refer to any rank over inspector[2] and in this specific context, detective inspector.

As an investigative practitioner with the Metropolitan Police Service for 29 years, I have been fortunate and privileged to have been involved in some of the most fascinating and challenging investigations in contemporary times. These include high-profile homicides, serious sexual offences, counter-terrorism, and serious crime investigations, including being the SIO for the post-investigation following the London disorders of August 2011. Over this long period I have seen the architectural structure of serious crime investigation develop from the card-

---

[1] Fictitious procedural US TV detective played by Peter Falk, 1968–2003.

[2] Constable, sergeant, inspector, chief inspector, superintendent, chief superintendent (also detective equivalent to each), then ACPO Ranks.

indexing, 'paper'-based, smoke-filled rooms of 'murder squads', into the clinical, sophisticated, complex, and technologically driven major incident rooms.

Techniques have ranged from knocking on doors and seeking out witnesses or informants, which, in my opinion, is still one of the most 'sophisticated', success-ful, but now sadly perhaps underused tactics in the investigator's toolbox, to the development of sophisticated, hi-tech covert tactics, the use of CCTV, and of course social media intelligence. I have been fortunate and privileged to have worked with and learnt from some of the most tenacious, inspirational, and modest detectives in modern times. Many of these individuals are not 'famous' or even 'of rank', but often display exemplary qualities of 'investigative leadership'. Quite often, like Columbo, using the building blocks of investigative history and the legacy of the theorists and detectives that came before, they work quietly and tenaciously, building their case, piece by piece, striving to ensure, as we shall see, that even today, almost 200 years later, the founding imperatives of policing are fulfilled.

The founding imperatives—using the literature to catch 'the bad guys'

Leading these professionals has been an inspirational experience, and understand-ing how they develop and contribute to the body of investigative epistemology is a necessary skill for the senior leader to acquire. The development of professional knowledge is a culmination of experiential practice developed over many years through a discursive dialogue of reflexive practitioner-based activity (Schon 1983). The rich philosophy of Michael Foucault helps us to understand just how such a constantly developing epistemological discourse can contribute to the shaping and development of investigative practice over many years (Foucault 1991). This concept solidifies how the founding imperatives of Peel, Rowan and Mayne, Bentham, and Colquhoun underpin or reinforce the investigative theories of the likes of Vincent (1881), Gross and Kendall (1934 [1893]), Vollmer (1936), Wilson (1950), and Moriarty (1955), and still remain relevant to SIOs today. At a time when increasing accountability at command level is prevalent, the key compo-nents that are found in these theories provide a robust structure for an SIO to reflect upon when devising strategic direction and hypothesis setting throughout each critical phase of an investigation. That is not to say that these alone are the sole solution, but as we shall see they are still an integral part of the reflexive leader's armoury.

Trying to unravel the complexities of an investigation within an academic framework is likely to distract investigative leaders from their task. Due to the rigours, complexities, and sometimes subjectivity of academic thinking, attempt-ing to apply an academic theory to an investigation can be like placing an intricate silk table doily over an antique dresser, where actually an industrialized protector is what is really required. But wider professional expectations are changing, and in order to professionalize the role of the investigator, the senior policing leader must start to engage with and understand academic thinking if they are to become as professionally credible as their peers in medicine, law, science, and academia.

I was encouraged by the then Deputy Assistant Commissioner, John Grieve, to start that journey several years ago. The impact it had upon my critical thinking and practitioner approach was significant in that I started to view the whole criminal justice process through a series of entirely different, long-term, and more complex lenses than just the linear 'results-driven' outcome. This has allowed me to lead and engage with senior stakeholders with a more precise focus when dealing with some of the wider, more entrenched, long-term policing challenges. As an example, the literature of Smith and Gray (1983), Anderson (2000), and Pitts (2008) can be used to explain that the increase of 'youth gang culture' is broader and more sociologically deep-rooted than just 'kids aspiring to be gangsters'. Academic research develops the criminological mosaic and can start to assist the practitioner not only with the 'who' and the 'what', but also develop a greater understanding of the 'why'.

State-of-the-art technology now sits at the heart of law enforcement. Hi-tech methods of surveillance and technical support, whilst heavily governed by a strict legislative framework, are still the primary tactical considerations for most investigators. However, one should never lose sight of the fundamental and founding principles that are hidden away in the literature, but reinforced through most training programmes. For example, I encourage any team I lead to underpin each investigation with these simple fundamental principles:

• *Assume* nothing;
• *Believe* no one;
• Check everything[3] (then check it again!)

I remind them that whilst 'whizzy' technological gadgets are impressive, even Eric Clapton had to learn the basic 'G C D' chords before he rose to greatness, chords he still very much relies on today!

The point is that the basic principles which arise from the theory, actually complement modern methods, as opposed to hindering them. For example, many years ago whilst investigating a series of serious sexual assaults I recall being mocked for tenaciously collecting and recording everything I found on the route to the point of entry of a victim's home, resulting in over a hundred exhibits and a collection of pocket book records. The case went unsolved. However, about 15 years later I received a call from a 'cold case' team who informed me that a single cigarette butt I had retrieved from that victim's shed had finally been linked through DNA to a man who had recently been arrested for an attempted rape. There are two important features here:

• the collection of evidence; and
• the recording of evidence.

---

[3] A slight variation on John's interpretation!

The phrase 'If it isn't written down it didn't happen' is often attributed in policing mythology to Michael Mansfield QC; however, it has been the mantra of the detective for many years. Its origins are irrelevant but it is perhaps THE most important facet of investigation management.

Managing upwards is also a critical area where first principles can be beneficial. I truly believe that—linked to the myth of the TV detective—many senior officers who have not been investigators believe the answer to every single crime sits within a police database somewhere. This perception is, of course, nonsense. Applying the first principles of GOYBAKOD (Get off your backside and knock on doors) is still one of the most effective tools in the senior investigator's armoury. To illustrate, I was investigating a serious assault with no leads—not even the identity of the victim, as his wallet had also been stolen. As it was a public holiday, I had limited resources. I formulated my strategy, but was hindered by a very senior officer who suggested that I use the staff to 'trawl' the police databases to 'look for clues'. Mindful of the 'golden hour' principles[4] and with no leads to go on, I took the informed decision to apply basic principles and deploy staff to revisit the core of the crime and conduct house-to-house and street inquires, and within two hours they had identified a significant witness. Assuming nothing, for a number of reasons, I did not *believe* the account this witness gave, so by complementing first principles with 'technological' solutions (CCTV) I tested and *challenged* their statement; it transpired they were actually involved in what subsequently became a murder investigation. This practical application of first principles combined with modern technological techniques resulted in the conviction of three people for murder and robbery.

Further evidence of the success of this unified technique can be found even in large-scale investigations. On 21 October 2013, Pavlo Lapshyn was convicted of the racist murder of Mohammed Saleem, which occurred on 29 April 2013, and also for deploying three improvised explosive devices (IEDs) between 21 June and 12 July 2013, in the West Midlands. He arrived in the United Kingdom from Ukraine on 24 April 2013 and within just five days committed the murder. The investigation had the might of the homicide and national counter-terrorism experts working around the clock, and whilst once again CCTV played a key role, it was 'boots on the ground', knocking on doors that identified and located Lapshyn, who incidentally was, with the exception of one minor misdemeanour in Ukraine, completely unknown to *any* global law enforcement agency (Beale 2013).

Reflection on time as a leader—leading the challenges

Since becoming a senior investigator in 2001, the landscape of criminal investigation has changed dramatically, bringing with it a number of significant fresh

---

[4] The principle that quick and effective response at the scene of crime is imperative to capture best evidence, especially in serious crime.

challenges for senior leaders. Failings in key investigations, such as those involving Stephen Lawrence (Macpherson 1999), Victoria Climbié (Laming 2003), and Baby P (Haringey Council 2009) have put the police service very much in the spotlight, both in terms of media, public scrutiny, and total accountability. With the abolition of police authorities and the introduction of police and crime commissioners (PCCs), the concepts and legacy of constabulary independence, police legitimacy, and police discretion (Reiner 2000: 167–98; Maguire et al 2007: 1025–8; Newburn 2007: 615–17) are now being vigorously challenged.

To meet these increasing challenges, now, more than ever, senior leaders need to be cognizant of their roles and responsibilities, both in terms of their own investigations, and of those under their command. The constant emerging thematic challenges include ethical leadership, trust and confidence, command and control, and the new phrase on the block, 'total grip', which very much reinforces the golden hour principles. In addition, a narrative of risk aversion has also become part of everyday policing practice (Heaton 2011; Houlihan and Giulianotti 2012; Smith 2012), where officers have to negotiate and plan for every possible outcome.

All of this takes time, knowledge, and understanding and SIOs have become the gatekeepers to risk. Whilst some risk is clear and present, it is the slow accrual of risk to which SIOs need to become acutely attuned. It is therefore so important that the senior leader invests time and commitment in themselves and their team to develop this skill to a high level through training, shadowing experienced investigators, applying best practice, and personal development, whether professional or academic. Managing expectations, particularly upwards, also brings fresh challenges. The ability to be strong, to articulate clearly, map out, and take responsibility for decisions, whilst at the same time being supportive to your team, coupled with an ability to challenge upwards based upon a grounded rationale, have become vital characteristics for the emerging or developing leader.

Not every eventuality can be foreseen and when it goes wrong the leader needs to step up, be honest, take responsibility, and look for ways to improve in the future. Therefore it is within this context that the senior policing practitioner needs to start aligning themselves more with the professions such as the law, medicine, or science, both in terms of practitioner- and academic practice-based development. Home Secretary Theresa May reinforced this in a keynote address to the College of Policing in October (May 2013), expressing a desire for police to actively publish in journals and lead on research. Whilst the College seeks to develop this skill through the concept of evidence-based policing, there is still much resistance to academia to be found at all levels with the service itself. Practitioner and epistemological development needs to be expanded beyond the 'training manual', as those leaders who wish to reach the top of their field need to understand that simply being a 'good old bill' will not be enough, they need to add 'a humble, honest, and learned leader' to their credentials in order to be viewed as a competent, credible, and professional leader in this fast-changing landscape.

Within the sanctuary of Reiner's 'canteen' (Reiner 2000: 85–107), a new phrase and challenge has emerged: 'hindsight policing'. As we witness an increasing appetite for the police service to be held to account for historic investigations and practices, such as Stephen Lawrence and Hillsborough (Scraton 2013; Ellison 2014), officers are beginning to feel vulnerable, criticized, and accountable for the acts of their predecessors. Whilst this undoubtedly contributes to low morale and a sceptical workforce, there is a real opportunity for the senior leader to build upon these issues in order to support and develop their teams, which can also make a significant contribution to professionalizing the role of the investigator. Whilst the challenge will be to bring the team along, this is not new territory for the leader to navigate; major police investigations and critical incidents have always been subjected to a level of scrutiny which in turn has resulted in significant policing change (Barrington and Peace 1985; Roycroft et al 2007). Tough as it may be, the message from senior leaders should be that public inquiry and accountability should be seen as instruments of review, learning, and reform.

Looking for new ways to innovate and operate that derive from the learning gained through such public and painful inquiries can only be a good thing. The way we record, map our conduct, and store investigation strategies should form the epistemological basis for future practice development. As with the great scientists, artisans, and philosophers, the senior investigator has a moral and ethical duty to leave behind a legacy of their lifetime of practice to those following on. To me this begins with the day-to-day interaction with the team and accepting that one organization cannot achieve everything alone; as Chief Constable Mike Cunningham notes in Chapter 4 of this work, honest, critical, and professional collaborative partnerships are the key to success.

The phrase 'partnership working', once a professional sound bite, now needs to be an intrinsic part of the investigative strategy. When setting the strategic direction, SIOs need to be thinking wider and deeper, using all the resources they may tap into. Taking risks and thinking outside the 'investigative box' should become key activities. Independent advice should be just that; all too often we turn to our 'critical friends' for advice, but that tactic too now needs to be reviewed. Investigators need to identify critical individuals who are considered hard to reach, invest time in those who will not engage, and be courageous and persistent in that challenge. Again, this is not a new concept and the notion of orientation and prior knowledge of communities (Gross and Kendal, 1934), good local knowledge and understanding of inhabitants (Vollmer 1936; Moriarty 1955), and the overlap of criminal investigation, risk management, community justice, and peacekeeping (Wright, 2002) can be found throughout the literature. It is therefore the responsibility of the leader to instil and encourage this cultural shift within their teams, provide guidance and the framework in which to work, and, most importantly, encourage and support their staff to do things differently, but to do things 'Kantianly' right (Rawls 1980).

'Oh, uh, just one more thing...'

It would be naive and foolhardy to suggest that if all aspiring senior investigators dashed off and got a degree, everything will be fine, in the same way that if they relied solely on databases or other technological wizardries, crime would be solved or reduced. What is suggested is that senior investigators open their minds to the rigours and potential of the theoretical and experimental application found in academic discovery, to adopt a synergistic approach to develop the existing theoretical frameworks and complement the current practice in order to develop an epistemological legacy upon which successors can build to bring policing in line with those professions such as the law and science, whose existence and credibility have been developed over many years on those very foundations.

As I near the end of my police service and reflect upon those leaders who I thought really made a difference, a number of key behaviours were evident in them all. They were not afraid to come out of their comfort zone; they were widely read, searching for innovative ideas from the literature of other professions; they would think outside the box by developing and trying new ideas. They were creative and considered unconventional by their peers, yet successful in terms of service delivery. They were not intimidated or afraid of academics, in fact they actively sought them out and collaborated with them. But for me one of the most important characteristics they shared was that they sought the advice and views of their teams, they did not hide behind their rank, and they pushed themselves and their teams to develop as professional practitioners. Any aspiring leader would do well to emulate these characteristics.

Shared Reflections

The investigation leader has a complex task that gets more complicated with each trial, each court of appeal judgment, each public inquiry, each political committee review, and each set of questions from the media. The joint thinking that has taken place in preparing this section has led to a further version of an earlier hybrid composite, layered, not to say laminated, model of ethical investigation leadership for the 21st century. It needs to continually review what it is to be lawfully audacious, at the cutting edge of what is possible, to be up to date in all the matters that may impact on the investigation. It is aided, as Rob Bhairam has pointed out, by rigorous academic thinking; in other words if it hasn't got a theory in it, it's not academic. What is significant is that the theory we have explored supports the practice and indeed supports the ideal in the traditional accounts of the investigator's task, either derived from practitioners (eg Beveridge 1959; Du Rose 1971; Barnett 1978) or practitioner/academics, or partnerships of the two (eg Gross and Kendal 1934 [1893]; or Williamson (Newburn et al 2007); or Alison and

Crego 2008), or pure academics (eg Innes 2003; 2007). Hans Gross (1934) and Tom Williamson (Newburn et al 2007; Stenning 2014) are our exemplars, practitioners who thought deeply and clearly about the investigative leadership process and the contributions academics could make. They both wrote it down and taught it with an academic rigour that was still accessible to practitioners.

So a hybrid model includes theory, research, experience, and practice. It includes research and experience of both investigative leadership and teamwork practice. The practice includes: 'there is always a team' who have to be led; there is a duty to understand, to reach for the truth; to do this is to be lawful but there is also the requirement to be audacious, ie up-to-date with the law, science, and technology in order to push the boundaries of evidential opportunities. There is a requirement to be 'healthily sceptical', the up-to-date version of the traditional *ABC* taught to the best investigators as 'accept nothing at face value', 'believe no one without checking', 'confirm or corroborate everything'; together with GOY-BAKODS, getting out there, talking to people, finding witnesses and evidential opportunities. The perfect example of this is Marcus Beale's (2013) counter-terrorist investigation.

At the same time, the leader has to remember and remind the team of John Fox and Lord Laming's 'investigative approach', which must be structured, analytic, rational, creative but also accountable, ie recorded accountable decisions and actions: 'Say it loud without a frown, Good investigators write it down!' This needs to be accompanied by Fox and Laming's requirement of 'an open mind', with all that entails for open questions—who, what, where, when, why, and how, with an updated version of Gross's 'orientation'; not just the crime scene but the wider community impact assessments and their relationship with victims and survivors. Some of this will be critical. There are many risks to be assessed: risks to any victims or survivors, to families, to justice or any criminal justice action, to the team, to the community, and to the organization. 'Concatenation' identified by Innes (2007) is right; the investigator has to find a path through what may appear to be the initial chaos, complexity, ambiguity, unknowns, not readily apparent risks or interested parties, and must then identify the important elements, priority actions, significant witnesses, and the evidence. This is often ambiguous with many choices, decisions to be made and written down, whether as witness statement, result of an action taken, policy to be followed, process or advice obtained. All these have risks to be assessed, and conclusions reached and recorded have often to be revisited systematically and sometimes changed.

'Oh, uh just one more thing . . . '—the leader has to think about legacy, not just not leaving a festering mess for their successors, not just about leaving stalled cases that can be readily picked up by others when the environment, knowledge, or context changes; but about handing on the torch of rigorous academic and practical knowledge, sharing their experiences, good and bad, leaving a record, mentoring and nurturing the next generation of investigative leaders. As Innes (2007) points out, it is about building knowledge. The way forward seems to us to be continuing collaborative research into investigative teams and their leaders, research that can contribute to consilient thinking, that is across multiple disciplines—academic rigour and artisan skilled crafts, science and professional investigative practice, philosophy, criminology, and shoe leather.

Recommended Reading

Brown, J (2014), *The Future of Policing* (London: Routledge). Many of the chapters explore the issues discussed here.

Gross, H (1962), *Criminal Investigation* (London: Sweet & Maxwell). There were many editions up to 1962. Still worth getting second hand to understand the basics, even if some of the prejudiced attitudes are outdated.

Harfield, C and Harfield, K (2012), *Covert Investigation* (3rd edn, Oxford: OUP) or any of the other volumes in the Blackstone's Practical Policing series (the titles on SIOs, Family Liaison, or Domestic Violence, for example).

Newburn, T, Williamson, T, and Wright, A (eds) (2007), *Handbook of Criminal Investigation* (Cullompton: Willan). The single most important milestone in the theory of investigation leadership and a must-buy for all those concerned with the development of investigation. Includes many chapters on issues covered here, not least that of Innes and Carson. The volume also includes much material of great importance not included in this chapter.

References

ACPO (2003), *Murder Investigation Manual*, Original version, ACPO, London

ACPO (2005), *Core Investigative Doctrine*, ACPO, London

Adair, J (1983), *Effective Leadership* (London: Pan Books)

Adlam, R and Villiers, P (2003), *Police Leadership in the Twenty-first Century: Philosophy, Doctrine and Developments* (Winchester: Waterside Press)

Alison, L and Crego, J (2008), *Policing Critical Incidents* (Cullompton: Willan)

Anderson, E (2000), *Code of the Street: Decency, Violence, and the Moral Life of the Inner City* (New York: WW Norton & Co)

Ascoli, D (1979), *The Queen's Peace* (London: Hamish Hamilton)

Barnett, J (1978), *Head of the Force* (London: Secker and Warburg)

Barrington, R and Peace, D (1985), 'HOLMES: The Development of a Computerised Major Crime Investigation System' 58 *Police Journal* 207

Beale, M (2013), 'Operation Clockface—The Investigation of Pavlo Lapshyn', Briefing to the Royal United Services Institute (RUSI) by ACC Marcus Beale West Midlands Police, 2 December

Beveridge, P (1959), *Inside the CID* (London: Evans Brothers and Pan Books)

Brain, T (2010), *A History of Policing in England and Wales from 1974: A Turbulent Journey.* (Oxford: OUP)

Brown, J (ed) (2014), *The Future of Policing* (London: Routledge)

Carson, D (2007), 'Models of Investigation', in Newburn, T, Williamson, T, and Wright, A (eds), *Handbook of Criminal Investigation* (Cullompton: Willan) 407

Carson, D, Milne, B Pakes, F, Shalev, K, and Shawyer, A (eds) (2007), *Applying Psychology to Criminal Justice* (Chichester: Wiley)

Chibnall, S (1977), *Law and Order News* (London: Tavistock)

Chesshyre, R (1989), *The Force* (London: Sidgwick and Jackson)

Chesshyre, R (2001), 'The Burden of Proof', *Daily Telegraph*, Saturday Magazine, 9 March, 48

Crego, J and Alison, L (2008), *Policing Critical Incidents* (Cullompton: Willan)

Critchley, TA (1967), *A History of the Police in England and Wales* (London: Constable)

Divall, T (1929), *Scoundrels, Scallywags and Some Honest Men* (London: Ernest Benn)

Du Rose, J (1971), *Murder was My Business* (London: WH Allen)

Ede, R and Shepherd, E (2000), *Active Defence* (London: Law Society)

Ellison, M (2014), 'The Stephen Lawrence Independent Review: Possible Corruption and the Role of Undercover Policing in the Stephen Lawrence Case', HC 1094, 6 March, Home Office, London

Foucault, M (1991), *Discipline and Punish: The Birth of the Prison* (A Sheridan (trans), New York: Penguin Books)

Grieve, J (2007), 'Behavioural Science and the Law: Investigations' in Carson, D, Milne, B, Pakes, F, Shalev, K, and Shawyer, A (eds), *Applying Psychology to Criminal Justice* (Chichester: Wiley) 39

Grieve, J (2014), 'Stephen Lawrence Inquiry: Complexity and Policing' in Pyecroft, A and Bartollas, C (eds), *Applying Complexity Theory: Whole Systems Approaches in Criminal Justice and Social Work* (Bristol: Policy Press) 141

Grieve, J, Harfield, C, and MacVean, A (2007), *Policing* (London: Sage)

Gross, H and Kendal, N (1934 [1893]), *Criminal Investigation: A Practical Textbook for Magistrates, Police Officers, and Lawyers Adapted from the System der Kriminalistik of Hans Gross* (London: Sweet & Maxwell)

Hall, N, Grieve, J, and Savage, S (eds) (2009), *Policing and the Legacy of Lawrence* (Cullompton: Willan)

Harfield, C and Harfield, K (2012), *Covert Investigation* (3rd edn, Oxford: Blackstone OUP)

Haringey Council (2009), 'Serious Case Review: Baby Peter', London: Local Safeguarding Childrens Board Haringey, at <http://www.haringeylscb.org/sites/haringeylscb/files/executive_summary_peter_final.pdf> (accessed 21 April 2015)

Heaton, R (2011), 'We Could be Criticized! Policing and Risk Aversion' 5(1) *Policing* 75

Herridge, R (1993), *Believe No One* (London: Little, Brown)

Home Office (2013), 'Crimes Detected in England and Wales 2012–2013', at <https://www.gov.uk/government/publications/crimes-detected-in-england-and-wales-2012-to-2013> (21 April 2015)

Houlihan, B and Giulianotti, R (2012), 'Politics and the London 2012 Olympics: The (In)security Games' 88(4) *International Affairs* 701

Innes, M (2003), *Investigating Murder: Detective Work and the Police Response to Criminal Homicide* (Oxford: Clarendon Press)

Innes, M (2007), 'Investigation Order and Major Crime Inquiries' in Newburn, T, Williamson, T, and Wright, A (eds), *Handbook of Criminal Investigation* (Cullompton: Willan) 255

Isaacson, W (2011), *Steve Jobs—The Exclusive Biography* (London: Little, Brown)

James, A (2013), *Examining Intelligence-led Policing: Developments in Research, Policy and Practice* (London: Palgrave Macmillan)

Laming, Lord (2003), 'Victoria Climbie Inquiry', TSO, London

McConville, M, Sanders, A, and Leng, R (1991), *The Case for the Prosecution: Police Suspects and the Construction of Criminality* (London: Routledge)

Macpherson, W (1999), 'The Stephen Lawrence Inquiry', HMSO, London

MacVean, A, Spindler, P, and Solf, C (2013), *The Handbook of Policing, Ethics and Professional Standards* (London: Routledge)

Maguire, M, Morgan, R, and Reiner, R (2007), *The Oxford Handbook of Criminology* (Oxford: OUP)

Mark, R (1978), *In the Office of Constable* (London: Collins)

Mawby, RC (2007), 'Criminal Investigation and the Media' in Newburn, T, Williamson, T, and Wright, A (eds), *Handbook of Criminal Investigation* (Cullompton: Willan) 146

May, T (2013), Home Secretary's address to the College of Policing, 24 May, at <https://www.gov.uk/government/speeches/home-secretary-college-of-policing-speech> (accessed 20 September 2014)

Moriarty, CCH (1955), *Police Procedure and Administration*: (London: Butterworth)

Morris, B (2007), 'History of Criminal Investigation' in Newburn, T, Williamson, T, and Wright, A (eds), *Handbook of Criminal Investigation* (Cullompton: Willan) 15

Newburn, T (2007), *Criminology* (Cullompton: Willan)

Newburn, T, Williamson, T, and Wright, A (eds) (2007), *Handbook of Criminal Investigation* (Cullompton: Willan)

NPIA (2005 to date) *Journal of Homicide and Major Incident Investigation*, published by NPIA/CofP for ACPO Homicide Working Group

Pitts, J (2008), *Reluctant Gangsters: The Changing Face of Youth Crime* (Cullompton: Willan)

Rawls, J (1980), 'Kantian Constructivism in Moral Theory' 7(9) *The Journal of Philosophy* 515

Reiner, R (2000), *The Politics of the Police* (Oxford: OUP)

Rose, D (2007), Tom Williamson Obituary, *The Guardian*, 14 March

Roycroft, M, Brown, J, and Innes, M (2007), 'Reform by Crisis: The Murder of Stephen Lawrence and a Socio-historical Analysis of Developments in the Conduct of Major Crime Investigations' in Rowe, M (ed), *Policing Beyond Macpherson: Issues in Policing, Race and Society* (Cullompton: Willan) 148

Savage, S (2007), *Police Reform: Forces for Change* (Oxford: OUP).

Scarman, L (1993), Private Correspondence with the author, unpublished letter

Schon, DA (1983), *The Reflective Practitioner: How Professionals Think in Action* (New York: Basic Books)

Schpayer-Makov, H (2011), *The Ascent of the Detective* (Oxford: OUP)

Scraton, P (2013), 'The Legacy of Hillsborough: Liberating Truth, Challenging Power' 55(2) *Race & Class* 1

Scruton, R (2003), 'A Kantian Approach to Policing' in Adlam, R and Villiers, P (eds), *Police Leadership in the 21st Century: Philosophy, Doctrine and Developments* (Winchester: Waterside Press) 76

Smith, DJ and Gray, J (1983), *The Police in Action* (London: Policy Studies Institute)

Smith, R (2012), 'Assessing the Role of "Entrepreneurial Policing" in Changing Times', Royal Gordon University, at <http://openair.rgu.ac.uk> (accessed 25 September 2014)

Stelfox, P (2007), 'Professionalising Investigative Processes' in Newburn, T, Williamson, T, and Wright, A (eds), *Handbook of Criminal Investigation* (Callumpton: Willan) 628

Stenning, P (2014), Book Review, 'Policing at the Top: The Roles, Values and Attitudes of Chief Police Officers' 16(1) *Police Practice and Research* 94

Summerscale, K (2008), *The Suspicions of Mr Whicher* (London: Bloomsbury)

Sydney-Smith, S (2002), *Beyond Dixon of Dock Green* (London: Taurus)

Vincent, CEH (1881), *Police Code: Manual of the Criminal Law* (London: Castellated, Petter, Galpin and Co)

Vollmer, A (1936), *The Police and Modern Society* (Berkeley, CA: University of California Press)

Wilson, OW (1950), 'The British Police' 40(12) *Journal of Criminal Law and Criminology* 637

Wright, A (2002), *Policing, An Introduction to Concepts Practice* (London: Routledge, 2002)

8

When Should They Get Engaged?

Police–Community Engagement

Martin Innes, Sarah Tucker, and Matt Jukes

Introduction

More than in most other jurisdictions, what the public thinks about the police *matters* to the British policing model. Indeed, it is threaded through the institutional DNA of UK policing. Although a 'foundation myth', the idea that Peel, Rowan, and Mayne defined the mission of the new police in the early years of the 19th century as being predicated upon 'policing by consent' and that the 'public are the police, and the police are the public' projected a particular notion of the relationship between police and policed.

The practicalities and pragmatics of such relations have been more difficult, however. Precisely how close and how responsive to public needs and concerns police should be has proved to be a perennial source of concern, debate, and problems. Throughout the 1830s and 1840s there was a high turnover of staff in the Metropolitan Police owing to misconduct (Reiner 1992), with similar issues resurfacing periodically since then. The fundamental challenge is that if officers become too close to the communities that they police then they are susceptible to corruption, which is harmful to public trust and confidence. Equally, if they distance themselves too much from the needs and concerns of the public, then their legitimacy decays and they lose public trust and support. As such, a series of critical questions for police leaders arises in terms of how, when, and why they and their officers should engage with the public.

In this chapter we consider these questions. We start by looking at what knowledge can be discerned from looking at the research that has been conducted into police engagement methods. To develop these insights we then set out a case study analysis based upon a five-year programme of research exploring some innovative methods for organizing police–community interactions. This evolves into an exploration of how new social media technologies are altering the information environment for policing and the associated social dynamics of engagement. The final section of the chapter seeks to distil some key issues for police leaders in terms of how they use and develop contacts with their communities.

Assessing Engagement Methods in Policing

Despite the importance, engagement is accorded in many contemporary policing plans and strategies and the amount of 'police talk' that attends to it, there is comparatively little research that has systematically tested the efficacy of different engagement methods to robustly establish 'what works' to increase the reach and effectiveness of these. Instead, discussions of engagement techniques are typically embedded in broader programme evaluations of specific initiatives— many of which are focused upon forms of community policing.

For instance, Skogan's (2006) assessment of the Chicago Alternative Policing Strategy is exemplary in documenting how innovative use of large-scale social surveys and regular police–community meetings drove reform of the delivery of policing, as part of a wider change programme. Similar engagement methods feature in the development and delivery of Neighbourhood Policing in the United Kingdom (Barnes and Eagle 2007). In both settings, these methods were intended to provide insights into what local public priorities for policing were, rather than police assuming that they knew what issues needed to be tackled. There is some evidence from the studies conducted of these initiatives that the engagement work resulted in: reduced levels of disorder and anti-social behaviour (ASB); increased feelings of safety; improved public confidence in the police; and changes to police officers' attitudes and behaviours (Myhill 2006; Tuffin et al 2006).

It would be misleading, however, to restrict the relevance and impact of engagement just to highly visible forms of community policing. A seminal finding of the early academic studies of policing was that one of the primary determinants of whether crimes are solved or not is the quality and quantity of information provided to the police about potential suspects by members of the public cast as witnesses (Reiner 1992). As such, maintaining channels of communication with citizens, in order that they can and want to provide such information to police when they need to, is an important element of thinking about the value of engagement to policing. It is not just about what is delivered in the here and now, but what communications infrastructure is developed that can be activated when needed.

A different perspective is gained by thinking about what happens when effective engagement is not present and policing is done to people rather than with them. This is a problem that has appeared most acutely and repeatedly in police relations with minority ethnic communities. For example, Lord Scarman's report (1982) into the major public disorders in Brixton in 1981 identified aggressive policing tactics and a failure of the police to account for their approach to the community as a primary cause of the violence. In response to this, police consultative groups involving 'leaders' from key Black communities were established in a number of urban areas in an attempt to institutionalize communication channels. However, in practice they were often fractious and fragile. As a model of engagement they were, to all intents and purposes, reinvented as Independent Advisory Groups in 1999, following the racist murder of Stephen Lawrence and the manifest failings of the police response to that crime (ACPO 2011). This tradition of 'small p' political engagement, whereby communities are engaged via contacts with representatives drawn from the purported 'leaders' of a particular grouping, has been carried over into the 'Prevent'[1] programme of the past few years, and much of the work that has been conducted with Muslim communities.

More recently, Stott et al (2013) have reinforced the importance of communication and dialogue in public order policing, and how it can diffuse the potential for disorder by de-escalating potentially tense situations. Work on the social psychology of collective behaviour in the context of crowd dynamics provides a concrete example of the ways engagement can be deployed with particular communities of interest that come together in particular moments and situations, rather than having a long-term sense of belonging and identity.

At the other end of the spectrum from these necessarily ephemeral and shallow forms of engagement is a set of much 'deeper' forms of 'participative policing', where people volunteer their time to get more directly involved in the work of the police.

Even from this cursory review, we are starting to piece together some of the ways in which police engage with the public across a variety of roles and situations, and using a diversity of methods (Lloyd and Foster 2009). Cutting across these permutations, it can be discerned that the variety of methods that police employ to connect, interact, and communicate with citizens and communities can be reduced to four principal motivations. Engagement can be designed: to enhance the intelligence base on crime and disorder problems and/or the people that cause them; to inform the public about aspects of policing; to listen to local communities' key concerns and issues; and to aid the response to particular situations and problems.

---

[1] Prevent is part of the government's counter-terrorism strategy, CONTEST. Its aim is to stop people becoming terrorists or supporting terrorism—see 'Prevent Strategy' (2011), at <https://www.gov.uk/government/uploads/system/uploads/attachment_data/file/97976/prevent-strategy-review.pdf> (accessed 26 January 2015).

Broadly speaking, the available research literature has been quite critical of how police typically seek to engage with various sectors of the public. Concern is regularly voiced about a police preference for consultation methodologies that are often relatively inflexible, lacking in nuance, and frequently unrepresentative (Jones and Newburn 2001; Myhill 2006). For whilst there are a multitude of methods that could be used to 'take the temperature' of public sentiment and opinion, overwhelmingly police tend to rely upon community meetings and quantitative public opinion surveys (Fielding and Innes 2006; Rousell and Gascon 2014). Any such doubts and worries are compounded by a growing awareness of the increasingly diverse and complex nature of many communities, rendering it increasingly challenging for police to harness methods that can adequately capture the range of views and perspectives that are a feature of today's fluid and morphing communities.

In one of the few attempts to synthesize and summarize the lessons learnt from all the research conducted, Myhill (2006) notes high rates of implementation failure (see also Neyroud 2001). What emerges from his structured review of the literature is that police organizations appear to find it very hard to sustain robust engagement that reaches across various communities and identities over time. Developing his analysis, he identifies several critical success factors for implementing community engagement, including:

- organizational commitment and culture change—because the police service is some way from understanding the benefits engagement can afford;
- mainstreaming—it needs to be seen as 'core work' rather than the responsibility of a particular department or project;
- sharing power with communities—too often engagement is done 'to' rather than 'with' communities;
- tailoring and local flexibility—local officers need to be afforded discretion about how to make engagement work in particular contexts, rather than being held to inflexible, generic standards of practice;
- performance management—performance assessments need to reward effective engagement work;
- training and capacity building—both police and public need 'up-skilling' to make engagement work;
- confidence and trust—engagement rarely happens in 'clean sites' and very often there is a legacy of poor relations, especially for minority ethnic communities, that police need to appreciate and work within;
- communication—partnerships need dialogue, not one-way broadcasting;
- partnership working—especially for community policing programmes, police need to engage their public sector partners as well as themselves, to tackle 'quality of life issues'.

Developing some of these themes, both Carr (2006) and Rousell and Gascon (2014) tease out some of the interactional difficulties involved in police–community engagements that serve to inhibit the efficacy of such initiatives.

Focusing in particular upon meetings, they note a police tendency to want to control the agenda, with the upshot that resistance from communities is generated.

One additional point worth flagging up concerns the general lack of awareness of the principles of political communication amongst police officers. There is a tendency to reach for familiar methods in familiar circumstances without seemingly taking account of what is known about the most effective and persuasive ways to communicate messages to people.[2] This lack of awareness is becoming increasingly problematic in the new media ecology, suffused as it is by social media communication platforms—a topic we will return to presently. In particular, there is often an assumption made by police that the public always wants to engage with them. It is an assumption that, as Herbert (2006) notes, creates unrealistic expectations about the capacity and capability of communities to engage in police programmes. Indeed, one of the key emergent learning points from studies of the ways police use social media as a community engagement method is how, rather than looking for an 'always on' relationship with the police, most citizens and communities prefer something more dynamic. They are frequently looking for engagement that can be turned 'off and on' as needed, often driven by local events.

From this scan of the available literature, it can be discerned that there are two critical questions that police leaders need to ask in seeking to assess the quality of activity: 'How are we engaging?' and 'Why are we engaging?'. The first of these attends to whether the methods are appropriate and whether they have sufficient 'reach' to encompass the variety of views that are 'out there' in the public sphere. The 'why' question seeks to clarify the purpose or intent of any engagement effort. To better understand the salience of these questions, we will turn now to a case study of research conducted to test the potential of an innovatively structured and systematic approach to engaging communities.

The Cardiff Community Engagement Field Trial

In 2008–09 South Wales Police undertook to implement a new community engagement methodology. The method had been designed to address three specific issues:

- to engage communities in a more structured, systematic, and intensive way than was frequently the case with most approaches police used;
- to capture data on peoples' perceptions and actual experiences of crime, disorder, and policing, rather than the more general attitudinal and opinion data typically generated by more orthodox survey instruments; and
- in so doing, to produce information that was operationally useful to the police, especially by being able to 'drill down' into key neighbourhoods by targeting the specific issues, in particular locations that were causing most harm to local people.

---

[2] A readable summary of this corpus of knowledge is contained in Cialdini (2001).

Blending a qualitative Geographic Information System software platform with the principles of cognitive interviewing, the methodology was about diagnosing the key drivers of collective neighbourhood insecurity in such a way that targeted treatment interventions could be introduced in response to these (Lowe and Innes 2012). Initially, 746 face-to-face interviews were performed across every neighbourhood in Cardiff by teams of researchers, Neighbourhood Policing officers, and police community support officers (PCSOs). In the second phase, the work was extended across the whole of the South Wales Police force so that, within the space of a year, a total of 4,300 in-depth interviews had been conducted to explore the local public understanding of crime, disorder, and policing. Subsequent to this initial field trial, South Wales Police have embedded this methodology in their engagement strategy, using it to gauge the impacts of policing operations against organized crime groups and the delivery of Prevent. An important component of the initial work was to compare the performance of the new targeted and intensive face-to-face engagement with the more orthodox approaches to engaging their communities that South Wales were utilizing at the time. Consistent with the findings of the literature outlined previously, they were using postal surveys with a Citizen's Panel of 1,500 Cardiff residents to gauge public sentiment and opinion. The Panel membership was selected to be representative of the demographic profile of the city as a whole. However, what police had omitted to test was just how engaged this membership was when they were sent the surveys to complete. The Cardiff University research team analysed how effective the postal survey of the Citizen's Panel actually was.

It identified that only 20% of those surveyed actually replied to the police (in line with standard response rates for this method), and of those who did, the vast majority lived in the lower crime, more affluent areas of the city, the obvious implication being that the segment of the public being engaged by the police through this method were not those most impacted by crime and disorder problems.

Alongside this test, an effort was made to appraise the efficacy of the Police and Community Together, or PACT meetings—the second most relied upon engagement method highlighted in the literature. Analysis of the minutes for a sizeable proportion of the PACT meetings held in Cardiff over the preceding 12 months found that well over half of the meetings had been attended by fewer than ten members of the public.

Analysis of the data generated by the new method fed both tactical and strategic problem-solving. The key strategic insight generated from engaging in this way was that at a city level, public concern was being influenced by a potent blend of crime, ASB, and physical disorder problems distributed across particular neighbourhoods. The public draw little distinction between those matters that are defined as criminal in law and those that are not. Indeed, it is because of this that effective engagement is so important for the police. It helps to sort out from amongst all the problems that can degrade and harm neighbourhoods and communities what are the most important ones from the public's perspective, at a particular moment in space and time.

For the purposes of public service delivery, Cardiff is divided into six neighbourhood management areas (NMAs). Table 8.1 lists the top five signal crimes (see Innes 2014) and disorder for each of the NMAs, ranked according to the frequency with which they were mentioned across all interviews in that area.

From Table 8.1 it can be seen that across all six NMAs it is a mix of crime and disorder that is animating citizens' concerns, but that the specific profiles of problems vary and are situationally shaped. In the different neighbourhoods of Cardiff, the collective sense of security is being harmed by different issues.

Table 8.1 Rank Order by Neighbourhood Management Area

	Canton & Ely	Rumney & St Mellons	Roath & Cathays	City & Bay	Fairwater	Llanishen & Llannedyrn
1	Youth disorder	Youth disorder	Parking	Youth disorder	Youth disorder	Youth disorder
2	Theft vehicles	Graffiti	Theft vehicles	Damage buildings	Speeding	Graffiti
3	Drug dealing	Burglary dwelling	Litter	Prostitution	Parking	Parking
4	Damage to vehicles	Speeding	Burglary dwelling	Drug dealing	Parking	Parking
5	Burglary dwelling	Damage bus shelters	Damage to vehicles	Theft vehicles	Graffiti	Speeding

Source: Innes et al (2009).

Connecting the Neighbourhood to the National

As mentioned earlier, in addition to contributing to a more general effort to improve neighbourhood security across the city, the engagement methodology has also been used to tackle thematic problems. In particular, at the time when the original interviews were being conducted, one of the key strategic policing priorities in Cardiff concerned tensions associated with delivery of the Prevent counter-terrorism programme. This was confirmed by the interview data collected, analysis of which also suggested that in an area of the city with a high proportion of Muslim residents there were very prominent concerns about the presence of drug dealing. In summary, the local community perceived they were being 'over-policed' as a source of potential suspects, and 'under-policed' in terms of the problems that they were encountering. By better understanding what the local community's concerns were and focusing some police activities around these drug-related concerns, more meaningful and productive interactions were facilitated. So rather than just focusing upon Prevent priorities, the officers involved came to understand that a way to initiate engagement with the communities was around tackling the drugs issues locally, because this was something that really mattered to local people. Once progress was made in this domain, some of the distrust and suspicion about the Prevent work was at least temporarily allayed.

Approaching community engagement to support Prevent in this way was important in helping to achieve a shift from just consulting with the community to co-producing social control responses to risks and threats with them (Innes 2006). Co-production is a highly engaged form of working, whereby public services and community representatives actively collaborate to solve problems of mutual concern. Blending informal and formal social control assets, it can be defined as having three principal dimensions:

- police and communities co-define the problem to be targeted;
- they then cooperate to co-design the solution; and then
- agents from the police and community groups co-deliver the response, both contributing to the work conducted.

It was precisely this highly engaged form of police-community collaboration that the field trial played a role in seeding in Cardiff. For example, when police acquired intelligence that a prominent radical preacher was planning to visit the city, they subsequently learned that the English Defence League were proposing to hold a concurrent counter-demonstration. Both police and Muslim community elders wanted to ensure that no confrontations took place that could be exploited by extremists on either side. The diversionary activities both parties enacted proved effective in diffusing the evident potential for tension and confrontation.

It is important not to overstate or inflate the impacts that were achieved by this initiative. Violent extremist radicalization remains a problem in the city, as it does across the United Kingdom and Europe. But what this example does evidence is the extent to which high-quality engagement efforts can play an important part in leveraging innovative and creative ways of tackling social problems that impact directly upon communities and the risks and threats to which they are exposed. More generally, the purpose of this detailed discussion of the Cardiff field trial has been to demonstrate that, if appropriately conducted and configured, community engagement methods can be used to direct operational policing in ways that render it more directly responsive to community needs and expectations.

Engaging the Future

More recently in South Wales, attempts have been initiated to blend this neighbourhood security-focused approach to engagement with emerging social media analytics tools, to enable new ways for police to key into particular communities. Debates about the potential and pitfalls of social media were brought into sharp relief by the riots in London in 2011, where several platforms in particular were attributed a critical role in terms of how those involved in disorder organized and mobilized (Procter et al 2013). The broader under-pinning point being that very rapidly, particular social media channels have become central mechanisms in terms of how many citizens interact and com-municate with each other. As such, they are important for the future of policing.

At the time of writing, whilst there are an increasing number of attempts across the police service to harness and utilize social media, we are not at the point of having anything approaching a robust evidence base concerning what works and what doesn't—we are still very much in the experimentation phase. Indeed, the scene is marked by a wide variation in the positions adopted by individual police forces. Some are constructing social media analytics principally as an intelligence tool, whilst others are positioning it more resolutely in the engagement space. This degree of variation is probably, in part, an artefact of how the potentials of social media are simultaneously being oversold and are insufficiently understood (Boyd and Crawford 2012). But what can be said with more certainty is that when compared with more familiar engagement methods, social media possess several unique qualities. These include its dialogic nature, in that platforms such as the micro-blogging site Twitter encourage interactions between users, rather than just one party 'speaking' and the other 'listening' (Tinati et al 2014).

In their analysis of the social reactions to the murder of Lee Rigby in Wool-wich in 2012, Innes et al (2014) attend to a second quality, whereby the presence of social media as a public communication channel effectively accelerated key aspects of the police response, when key developments at the crime scene were being 'live tweeted' by members of the public. Consequently, whilst there is ubiquitous talk of big data, the key implication for the police of social media may actually be in creating 'fast data'—public awareness of police work, both good and bad, travels further and more rapidly than was ever hitherto imaginable.

What this points to is that there are liable to be complex effects upon the processes and systems of policing in general, as these new technologically medi-ated forms of interactive engagement become increasingly embedded into the routines and rhythms of police work. Such technologies are 'interventions', rather than simply solutions. That they tend to induce unintended consequences is one of the primary lessons of history. In their analysis of the professional policing model of the 1960s, Sparrow et al (1992) identify how the twin reforms of telephone crime reporting and the introduction of the police patrol car irrev-ocably altered the ways in which the public came to engage and interact with police. According to their narrative, community policing had to be invented to compensate for the increased social distance that these technological interven-tions created. Social media is having a transformative impact upon the processes of social order in society, and as such, it is inevitably freighted with profound consequences for how, when, and why police engage with citizens and commu-nities in the future.

Conclusion

The preceding discussion has documented that effective police–community engagement is complex and difficult. It is, though, also an integral component of many key policing disciplines and how policing services are delivered to the public. Communities are increasingly complicated and can be delineated along a number of dimensions of social identity and belonging. This is reflected in the numerous accounts in the literature of engagement implementation failures. There is, however, growing research evidence to suggest that if properly structured, police–community engagement can help to configure a more democratically responsive style of policing.

The current challenge for police leaders is how to maintain these channels of communication in an era where significantly reduced police funding is 'the new normal' (Innes 2011). That said, whilst the economics of public austerity are likely to constrain and inhibit the adoption of some engagement models, these are balanced by counteracting social forces that are pushing for more engagement. Most notably these include the changing accountability landscape for policing, alongside the make-up of the new information environment.

Over the next few years, it is likely that social media channels will play an increasingly prominent role in terms of how police think about their interactions with local communities and their wider public audience. But this will, of course, induce new challenges for police leaders. The introduction of increasingly sophisticated text-mining algorithms with the capacity to scan large swathes of social media clearly has the potential to establish the equivalent of a 24/7 'always on' form of community impact assessment. This would allow police decision-makers to have a 'near real-time' update of emerging problems and almost instantaneous feedback on community perceptions of any police interventions. But the defining issue will be whether the organizational structures and processes of police bureaucracies can be engineered so that they are sufficiently agile to engage with and respond to such data (Innes et al 2014).

As these new disruptive technologies come to play an increasingly prominent role in the ways police engage and interact with the communities they serve, it will be incumbent upon their leaders to think through not only how they engage these methods, but why they want to use them. For one thing that studies of the adoption processes for other technologies has demonstrated is a generic tendency for societies to overestimate the near-term effects of new technologies, and underestimate their power to change social relations over the longer term.

Practitioner's Perspective

'Co-production' sounded to me like a pretty academic concept when I first encountered the term. I arrived in South Wales as Professor Martin Innes was completing and reporting his research in the communities of Cardiff (Innes et al 2011). Over time, this has led me to reflect on how as senior police leaders we approach our partnerships with researchers and how concepts of co-production can be applied to the most 'wicked' and risk-laden aspects of policing. In an age of austerity, we are bound to ask whether current models of community engagement are affordable and whether, in the digital age, they need to evolve to remain relevant.

The work of the Universities' Police Science Institute (UPSI) in Cardiff's neighbourhoods was introduced to me by new colleagues as innovative and important. As an assistant chief constable, I wanted to know if it had made a difference, any *real* difference, to policing our communities. My past experience of working with academia was mixed. The challenge, I felt, was for research to report in a timescale and in a form that could inform and potentially change contemporary police practice. I had seen research do this and I had seen it fail. However, I was increasingly aware that the prospects of success were cast as much in the willingness of police leaders to commit to a continuous, mutually challenging relationship to shape and steer research. Co-production, if you will.

Research into practice

A good part of my career to date has been spent in or around security and intelligence, counter-terrorism, and its relationship to community policing. A Masters' degree (started whilst a detective inspector) was a challenge, but aspects of my research on police culture (and its impact on offender management) came back to inform my thinking, as I started working with UPSI. The work described in the previous section was challenging the police to do something different and that, by the very nature of police organizations, is not easy. The literature shows that modern police culture is remarkably consistent, across the decades and across nations (Johnston 2000), and notably conservative (Waddington 1999: 101). Academia is not helped in penetrating or influencing policing by a strong trait of pragmatism in police officers, which values 'common-sense' over theory (Crank 1998; Reiner 2000). That might prompt despair in some quarters, but I have a different sense. Cultural traits are rarely completely negative or positive. They have 'Janus faces'—isolation and secrecy can be the shadow side of teamwork and esprit de corps; an unwavering 'moral imperative' can be used to justify abhorrent actions, but it can also be the foundation of a sense of mission and duty. And so it is with police pragmatism. On the one hand, it might lend substance to a rejection of 'book learning' but on the other, it gives rise to a 'thirst for action' (Reiner 2000), and turning research into action, is surely where this form of co-production hits the streets. 'Very interesting. What are we going to do?' is not a bad question.

Research on the streets has literally been the model in Cardiff, and increasingly in sensitive areas of policy and practice. Counter-terrorism policing necessarily has a 'secret' component, but very explicitly since the development of the CONTEST strategy (see footnote 2), developing intelligence within communities and working with them to prevent violent extremism have been priorities (the so-called 'Prevent' element of the CONTEST strategy). Set against the very real risk that intelligence and law enforcement activity is viewed as 'targeting' particular communities, we need to give communities, whether in our towns and cities or in the digital space, confidence that we are finding an appropriate balance between privacy, freedoms, and security. In exploring this balance, research is made more difficult by the subject matter and the range of partner agencies. Few outsiders have gained the type of access required to support and inform police leaders in their decision-making on counter-terrorism. With the support of national and local partners, academics have done this in South Wales and elsewhere, and the results are informing policing practice, even as I write.

It has taken a little courage in some quarters to do this. Vetting and accrediting researchers to work with the Welsh Extremism and Counter-Terrorism Unit was relatively easy to achieve, but understanding how to shape their work to inform national agendas, local partnerships, and ultimately the public, is a work in progress. In the context of policing this is a question not just of security but, as I have touched on, of culture. There is a Welsh maxim: 'Constant tapping breaks the rock', and so it has been with attitudes to our joint work with academia. The chief constables who over almost a decade have been the architects of the wider partnership, set the tone of openness very clearly and in a very positive sense over time. Through events such as master classes with police leaders, academic work has been 'socialized' and barriers have been broken down. This academic presence in our working lives culminated in events at which academic research, the perspectives of MI5, and insights from the media were debated. Whilst such events have long been the stuff of Chatham House or other esteemed institutes, this discussion was distinctively local and specific, and formed part of a continuing partnership with its feet firmly in our communities. Whilst I had taken part in some of those grander events, I welcomed a conversation where the possibility of connecting theory with practice—to answer the 'So what?' question—was so immediate.

Operational perspectives

We are not necessarily, of course, going to effect any change in a room amongst academics and officials. The 'So what?' question was brought to life for me in late 2010. In the biggest counter-terrorism operation of that year, arrests took place in Wales, the Midlands, and London. Amongst a wider group, three men from Cardiff were subsequently convicted of terrorism offences. During the peak of the operation, with multiple addresses being raided (most of them family homes), the groundwork of community engagement over preceding years could clearly be seen to be yielding benefits. Initially, this had helped me inform national and local approaches to operational tactics and to media issues with a rich picture of our communities' perspectives, drawn from the Cardiff neighbourhood research and police intelligence. Publicly and privately the Muslim communities affected were supportive of the police actions and the steps taken to avoid a 'media circus'.

During the operation I was bound to reflect on my earlier involvement in counter-terrorist policing. Contact and intelligence from the community has long been a part of the policing of threats to national security. As a detective inspector, I had worked with Special Branch officers who would maintain confidential sources within communities; some acting as paid informants, others motivated by the desire to keep the public safe from the violent fringes of various organizations. Away from these clandestine actions there had been some discussion publicly, or at least discretely within communities, about ongoing operations. This was often through conversations in which information flowed from the police to the community in the form of 'just in time' briefings to community leaders, as operations were about to move to their 'executive' phase of raid and arrests. The introduction of these briefings was in itself a step-change in police communication but it was perhaps a discrete broadcast rather than a conversation.

The 2010 operation benefited from something more akin to a conversation with our communities but it was not generated by that exchange. By early 2012, with the trial of those charged from the earlier operation still pending, I was overseeing an operation which led much more directly from a distinct and quietly demanding view from the same communities that a residual group of extremists needed to be addressed. Community members came forward to raise concerns that meetings at a community hall near to the centre of Cardiff were being used for radicalization,[3] and they did this through channels of communication that had been established during the earlier operations and other work on 'Prevent'. Through partnership with the city's council, police and stakeholders in the community agreed that withdrawal of the group's permission to use local authority facilities was necessary and proportionate. Whilst the intervention was not without challenge (one man present threatened to behead police officers, later being convicted of public order offences),[4] the contribution to the disruption of the group was widely welcomed.

Although this action engaged some statutory powers, it was essentially an intervention shaped around the ethos of 'Prevent', with community engagement surfacing a desire for action from, in this case, Muslim communities. For this operation, a deliberately high profile was established in the media, showing partner agencies and communities working together. It achieved the disruption rather than the dismantling of a potentially troubling group but it was an important action, developed by a range of partners. Supported as it was by communities, it played a part in mobilizing co-production of a response, which sadly is still required today.

---

[3] See <http://www.bbc.co.uk/news/uk-politics-21790569> (accessed 31 May 2014).

[4] See <http://www.bbc.co.uk/news/uk-wales-south-east-wales-16665008> (accessed 31 May 2014).

Counter-terrorism: frontline community engagement

The threat of international terrorism in the United Kingdom, and now emanating from the United Kingdom is clearly enduring. Young men from several towns and cities, including Cardiff, have travelled to join terrorist groups, most recently in Iraq and Syria. Some of these individuals are using new technologies and social media as a key tool to glorify and organize their terrorist activity. On a pragmatic level, we have not relied on 'Prevent' in isolation to meet this challenge, and our relationships with intelligence agencies, paid informants, and technical surveillance (subject to increasing scrutiny in the post-Snowden age) are still essential tools. This presents something of a challenge for police leaders, whether they are counter-terrorist experts, local commanders, or the officers taking forward 'Prevent' on the ground on a daily basis. Sitting in mosques and community halls, there has rarely been a member of an intelligence agency or the national government alongside me, as I have sought to account for and give confidence in the use of the most draconian legal powers available to the police, whilst at the same time attempting to foster the co-production of sustainable solutions in communities. There is no academic reference or professional doctrine that can do more than guide or inform police leaders in these situations. The unique role of policing demands a resourcefulness to respond to global grievances, played out locally. For senior leaders, this requires a coherence of approach between command rooms and government crisis meetings, through to a personal role in town halls and community settings.

These are important conversations and almost bound at times to be uncomfortable, taking us beyond 'traditional' community leaders. At least some of our efforts around co-production need to take place closer to the threat of violent radicalization and involve people who are progressing towards violent extremism. Inevitably, these efforts cannot always be successful, and for the police and security service the prospective headlines loom. Somebody approached for information or an individual subject to 'soft' interventions to tackle their apparent extremism might go on to engage directly in terrorism, with potentially devastating implications for the public. 'Prevent' can never be relied upon to contain a real and present threat but it offers a response to cases which fall below this threshold.

Against the very serious implications of misjudging an individual's risk to others, the prospect of overly defensive practices and a 'blame culture' are ever-present (Kemshall 2003). Done badly, counter-terrorism work clearly has the potential to increase a sense of grievance and fuel radicalization. To navigate these dilemmas with the consent of the public and politicians requires a high level of confidence in the legitimacy of policing, not just in the communities affected but in the public discourse. The consensus around the legitimacy of British policing is being questioned, with trust and confidence in the police seen as damaged, but not broken according to recent comments by the Her Majesty's Chief Inspector of Constabulary (HMIC 2014). On this analysis, engaging the public explicitly in the most complex and sensitive areas of our work seems to be of more fundamental importance than ever, but that will not make the conversations any easier.

Austerity and the digital age

One thing is for certain, this discussion now takes place after a period of austerity in policing, unprecedented for a generation of police leaders, who find that the expensive investigative resources that we expanded in the past two decades are now under ever greater pressure. The difficult decisions around funding prioritization have given renewed focus to the 'what works' discussion and evidence-based policing. In the context of engagement and security, the role of neighbourhood policing has been propounded as key, as have 'softer' engagement roles and the Prevent initiative.

In an era when 'what works' can shape budgets, we know with some certainty that assertive, intrusive policing can at one level be shown to work (whatever its long-term effects, terrorists in prison are a good deal less dangerous to the public than those in the community). On another level, we are bound to ask whether the investment in neighbourhood policing—at least so far as it is seen as valuable to tackling serious crime and terrorism—is sustainable on equally strong evidence. The truth is that this evaluation is relatively underdeveloped and whilst some evidence exists, the barrier presented by 'secrecy' will need to be navigated and we will need to find ways of being bolder in enabling research into and evaluation of the long-term efficacy of both conventional law enforcement and Prevent or counter-terrorism community engagement.

As individual police leaders, we will need to understand not just 'what works' in an isolated sense ('Was this project more useful than that one?') but to bring that raft of responses required by the broad police function together in a way that is coherent and affordable. This will take time, with only the most tactical of actions likely to be understood in the short term. To return to police culture, it is not by nature attuned to waiting and reflecting. Police leaders—as contrary to the prevailing culture as it is—will have to display patience and stretch the horizon of the discussion on 'what works'.

Perseverance and dogmatic resistance are perhaps another example of 'two sides of the coin'. Counter-terrorism policing and the wider partnership around it could easily have been deflected by internal and external critics of the Prevent approach. Earlier iterations of the strategy were not entirely effective and were less well received by communities (Innes 2014), who saw it as more evidence of 'spying' (Casciani 2009). It survived not because of political rhetoric or its strategic elegance, but fundamentally because United Kingdom police forces, along with other partners in national and local government, sincerely believed that at the same time as pursuing unrelenting intelligence and law enforcement operations (and military operations overseas), there was a place in any counter-terrorism strategy for diverting individuals from the path towards violent extremism. Spending money on this and investing organizational capital was a risk and required perseverance at personal and organizational levels, but not dogmatism. The strategy remains controversial, but has evolved and responded to new threats over a decade (Casciani 2014). However its effectiveness is measured, Prevent has certainly become more complex and sophisticated, as well are more focused over this period (Innes 2011).

That same responsiveness may also require police leaders, as well as police and crime commissioners (PCCs) to reframe what has become one of the paradigms of late 20th-century policing. Neighbourhood policing, seen as the 'ground-level' of the golden thread linking global threats to local communities, has been articulated (by both politicians and police leaders) as almost unassailable since the late 1970s (Waddington 1999). But the predominant model, now essentially a handful of police officers and PCSOs, dedicated to a geographical neighbourhood, may for many 21st-century Britons suggest a type of 'parish pump' locality that is increasingly unrepresentative of their lives. Whether diverse communities connect across cities through ethnicity or religion, or people are connected by their politics, hobbies, or occupations, we increasingly live in communities of interest, as well as in physical neighbourhoods. For many this means an increasingly dispersed life, with work and home farther apart (or conversely, in the same building) and more of life lived through digital associations, rather than communities of location around the village green or its urban equivalent.

What does this mean for police leaders?

In an era where, despite technology, neighbourhood policing is still essentially a collection of 'boots on the ground', policing like other forms of public service needs to find a model for providing the same contact, visibility, and reassurance in communities that have been atomized into myriad networks of individuals and groups. In many positive examples, the boots on the ground do have a digital platform of social media to reach their more conventional geographical communities. More challenging for policing will be finding an expression of the same sense of presence and security that flows from the best neighbourhood policing models in communities that have no geography. What does a PCSO offer an online community?

Whilst there is a basis of literature to inform police leadership, even the most recent reviews seem locked in some 20th- or even 19th-century conceptions of community.[5] At the same time, and certainly with unsurprising evidence that social deprivation and 'digital exclusion' are linked (Burton 2013), the concept of 'local policing' remains of real significance in many communities (Lowe and Innes 2012). We cannot have one or the other, but need perhaps to understand 'laminated' lives; operating in digital communities, dispersed social groups, and

---

[5] See eg Lloyd, K and Foster, J, 'Citizen Focus and Community Engagement: A Review of the Literature' (2009), at <http://www.police-foundation.org.uk/uploads/catalogerfiles/citizen-focus-and-community-engagement-a-review-of-the-literature/citizen_focus.pdf> (21 April 2015).

global networks but nonetheless, still living in homes and streets, around schools and parks.[6]

This is potentially 'baby and bathwater' territory and, as noted above, it is easy to get ahead of ourselves in the excitement to pursue new technologies and forget the daily, local, and very real-world experiences that impact on sense of security. As we reorganize to respond to financial challenges and an evolving society, community engagement will need to evolve if it is to remain relevant to increasingly complex communities who deserve to feel secure in the spaces they inhabit, whether physically or virtually. If ever there was a need for co-production between communities, policing, and academia, it is here and it needs to move quickly to keep pace.

There is real evidence of forces and individual officers trying to respond to this challenge (witness the number of police officers and teams tweeting). Social media, as so very distinct from conventional media, are two-way. The best police use of it reflects this. Perhaps the most exciting opportunities lie where, as we did in the evolving counter-terrorism engagement, we shift from broadcast to dialogue, and empower interaction with the real potential for communities to inform and shape our responses or, better, respond together in a form of digital co-production.

Shared Reflections

Policy and practice development in policing too often pivots around 'ideal type' examples that occur under a set of 'perfect' conditions, rather than attending to and capturing the complex, contingent decisions and behaviours that are a defining feature of much police work 'in action'. To put it another way, the accounts that seek to define and model best practice tend to describe what *should* happen, rather than what more typically actually *does* happen.

This is an artefact of how much professional doctrine is devised. Subject matter experts tasked to develop a manual of effective practice sit in a room using past experiences to codify instructions, checklists, and process models to guide the actions of other professionals. The results tend to elide and neglect the 'grit' and challenge present in 'actual' as opposed to 'theoretical' policing practice.

This approach to improving policing practice is one that the emergent evidence-based policing movement could usefully challenge and reset. Rather than seeking to apprehend some perfect model of what ideal police performance might be, instead, evidence could: outline a framework of what to do and not do; understand how and why police behave in particular ways in particular situations; and establish what can be done to prevent or mitigate the worst forms of implementation.

Such general reflections on the dynamics and mechanics of operational police reform are especially apposite for thinking about the future of the community

---

[6] These issues are addressed in the collection of essays published by Orton-Johnson and Prior (2013).

engagement function. For although such work often draws upon similar methodologies to those employed by academic researchers, it does not necessarily require the same levels of rigour. Policing is manifestly a practical profession; as Egon Bittner (1974: 30) famously noted, it revolves around 'something that ought not to be happening and about which someone had better do something now!'. Given this, it would seem that rather than focusing upon pursuit of optimum models of engagement, and feeling constrained by these in terms of trying to engage communities in policing, a more realistic and achievable outcome would be to ensure that police efforts in this domain are 'good enough'.

What police engagement methods do need is sufficient validity and reliability that they reasonably accurately diagnose an issue or problem so that appropriate treatment interventions can be delivered. Viewed in this way, the role of the senior police leader is to provide clarity about why a particular mode of engagement is being engaged, and to test how it is being practically implemented by accessing the full range of perspectives and voices that need to be heard. This might include, for instance, checking that officers are not repeatedly seeking the views of those groups who are more naturally inclined to be well disposed to the police. The contribution of the research evidence base to such an effort would be in aiding police leaders' understanding about how and why officers might 'game' any formal standard operating procedures used to scaffold engagement activities, and hence where to check for the more egregious departures between strategic intent and action.

This more realistic sense of what engagement can and cannot do is certainly needed in respect of some of the most challenging problems for contemporary policing, such as Prevent. As was noted in the preceding sections, for some problems there simply isn't a 'right' answer that will satisfy all constituencies. Indeed, it is in relation to such complex situations, that the ability to engage effectively with different communities becomes of most value and import to the pre-eminent task of maintaining social order. Moreover, as has happened in the 'Prevent space', problems evolve and adapt, with the consequence that what was a 'perfect fit' solution for an earlier problem becomes less effective over time. The danger inhering in the models of perfected optimum forms of engagement is that they may discourage officers from attempting to engage at all because the aspiration appears unachievable—when, on balance, some 'imperfect' effort, would be of more benefit than is achieved by complete absence. The systematic, structured, and intensive approach to engagement implemented in Cardiff was undoubtedly resource intensive. But the public value accrued in terms of providing robustly evidenced insights into the specific problems acting as drivers of neighbourhood insecurity was the return on the investment.

For understandable reasons, strategic police thinking over the past five years fixated upon reducing spending. Now that it has become clear that for the foreseeable future a smaller police service is the 'new normal', the discussion needs to move on to what comes 'after austerity'. So where the mantra of austerity has been 'doing more with less', serious consideration now needs to be given to 'doing less with more'—police intervening less often in social life, but with more impact; and acknowledging that with fewer officers, they will need to be more agile and skilled. The leadership task then, is in shifting from making policing smaller, to making it better.

The new media ecology instantiated by the introduction of Web2.0 technologies, mobile computing, and the widespread uptake of social media platforms, affords new opportunities for more effective and cost-efficient police–community engagement. Albeit police haven't been early adopters of these developments, evidence is starting to be generated of how these technologies can improve how cops interface with communities.

We should not get carried away though. There is a remarkable diversity of positions amongst different forces, in terms of their current capacity and capabilities to use social media. Questions abound about how publics will respond to such developments and where they see the balance between privacy and security. Given the accent that is placed upon policing by consent in this country, it is imperative to evidence where the thresholds of public permission lie in respect of the new digital policing techniques and technologies that are coming on stream. For which problems and situations do the public perceive the application of such approaches as legitimate and appropriate?

Just because police can track and trace public conversations taking place on social media channels, this doesn't mean they necessarily always should. Senior police leaders need to start thinking about what is required for a framework that enables digital policing by consent. Engaging with the public to determine which policing problems and situations they would see the application of big data analytics as legitimate and appropriate is a necessary condition for sustaining the tradition of policing by consent.

Recommended Reading

Fielding, N (1995), *Community Policing* (Oxford: Clarendon Press)

Kleinig, J (1996), *The Ethics of Policing* (Cambridge: Cambridge University Press)

Lowe, T and Innes, M (2012), 'Can We Speak in Confidence? Community Intelligence and Neighbourhood Policing v2.0' 22 *Policing and Society* 295

Myhill, A (2006), 'Community Engagement in Policing: Lessons from the Literature', Home Office, London

Reiner, R (2010), *The Politics of the Police* (Oxford: OUP)

Tuffin, R et al (2006), 'The National Reassurance Policing Programme: A Six Site Evaluation' Home Office, London

References

ACPO (2011), 'Independent Advisory Groups: Advice and Guidance', ACPO, London

Barnes, I and Eagle, T (2007), 'The Role of Community Engagement in Neighbourhood Policing' 1(2) *Policing* 161

Bittner, E (1974), 'Florence Nightingale in Pursuit of Willie Sutton: A Theory of the Police' in Jacob, H (ed), *The Potential for Reform of Criminal Justice* (Beverly Hills, CA: Sage)

Boyd, D and Crawford, K (2012), 'Critical Questions for Big Data: Provocations for a Cultural, Technological and Scholarly Phenomenon' 15(5) *Information, Communication and Society* 662

Brant, R (2013) 'TPims: Terror Watchdog Urges Higher Standard of Proof', *BBC News*, 14 March, at <http://www.bbc.co.uk/news/uk-politics-21790569> (accessed 31 May 2014)

Burton, L (2013), ' "Low Income and Digital Exclusion", Poverty and Social Exclusion', at <http://http://www.poverty.ac.uk/editorial/low-income-and-digital-exclusion (accessed 21 April 2015)

Carr, P (2006), *Clean Streets* (New York: New York University Press)

Casciani, D (2009), 'Terrorism Strategy Lacks Clarity, Says Minister', 8 December 2009, at <http://news.bbc.co.uk/2/hi/uk_news/8400734.stm> (accessed 21 April 2015)

Casciani, D (2014), 'Analysis: The Prevent Strategy and its Problems', 26 August, at <http://www.bbc.com/news/uk-28939555> (accessed 21 April 2015)

Cialdini, R (2001), *Influence: Science and Practice* (4th edn, Boston, MA: Allyn and Bacon)

Crank, JP (1998), *Understanding Police Culture* (Cincinatti, OH: Anderson Publishing)

Fielding, N and Innes, M (2006), 'Reassurance Policing, Community Policing and Measuring Police Performance' 16 *Policing and Society* 127

HMIC (2014), 'State of Policing: Annual Assessment of Policing in England and Wales 2012/13', Home Office, London

Herbert, S (2006), *Citizens, Cops and Power* (Chicago, IL: University of Chicago Press)

Innes, M (2006), 'Policing Uncertainty: Countering Terror through Community Intelligence and Democratic Policing' 605 *Annals of the American Academy of Political and Social Science* 222

Innes, M (2011), 'Doing Less with More: The New Politics of Policing' 8(2) *Public Policy Research* 73

Innes, M (2014), *Signal Crimes: Social Reactions to Crime, Disorder and Control* (Oxford: OUP)

Innes, M, Abbott, L, Lowe, T, Roberts, C, and Weston, N (2009), 'Signal Events, Neighbourhood Security, Order and Reassurance in Cardiff', Cardiff University, Cardiff

Innes, M, Roberts, C, and Innes, H, with Lowe, T and Lakhani, S (2011), 'Assessing the Effects of Prevent Policing', ACPO, London

Innes, M, Roberts, C, and Rogers, D (2014), 'Critical Timing: Social Media and the Golden Hour', *Police Professional Magazine*, 16 January

Johnston, L (2000), *Policing Britain: Risk, Security and Governance* (Harlow: Pearson Education)

Jones, T and Newburn, N (2001), 'Widening Access: Improving Police Relations with Hard to Reach Groups', Police Research Series, Paper 138, Home Office, London

Kemshall, H (2003), *Understanding Risk in Criminal Justice* (Maidenhead: Open University Press)

Lloyd, K and Foster, J (2009), 'Citizen Focus and Community Engagement: A Review of the Literature', The Police Foundation, London

Lowe, T and Innes, M (2012), 'Can We Speak in Confidence? Community Intelligence and Neighbourhood Policing v2' 22(3) *Policing and Society* 295

Myhill, A (2006), 'Community Engagement in Policing: Lessons from the Literature', Home Office, London

Neyroud, P (2001), *Public Participation in Policing* (London: IPPR)

Orton-Johnson, K and Prior, N (2013), *Digital Sociology: Critical Perspectives* (Basingstoke: Palgrave Macmillan)

Procter, R, Crump, J, Karstedt, S, Voss, A, and Cantijoch, M (2013), 'Reading the Riots: What Were the Police Doing on Twitter?' 23(4) *Policing and Society* 413

Reiner, R (1992) *The Politics of the Police* (2nd edn, Hemel Hempstead: Harvester Wheatsheaf)

Reiner, R (2000), *The Politics of the Police* (3rd edn, Oxford: OUP)

Rousell, A and Gascon, L (2014), 'Defining "Policeability": Cooperation, Control and Resistance in South Los Angeles Community-Police Meetings' 61(2) *Social Problems* 237

Scarman, L (1982), *The Scarman Report: The Brixton Disorders April 10–13 1981* (London: Pelican)

Skogan, W (2006), *Police and Community in Chicago* (New York: OUP)

Stott, C, Scothern, M, and Gorringe, H (2013), 'Advances in Liaison based Public Order Policing in England: Human Rights and Negotiating the Management of Protest?' 7(2) *Policing* 212

Sparrow, M, Moore, M, and Kennedy, D (1992), *Beyond 911: A New Era for Policing* (New York: Basic Books)

Tinati, R, Halford, S, Carr, L, and Pope, C (2014), 'Big Data: Methodological Challenges and Approaches for Sociological Analysis' 48 *Sociology* 663

Tuffin, R, Morris, J, and Poole, A (2006), *An Evaluation of the Impact of the National Reassurance Policing Programme*, Home Office, Development and Statistics Directorate, London

Waddington, PAJ (1999), *Policing Citizens* (London: UCL Press)

9

Police Leadership in Fractured Societies

Aogán Mulcahy and Hugh Orde

Introduction

Despite the significance of their role within police organizations, and society generally, for many years chief constables largely escaped the attentions and intrusions of researchers, certainly to a greater extent than rank-and-file officers did. Some authors did highlight concerns over the powers of chief constables and related issues (eg Brogden 1982; Jefferson and Grimshaw 1984), but only relatively recently has a body of work emerged focusing specifically on chief constables and police leadership.[1] That literature has addressed a range of issues, including background, selection, and progression; values and attitudes; management styles; and structures of governance (Reiner 1991; Wall 1998; Savage et al 2000; Loader and Mulcahy 2001a, 2001b; Caless 2011; Silvestri et al 2013; Pearson-Goff and Herrington 2014). However, and with some important exceptions (eg Murphy 2013), the role of senior officers in fractured societies and contexts of social division has generally received little academic attention.

This omission is important for two main reasons. First, the significance of police actions in those contexts—particularly in terms of the use of contentious powers, tactics, and technologies—is likely to be more far-reaching than in contexts of 'routine' policing. Second, social division is itself becoming a more prominent part of police debate, whether through the challenges of political

---

[1] For insightful discussions of aspects of police leadership and management below the level of senior officer, see Punch (1983) and Young (1994).

violence, racial conflict, and urban unrest, or the new security environment post-9/11. Although researchers might have largely neglected this topic, it is clear that from the 1970s onwards in particular, it became an increasingly prominent issue for chief constables. The title of Robert Mark's *Policing a Perplexed Society* (1977) alludes, at the very least, to the loss of social cohesion, while in the 1980s the contrast between the 'law-and-order' approach advocated by James Anderton (Prince 1988), and the 'community policing' approach championed by John Alderson (1979)—particularly in the context of urban disorder, and relations between the police and marginalized social groups—gave these issues a new prominence in wider public debate (Reiner 1991).

This chapter seeks to contribute to our understanding of the challenges of police leadership in fractured societies, drawing on Northern Ireland as a case study. I begin the discussion by considering the nature of policing in fractured societies generally, and the impact that state security has on police practice and relations with the public. I then look at three dimensions of leadership within the context of Northern Ireland. First, I consider issues of identity and affiliation. Second, I highlight the tensions between security policy and legitimacy. Third, I examine the opportunities and challenges arising from processes of police reform.

Policing and Social Division

Crisis situations can shed important light on the underlying dynamics of the criminal justice system which, during periods of stability, may remain opaque. As Balbus (1977) noted in his study of the US court system's response to widespread disorder and race riots during the 1960s, the various organizations which form the criminal justice system face an inherent tension between different and overlapping imperatives. First, they must be attentive to their mandate, and seek to achieve their stated goals. Second, in doing so, they must operate within an organizational context of finite resources and within the limits of operational effectiveness. Third, they must seek to ensure their legitimacy in the eyes of the public. The difficulty, of course, is that there is an inherent tension between these various elements, and action or change in one sphere is likely to affect the others in potentially significant ways. This is fully evident when we consider policing in fractured societies.

'Fractured societies' are characterized by a major schism or rift between different social groups, often based on or reflecting fundamental differences in their orientation towards the state, and taking the form of dominant/subordinate relations (Guelke 2012). The difficulties of policing in such societies are considerable, and, for several reasons, the dynamics of conflict often revolve specifically around policing and related issues of security and justice (Mulcahy 2015). First, as a state agency, the police tend to be indelibly associated with the dominant political order, and they occupy a highly symbolic role as an expression of the state and a means of ensuring its security. Second, the police may provide a range of civil policing services, but primacy is given to ensuring the security of the state. Third, because of the foregoing, relations with the dominant and subordinate groups tend to be shaped by this priority: the dominant group tends to view the police as 'theirs', while the subordinate group tends to be cast as inherently disloyal and thus largely as a potential threat to be managed and controlled. This gives rise to the 'over-policing' of the subordinate group through extensive police scrutiny and abrasive police practices, which in turn sustains and exacerbates the existing divisions, adding fresh grievances to existing ones. As Weitzer (1995: 5) noted, these factors ensure that 'conflict over policing is endemic in these societies', both as a key dimension in the development of conflict, and as in its ongoing dynamics.

Brewer and Weitzer suggested that policing in fractured societies is characterized by specific features that distinguish it from policing in more stable or democratic contexts, and their models are outlined in Table 9.1.

Notwithstanding the differences between their models, Brewer and Weitzer highlight how the contested nature of fractured societies (even in contexts where this is not evident in public protests or political violence) tends to ensure that police action is focused on the issue of state security, and this can cloud all other aspects of policing with important implications for police efforts to attract the support of communities who already may find themselves subject to disproportionate police attention.

While it is important to consider the role of police leadership in fractured societies as a matter of significance in its own right, these issues also have a clear relevance for policing internationally. Conflicts may be local in origin, but their impact can extend far beyond that jurisdiction. For example, since the start of the Northern Ireland conflict there has been considerable traffic between Northern Ireland and Britain at senior officer level (Mulcahy 2005). Some chief constables of the Royal Ulster Constabulary (RUC) went on to play central roles in the field of policing in Britain; while senior officers in other British forces also shaped Northern Ireland's policing landscape in important ways. Sir Robert Mark, prior to becoming Metropolitan Police Commissioner, was a member of the 1969 Hunt Committee into policing in Northern Ireland. Sir Kenneth Newman, RUC Chief Constable from 1976 to 1980, went on to become Commissioner of the London Metropolitan Police. Sir John Stevens, also a former Commissioner, was tasked with investigating allegations of collusion between loyalist paramilitaries and the security forces. Sir Hugh Orde, a senior member of the Stevens Inquiry, was subsequently appointed PSNI Chief Constable, and until recently was the President of the Association of Chief Police Officers (ACPO). Sir Ronnie Flanagan, Chief Constable of the RUC/PSNI from 1996 to 2002, subsequently was appointed Her Majesty's Chief Inspector of Constabulary for England and Wales in 2005, and has also been a policing and security adviser in a number of different contexts. Moreover, as the reform programme in Northern Ireland came to assume the mantle of an international success story—described by Chris Patten (2010: 25) as 'the best working example of

Table 9.1 Features of Policing in Fractured Societies

Brewer (1991)	Weitzer (1995)
• Selective enforcement of the law in favour of the dominant group • Discriminatory practices which limit the exercise of the rights of the minority • Political partisanship in upholding and enforcing the distribution of political power by allowing unequal rights to political protest • A lack of autonomy from the political system • An absence of effective mechanisms of public accountability • Relatively unrestrained use of force • A dual role which arises from responsibility for ordinary crime and internal security, although as threats to internal order have grown, security tends to dominate police activities, strategic planning, and leadership • The polarization of attitudes towards the police and their conduct • A social composition biased towards the dominant group because of an inability or unwillingness to recruit from among the minority communities • Chronic and endemic manpower shortage • The diffusion of policing functions throughout the dominant group, as volunteer groups and other compatible agencies are drawn into a policing role • Close operational links between the police and the military	• Systematic bias in law enforcement • Politicized policing, including strong police identification with the regime and vigorous police actions against the regime's political opponents • Dominant-group monopoly of the top positions in the police force • Dual responsibility of the police for internal security and ordinary law enforcement • Legal or extralegal powers giving the police great latitude, including in relation to the use of force • An absence of effective mechanisms of accountability with respect to police abuses of power • Polarized communal relations with the police, with the dominant group as a champion of the police and the subordinate group largely estranged from the police

Source: Adapted from Brewer (1991) and Weitzer (1995).

how to police a fractured community'—many former and serving PSNI officers played an active role in advising other societies on developments in Northern Ireland and became de facto 'sponsors' of policy transfer (see generally Ellison and O'Reilly 2008; Sinclair 2012). This flow of personnel and expertise ensures that the nature of police leadership in fractured societies is informed by, and also itself informs, the nature of policing in other jurisdictions.

Identity and Affiliation

It would be a mistake to characterize senior officers as conflict-brokers, peace-makers or otherwise, given that their role is largely to enforce the law whether in relation to conflict management or conflict resolution. Equally, though, it would be disingenuous to suggest that senior officers are simply cogs within a vast governmental apparatus, and that their significance is limited to issues of organizational efficiency and effectiveness. The police represent the most routinely visible expression of state authority and the coercive powers underpinning it, and for many communities their relationship with the police is the primary means through which wider issues of safety and security, inclusion and exclusion, and identity and affiliation, are mediated. Police leaders, then, play a public and prominent role, and one that is of inherent significance in any society; hence the selection of chief officers in fractured societies is itself a controversial issue from the outset, as is evident in the case of Northern Ireland.

Within Britain, there has been a clear trend towards greater governmental control in the selection of chief officers, partly in an effort to prevent the emergence of idiosyncratic chief officers whose high profile was often deemed a liability for the wider field of police governance, and partly to ensure greater homogeneity in outlook and approach, and thus greater central control over policing outcomes (see generally Reiner 1991; Loader and Mulcahy 2001a, 2001b). While senior officers were encouraged to curb their individual voices, their corporate voice gained in prominence, although more within institutional settings such as ACPO than in public discourse (Savage et al 2000). In fractured societies, however, the prominence of policing ensures that the role of police leaders comes under particularly close scrutiny (both during periods of overt conflict and processes of conflict resolution) in terms of the perception of any underlying bias.

The historical alignment between the RUC and unionism—the largely Protestant political bloc favouring continuation of the union between Northern Ireland and Britain—ensured that senior officers were assumed to have such an affiliation. As widespread disturbances broke out across Northern Ireland in the late 1960s, the Hunt Committee was established in 1969 to review policing. Following its report, Sir Arthur Young—then Commissioner of the City of London Police—was appointed Chief Constable of the RUC. Within the RUC and the Northern Ireland political establishment, he found that as an outsider he was viewed with considerable surprise and hostility, as someone who 'if he wasn't an enemy was certainly an alien ... It was rather like the Metropolitan Police having a Japanese general for their commissioner, as I discovered afterwards!' (cited in Alderson 1998: 116). His role in implementing the Hunt recommendations (including the disbandment of an auxiliary police force, the 'B' Specials) generated enormous hostility from loyalists and unionists, who viewed him as undermining 'their' police force:

> After a month or two, it got extremely difficult for me to get out and about because as soon as I was seen anywhere publicly by Protestants they began a demonstration and sticks and stones were thrown. I am sure if they could have they would have killed me. In Lurgan ... they made an effigy of Arthur Young and I was burnt publicly (cited in Alderson, 1998: 119).

This issue was complicated by the institutional relationship between police and the political establishment. For instance, Robert Mark noted that his involvement in the 1969 Hunt Committee had left him 'full of admiration for the rank and file of the RUC and without any admiration at all for most of its leaders' (Mark 1978: 110). He also identified the importance of ensuring that officers had scope to make meaningful representations on their conditions of service: 'In particular, we managed to give them negotiating machinery with real teeth, so that they were no longer dependent on the patronage of Northern Ireland's government at Stormont' (Mark 1978: 112; see also McGarry and O'Leary 1999: 29).

While a range of internal and external candidates were appointed to the position of RUC Chief Constable over the years, from the early 1970s onwards an overt affiliation with unionism was untenable. But it is hardly surprising to note that the various political constituencies in Northern Ireland could still view a senior officer through the prism of their political outlook. Sir Hugh Orde, for instance, was appointed over the opposition of unionist members of the Policing Board who did not attend the press conference announcing his appointment, and his appointment itself was described by one unionist Board member as 'surprising' and 'political' (Murphy 2013: 23).

But if affiliation with political blocs was no longer an overt dimension of policing, the nature and scale of the conflict gave greater weight to organizational cohesion, particularly in terms of how senior officers understood and empathized with the activities and concerns of rank-and-file officers within the organization. Whether for internally or externally appointed chief constables, the need to support one's officers as they carried out what was a difficult and enormously dangerous occupation was fully apparent. For example, in Northern Ireland during the conflict, over 300 officers were killed, and thousands suffered serious and debilitating injuries; others suffered mental trauma that, while largely unremarked on throughout the conflict, surely damaged their lives in profound ways. When Kenneth Newman was appointed RUC Chief Constable in 1976, he attended 'the funerals of seven murdered officers in his first month in office...Attending funerals was one of the most harrowing and routine duties for any RUC chief but it was an important factor, especially for an outsider to the close-knit RUC circle, in removing the remoteness between the officers at the top and those at the bottom' (Ryder 2000: 143–4). John Hermon, Newman's successor, also noted that in the drawer of his office desk he kept a copy of *Police Beat* magazine open to the page where it listed, with names and photographs, the nine RUC officers who were killed in a mortar attack in 1985 (Hermon 1997: 169).

Facing danger on such a scale undoubtedly contributed to a strong sense of solidarity among police officers. Yes, as the conflict progressed, there was a shift from an overt affiliation with unionism to a greater emphasis on professionalism, a process undertaken to enhance the force's legitimacy and to secure recognition as an impartial entity. In terms of police leadership, this involved negotiating a number of different challenges. On the one hand, by prioritizing impartiality above community affiliation, it involved distancing the organization from the political background of the vast majority of its recruits. It also involved maintaining organizational solidarity and cohesion even as its new role placed its officers increasingly in the frontline of security policing, with all of the attendant dangers that entailed. I now turn to those issues in more detail.

State Security, Operational Policing, and Public Legitimacy

By the mid-1970s and with no political solution in sight, the British government began to pursue a conflict management strategy based around policies of containment and normalization, involving a concerted effort to portray the conflict as a 'law and order' problem rather than a challenge to the state's legitimacy. This included phasing out some of the emergency measures that had proved so controversial ('special category status' for individuals convicted of offences related to the conflict, and the use of internment without trial, for example) in favour of a greater reliance on the rule of law and the 'normal' (albeit with considerably enhanced powers) criminal justice system, particularly through court convictions and greater use of standard imprisonment. At the heart of this lay an enhanced role for the police whereby they would assume primary responsibility for law and order (the army largely moving to a supporting role), and Sir Kenneth Newman (1978) was very influential in developing this policy (Mulcahy 2006). This strategy required the RUC to enhance its professionalism in two, often contradictory, ways. First, it involved the RUC increasing its effectiveness in dealing with paramilitary violence and public disturbances through a huge increase in personnel and improvements in training and equipment. Second, it entailed seeking to improve public trust in the police, by demonstrating the RUC's impartiality and its commitment to serving all communities equally. This strategy, however, brought its own dilemmas.

One strand of the RUC's efforts to secure its legitimacy involved seeking to promote itself as impartial. While in abstract terms this involved treating both communities equally, in practical terms it involved a major shift in the RUC's traditional relationship with the broad unionist community, situating the RUC—in Hermon's (1997) terms—as 'the third religion in Northern Ireland'. Unionist protests against the 1985 Anglo-Irish Agreement brought the RUC into unprecedented conflict with the broad Protestant community. Over 500 attacks on police officers' homes were recorded in 1986, and over 120 officers' families were intimidated from their homes. Hermon (1997: 193) maintained that the RUC's determination to 'hold the line' under such circumstances represented 'the turning point: it marked the emancipation of the RUC from the yoke, whether real or imagined, of unionist/loyalist influence'.

Such events undoubtedly enhanced the RUC's legitimacy in terms of impartiality (despite alienating some sections of unionism and generating significant criticism from within the force, as many officers were bitterly opposed to the

RUC assuming such a militarized role). The RUC's enhanced role in dealing with paramilitary organizations came at the cost of involving the police more closely in counter-insurgency strategies that had been so detrimental to the army's reputation, and to public trust in the criminal justice system generally. The priority attached to addressing republican paramilitary violence inevitably ensured that the broad Catholic community came under greater police scrutiny and was disproportionately subject to police action.

Perhaps robust accountability measures might have protected the RUC from some of the controversy it received for its enhanced security role from the mid-1970s onwards, but there appears to have been little appetite within government to ensure that this was the case. The Police Authority was one possible means of doing so, but it proved largely ineffectual in holding the police to account. One former member highlighted the Authority's shortcomings as an accountability mechanism, in relation to the scandal over the alleged use of violence during police interrogations during the late 1970s:

> We had called for a report on assaults and after waiting for a long time, the Chief Constable eventually came along to deliver the report. So he opened the report, read out a list of statistics at phenomenal speed—it was like speed reading, you wouldn't think that people could talk that fast—and of course no-one could make sense of what he was saying, he was just reading out a bundle of numbers. Then he closed it, said he had fulfilled his statutory obligation to the authority, and walked out. He didn't even leave us a copy of the report. Can you imagine that? And this is the body he is supposed to be accountable to? (quoted in Mulcahy 2006: 40)

In later years, other authority members also resigned, alleging that it was more of a 'performing poodle' than an effective watchdog. Within police circles, the Police Authority certainly was viewed as a less-than-robust entity. In 1994, RUC Chief Constable Hugh Annesley described the Police Authority as 'a well-intentioned bunch of amateurs' and stated that 'he would pay as much attention to a letter to the Irish News [newspaper] ... as he would to the police authority' (Hamilton et al 1995: 24).

Overall, in the balancing of different organizational imperatives, the strategies pursued by chief constables throughout the conflict suggest that the mandate of state security trumped concerns over police legitimacy. Special Branch, the unit tasked with countering paramilitary organizations, appeared to operate with considerable latitude and in conditions of near-impunity. Even in 2007, a Police Ombudsman report stated that 'a culture of subservience to Special Branch developed within the RUC ... [to the extent that] it acquired domination over the rest of the organisation' (2007: 144). Security force measures taken during the conflict—including collusion between the security forces and loyalist paramilitaries (see generally Stevens 2006; Punch 2012)—cast a long shadow indeed.

For these reasons, while the RUC attracted considerable support for its role in dealing with ordinary crime, its support levels among Catholics plummeted in relation to its security role. Surveys repeatedly demonstrated the gulf in Catholic and Protestant attitudes towards security measures, which largely reflected differences in political outlook, and direct experience (Weitzer 1995; Ellison and Smyth 2000; Mulcahy 2006). As Whyte (1990: 88) noted: 'There is an even greater degree of disagreement between Protestants and Catholics on security policy than there is on constitutional questions. Security issues remain an unhealed sore.'

Enduring concerns over security policy ensured that regardless of the RUC's considerable moves towards greater professionalization, policing would continue to be a key element of any political settlement. As a consequence, the role of the chief constable remained hugely prominent, both in terms of assuming responsibility for driving and managing that process within the police organization, as well as communicating those developments to an often polarized and sceptical public audience.

The Opportunities and Challenges of the Reform Process

For a police force which had been at the forefront of an armed conflict, and which had seen so many of its members killed or injured, the peace process culminating in the 1998 Belfast Agreement held out the promise of a future in which policing would no longer be so controversial and divisive, nor so profoundly dangerous. From the policing arrangements outlined in the Patten Report (Independent Commission on Policing in Northern Ireland 1999), a new set of challenges arose for police leaders.

First, the advent of a permanent peace and a political settlement brought closer the day when many police officers would lose their jobs. For the exchequer, one of the 'peace dividends' was a major reduction in security expenditure, largely to be achieved through a reduction in personnel within the security sector. This had been anticipated for many years, but it was crystallized in the Patten Report's recommendation to reduce the size of the police force from 13,000 to 7,500 officers (largely to be achieved through a generous severance package) while simultaneously increasing the proportion of Catholics within the police service by introducing a 50:50 recruitment system for Catholics and non-Catholics (Mulcahy 2013).

Second, the reform programme was dripping with symbolism. Many within the RUC felt that having 'policed the war', the force had earned the right to 'police the peace', but the proposal to have a new name for the force—it duly became the Police Service of Northern Ireland (PSNI) in 2001—was perceived as a rejection of the RUC's claims concerning its role and performance, and it caused enormous affront within the force. Despite the many far-reaching changes proposed in the Patten Report, it was the name change which caused most public anguish, and around which most critics of the Patten programme coalesced.

Third, the range of new institutions which emerged from the Patten Report—including the Policing Board, District Policing Partnerships, the Policing Ombudsman, and the Oversight Commissioner—involved a level of transparency and oversight, and liaison and relationship-building, that simply was of a different order to what prevailed during the conflict.

Fourth, the new political environment was also evolving in parallel to the police reform programme. In addition to an ongoing level of paramilitary threat (particularly from republicans opposed to the peace process), disturbances in relation to parades, the flying of flags, and other matters, all contributed to the political uncertainty of the time. This ensured that rolling out the new policing institutions and arrangements was a protracted process, each element of which nevertheless had an extremely high profile (including symbolic events such as the first meeting between the chief constable and the leader of Sinn Féin in 2004).

Fifth, despite the euphoria of peace and the promise of new policing arrangements, the PSNI still operated within a finite resource environment. Public expectations of the new policing era were extremely high, and far exceeded the ability of the police to meet them. Moreover, the deployment of police resources was also shaped by the tension between addressing past controversies (particularly through the establishment of the Historical Enquiries Team to investigate the many unsolved murders related to the conflict) and meeting present-day demands.

Addressing these various issues is an unfolding story, but given the scale of the transition from RUC to PSNI and the uncertainty it generated within the police, communication and persuasion on the part of police leaders proved to be an important aspect of this process. Sir Ronnie Flanagan, for instance, displayed a willingness to publicly engage with other stakeholders about policing and the reform process in a manner that had not previously occurred (Mulcahy 2006; Murphy 2013). Flanagan was widely viewed as an articulate proponent of change, but also as someone attentive to the concerns of rank-and-file officers. Similarly, Orde noted his commitment to 'getting out and about' among his officers (Orde 2010: 100) and meeting with them to address their concerns and secure their support for the new policing arrangements. But given the controversial nature of policing historically and its centrality to the peace process in Northern Ireland, it is also important not to overlook another key feature of the reform process—opposition and resistance. This is not to imply bad faith, but simply to recognize that any process of change can inherently undermine the certainties that shaped one's outlook—particularly in the context of what constituted 'normal policing' (Mulcahy 1999)—and thus can generate significant resistance both within and without the police organization, as was clearly the case in Northern Ireland (Murphy 2013). As such, one should not assume that immediate agreement necessarily can be reached. In that case, police leadership requires attentiveness to the long-term goal of reform, and a willingness to persevere even in the face of resistance. As Orde noted: 'Resilience . . . is a key requirement in leading change' (Orde 2010: 102).

Practitioner's Perspective

This section is in part a response to the observations of Dr Mulcahy and in part my own observations based on the experience of being the Chief Constable of the PSNI for exactly seven years, between September 2002 and September 2009. For the two years prior to my appointment as Chief Constable, between 2000 and 2002, I was in day-to-day command of Sir John (now Lord) Stevens' Enquiry into the murder of Patrick Finucane, a solicitor murdered during the Troubles. The lessons and experience of leadership are built up en route to the top—ie one steps into the difficult territory en route. This allows one to experience the challenges of risk and decision-making at lower levels and provides essential experience and greater confidence when faced with wicked issues as the leader of a large force.

Before my involvement in Northern Ireland I policed some of the most difficult territory in London, in particular protecting the diverse communities of the capital from serious and organized crime; and developing Operation Trident, a long-running operation focused (then) on crack cocaine and murder within the black communities of London. It was during that part of my career in leadership that I began to better understand the critical importance of legitimacy and in particular, the skill of listening—in quiet conversations—to those who truly represented their communities in order to understand them better.

The notion that police are simply law enforcers within a model based on policing by consent is flawed at every level. Consent requires an approach that builds legitimacy and trust in order that when power is exercised over fellow citizens as necessary, it is understood and accepted. Several thousand police cannot dominate 1.5 million people. In the context of Northern Ireland and its unique policing challenges, that is a statement of the blindingly obvious.

Leadership and consent

The role of leadership in building consent is in my experience the essential element. The clear determination to police against a set of principles that is made explicit at a strategic level must be declared in an open and transparent way, coupled with an empowering approach that gives permission to subordinates in the leadership chain to translate that broad ambition into the local reality in which they operate. This is difficult to achieve both culturally and hierarchically. Senior leaders are used to giving orders, and junior leaders are used to receiving them! In the context of Northern Ireland that hierarchy was well established, for very understandable reasons.

I remember the press conference announcing my appointment,which Aogán refers to very well. Despite the behaviour of some politicians, I used it to clearly state my determination to work with the Northern Ireland Policing Board (NIPB) and the Police Ombudsman to implement the Patten Report and deliver world class policing at the earliest possible opportunity. I believe there is a very short window of opportunity for an incoming leader, regardless of rank, to state clearly how they intend to do business, and how they expect business to be done. The intentions I stated underpin Aogán's observations around the importance of oversight and accountability. The willingness of leaders to engage publically with outside agencies offering accountability and challenge is critical to effective leadership, however uncomfortable it may be on occasions.

A commitment to transparent oversight has to be broadly drawn and interpreted. In addition to the NIPB and Police Ombudsman, I saw the human rights advisers to the Board, the Oversight Commissioner, and select committees as essential stakeholders, to be accorded the respect and attention they deserved as of right. But I see oversight extending far beyond other public bodies. The media, together with third-sector organizations and interest groups, all have a part to play, and a willingness to engage across this spectrum, however challenging and difficult it may be, sends a clear message both internally and externally about an open approach to engagement. In my experience, it also gives permission for a similar approach to be taken at the local level. In Northern Ireland, District Policing Partnerships secured citizen engagement between local commanders and their communities through statutory meeting arrangements. I would also attend these meetings from time to time.

Within the new arrangements set out by Patten, I would highlight the Policing Board as the primary accountability mechanism. This forum was well resourced and broadly reflected the communities I was responsible for policing. I was operationally responsible for policing, the Board was charged with holding me to account. The Police (Northern Ireland) Act 2000 gave the Board powers to require me to attend; however, my sense was that to be compelled would indicate an unwillingness to be open, transparent, and accessible, and I ensured that every request to attend was met with an immediate agreement, whether it came from the full Board or any subcommittee. In the wider context of UK policing and the new arrangements for governance which introduced police and crime commissioners (PCCs), police leaders must be equally open to scrutiny. This is of particular relevance when the conditions of fractured societies identified at Table 9.1 apply.

Leadership and empowering others

As mentioned, the strategic approach must mesh with the tactical; this introduces the concepts of empowerment and risk into the leadership equation. We have to acknowledge that we are operating against a backdrop of intolerance for failure, regardless of its reason. In addition, we are seeing growing demand for historic investigations. The impact can drive people towards risk-averse compliance approaches based on creating policy and procedure, rather than encouraging them to innovate, take citizen-specific approaches, or embrace risks.

Even so, leaders must allow their subordinates to operate with sufficient freedom to deliver policing bespoke to the local communities, and underwrite that risk against a clear set of principles, not an over-complicated and rigid set of policies and procedures. In Northern Ireland, these principles were very simple: a human rights-based approach to policing together with a code of ethics that covered how we would deliver policing. I think we were ahead of the game; certainly the new Code of Ethics established by the College of Policing in 2014 adopted much of our work. The European Code of Police Ethics (Counsel of Europe) is also important reading (Council of Europe 2011). Communicating the message around this ambition becomes more challenging when the geography of a large force encompasses diverse communities with different expectations and experiences of policing, as evidenced by Weitzer (1995). The current climate of growing demand to be accommodated within fewer resources, adds even more complexity.

As a senior leader I found such empowerment to be a critical success factor, but very challenging. It was about being comfortable with not knowing everything that was going on, and confident that the trust within the team was such that events I needed to know about came to my attention quickly. This is not a precise science and on occasions will inevitably go wrong, sometimes even spectacularly wrong. By way of example, shortly after my appointment, came the infamous PSNI 'raid' on Stormont on Friday 4 October 2002, following allegations of republican intelligence gathering inside the Northern Ireland Office. After PSNI officers conducted a search of Sinn Féin offices, power-sharing arrangements were suspended and the force was accused of having a political motive.

In essence, a large number of officers were deployed to support the search of one office, in an operation that could be described as clumsy. Bearing in mind the symbolic location and the foreseeable consequences of such an event, to be unsighted was inexcusable. The impact internationally was immense, and exacerbated by the live news coverage from a television crew who merely by chance, happened to be on the scene to report a far more mundane event. Notwithstanding the internal issues that needed to be dealt with, this event was seen very differently by the two communities. One Democratic Unionist Party politician described it as a '****ing good Friday', reflecting their general views on parts of the peace process. Meanwhile, Sinn Féin, who were yet to engage formally in policing, were predictably outraged.

Whilst a stark example, the potential damage to a delicate peace process and to confidence building in policing required a prompt and clear response. I was very clear that in my judgment we had clearly got this badly wrong. I chose to recognize this quickly on live television, and acknowledge that the search, whilst lawful and part of a wider investigation, was poorly executed. I also observed that the officers deployed were undertaking that which they had been told to do. Leaders have to be conscious in situations such as these of the many different audiences that they will be addressing with one message. The audiences included my own officers, many of whom felt let down by their leader. Again, leadership requires complete honesty with our own people, and it took a challenging, yet very useful debrief led by me personally, to give officers an opportunity to engage with the leadership and express their views.

So what was the learning?

1. Honesty, and acknowledgement of different perspectives even in quite unforgiving environments is the proper and ethical way forward. It has to be genuine and meaningful to be effective.
2. Operationally independent police leaders have to speak in an unintimidated and unfettered way, yet mindful of the potential political consequences of their statements.
3. There is no such thing as good timing. To delay, obfuscate, or disappear in such a situation would allow the agenda to be set by others. Taking the high ground quickly is essential.
4. On occasions such as these, delegation is not an option. Visible leadership is important.
5. Whilst sometimes quite challenging, authentic engagement with our own people post-event is a crucial element in preventing resentment and repeats.
6. Citizens understand that we are human and will tolerate error. They will not tolerate defending the indefensible.
7. Moving from entirely understandable but rigid procedures to a more thoughtful and bespoke approach takes time.

Engaging with fractured communities

Finally, without thoughtful follow-up, in particular with the formal accountability mechanisms, initial statements lose value very quickly. I would further argue that particularly when dealing with fractured communities, such calamitous events require wider engagement. I touched earlier on the significance of what I termed quiet conversations. In the context of Northern Ireland, it was clear that many individuals who clearly knew the pulses of their communities were prepared to engage with policing, sometimes through third parties, in ways that allowed me to better understand the impact of policing, expectations for the future, and the burdens of the past.

My starting point was that I would talk to anyone who wanted to make a difference to policing. I found such conversations of immense value in understanding the issues covered in Aogán's section on policing and social division. Policing in my experience is as much about emotion and thoughtfulness as it is about science and evidence; it is as much about perception as it is about reality. I remember one quiet conversation where individuals, with terrorist histories from across the divide, explored and dismantled the different constructions of their respective realities during the troubles in an extraordinary and emotional way. Their shared distrust of the police was the only area of common agreement!

I learned more about the struggle of working-class Protestants and their relationship with policing from a quiet conversation with a convicted loyalist terrorist who has now passed away, sitting in a neutral place provided by a facilitator and eating fish and chips, than from anyone else. Similarly, with the Republican side, it was quiet conversations with people that helped me to understand how the communities saw the organization I led. The point I make here is that effective policing in fractured communities requires leaps of faith from both the police and the community, and likewise it demands an appetite for risk. It also requires trust, which can only be earned and built up through the courage to take such leaps of faith. Police leaders should feel under an obligation to seek out the conversations that will help them to engage with and understand communities, being prepared to accept rejection on occasions, yet try and try again to secure the shared understanding that underpins effective policing. Despite so many conversations, I was never compromised as a consequence of these meetings, nor did I ever compromise those who met me.

Again, what works at the strategic level often has application tactically. Many difficult conversations were held in a similar way by police commanders and leaders generally within communities at the local level. The power of such engagement should not be underestimated and it can play a major part in narrowing the gap between a community which is over-policed and one which is under-policed.

In Trident,[2] the leadership challenge was convincing communities that we were capable of protecting them from extremely violent and dangerous killers. The impact of crimes such as the murders of Avril Johnson, Michelle Carby, and Patrick Ferguson, all within the space of a single month in 1988, shook the confidence of a community.

One traditional police approach to dealing with such a cycle of violence is to set up a squad, fix the problem, and then disband. Trident adopted a different approach; it worked with the communities in a far closer way to protect them. It listened and engaged with individuals who previously would have been seen as too high risk. Through an advisory group, it identified further players who could help and built a network across parts of London that played a major part in the investigation.

By openly declaring that I would speak to anyone who wanted to make a difference, we created a space for community members to meet us with a shared objective, without any baggage from history. The fact that Trident continues to this day is a testament to this approach and the confidence it has built over time. I repeated the pledge in Northern Ireland when challenged about whether I should meet individuals with terrorist histories. While it was an unusual question to be asked within the UK policing environment, my answer remained the same. I met with many over my seven years, some privately and some publically,

---

[2] Operation Trident was a determined effort by the Metropolitan Police to create a standing team of experienced detectives to combat so-called black-on-black crime. It started following some very violent murders within that community and was linked primarily to crack cocaine and Jamaica.

but without question those conversations overwhelmingly contributed to build-ing confidence in policing.

One of my chief concerns around meeting some of the more high-profile individuals was the view which would be taken by my own officers. In fact, I learned that one should never ever underestimate those who we lead. In simple terms they understood the principle and recognized why it was the right thing to do. This rationale can in my experience be applied to the routine of policing: the vast majority of officers come into work each day determined to do a good job for the public and they can be trusted to make those difficult decisions.

Dealing with the past

Confidence in policing is not always a function of the present, but also can depend on a willingness to deal with the past. While this subject may not at first pass be seen as relevant to leadership, I would argue the opposite. While there are unique and exciting challenges for the future of policing in Northern Ireland, there is also a unique legacy of pain and suffering associated with its difficult history. This is an issue that permeates every aspect of life, a shadow across politics, organizations, communities, and families. As a police officer interacting with the public it is impossible to remain unmoved by the terrible individual tragedies that underpin this debate.

In fractured communities generally, this becomes more intense and often complicated by many different legal approaches to individual cases, creating a hierarchy of death, for example those who have investigations, inquests, and public inquiries, or at least some support through interested parties or pressure groups, and those who have nothing. In modern policing terms, historic issues are no longer simply an issue for Northern Ireland (think about Hillsborough, for example, and the Saville Inquiry), and their impact on confidence in policing is substantial if left unaddressed.

The role for leaders is aptly described thus:

> History, despite its wrenching pain
> Cannot be unlived, and if faced
> With courage, need not be lived again.
> *On the Pulse of Morning*,
> Maya Angelou (1993)

The impact of the past on the present is no longer unique to Northern Ireland, although it is there that some learning can be found. Currently, it is growing unabated, and the spectrum is widening. Investigations into child abuse in North Wales, new inquests and further investigation into the Hillsborough tragedy, investigations around the murder of Stephen Lawrence, a criminal investigation into Bloody Sunday, together with thematic concerns around issues challenging policing such as deaths in custody; all these will reach into the future, as the many different but broadly legal and judicial approaches grind on.

The impact on community and police relationships should be a key concern for leaders in policing. Any notion that such issues will simply fade over time without being faced are flawed, and courageous decisions are required. Different approaches (that are without question high risk), which focus on victims and their families, have been critical to developing confidence in policing in Northern Ireland.

I was responsible for leading such an approach in Northern Ireland, through creating the Historic Enquiries Team (HET). Over 3,260 deaths were attributed to the Troubles between 1968 and 1998, of which 2,002 were never solved. The common strand across all those who had lost loved ones was the desire to know more about what happened. The HET was an attempt to do something to meet those concerns, based on maximum permissible disclosure of information, about what was known to have happened and what had been investigated.

I always envisaged that it would be but a part of a wider process. My hope was that other approaches would run in parallel, providing alternative solutions to our approach. While far from perfect, the work of the HET represented a genuine and committed attempt to help families of victims of the Troubles to find a measure of resolution. It is a matter of huge regret that the difficulties of investigating cases involving the state have now helped to undermine the work of the HET. Dealing with the past is not just a policing and justice issue, but one for government and civic society. Yet no other body has followed the PSNI in making an attempt to face it.

The learning is that in fractured communities, different approaches need to be subject to different oversight and are vulnerable to naive interpretation and complex politics. Furthermore, courage can be a critical dimension of leadership. On occasions in my experience a sincere and deep belief that one is doing the right thing for citizens can, over time, fall victim to changing circumstances and perspectives. The more radical the solution, the easier it can become to challenge it. The inevitable consequence is that it requires more courage to be radical and forward looking, as risk taking can become subordinated to what is routine, but safe. The skill to operate in a politicized environment is to be prized and to a degree I think much of it can be learned. Courageous leaders who care for their communities should be prepared for such assaults. As Aogán observes, resilience will remain a key requirement in leading change.

Shared Reflections

Having outlined separately, drawing on academic debates and professional experience, some of the key concerns relating to police leadership in fractured societies, here we offer some brief shared reflections on these issues in light of the earlier discussion.

Within much academic debate on policing, issues of social structure and socio-political environments tend to predominate as explanatory factors. Police officers themselves have almost been viewed as an inconvenience, an anomaly within otherwise robust explanatory frameworks. Occasionally, reforming officers may be characterized as lone rangers of sorts, but this confirms their role as iconoclasts, the exception that proves the structural rule. Yet in debates on police reform, police officers typically have been cast as the villain of the piece (while often being simultaneously characterized as the victims of a rapacious occupational culture and/or an 'impossible' mandate). There is now a greater appreciation of the role that police officers can play in improving policing—such as the literature on 'police reform from below' and on rank-and-file officers as 'change agents' (see eg the special issue of *Policing and Society* (2008) 18(1))—and discussion of chief constables in other contexts highlights the different orientations they bring to the role (Reiner 1991; Murphy 2013). In that spirit, it would be no bad thing if commentators showed a greater awareness of the role that human agency and contingency can play in these processes.

Related to this, given the centrality of policing to the social and political dynamics of fractured societies, we also highlight the role that police reform can play in consolidating any process of conflict resolution or political transition. Few issues carry such symbolism and are as prominent in public debate as an unfolding programme of police reform. The tone of senior officers' comments and their willingness to engage with a range of parties are important cues within the police organization, but their importance extends far beyond that, and in significant ways may contribute to public support for new policing arrangements, as well as being a tangible sign of progress in respect of a peace process itself. Here also it is important to recognize the importance of building productive relations with any new institutions of police governance; and 'productive' does not imply a cosy chat (or 'capture', of which the Oversight Commissioner warned). Rather, it can entail a very challenging engagement, but one which serves the wider purpose of ensuring police oversight, and demonstrating it to be a tangible entity.

While we are in clear agreement over the centrality of legitimacy, the means to generate and maintain it is, of course, complex. Recent research suggests that the public places great store on police adherence to standards of procedural justice (Jackson et al 2012). While this may be the case in contexts of tranquillity and stability, in times of crisis there is a real danger that 'rights' become secondary to security, that they are viewed as an optional extra which can be written off in pursuit of the 'obvious' goal of security. Clearly, we recognize the real pressures that are generated during conflict situations, and certainly police leaders in contexts other than that of Northern Ireland seem to view their legitimacy as based on 'crime control' rather than procedural justice (Jonathan-Zamir and Harpaz 2014). However, to view rights in this way, as something which can be rolled back when under duress, and then, perhaps when these pressures recede, reinstated on the basis that the state can 'afford' them once again, is of course to make a mockery of them. It also overlooks the historical tendency for 'exceptional' or 'emergency' powers to become 'normalized' within criminal justice, remaining in place long after the putative crisis has passed (Hillyard 1987;

Mulcahy 2005). In response to this commonly stated position, we simply note that to treat human rights (including those of criminal suspects) as 'optional' is itself to sow the seeds of future insecurity. Perceptions of injustice on the part of the police and security forces can fuel a conflict much more than, say, initial concerns over discrimination in housing allocation or constituency gerrymandering. This is one of the primary lessons to be learnt from analysing the Northern Ireland conflict. In respect of the specific issue of police leadership, it means that senior officers play a vital role in supporting human rights and in resisting any pressure (political or otherwise) to prioritize security outcomes over rights.

Finally, we note the significance of the legacy of the past. In fractured societies, it is a live and consequential phenomenon. The sheer scale of the conflict and the disputed nature of the political backdrop may help to ensure that any claim over the public sphere is likely to be contested. Moreover, the covert nature of protagonists' actions, the use of 'proxy' actors, and widespread strategies of 'othering' and denial all ensure that the past is inherently unresolved (Cohen 2001; Jamieson and McEvoy 2005). Continued obfuscation may appear politically advantageous in the short term, but at an unknown cost in terms of solidarity and reconciliation. However, regardless of the location, damage is damage and pain is pain; and whether societies may be characterized as fundamentally fractured or not, perceptions of injustice can shape entire communities' engagement with the state, and their sense of belonging and recognition within it. The experience of Northern Ireland demonstrates the damaging effect that failing to address past controversies can have (Hearty 2014; Lawther 2014), and that salutary lesson holds true for other societies also.

Recommended Reading

Alison, L and Crego, J (eds) (2012), *Policing Critical Incidents: Leadership and Critical Incident Management* (Abingdon: Routledge)
Mark, R (1977), *Policing a Perplexed Society* (London: Allen & Unwin)
Murphy, J (2013), *Policing for Peace in Northern Ireland: Change, Conflict and Community Confidence* (Basingstoke: Palgrave Macmillan)

References

Alderson, J (1979), *Policing Freedom* (Plymouth: Macdonald and Evans)
Alderson, J (1998), *Principled Policing* (Winchester: Waterside Press)
Angelou, Maya (1993), 'On the Pulse of Morning'. Poem read at the inauguration of President Bill Clinton
Balbus, I (1977), *The Dialectics of Legal Repression: Black Rebels before the American Criminal Courts* (revd edn, New Brunswick, NJ: Transaction Books)
Brewer, J (1991), 'Policing in Divided Societies: Theorising a Type of Policing' 1(3) *Policing and Society* 179
Brogden, M (1982), *The Police: Autonomy and Consent* (London: Academic Press)

Caless, B (2011), *Policing at the Top: The Roles, Values and Attitudes of Chief Police Officers* (Bristol: Policy Press)

Cohen, S (2001), *States of Denial: Knowing about Atrocity and Suffering* (Cambridge: Polity)

Council of Europe (2011), 'International Standard: The European Code of Police Ethics, Democratic Control of Armed Forces', Committee of Ministers, Brussels

Ellison, G and O'Reilly, C (2008), ' "Ulster's Policing Goes Global": The Police Reform Process in Northern Ireland and the Creation of a Global Brand' 50(4–5) *Crime, Law and Social Change* 331

Ellison, G and Smyth, J (2000), *The Crowned Harp: Policing Northern Ireland* (London: Pluto)

Guelke, A (2012), *Politics in Deeply Divided Societies* (Cambridge: Polity)

Hamilton, A, Moore, L, and Trimble, T (1995), *Policing a Divided Society* (Coleraine: Centre for the Study of Conflict)

Hearty, K (2014), 'A Shared Narrative? A Case Study of the Contested Legacy of Policing in the North of Ireland' 54(6) *British Journal of Criminology* 1047

Hermon, J (1997), *Holding the Line: An Autobiography* (Dublin: Gill and Macmillan)

Hillyard, P (1987), 'The Normalization of Special Powers: From Northern Ireland to Britain' in Scraton, P (ed), *Law, Order and the Authoritarian State* (Milton Keynes: Open University Press) 279

Independent Commission on Policing in Northern Ireland (1999), 'A New Beginning: Policing in Northern Ireland' (the Patten Report), HMSO, Belfast

Jackson, J, Bradford, B, Stanko, B, and Hohl, K (2012), *Just Authority? Trust in the Police in England and Wales* (Abingdon: Routledge)

Jamieson, R and McEvoy, K (2005), 'State Crime by Proxy and Juridical Othering' 45(4) *British Journal of Criminology* 504

Jefferson, T and Grimshaw, R (1984), *Controlling the Constable: Police Accountability in England and Wales* (London: Frederick Muller/Cobden Trust)

Jonathan-Zamir, T and Harpaz, A (2014), 'Police Understanding of the Foundations of Their Legitimacy in the Eyes of the Public: The Case of Commanding Officers in the Israel National Police' 54(3) *British Journal of Criminology* 469

Lawther, C (2014), *Truth, Denial and Transition: Northern Ireland and the Contested Past* (Abingdon: Routledge)

Loader, I and Mulcahy, A (2001a), 'The Power of Legitimate Naming: Part I—Chief Constables as Social Commentators in Post-War England' 41(1) *British Journal of Criminology* 41

Loader, I and Mulcahy, A (2001b), 'The Power of Legitimate Naming: Part II—Making Sense of the Elite Police Voice' 41(2) *British Journal of Criminology* 252

McGarry, J and O'Leary, B (1999), *Policing Northern Ireland: Proposals for a New Start* (Belfast: Blackstaff)

Mark, R (1977), *Policing a Perplexed Society* (London: Allen and Unwin)

Mark, R (1978), *In the Office of Constable* (Glasgow: Collins)

Mulcahy, A (1999), 'Visions of Normality: Peace and the Reconstruction of Policing in Northern Ireland' 8(2) *Social and Legal Studies* 277

Mulcahy, A (2005), 'The "Other" Lessons from Ireland? Policing, Political Violence and Policy Transfer' 2(2) *European Journal of Criminology* 185

Mulcahy, A (2006), *Policing Northern Ireland: Conflict, Legitimacy and Reform* (Cullompton: Willan)

Mulcahy, A (2013), 'Great Expectations and Complex Realities: The Impact and Implications of the Police Reform Process in Northern Ireland' in Brown, J (ed), *The Future of Policing* (Abingdon: Routledge) 476

Mulcahy, A (2015), 'Policing in Divided Societies' in Richard Wright, R (ed), *International Encyclopaedia of the Social and Behavioural Sciences*, Vol 18 (2nd edn, Amsterdam: Elsevier) 266

Murphy, J (2013), *Policing for Peace in Northern Ireland: Change, Conflict and Community Confidence* (Basingstoke: Palgrave Macmillan)

Newman, K (1978), 'Prevention in Extremis: The Preventative Role of the Police in Northern Ireland' in Brown, J (ed), *The Cranfield Papers* (London: Peel Press) 13

Orde, H (2010), 'Leading the Process of Reform' in Doyle, J (ed), *Policing the Narrow Ground* (Dublin: Royal Irish Academy) 99

Patten, C (2010), 'Personal Reflections on Chairing the Commission' in Doyle, J (ed), *Policing the Narrow Ground* (Dublin: Royal Irish Academy) 13

Pearson-Goff, M and Herrington, V (2014), 'Police Leadership: A Systematic Review of the Literature' 8(1) *Policing* 14

Prince, M (1988), *God's Cop: The Biography of James Anderton* (London: Frederick Muller)

Punch, M (ed) (1983), *Control in the Police Organisation* (Cambridge, MA: MIT Press)

Punch, M (2012), *State Violence, Collusion and the Troubles: Counter Insurgency, Government Deviance and Northern Ireland* (London: Pluto)

Reiner, R (1991), *Chief Constables: Bobbies, Bosses or Bureaucrats* (Oxford: OUP)

Ryder, C (2000), *The RUC 1922–2000* (4th edn, London: Arrow)

Savage, S, Charman, S, and Cope, S (2000), *Policing and the Power of Persuasion* (London: Blackstone)

Silvestri, M, Tong, S, and Brown, J (2013), 'Gender and Police Leadership: Time for a Paradigm Shift?' 15(1) *International Journal of Police Science and Management* 61

Sinclair, G (2012), 'Exporting the UK Police Brand: The RUC-PSNI and the International Agenda' 6(1) *Policing* 44

Stevens, J (2006), *Not for the Faint-Hearted* (revd edn, London: Phoenix)

Wall, D (1998), *The Chief Constables of England and Wales: The Socio-legal History of a Criminal Justice Elite* (Aldershot: Dartmouth)

Weitzer, R (1995), *Policing under Fire: Ethnic Conflict and Police–Community Relations in Northern Ireland* (Albany, NY: SUNY Press)

Whyte, J (1990), *Interpreting Northern Ireland* (Oxford: Clarendon)

Young, M (1994), *In the Sticks: Cultural Identity in a Rural Police Force* (Oxford: Clarendon)

10

Women in Police Leadership

Marisa Silvestri and Colette Paul

Introduction

Recent decades have witnessed a significant level of interest in police leadership, yet our knowledge of the specificity of experience inherent in the role and work of police leaders remains relatively limited. As a result, police leaders have for the most part been presented as a fairly homogenous group. With a preponderance of (white) men serving in senior ranks, and a persistent and enduring presence of a 'masculine ethos' within policing (Loftus 2010; Barrie and Broomhall; 2012; Dick et al 2013); gendered analyses of police leadership, either in relation to masculinity or femininity, remain scarce. A review and analysis of the key literature on women working in police leadership is thus fundamental to the study of police leadership. Given the relatively small evidence base, it draws upon international work to develop its analysis. Indeed, there is much to suggest that policewomen in Britain share much in common with their global counterparts. In trying to make sense of the 'here and now', the chapter also adopts a historical approach through a consideration of women's engagement with police leadership over time. The chapter is made up of five key parts. First, it considers the presence and legacy of pioneering women police leaders in the early 20th century. Second, it outlines the broader context of 'crisis' that has shaped much of the discourse in calling for more women police. Third, it reports on some of the key challenges that women face in navigating their climb to the top of policing. It then explores what we know about how women '*do*' police leadership, and finally, Chief Constable Colette Paul of Bedfordshire Constabulary reflects on her career and her role thus far as a police leader.

Pioneers in a Past Life

Whilst contemporary discourses on women in police leadership often begin with the appointment of Pauline Clare as Chief Constable of Lancashire in 1995, women's engagement with police leadership extends well over a century. Histories document considerable resistance towards women's entry and progression within policing which was vigorously fought, resisted, and undermined on legal, organizational, informal, and interpersonal levels (Martin 1980; Carrier 1988; Schultz 1995; Segrave 1995; Miller 1999). With a focus on social and welfare work, women police leaders in the early part of the 20th century lobbied hard and fought vigorously on a global stage to establish a permanent place for women in policing and for 'women's issues' (Lock 1979; Carrier 1988; Appier 1998; Schultz 1995; Heidensohn 2000). Heidensohn (1992) documents the ways in which senior policewomen worked tirelessly, pursuing their cause, 'proselytizing' their case, urging others to follow their example. Margaret Damer Dawson (Commandant and co-founder of the Women's Police Service in 1914) addressed numerous meetings of local committees and societies. Her successor, Mary Allen, also dedicated much time to advocating the cause of women police (Lock 1979). Indeed, Heidensohn (2000: 57) remarks that many of the skills that Allen and her colleagues sustained and developed were remarkable, resembling those of 'contemporary spin doctors'. In making sense of such activism, the campaign for women police most certainly came from women who were in some shape or form connected to the suffrage movement (Carrier 1988). Often 'committed feminists' (Heidensohn 1992), these pioneering women police leaders worked to construct the concept of an 'international woman police officer', working collectively and in an organized way with women police across the globe. This is not to suggest that women worked effortlessly within a framework of 'sisterhood' without disagreement. On the contrary, there is much evidence to suggest disagreement and conflict between women police leaders about how they should progress the agenda for women police (see Lock 1979 for an account of this).

As the century progressed, the appointment of women police in England and Wales continued on a piecemeal basis and women moved from a separate women's sphere to integration into mainstream policing in 1973. Hailed as a moment of 'progress' and 'gain' in the journey towards gender equality, commentators have observed the considerable and simultaneous losses experienced by women police leaders (Schultz 1995; Miller 1999). In a review of career advancement during this time, Brown (2006) argues that women officers fared worse in achieving promotion when compared to men. She suggests that this was because women were now competing against the total number of eligible officers instead of being considered in terms of the number of appropriately qualified women from the previously separate Police Women's Department. Moreover, women who had reached senior positions in the separate policewomen's service were forced to relinquish them as they joined forces with men. Brown and

Heidensohn (2000: 4) describe the move towards integration as '... the striking of a somewhat Faustian bargain', with the price of admittance resulting in a loss of a radical agenda and the acceptance of male definitions and methods of control. Since integration, there have been a number of important and welcome changes in equalities policy, and substantial inroads have been made to the advancement and position of women in policing (ACPO 2010). Figures for England and Wales show that women currently account for 28% of the total number of officers, with women in leadership roles standing at 19% (BAWP, 2014).

The Call for More Women Police—in Times of 'Crisis'

Change brought about by equalities policy and legislation has done much to improve women's position in society. The Equal Pay Act 1970 and the Sex Discrimination Act 1975, represented significant gains for women's rights in the areas of employment, training, education, protection from harassment, and the provision of goods and services. Since that time, much policy and legislation has been directed at improving the position of women in the workplace. The establishment of the Equal Opportunities Commission in 1975, the creation of a Minister for Women and Equalities and the Equalities Office in 1997, the introduction of the Gender Equality Duty (GED) in 2007, the creation of the Equality and Human Rights Commission (EHRC) in 2007, the Equality Act 2010[1] and the Equality Duty (2011) have all strengthened the equalities architecture in the United Kingdom over the past 40 years. More significantly, such developments have firmly shifted the onus of responsibility for gender equality from individuals to public bodies, requiring public bodies to review proactively their policies and practices on gender equality, collect and monitor equality data, and tackle institutionalized gender discrimination.

Although such policy and legislation have contributed much to the progression of women into mainstream policing, women's entry to policing was often precipitated by a 'crisis' (Brown 2007; Natarajan 2008; Prenzler and Sinclair 2013). At moments of crisis the police service often turns to women as 'a desperate remedy' to offset staffing shortages, avert criticism, as an antidote to corruption, or symbolically to demonstrate a softer side to policing (Heidensohn 1992; 2000). The influence of such 'crisis'-based discourse continues to hold much resonance for contemporary calls to recruit more women into police leadership roles. Plagued by a series of high-profile events and chief officer resignations in

---

[1] The Equalities Act 2010 has brought together and combined all previous anti-discrimination legislation, adding legal protections against discrimination on the grounds of age, disability, gender reassignment, pregnancy and maternity, race, religion or belief, sex, and sexual orientation—the Equality Duty 2011 replaces the previous race, disability, and gender equality duties.

England and Wales, the past decade has witnessed a growing disquiet over the failures of police leaders and of the need to transform and diversify the police workforce, particularly those working in leadership (HMIC 1996; Condon 1997; HMIC 1999; House of Commons Home Affairs Committee 2013). The race to appoint a new London Metropolitan Police Commissioner in September 2011, for example, saw much media speculation about the possible appointment of a woman chief to address the 'crisis in policing'. In predicting possible successors, the *Evening Standard* newspaper, of 19 July 2011, ran a double-spread feature on potential female candidates entitled 'Can These Women Save the Met? Restoring Trust Lies with Senior Females' (Lydall 2011). Such calls for more women to 'clean up' policing has become a familiar mantra in times of crises, controversies, and 'integrity lapses' (Fleming and Lafferty 2003). Pruvost's research (2009: 42) reminds us that the French government has come to depend on an emblematic female Commissarie to 'promote their reforms and to reassure public opinions about police methods'. The appointment of South Africa's first female police chief, Mangwashi Victoria Phiyega, in 2012, was also firmly located within such a discourse, being cited as 'South Africa's hope, the saviour of the nation's corruption-riddled, scandal-plagued police service' (*The Guardian*, 13 June 2012). Increasing women's presence in policing in this respect forms a crucial strategy in professionalizing the police. In these cases 'women are "allowed in" at particular historical points when agencies wish to (re)legitimise their practices' (Prenzler and Wimshurst 1996: 16).

The appointment of women to leadership positions against such a backdrop holds serious consequences for how women's performance in leadership is perceived. Extensive research by Ryan, Haslam, and colleagues (Ryan and Haslam 2005, 2007; Ashby et al 2007; Haslam and Ryan 2008; Ryan et al 2010; Ryan et al 2011) has demonstrated that leadership appointments made in a time of crisis are typically different from those made when all is 'going well'. Investigating the circumstances surrounding the appointment of directors of companies in Britain in 2003, Ryan and Haslam (2005) examined the share price performance of FTSE 100 companies both immediately before and after the appointment of a male or female board member. What was striking in the data was not that the appointment of a man or a woman had a differential effect on company performance, which would suggest that there were gender differences in leadership abilities, but rather that company performance leading up to the appointment of a director was very different depending on the gender of the appointee. They argue that for companies that appointed men to their boards of directors, share price performance was relatively stable, both before and after the appointment. However, in a time of a general financial downturn in the stock market, companies that appointed a woman had experienced consistently poor performance in the months preceding the appointment. In this extensive data set it was therefore apparent that men and women were being appointed to directorships under very different circumstances, with female leaders more likely to be appointed in a time of poor performance or when there is an increased risk of failure. To characterize the nature of this difference, Ryan and Haslam (2005, 2007) extend the metaphor of the glass ceiling to suggest that women are more likely than men to find themselves on a 'glass cliff'—an allusion to the fact that their leadership positions are relatively risky or precarious, since they are more likely to involve management of organizational units that are in crisis. Such appointments, the researchers argue, are potentially dangerous for the women who hold them, as companies that experience consistently bad performance are likely to attract attention, both to their financial circumstances and to those on their boards of directors. As a consequence, when compared to men, women who assume leadership positions may be differentially exposed to criticism and in greater danger of being apportioned blame for negative outcomes that were initiated well before they assumed their new roles (McGarty et al 1993; Haslam et al 1996). Such work provides instructive messages for women seeking progression within policing in times of crisis.

'Doing' Time

In thinking about women's experiences of climbing the police career ladder, my aim here is to critically consider the organizational arrangements for progression within policing and how they impact on women looking to rise through the ranks. Notwithstanding the recent changes enabling direct entry to the rank of superintendent (Winsor Review 2012) and the recently implemented 'fast-track' career options for identified officers, the police organization in England and Wales remains attached to the idea of a strict linear organizational career model, with progression through the ranks enabled through a structured career ladder. I have argued elsewhere (Silvestri 2003, 2006, 2007) that the 'ideal type' of police leader is constructed through the accumulation of a 'full-time and uninter-rupted' career profile and as such has an 'inbuilt' male bias. Senior policewomen I have interviewed suggest an 'irresolvable conflict' between fulfilling the demands of work and life beyond. Women's reported pressure to 'give time' stemmed not only from increased workloads and reduced staffing levels but also from a growing managerial culture that places a high premium on doing so. In this way, time-serving is a core constituent of the 'smart macho' management culture that characterizes police leadership and is a fundamental resource for building the identity necessary for the police leader (Silvestri 2003).

Whilst the police service has done much in recent years to develop alternative ways of working, through the provision of 'part-time' and 'flexible' arrangements, research overwhelmingly indicates a strong belief amongst women in policing that engaging in such arrangements adversely affects their promotion and career opportunities, calling into question their commitment to a police career (Stone et al 1994; Gaston and Alexander 1997; Holdaway and Parker 1998; Adams 2001; Charlesworth and Whittenbury 2007; Dick and Metcalf 2007; Silvestri 2007; Whittred 2008; Archbold and Hassell 2009; Turnball and Wass 2012).

Enabling alternative routes to police leadership through 'direct entry' and the 'fast tracking' of officers therefore symbolizes a number of important challenges to the configuration of 'time' within policing, the composition and culture of police leadership (Silvestri et al 2013). In a global review of women's progression within policing, Brown et al (2014) argue that female police officers are more likely to access higher ranks from outside than by moving up internally from the lower ranks. The impacts of such alternative systems on increasing the number of women in policing have been particularly significant in Sweden. With a strong reputation for gender equality, the Swedish police service has done much to attract women into policing and into leadership positions through appointing them as non-sworn employees—about 40% of all employees in the Swedish Police are women and among police officers specifically, they form 25%. The number of female leaders in Sweden has also increased this past decade and in 2010, approximately 22% of police officers were women who were leaders at different levels (The National Police Board 2008, cited in Osterlind and Haake 2010).

Research by Metz and Kulik (2008) on Victoria Police Force's (VPF) first female commissioner, Christine Nixon, notes the 'distinct' advantages that come with being an 'outsider'. Reflecting on the considerable organizational and cultural change achieved under Commissioner Nixon's leadership in a short time, they argue that whilst she was not a classic example of an 'outsider', in that she was a sworn officer rising through the ranks, her career background bore many of the hallmarks of an 'outsider'. Nixon's work experience came from a state outside Victoria, she had an academic background, and she was perceived to lack operational experience—particularly by the state's powerful police union. Through adopting a consultative and inclusive leadership style, Nixon introduced a 'blitz of changes' designed to address discrimination and improve diversity within the VPF, at policy, structural, and cultural levels. However, following her resignation in 2009, many of her reforms have been reversed and the recruitment of women has slowed (see also Fleming 2008).

While such recruitment strategies might enable women to take an alternative route into police leadership, our knowledge of the importance that police officers attach to 'organizational belonging', together with their long tradition of exercising resistance to organizational change initiatives (Skolnick and Bayley 1988), provide valuable and instructive lessons. Rowe (2004) points to the 'considerable internal resistance' that the non-sworn leader faces. In relation to women, such findings are echoed by Stenmark (2005) and Osterlind and Haake (2010) in their work on Sweden, in which they report that non-sworn police leaders express difficulty in commanding respect and authority to the same degree as their sworn counterparts. With women already constructed and conceived of as 'outsiders' to the project of policing (Brown and Heidensohn 2000), lacking in both 'credibility' and 'commitment' (Silvestri 2007), recruiting non-sworn women to leadership ranks may risk pushing women even further into the role of 'outsiders'. So, for those women who have secured a place in police leadership, what do we know about how they engage with the task of leadership?

'Doing' Police Leadership

Though our knowledge of how women *do* police leadership is limited, an insight into some key findings in relation to how women undertake the policing task more generally provides an important starting point. Studies overwhelmingly indicate that women officers demonstrate a strong 'service-oriented' commitment to policing, emphasizing communication, familiarity, and the building of trust and rapport with communities (Heidensohn 1992; Miller 1999; Patten Report 1999; Davies and Thomas 2003; Brown et al 2009; Fleming and McLauchlin 2010; Brown and Wolfenden 2011). In their interactions with apprehending potential or actual perpetrators of crime, research shows that, when compared to men, women police appear to be less 'trigger happy' and much less likely to use deadly force (Waugh et al 1998; Brown and Langan 2001; McElvain and Kposowa 2008), utilize threats, physical restraint, and arrest (Grennan 1987; Belknap and Shelley 1992; Braithwaite and Brewer 1998; Schuck and Rabe-Hemp 2005; Rabe-Hemp 2008), and are less likely to abuse their power and attract complaints and allegations of misconduct (Waugh et al 1998; Brereton 1999; Lonsway et al 2002; Fleming and Lafferty 2003; Corsianos 2011). Positive outcomes can also be found in relation to policewomen's interactions with victims of crime, particularly those that have experienced sexual offences and domestic violence. Women officers are more likely to believe victims, show empathy, attribute less blame to the victim, and be less accepting of rape myths than their male counterparts (Brown and King 1998; Schuller and Stewart 2000; Page 2007; Sun 2007; Rabe-Hemp 2008, 2009; Brown 2012). Such positive accounts of women's enactments of everyday practices offer considerable opportunities for building greater trust, confidence, and, ultimately, greater consent and legitimacy in policing (Miller 1999; Brown et al 2006; Murphy et al 2008; Prenzler et al 2010).

In relation to the study of women and leadership more generally, a number of works have emphasized women's greater association with transformational leadership styles (Rosener 1990; Alimo-Metcalfe 1995; Carless 1998; Eagly et al 2003). Evidence of women 'doing' and 'championing' a transformational leadership style in policing can also be found in the literature. In my own work, I argue that senior policewomen adopt a more holistic style of leadership, not traditionally associated with the police organization (Silvestri 2003). Senior women I have interviewed associate themselves strongly with a transformational approach, engaging with behaviours that emphasize participation, cooperation, consultation, inclusion of staff in decision-making processes, team orientation, flexibility, and supporting staff with family commitments. Such leadership styles were evidenced in the rigorous, thoughtful, and consultative approach adopted in their decision-making when taking account of subordinate staff as individuals with obligations and lives that extend beyond their jobs. Senior women here, were 'conscious and active' in providing support for officers with family commitments to work more flexibly wherever possible. Whittred's (2008) findings concur with these, further emphasizing high levels of 'emotional intel-ligence' among senior policewomen. The benefits of such a style have been emphasized by a number of police commentators looking to secure successful long-term change in policing and move the service into line with a greater 'ethical' and 'quality-of-service' culture (Densten 1999; Adlam and Villiers 2003; Villiers 2003; Dobby et al 2004; Marks and Fleming 2004; Casey and Mitchell 2007; Wood et al 2008; Dick 2009). The importance of such leadership practice takes on additional significance in light of the recent finding by the *Independent Police Commission into the Future of Policing*, that four in ten women police officers have considered leaving the force because of low morale, concerns regarding flexible working, and child care considerations (Dick et al 2013).

Despite demonstrating positive ways of working, women police leaders do encounter a great deal of resistance, expressing particular concern over the issue of sharing power with peers and subordinates. At the heart of women's experience is a message that clearly spells out the difficulty of applying demo-cratic principles to the work of policing without endangering the structure and hierarchy by which the police organization is so strongly governed (Silvestri 2003, 2007). Bayley (1994: 61) reminds us that 'decision making in policing is rarely participative or collegial across rank lines'. In adopting more participatory approaches to leadership, senior women report being constructed as the 'weak' and 'soft' link in the managerial chain. The culture of police leadership manage-ment demands quick decision-making and decision-makers; the transform-ational approach takes too long and is therefore perceived to be ineffective by superiors when performed by women. Those women who engage with develop-ing alternative conceptions of police leadership come to be labelled 'not as progressive or innovative, but as weak, passive, over-sensitive and unable to withstand the rigours and demands required of the police leader' (Silvestri 2007: 43). Despite a discourse that suggests otherwise, the police organization continues to value and reward the transactional approach underlined by com-petitiveness and individualism.

Mindful of the 'pioneering' narratives of early women police leaders in driving forward women's status within policing, over a century later, a 'pioneering' theme can still be observed in the narratives of contemporary policewomen. This time, however, being the 'first and only' does not appear to be accompanied by a sense of gender activism. Senior policewomen report experiencing an increased sense of isolation once in leadership ranks. The high visibility that comes with being a 'pioneer' in the 21st century creates a state in which women report a heightened perception of surveillance over their work by both male and female colleagues; which in turn, increases a consciousness of their own suc-cesses and failures. As a result, women in leadership roles understandably report a reluctance to speak the 'gender speak' or to stand as beacons for all women. Unlike their historic counterparts (who were positioned 'outside' mainstream policing in a separate women's police service), contemporary women are an embedded and integrated part of the police service. Serving alongside their male colleagues, it is perhaps not surprising that senior women report feelings of 'disloyalty' when advocating gender issues. Here, 'rank gets in the way' of developing any notion of 'sisterhood' and it is loyalty to rank and not loyalty to other women that takes precedence (Silvestri 2003: 157, 160).

Practitioner's Perspective

Within a context of scandals about MP's expenses, abuses by catholic priests, excesses by bankers, and integrity failings by senior police leadership, there has never been as much public interest in leadership in the public sector and in the public domain. There has never been as much transparency and public accountability, and the internet and social networking has certainly seen a 'shift of power to the people', as noted by Ed Miliband (Richards 2014). It is within this complex context that I would argue that women's leadership skills have never been more relevant and required. I think it is pertinent that the scandals just mentioned have generally been perpetrated by men. It is telling that Chief Constable Jacqui Cheer has been chosen to lead Cleveland Police after her predecessors, the chief constable and the deputy chief constable were suspended and then sacked for unethical behaviour. She has used her experiences to lead on the code of ethics for the service.

With the policing landscape changing, and public expectation and demands becoming more exacting, leaders need to be adaptable and flexible to meet the new challenges. The remit is much broader, the ability to communicate, collaborate, cede sovereignty, and work in partnership is a necessity, not a nicety, and in general terms women find this much easier to do. Gone are the times when a chief constable solely led 'his' force, with little accountability, and was almost seen as a 'god' in a hierarchical world. This cult of the personality or individual is not a model that can survive in a world that is complex and more nuanced. With the election of police and crime commissioners (PCCs) in 2012 and the nature of 24-hour news and knowledge, a broader leadership mission is required, one that connects policing to the public, is more transparent, and more publicly accountable. Baroness Hood said, 'plant trees under whose shade you will not rest'. It is selflessness, the mentoring of other talent, the building of the team to deliver and the recognition that each and every one of our staff are leaders in their own right, are brand ambassadors, and that leadership needs to be dissipated throughout the organization rather than simply vested in the leader. As a chief constable I have set a clear vision and created the space for people to develop and deliver the service that helps policing to meet the complex challenges we now face.

Leadership is about embracing change and relishing it and being adaptable and flexible to absorb the challenges and seize the opportunities. I am impressed with the First Direct and the John Lewis approach; very customer focused, whereby their staff are empowered and rewarded to deliver the best service they can. Other businesses have a flexible and evidence-based and technological approach that is predictive and can be a useful model for delivering technological and business transformation and ultimately cultural change in policing. Being empathetic and flexible is not about being soft and fluffy. It is good business sense to listen and respond to encourage more people to report crime, to come forward with intelligence to help in the mission to keep people safe. The Peelian principles that have defined the relationship between the public and police are now being further refined as public expectations and demands are encouraging an extension of this relationship. With cuts in resources, empowering and enabling communities to take responsibility to help themselves and keep others safe by working with the police, not just allowing them to be passive recipients of policing services, makes sense. This surrendering of leadership and power on the frontline can also be seen in the ceding of power in partnerships, either with other local public services, where leading without authority is a critical leadership skill, or in collaboration with other forces, where leadership is passed to others, whilst the chief constable is still accountable, but without direct ownership of the resources. This brave new world requires different skills, which women leaders are ideally suited to, but many men have too.

I am now going to go back in time to when I joined the police service in 1982, and the caveat to what I am going to say is that I have worked, and do work, with some really great men who have been supportive, but I want to describe some experiences of being a woman in a man's world. When I joined the police service, there were very few women; I was one of two on my shift. I make reference to a couple of clear memories that influenced my approach. I couldn't be deployed to police the miner's strike as women couldn't train in public order and I remember thinking how unfair this seemed and that I was determined to have an active career which would give me the opportunity to experience all aspects of policing. Even as a young police constable, this first experience encouraged me to take risks and to move out of any comfort zone, as I wanted to prove that I was capable of delivering in any policing context.

On a different matter, I clearly recall being shocked when I saw how we dealt with domestic abuse; we saw it as a private matter and felt that policing was for the public areas of life. This was how it was perceived by society too, that policing dealt with public space, but the private space was private. I remember with such clarity thinking how can we get away with it, how can we as police officers leave victims and their children without our help? From the very first, public service— and protecting the vulnerable—was at the heart of my wanting to be a police officer.

In the aftermath of the Broadwater Farm riots in 1985, I seized the opportunities caused by the burning platform of a riot and the horrific murder of Police Constable Keith Blakelock, to help to build bridges with the local community. I recognized that in the deprivation in Tottenham, domestic violence was rife and women and children were looking for help. Change was needed and confidence between the police and the community needed to be restored. As a sergeant, I seized the opportunity to set up the first domestic violence unit to make a difference to those victims and witnesses and to build confidence in the police service. I recall being at a Home Office working party, and that I represented the Metropolitan Police Service, and that a chief constable represented the lead for policing outside the London area.

The policing world I joined in 1982 was very different for women, as described by Marisa earlier, but it was a reflection of general society too. I was asked directly by the chief superintendent if I had joined the police to find a husband. I remember being affronted and saying very directly that if that had been my plan I would have found one at university! I was told that I was very confident as I could talk to higher ranks, which was unusual in such a hierarchical organization, but I had come from university and had been taught to think and to challenge. I knew that further education was important, but at that stage it wasn't really valued by the police service, although that has since changed, particularly as evidence-based policing is more valued, and with the advent of fast-track and direct-entry admission. I soon learned that it was best to hold my counsel, watch and see, and then choose my moment to act, which is why I worked hard to introduce a different approach to domestic violence and set up the first unit in the United Kingdom when I had that opportunity to make a difference.

Empowerment, protecting human rights, and service delivery was an important part of my psyche. I joined policing in the aftermath of the largest clean-up of corruption, so all the references back to 'the good old days' were just not applicable. As Marisa has suggested, policewomen have come a long way since I joined, in spite of the headlines. There have never been more women chief constables and less corruption. I think having more women chief constables has helped with this and I will be controversial and say that PCCs, as the elected bridge between the police and the public, have selected more women chief constables than their predecessors. It could be that they see the value that women bring to the more citizen-focused approach now demanded by the public.

Strong leadership with a moral compass and an ability to make difficult and unsentimental decisions have moved police leadership from the selfish cult of the personality of the 1980s and 1990s to the new breed of chief constables we see today. Authentic leadership is one of the most important parts of leadership and I had to learn this. A useful book to consult in this respect has been *Living Leadership: A Practical Guide for Ordinary Heroes* by Binney et al (2012) because it shows how to become the best performing leader that you can be. I think that early on in my career, I was professional, dedicated, and worked hard but I did not bring 'myself' to work; I almost had a professional mask. I remember not really understanding when a senior officer told me that I did a great job but they didn't know who I was. It took taking a career break to Canada to make me realize that my identity was very much tied up with my work. I was the detective chief inspector at Hackney, and it took me six months to realize that I had actually got 'me' back, and that I would be more effective if the authentic me went back to work. I needed to stop protecting myself in a male world and actually be myself, so the 'warts and all self' came back to work and I think it made me more effective as an authentic leader, as a detective chief inspector. I believe a good leader needs to have moral courage, resilience, and a positive outlook, and also to be authentic. Enthusiasm and passion enthuses and motivates others. People need to see that you are approachable and supportive, but at the same time that you are fair, objective, and willing to be truthful and not avoid difficult conversations or decisions. I agree with recently retired Deputy Chief Constable Judith Gillespie from the Police Service of Northern Ireland, who quotes Shakespeare's Hamlet: 'To thine own self be true'. This can be difficult for women leaders who have a range of coping mechanisms, often emulating their male colleagues to be able to cope in a man's world and articulated in the literature discussed earlier.

I have a recollection that I always got posted to difficult areas, but this made me stronger. As a new detective chief inspector, I was posted to Hackney, East London, a really challenging policing role, whilst my male colleagues got less challenging postings. I relished the challenge and loved my time in Hackney and it gave me real confidence that I could work anywhere. I always had a belief that the only way you can develop leadership skills is by taking on the tough challenges, learning from successes and, more importantly, from the difficult times. It is easy to be a leader when all is going well, but the real test is when you have to overcome obstacles and difficulties. The mixture of practical leadership experience, coupled with good academic leadership training at Bramshill, and the challenge, stretch, encouragement, and faith of mentors and role models such as Lord Stevens (Metropolitan Police Commissioner), Barbara Wilding (Chief Constable South Wales), and Hugh Orde (ACPO President) have all helped me to develop the necessary resilience to lead through difficult times. I really admire (recently retired) Assistant Commissioner Cressida Dick (Metropolitan Police). who lives and breathes this approach and has had the resilience to deal with difficult issues with dignity.

I have considered how being a woman leader made a difference. When I joined the Anti-Terrorist Branch, I did two things that were different from my male colleagues. When I dealt with terrorists, I always made sure that I looked after their families, as by treating them fairly and with dignity, it demonstrated fairness and consideration. They were not the terrorists and I felt this approach would encourage them to come to the police if they had any doubts about their sons or daughters and needed help, because they knew we would be fair. I don't believe my male colleagues really considered such an approach at this stage. Additionally, when I dealt with any terrorist investigations, I always ensured that I attended meetings locally in London to reassure the local community about what we were doing. My colleagues viewed themselves as specialists that did not connect with local people; they saw that as being the job of local officers. This has changed in recent years and a much more holistic approach has been taken by the police service, but I believe—and the literature cited earlier seems to bear this out—that women have emotional intelligence and have influenced an empathetic approach to some difficult policing issues.

As part of my national responsibilities, I am currently the national lead for 'International Policing' and the deployment of police officers to fragile conflict-affected states and other challenging zones. I have scoured the literature and there is surprisingly little on women police leadership in this area, as there are very few examples of senior-ranking women in these places. The cultural and social norms in many of these predominantly patriarchal contexts make it very difficult for women to be promoted to leadership roles. Put simply, often basic working conditions are not conducive to women even joining the police, an example being Sudan, where they stopped recruiting women for a while because they could not stop them being raped by male instructors and peer recruits. A good example of leadership by women is Colonel Jamilla Bayaz, who was appointed to run a major police station in Kabul in January 2014.

Women can really make a difference in conflict-ridden and damaged societies. I am constantly encouraging senior women from the United Kingdom to work in conflict zones. Janice McClean is a great example of a role model whose collaborative and team working approach was well received when she was Commissioner in Sierra Leone. To encourage women to follow Janice's example, I have dropped the seniority required for working in such zones, as this was a block to women going into such roles as there were insufficient women of seniority to take them. I have had to be lawfully audacious to do this for women rather than both sexes, as a genuine occupational qualification. Serving overseas is almost seen as a barrier to professional development and progression, so I am now working with the College of Policing to look at accrediting service overseas to ensure that it is a seen as a valuable and worthwhile leadership experience. Leaders in international policing need to be resilient, have moral courage, a collaborative approach, and all the qualities that I think many women police leaders have in abundance. Angelina Jolie has recently highlighted the impact of sexual violence internationally, and this work demonstrates why it is so important that women leaders take on challenging international roles, not just as role models to their colleagues (which is important), but also to set an example for and to help protect other women who live in patriarchal countries. I want those male leaders to see just how valuable the contribution of women in leadership positions is. I have tried to demonstrate that—in a complex world, with an environment of greater accountability and increasing demands—both internationally, nationally, and locally, women have leadership skills that are modern, relevant, and deliver huge value in dealing with multifaceted policing challenges. Such skills are equally important in conflict and fragile states that need good leadership to deliver difference.

Shared Reflections

Often accused of standing at polar opposites, the value of bringing together both academic and practitioner reflections is clear. The preceding commentaries demonstrate both a shared narrative and points of departure, useful for informing both theoretical and practical debates on gender and police leadership. Perhaps one of the most striking themes that chime within both our accounts is the extent to which women make a difference to police leadership as 'women'. Indeed, the extent to which we should emphasize the concept of 'women' as leaders remains a key and controversial issue within discussions about organizational leadership. The focus on the idea that women bring something different than men relies heavily on essentialist arguments about women. With an undeniable tension and near 'discomfort' within some academic and police practitioner narratives about emphasizing the 'difference' between women's and men's contributions to police leadership, the honest and 'authentic' voice within this piece, through reflections of a real and 'lived' experience, acts as an instructive reminder that on the ground, gender matters. A continued focus on maintaining gender as a focal point of investigation and discussion may also work to counter any discomfort in emphasizing a growing and strong evidence base that suggests that women do bring much transformative potential to the work of policing, and to the work of police leadership more specifically. Moreover, it may also serve to inject greater specificity into debates about diversity, in which the issue of gender has been significantly diluted through talk of gender mainstreaming. Changes to equalities law have witnessed the abolition of the Gender Duty, and the arrival of a broader and all-encompassing Equality Duty (2011), in which all diversity characteristics are protected. Hailed by some as indicative of diversity success, in that there is no longer any need to identify particular inequalities, the mainstreaming of gender within an overarching concept of equality has led some commentators to express a more critical interpretation of such developments. McRobbie (2012) argues that in subsuming gender into the broader notion of 'equality', we can observe a simultaneous 'undoing of gender' in that process. In merging inequalities of gender alongside race and disability, the process of mainstreaming may serve to dilute the importance attached to gender inequality and risks a failure to identify the specifics of inequality raised by gender (or any other inequality for that matter). It is within this landscape that all things are presented as equal, enabling a culture and environment in which it becomes 'uncomfortable' to draw out the significance of gender.

In emphasizing an increased appreciation of the positive 'difference' that women may bring to policing, we add some caution here. We would encourage readers to go beyond the preoccupation with counting how many women have been recruited, retained, and promoted within policing. The mantra of calling for more women to be brought into police leadership will no doubt be echoed as organizational crises continue to plague the police. The recruitment of more women, of more senior policewomen, although welcome, will not in and of itself impact upon the deep-rooted gendered assumptions upon which policing and, more generally, management practice, more specifically, are based. Pruvost's (2009: 40) study of the high number of women serving in the leadership rank of Commissaire in France demonstrates quite forcefully that despite being an atypical example of women's upward mobility within policing, the female Commissaire has not modified the ideal type of the police leader, but is 'a quite perfect empirical example of how women have become more masculine over time'. An awareness and willingness to act upon the discriminatory ways in which gender is embedded within policing is central to securing a more legitimate future for the police service. It is true that policewomen in England and Wales no longer face or experience the visible and audible hostility of the past; they do, however, continue to experience the processes of gendered inclusion and exclusion—albeit in more subtle ways. And whilst for many officers the battle for equality may appear to have already been won, the task ahead is to make known the inconspicuous yet strongly embedded forms of gendered discrimination that all officers, both male and female, might encounter as they rise through the ranks.

Exploring more fully how leadership behaviours and characteristics are themselves constructed through gendered ideals is also central to our observation. It has been noted here that being empathetic and flexible is not about being 'soft and fluffy', but rather is about 'good business sense'. The current policing landscape, with all its attendant crises, offers an important opportunity to develop policing skills, bringing in 'alternative' and 'different' skills which both women and men possess. Bringing the 'authentic' leader to the role of police leadership is an excellent starting point. A greater self-perception and self-awareness of how one's role is inextricably bound up with one's own identity is central to bringing about change. In thinking about possible impacts with communities, we have emphasized the very real differences that women can and do bring to the work of policing. The setting up of the first Domestic Violence Unit in England and Wales by Chief Constable Paul, and her proactive and conscious work on emphasizing respect when dealing with the families of terrorists, are indicative of her need to make a difference, whilst simultaneously building confidence in the police service—it is also indicative of what a woman brings to the role of Chief Constable, and leadership generally.

We have also emphasized the importance of women police working collectively. Heidensohn (2000) reminds us of the importance of 'organizing' and 'collective action' in bringing about change, noting that national and international alliances and networks that women forged throughout the 20th century were instrumental in developing their roles and their cause. Early women leaders worked strategically to keep plugged into the 'mains', with the support of both women and men (Heidensohn 2000). There is also much evidence to suggest that their contemporary counterparts are also working collaboratively to improve the position of women in policing. Opportunities to network and consider the unique contribution of women in the delivery of an effective policing service can, for example, be seen in the 2014 'Senior Women in Policing' conference, held in Belfast. The recent publication of the 'Gender Agenda 3' by the British Association for Women in Policing further demonstrates a continued commitment to raising awareness of the importance of gender within policing (BAWP,

2014). The challenge for those seeking to develop more women in police leadership, then, will be to reach out and harness the support of all officers who might
be the beneficiaries of improved equality. Reform has to be championed and
supported, and reformers must be able to develop a sense that change can be
brought about. Of crucial importance here, is the need for women to extend and
develop a collective and shared interest with each other and with men (Dick et al
2013). With a renewed focus on campaigning and combatting global violence
against women, contemporary conditions offer significant opportunities for the
development of stronger and more strategic links between women police on a
national and international stage.

Recommended Reading

Binney, G, Williams, C, and Wilke, G (2012), *Living Leadership: A Practical Guide for
Ordinary Heroes* (3rd edn, London: FT Publishing International)

Dick, G and Metcalfe, B (2007), 'The Progress of Female Officers? An Empirical Analysis
of Organizational Commitment and Tenure Explanations in Two UK Police Forces'
20(2) *International Journal of Public Sector Management* 81

Dick, P, Silvestri, M, and Westmarland, L (2013), 'Women Police: Potential and
Possibilities for Police Reform' in Brown, J (ed), *The Future of Policing* (London:
Routledge)

Ryan, M, Haslam, S, Hersby, M, and Bongiorno, R (2011), 'Think Crisis—Think
Female: the Glass Cliff and Contextual Variation in the Think Manager—Think
Male Stereotype' 96(3) *Journal of Applied Psychology* 470

Silvestri, M (2003), *Women in Charge: Policing, Gender and Leadership* (Cullompton:
Willan)

Silvestri, M (2006), ' "Doing Time": Becoming a Police Leader' 8(4) *International Journal
of Police Science and Management* 266

Silvestri, M (2007), ' "Doing" Police Leadership: Enter The "New Smart Macho" ' 17(1)
Policing and Society 38

References

ACPO (2010), 'Equality, Diversity and Human Rights Strategy for the Police Service',
ACPO, APA, and Home Office, London

Adams, K (2001), *Women in Senior Police Management* (Payneham: Australasian Centre
for Police Research)

Adlam, R and Villiers, P (eds) (2003), *Police Leadership in the Twenty-first Century:
Philosophy, Doctrine and Developments* (Winchester: Waterside Press)

Alimo-Metcalfe, B (1995), 'An Investigation of Female and Male Constructs of Leadership and Empowerment' 10(2) *Women in Management Review* 3

Appier, J (1998), *Policing Women: The Sexual Politics of Law Enforcement and the LAPD*
(Philadelphia, PA: Temple University Press)

Archbold, CA and Hassell, KD (2009), 'Paying a Marriage Tax: An Examination of the
Barriers to the Promotion of Female Police Officers' 32(1) *Policing* 56

Ashby, J, Ryan, M, and Haslam, S (2007), 'Legal Work and the Glass Cliff: Evidence that Women are Preferentially Selected to Lead Problematic Cases' 13 *Journal of Women and Law* 775

Barrie, D and Broomhall, S (2012), *A History of Police and Masculinities 1700–2010* (Cullompton: Routledge)

BAWP (2014), 'Gender Agenda 3', at <http://www.bawp.org/GA3> (accessed 28 April 2015)

Bayley, D (1994), 'It's Accountability, Stupid' in Bryett, K and Lewis, C (eds), *Un-peeling Tradition: Contemporary Policing* (South Yarra: Centre for Australasian Pubic Sector Management, Macmillan Education) 64

Belknap, J and Shelley, JK (1992), 'The New Lone Ranger: Policewomen on Patrol' 12 *American Journal of Police* 47

Binney, G, Williams, C, and Wilke, G (2012), *Living Leadership: A Practical Guide for Ordinary Heroes* (3rd edn, London: FT Publishing International)

Braithwaite, H and Brewer, N (1998), 'Differences in Conflict Resolution of Male and Female Police Patrol Officers' 1(3) *International Journal of Police Science and Management* 276

Brereton, D (1999), 'Do Women Police Differently? Implications for Police-Community Relations', paper presented to the Second Australasian Women and Policing Conference, Brisbane, July

Brown, J (2006), 'Integrating Women into Policing: A Comparative European Perspective' in Pagon, M (ed), *Policing in Central and Eastern Europe: Comparing Firsthand Knowledge with Experience from the West* (Ljubljana: College of Police and Security Studies) 627

Brown, J (2007), 'From Cult of Masculinity to Smart Macho: Gender Perspectives on Police Occupational Culture' in Sklansky, DA (ed), *Police Occupational Culture: Sociology of Crime, Law and Deviance*, Vol 8 (Bingley: Emerald) 72

Brown, J (2012), 'Facing the Future' *Police Magazine*, at <http://www.policemag.co.uk/editions/709.aspx> (accessed 28 April 2015)

Brown, J and Heidensohn, F (2000), *Gender and Policing* (London: Macmillan)

Brown, J and King, J (1998), 'Gender Differences in Police Officers' Attitudes towards Rape: Results of an Exploratory Study' 4(4) *Psychology, Crime and Law* 265

Brown, J and Langan, P (2001), 'Policing and Homicide, 1976–98: Justifiable Homicide by Police, Police Officers Murdered by Felons', US Department of Justice, Washington, DC

Brown, J and Woolfenden, S (2011), 'Implications of the Changing Gender Ratio amongst Warranted Police Officers' 5(4) *Policing* 356

Brown, J, Hegarty, P, and O'Neill, D (2006), 'Playing with Numbers: A Discussion Paper on Positive Discrimination as a Means for Achieving Gender Equality in the Police Service in England and Wales', Department of Psychology, School of Human Science, University of Surrey

Brown, J, Fielding, J, and Woolfenden, S (2009), 'Added Value? The Implications of Increasing the Percentages of Women in the Police Service by 2009', A report commissioned by the British Association for Women Policing

Brown, J, Prenzler, T, and Van Ewijk, A (2014), 'Women in Policing' in Bruinsma, RG and Weisburd, D (eds), *Encyclopaedia of Criminology and Criminal Justice* (New York: Springer) 5548

Carless, S (1998), 'Gender Differences in Transformational Leadership' 39(11/12) *Sex Roles* 165

Carrier, J (1988), *The Campaign for the Employment of Women as Police Officers* (Aldershot: Avebury Gower)

Casey, J and Mitchell, M (2007), 'Police–Community Consultation in Australia: Working with a Conundrum' in Ruiz, J and Hummer, D (eds), *Handbook of Police Administration* (Boca Raton, FL: CRC Press) 335

Charlesworth, S and Whittenbury, K (2007), 'Part-time and Part Committed? The Challenge of Part-time Work in Policing' 49(1) *Industrial Relations Journal* 31

Condon, Sir Paul (1997, April), 'The Leadership Challenge', Address given to the Strategic Command Course, The Police Staff College, Bramshill

Corsianos, M (2011), 'Responding to Officers' Gendered Experiences through Community Policing and Improving Accountability to Citizens' 14(7) *Contemporary Justice Review* 7

Davies, A and Thomas, R (2003), 'Talking COP: Discourses of Change and Policing Identities' 81(4) *Public Administration* 681

Densten, IL (1999), 'Senior Australia Law Enforcement Leadership under Examination' 26(3) *Policing* 400

Dick, P (2009), 'Bending Over Backwards? Using a Pluralistic Framework to Explore the Management of Flexible Working in the Police Service' 20(1) *British Journal of Management* 182

Dick, P, Silvestri, M, and Westmarland, L (2013), 'Women Police: Potential and Possibilities for Police Reform' in Brown, J (ed), *The Future of Policing* (London: Routledge)

Dick, G and Metcalfe, B (2007), 'The progress of female police officers?' *International Journal of Public Sector Management* 20(2) 81

Dobby, J, Anscombe, J, and Tuffin, R (2004), 'Police Leadership: Expectations and Impact', Home Office 20/04, Research Development and Statistics Office, London

Eagly, A, Johannsen-Schmidt, M, and Van Egan, M (2003), 'Transformational, Transactional and Laissez-faire Leadership Styles: A Meta-analysis Comparing Women and Men' 129(4) *Psychological Bulletin* 569

Fleming, J (2008), '"Managing the Diary"—The Role of Police Commissioner' 86(3) *Public Administration (UK)* 679

Fleming, J and Lafferty, G (2003), 'Equity Confounded: Women in Australian Police Organisations' 13(3) *Labour and Industry* 37

Fleming, J and McLaughlin, E (2010), '"The Public Gets What the Public Wants?" Interrogating the "Public Confidence" Agenda' (Special issue: Public Confidence in the Police) 4(3) *Policing* 199

Gaston, KC and Alexander, A (1997), 'Women in the Police: factors influencing managerial advancement', *Women in Management Review*12(2) 47

Grennan, SA (1987), 'Findings on the Role of Officer Gender in Violent Encounters with Citizens' 15 *Journal of Police Science and Administration* 78

Haslam, SA and Ryan, M (2008), 'The Road to the Glass Cliff: Differences in the Perceived Suitability of Men and Women for Leadership Positions in Succeeding and Failing Organisations' 19 *The Leadership Quarterly* 530

Haslam, SA, McGarty, C, and Brown, P (1996), The Search for Differentiated Meaning is a Precursor to Illusory Correlation' 22 *Personality and Social Psychology Bulletin* 611

Heidensohn, F (1992), *Women in Control: The Role of Women in Law Enforcement* (Oxford: OUP)

Heidensohn, F (2000), *Sexual Politics and Social Control* (Buckingham: Open University Press)

HMIC (1996), 'Developing Diversity in the Police Service: Equal Opportunities Thematic Inspection Report', Home Office, London

HMIC (1999), 'Police Integrity: Securing and Maintaining Public Confidence', Home Office, London

Holdaway, S and Parker, S (1998), 'Policing Women Police: Uniform Patrol and Representation in the CID' 38(1) *British Journal of Criminology* 40

House of Commons Home Affairs Committee (2013), 'Leaderships and Standards in the Police', TSO, London

Lock, J (1979), *The British Policewoman; Her Story* (London: Hale)

Loftus, B (2010), 'Police Occupational Culture: Classic Themes, Altered Times' 20(1) *Policing and Society* 1

Lonsway, K, Wood, M, and Spillar, K (2002), 'Officer Gender and Excessive Force' 50 *Law and Order* 60

Lydall, R (2011), 'Can these women save the Met? Restoring trust lies with senior females', 15 July, at <http://www.standard.co.uk/news/can-these-women-save-the-met-restoring-trust-lies-with-senior-females-6422510.html> (accessed 1 July 2015)

McElvain, JP and Kposowa, AJ (2008), 'Police Officer Characteristics and the Likelihood of Using Deadly Force' 35(4) *Criminal Justice and Behavior* 505

McGarty, C, Haslam, SA, Turner, JC, and Oakes, PJ (1993), 'Illusory Correlation as Accentuation of Actual Intercategory Difference: Evidence for the Effect with Minimal Stimulus Information' 23 *European Journal of Social Psychology* 391

McRobbie, A (2012), *The Aftermath of Feminism* (London: Sage)

Marks, M and Fleming, J (2004), 'As Unremarkable as the Air They Breathe?' Reforming Police Management in South Africa' 52(5) *Current Sociology* 784

Martin, S (1980), *Breaking and Entering: Policewomen on Patrol* (Berkeley, CA: University of California Press)

Metz, I, and Kulik, C (2008), 'Making Public Organisations More Inclusive: A Case Study of the Victoria Police Force' 47 *Human Resource Management* 367

Miller, SL (1999), *Gender and Community Policing: Walking the Talk* (Boston, MA: Northeastern University Press)

Murphy, K, Hinds, L, and Fleming, J (2008), 'Encouraging Public Cooperation and Support for Police' 18(2) *Policing and Society* 136

Natarajan, M (2008), *Women Police in a Changing Society* (Aldershot: Ashgate)

Osterlind, M, and Haake, U (2010), 'The Leadership Discourse amongst Female Police Leaders in Sweden' 30(16) *Advancing Women in Leadership Journal* 1

Page, AD (2007), 'Behind the Blue Line: Investigating Police Officers' Attitudes toward Rape' 22(1) *Journal of Police and Criminal Psychology* 22

Patten Report (1999), 'A New Beginning: Policing in Northern Ireland', The Independent Police Commission on Policing in Northern Ireland, Belfast

Prenzler, T, and Sinclair, G (2013), 'The Status of Women Police Officers: An International Review' 41(2) *International Journal of Law, Crime and Justice* 115

Prenzler, T and Wimshurst, K (1996), 'Reform and Reaction: Women and Politics in the Queensland Police, 1970–1987' 44(4) *Journal of Australian Studies* 42

Prenzler, T, Fleming, J, and King, A (2010), 'Gender Equity in Australian and New Zealand Policing: A Five Year Review' 12 *International Journal of Police Science and Management* 584

Pruvost, G (2009), 'A Profession in Process: The Atypical Rise of Women to the High Rank of Police "*Commissaire*" in France' 51 *Sociologie du Travail* 34

Rabe-Hemp, C (2008) 'Female Officers and the Ethics of Care: Does Officer Gender Impact Police Behaviours?' 36 *Journal of Criminal Justice* 426

Rabe-Hemp, C (2009), 'POLICEwomen or PoliceWOMEN? Doing Gender and Police Work' 4 *Feminist Criminology* 114

Richards, S (2014), 'Ed Miliband will shift power from London – but there's a catch' *The Guardian*, 9 April 2014, at <http://www.theguardian.com/commentisfree/2014/apr/09/ed-miliband-shift-powers-london-cities> (accessed 1 July 2015)

Rosener, J (1990), 'Ways Women Lead' 68(6) *Harvard Business Review* 119

Rowe, M (2004), *Policing, Race and Racism* (Cullompton: Willan)

Ryan, M and Haslam, S (2005), 'The Glass Cliff: Evidence that Women are Over-represented in Precarious Leadership Positions' 16 *British Journal of Management* 81

Ryan, M and Haslam, S (2007), 'The Glass Cliff: Exploring the Dynamics Surrounding Women's Appointment to Precarious Leadership Positions' 32 *Academy of Management Review* 549

Ryan, M, Haslam, S, and Kulich, C (2010), 'Politics and the Glass Cliff' 34 *Psychology of Women Quarterly* 56

Ryan, M, Haslam, S, Hersby, M, and Bongiorno, R (2011), 'Think Crisis—Think Female: The Glass Cliff and Contextual Variation in the Think Manager—Think Male Stereotype' 96(3) *Journal of Applied Psychology* 470

Schuck, AM and Rabe-Hemp, CR (2005), 'Women Police: The Use of Force By and Against Female Officers' 14(4) *Women and Criminal Justice* 91

Schuller, RA and Stewart, A (2000), 'Police Responses to Sexual Assault Complaints: The Role of Perpetrator/Complainant Intoxication' 24 *Law and Human Behavior* 535

Schultz, D (1995), *From Social Worker to Crime Fighter: Women in United States Municipal Policing* (Westport: Praeger)

Segrave, K (1995), *Policewomen: A History* (Jefferson, NC: McFarland)

Silvestri, M (2003), *Women in Charge: Policing, Gender and Leadership* (Cullompton: Willan)

Silvestri, M (2006), ' "Doing Time": Becoming a Police Leader' 8(4) *International Journal of Police Science and Management* 266.

Silvestri, M (2007), ' "Doing" Police Leadership: Enter the "New Smart Macho" ' 17(1) *Policing and Society* 38

Silvestri, M, Tong, S, and Brown, J (2013), 'Gender and Police Leadership: Time for a Paradigm Shift' 15(1) *International Journal of Police Science and Management* 61

Skolnick, J and Bayley, D (1988), 'Theme and Variation in Community Policing' in Tonry, M and Morris, N (eds), *Crime and Justice. A Review of Research*, Vol 10 (Chicago, IL: University of Chicago Press) 1

Stenmark, H (2005), 'Polisens Organisationskultur: En Explorative Studie' ['The Organizational Culture of the Police: An Exploratory Study'], PhD, Umeå University, Sweden

Stone, R, Kemp, T, and Weldon, G (1994), 'Part-time Working and Job Sharing in the Police Service', Police Research Series Paper 7, Home Office, London

Sun, IY (2007), Policing Domestic Violence: Does Officer Gender Matter? 35 *Journal of Criminal Justice* 581

Turnball, P and Wass, V (2012), 'Time for Justice? Long Working Hours and the Wellbeing of Police Inspectors, Report, Cardiff Business School

Villiers, P (2003), 'Philosophy, Doctrine and Leadership: Some Core Beliefs' in Adlam, R and Villiers, P (eds), *Police Leadership in the Twenty-first Century: Philosophy, Doctrine and Developments* (Winchester: Waterside Press) 223

Waugh, L, Ede, A, and Alley, A (1998), 'Police Culture, Women Police and Attitudes Towards Misconduct' 1(3) *International Journal of Police Science and Management* 289

Whittred, J (2008), 'A Qualitative Exploration into the Transformational Leadership Styles of Senior Policewomen', unpublished MSc in Police Leadership and Management, University of Leicester

Winsor Review (2012), 'Independent Review of Police Officer and Staff Remuneration and Conditions, Part 2', at <https://www.gov.uk/government/uploads/system/uploads/attachment_data/file/250812/8325_i.pdf> (accessed 1 July 2015)

Wood, J, Fleming, J, and Marks, M (2008), 'Building the Capacity of Police Change Agents: The Nexus Policing Project' 18(1) *Policing and Society* 72

11

Contested Knowledge

Learning to Lead in a Policing Context

Mark Kilgallon, Martin Wright, and Adrian Lee

Introduction

The motto of the Royal Military Academy, Sandhurst is well known and entreats cadets to 'Serve to Lead'. For policing leaders such a calling is very well placed—for service to others sits at the heart of the vocational beliefs of those who have served in the office of constable. Leadership is, though, not an attribute of rank or position; rather, it is required of everyone that joins the police service, either as a police officer or a member of police staff. The unique role that policing holds in society is mirrored by the level of public interest in all it does and the high standards that the public and the service expect of each member. The police service requires all staff to be leaders in their own right because they have chosen to be part of a highly demanding and complex occupation that requires leadership decisions to be taken against a backdrop of conflicting and competing demands. This chapter therefore seeks to examine some of the literature and explore the history and context of how police learning and development and engagement with training and education assists leaders in their roles of providing the best service possible to the communities they seek to serve.

Developing policing leadership is a political event, and as successive governments have been elected to power, policing leadership development, directly or indirectly, has been influenced by the political hue of the moment. The leaders of one of the most powerful organizations in a liberal democracy are rightly never far from the public or media gaze. Developing their learning agenda therefore becomes increasingly important the more complex a post-modern society becomes. Herbert states that police organizations are:

> ...sites of ongoing political struggles over how to define and trumpet different normative orders, struggles that fundamentally shape the daily practices of officers, the overall orientations of departments, and the state of police-community relations (Herbert 1998: 364).

If this is the case, so too are the 'learning sites' within which the policing organization is explored, tested, and ratified by its current and future leaders. It is not by chance that consecutive Home Secretaries have sought to address the Strategic Command Course (SCC) and the Fast Track, High Potential Development Scheme (HPDS), the two programmes for high-performing future strategic leaders of the service. They want to give a view on the critical issues facing policing and its leadership from their personal and political perspectives.

We know that police leadership development has been of significant interest for consecutive governments, and in Hurd (2008) we are made aware of the fact that from the very outset Peel was conscious of the importance of leadership development as the key element of policing success. According to Peel, it was not so much the legal powers that were awarded to the new police that were important; rather it was the 'quality of the men [sic] picked to staff it' (Hurd 2008: 103). Peel was committed to the day when all promotions would come from those who were *serving police officers*. This, however, is not the position adopted by the current HM Chief Inspector of Constabulary, Sir Tom Winsor. He states: 'I do not accept that every officer must start as a constable and work his[1] [sic] way through every rank before reaching the highest ranks' (Winsor 2012: 18). To add value to the policing leadership debate, this chapter takes a comprehensive look at the historical context of leadership development, the theory and practice of policing, exploring successes and failures as well as sharing our own experiences.

History of Police Learning Institutions in the United Kingdom

It was not until 1948 that a centre of leadership learning—the Police College—was opened in Ryton-on-Dunsmore, near Coventry. The case for the college had been made by the Police Post-War Committee, and was published in 1946. The primary focus of the Police College centred on assisting currently serving police officers to develop their leadership qualities in order to be promoted within the service (Adlam 2000). The curriculum focus therefore was on encouraging inspectors and above to have a 'broad outlook, the quality of leadership and the

---

[1] The gender-specific language is both interesting and disappointing!

independent habits of mind' (Adlam 2000: 22). Officers were also encouraged to develop a professional interest in research and reasoning. Interestingly, though research was considered a priority, the current (re)introduction of the 'new' evidence-based practice agenda by the College of Policing may suggest that scholarly reflection and inquiry has never been fully embedded into the culture!

The new Police College was described by the then Home Secretary as a 'landmark in the history of the police of England and Wales' (Harris 1949: 217) and if successful would be progress towards imbuing policing with a professional status as well as enhancing its prestige within society at large (Harris 1949: 222). Moving from a craft focus towards a more educational approach, the subsequent 1948 White Paper confirmed the need for police leaders to benefit from the 'virtues of liberal education' within a value framework at the core of liberal democracy (Harris 1949; Adlam 2000).

Following a call for a more permanent base for a national police college from the then Commissioner of Policing, Sir Harold Scott, supported by Sir Frank Newsam the Permanent Secretary to the Home Office, Bramshill was purchased by the Home Office in 1960. The newly named National Police College focused on a national approach to leadership development for inspectors and above and remained in place until the inception in 1988 of National Police Training (NPT).

NPT had a far broader remit: continuous leadership development, a core curriculum, a qualifications framework, the establishment of one central police college and a cluster of other colleges, quality assurance for courses and training providers, and greater use of IT. NPT was in turn replaced by the Central Police Training and Development Authority—better known as Centrex—established as part of the Criminal Justice and Police Act of 2001.

The focus of Centrex was to deliver not only leadership development opportunities for inspectors and above, but also probationer training and investigator training. It was the consolidation of learning with the added responsibility of assessing recruits, and developing probationer suitability tests as well as national police promotion exams. Centrex, however, was short lived (see later) and was replaced in April 2007 by the National Policing Improvement Agency (NPIA).

The NPIA, led by a serving Chief Constable, Peter Neyroud, arguably moved the leadership and development mandate within policing towards a more professional footing and thus, in some ways, reverted back to the original concept envisioned for Ryton in 1948. However, the NPIA was always intended as a 'stopgap' agency, given that the debate on the professionalization of policing was growing in momentum and the move towards the concept of an 'independent' professional body was being discussed politically by all three major political parties. The NPIA was also a Quango,[2] the number of which government had pledged to reduce in order to address its increasing costs.

---

[2] An organization to which government has devolved power (a quasi-autonomous non-governmental organization).

The College of Policing was created in 2012, adopting much of the direction initiated by Neyroud in his Leadership Review report (2013). The College of Policing has shown early results that indicate a more positive, evidenced-based research agenda—'what works in policing', and a 'renewed emphasis on engaging with other academic institutions, particularly universities and the private sector' (Brain 2013: 150).

From the Police College of 1948 to the College of Policing in 2015, different educational approaches and ideologies with respect to content, focus, partnerships, and delivery methods have emerged, all with the genuine intention of helping Policing leaders to be more effective in their roles. However, intention has never been a reliable indicator of success and therefore we need to consider in closer detail the provision of some of these services in order to establish what has worked from an educational as well as a practical perspective, and what type of learning environment might best suit the future demands of policing leadership.

The Cordner and Shain Questions

In their editorial on *Police Practice and Research*, Cordner and Shain (2011) ask readers to consider some critical questions regarding the education and development of policing leadership. We would like to adapt and utilize aspects of these questions to systematically address our own focus on what works in policing leadership development and how we as academics and practitioners can best help the future leaders of policing to develop in the most effective and authentic manner.

Cordner and Shain ask:

1. What is the proper distinction between police education and police training?
2. What are the responsibilities of individuals in obtaining an initial police education/training and ongoing police education/training?
3. What institutions are best suited to provide police education and police training?
4. What methods of instruction are most effective for delivering police education and training?
5. In what substantive areas is police education and training currently in need of improvement?

From an academic perspective, we would like to adapt questions 4 and 3 with the intention of outlining: the direct correlation between how policing leadership development is delivered and the capacity of officers and staff to consume the learning; and the significant impact that both positive and negative institutions can have in creating an environment within which leaders can flourish. Chief Constable Adrian Lee covers aspects of the remaining questions, from an informed practitioner's perspective.

What methods of instruction are most effective for delivering police education and training?

In addressing aspects of this question we are cognizant of the 'what works' agenda set by the College of Policing and the need for current and future provision of leadership development programmes to connect the theory of policing with the practice of leadership. We have identified four areas of interest, as follows.

Establishing knowledge: a learning partnership

The policing operational culture has been explored and debated extensively within criminological literature (Skolnick 1975; Manning 1977, 1989; Holdaway 1983; Reiner 1992; Chan 1996; Waddington 1999; Loftus 2009), the idea of rules and principles, values and norms, rationales and beliefs, operational credibility and working personalities that are closely aligned to the role of policing. However, these habits of behaviour that are created within the cultures of policing 'can be efficient, [but] they are not always necessarily effective' (Rowson and Lindley 2012: 6).

In any policing learning environment there needs to be recognition of the cultural norms that officers bring with them into an educational setting. An almost disproportionate (self-) respect and (self-) recognition of operational experience is just one example of a cultural norm that a policing learning environment needs to acknowledge. Policing cultures are believed to attach value to being 'action centred' (Manning 1989), for police leaders to be sophisticated judges of 'operational competence' (Van Maanen 1978). Police culture is thought not necessarily to engage with theoretical constructs produced in a learning environment unless what is being conveyed has direct operational utility. Policing education therefore needs to be embedded within the organization's culture (Kodz and Campbell 2010). Policing leaders bring into the learning environment knowledge and experience that is culturally recognized as valuable; educational methods must engage with this and not treat it as a form of subjugated knowledge (Foucault 1972; Hartman 1992).

Furthermore, there needs to be a carefully crafted relationship between the perceived educator and those seeking to share learning experiences. Cordner notes that some research indicates that 'Higher education (university) often relies on one-way learning, based on the assumption that the instructor is the sole source of knowledge and the students are mere empty vessels to be filled with information' (Cordner and Shain 2011: 284). In policing educational terms this would be fatal—for there is a direct correlation between the ability and cultural credibility of the member of staff and the participants' readiness to accept the message being conveyed.[3] There is, to some extent, an informal learning contract

---

[3] See the later section by Chief Constable Adrian Lee (Practitioner's Perspective). Recognizing this credibility debate, it was important for him to have a sound operational background when teaching ethics to police leaders.

in existence that outlines 'whose claims concerning what issues will be temporarily honoured' (Goffman 1959: 21). Recognition that 'one-way learning' (Cordner and Shain 2011) is not an option and that participants require their own experiences and knowledge to be recognized and valued (Foucault 1972) are essential aspects for the provision of leadership and educational services in policing. If this is not achieved, then participants rightly or wrongly believe that they are receiving some form of 'official line' from the Home Office[4] (Adlam 2000). Police learning professionals therefore need to 'be open to local knowledge, to the narratives and truths of "our clients"' (Hartman 1992: 484).[5]

From an academic perspective, Sherman (2011) outlines the value of a learning partnership approach that acknowledges both the cultural capital that policing leaders bring with them and the integration that academic expertise can provide to police leadership development. He proposed that universities should encourage the creation of 'Faculties of Policing' to steward 'complex knowledge'[6] that will help to create a culture of 'evidence-based policing'. He believes that the police should invade universities, demanding the best science available to enhance police performance (Sherman 2011: 7). The alignment of academic knowledge and credible learning professionals with police praxis and knowledge is therefore critical for a policing learning environment. Neyroud acknowledged the symbolic and practical aspects of this in his 2011 review:

> Similarly, the Strategic Command Course (SCC) in contrast to ten years ago when the vast majority of directing staff were not senior police officers, is now wholly directed by a Chief Constable and a group of serving Assistant Chief Constables, supported by an academic staff (Neyroud 2013 112).

This model has since been recognized and repeated in the recently redesigned Leading Powerful Partnerships Programme.[7] Clearly, there is a strong coaching and mentoring aspect embedded in this approach. Where then does that leave non-police academics and other informed experts? Guest speakers have been an integral part of any leadership development programme, and policing is no different. Bringing with them their expert knowledge and educational credibility, speakers frequently engage at a very effective level with senior policing leaders. A negotiated agreement is achieved between the sharing of academic and practitioner knowledge. As Schafer notes, 'good educational and learning experiences are viewed as a process best achieved through a complementary mix of education reinforced by practical application with constructive feedback' (Schafer 2009: 253).

---

[4] Or indeed the College of Policing.

[5] This is not to deny that there are officers and staff who are open to all forms of learning and development, but rather the need to recognize the role that knowledge plays in a learning and development policing context.

[6] From the 2011 Benjamin Franklin Medal Lecture by Professor Lawrence Sherman.

[7] It is also of interest that many universities recognize the importance of this point by employing ex- or retired police officers on their pre-employment policing degree programmes.

Establishing programme content and 'pitch'

Many senior leaders within policing have undergraduate, post-graduate, and even doctoral qualifications. Finding the appropriate pitch has therefore been vital in successfully engaging with educational learning outcomes. The NPIA response to the government's Green Paper of 2008 stated, 'Bramshill will not be a technical college; nor will it be a theoretical academic institution. Rather, it will be a learning establishment that focuses upon applied police leadership development that helps to deliver great leaders.' In other words, the NPIA emphasized the importance of a theory-to-practice approach.

Keith Grint, who was a frequent visitor to Bramshill, adopts an Aristotelian stance in trying to combine knowledge of 'what works' in leadership with how to articulate this in a learning environment. He suggests that we may need to re-think how we educate police leaders by acknowledging the dangers of conflating knowledge (*techne*), analytical skills (*episteme*), and wisdom (*phronesis*) (Grint 2007: 336). Grint argues for the provision of different frameworks for the pursuit of learning; and carefully aligning knowledge sharing with the ability of learners to experience leadership practically. Provocatively, Grint asks 'should we build more anxiety and risk into learning events in order to create opportunities for leaders to fail, thus more accurately replicate reality?' (Grint 2007: 242)

If policing is to be taken seriously and recognized as having moved beyond the 'craft' level, then there needs to be investment in appropriate academic and practical leadership learning environments in order to prepare leaders for the complexity of strategic challenges that may exist in the future.[8] However, we also need to note that leaders within organizations cannot learn solely by drawing on their past experiences and applying them to current and future scenarios. Any future provision of content to policing leadership at an educational level needs to be cognizant of the 'adaptive nature of policing challenges' and the need for leaders to develop 'self-awareness and a personal mental complexity' (Rowson and Lindley 2012: 8). As Heifetz et al suggest, 'adaptive challenges can only be addressed through changes in people's priorities, beliefs, habits and loyalties' (2009: 19).

The content of any learning event therefore needs to strike a fine balance between increasing current knowledge and replicating workplace scenarios. It should encourage leaders to think and behave differently in order to meet the adaptive challenges that directly impact on workplace performance (Kleinig 2013). High-performing leaders can therefore achieve an entirely new under-standing of the world (Harris and Kuhnert 2008).

---

[8] See the later section by Chief Constable Adrian Lee (Practitioner's Perspective), and his argument for leadership development that focuses on a multi-leader approach rather than the historical single or partner leader approach.

Establishing governance

Over the past decade, the Association of Chief Police Officers[9] and the Superintendent's Association have become increasingly engaged with leadership development, adding a professional authenticity to leadership products. In particular, the SCC has established a Professional Reference Group whose membership is both culturally significant and impressive.[10] The design team of each programme is held to account four times a year in terms of content, delivery, and partnership engagement. The Group also creates the learning outcomes.

The effectiveness of aligning programme design with operational need was so successful that Chief Constable Adrian Lee established a similar model for the Senior Leadership Development Programme (now the Leading Powerful Partnerships programme). Governance ensures that current leaders have the opportunity to pass comment, guide and influence, or reject the content and design of any product. Participants on a programme are thus guaranteed a form of professional quality assurance endorsed by their strategic leaders.

There is little doubt that drawing on their professional experience, informed stakeholders (ex-Chief Constables or senior operational leaders from the Superintending ranks, Home Office officials, for example) can add real value to any leadership development programme. They can also be problematic if they are omitted from the process (see the later discussion of Centrex).

Establishing professional self-confidence

The past and current educational learning principles that have helped to develop policing leadership in the United Kingdom are based on reflective practice. And while leaders in an 'action-centred culture' may initially react negatively against the pace of reflective practice; nevertheless, it has a crucial role in helping to embed learning principles into policing (Kodz and Campbell 2010). As outlined later by Adrian Lee, 'emotional intelligence' is a leadership model that has endured the test of time. Its emphasis on self-awareness and the move away from self-centeredness, alongside its ability to assist with self-confidence, has been an essential and on-going part of leadership development (Goleman 1998b).

However, it needs to develop at an even deeper level. We would argue that policing leaders have not sufficiently developed their self-assurance in order to appropriately defend their professional mandate. If policing is a profession, would any other professional body allow external agencies, be they the Audit Commission, Home Office, or academics, to apply 'labels', with all that these

---

[9] The National Police Chiefs Council replaced ACPO in April 2015. Sara Thornton is the Chair of the new body.

[10] Eg the minutes from a 2007 Professional Reference Group meeting shows in attendance: the Chief HMI, President of ACPO, two chief constables, head of HR for the MPS, two members of the Association of Police Authorities, one ACC, the head of Operational Services (NPIA) and apologies from the Commissioner, two chief constables, the deputy director of the Scottish Police College and the Chief People Officer (NPIA).

imply, to their practice and status? Can it be imagined surgeons would accept they engage in 'reassurance surgery'; teachers in 'intelligent education'; social workers in 'zero-tolerance' therapeutic interventions? Arguably, these examples suggest an absence of professional self-confidence and self-belief by policing, even undue deference (Waddington PAJ, personal communication), to external bodies. In the context of this chapter, therefore, an additional 'knowledge need' should be added to the list proposed by Fyfe and Wilson (2012: 307), ie 'knowledge of knowledge'.

It is here argued that the 'body of police professional knowledge' is not restricted to a specific locus of ownership, neither is it derived from a policy development or academic research methodology. For policing to (re)gain a professional 'voice', one that critically engages with government and others (Police and Crime Commissioners (PCCs), and the Independent Police Complaints Commission, for example), there is a pressing need for its current strategic (ACPO) and operational (superintending ranks) leaders, and those supportive of the police, to engage with and draw strength from police's 'knowledge of knowledge'.

What institutions are best suited to provide police education and police training?

Recognizing the value in establishing a knowledge partnership, effective programme content, appropriate governance, and a professional self-confidence allows us to move towards addressing the question of suitable instututions— who is actually best placed to develop policing leaders?

The diversity of approach

The desire (and necessity) to engage policing praxis with rigorous academic thinking is not new. The concept of valuing research, evidence-based policing, or 'what works' is something that policing has been considering for decades. As far back as the 1950s, informed police commentators and practitioners were calling for an increased capacity for research within law enforcement. Olsen suggested that 'the function and study of law enforcement as an instrument of social defence is hindered by a lack of valid, easily accessible, and pertinent data'(1959, 296). The recent Strategic Intent document from the College of Policing supports this point:

> A fundamental element of our role as a professional body is to be a catalyst for the development and use of knowledge and research by and for those working in policing. This will ensure that the best available evidence of what works is accessible for practitioners when making decisions (College of Policing 2013).

The issue, however, will be how to connect the 'evidence' with the provision of leadership programmes. As we have observed, it is one thing to have the evidence; it is another to find appropriate bespoke learning opportunities that can connect evidence and theory to practice. What could possibly be worse than to find an organization that invests in research but does not take the time to find appropriate learning methods (as outlined earlier) to disseminate the knowledge?

Equally, the current move to take leadership development out of a pure learning environment and into the workplace in order to deliver learning closer to reality is a concept that has been around for some considerable time. Clift's ideas about 'on-the-job training', rooted in 1950s America, and now echoed by the College of Policing, state that 'On-the-job training is the secret of really good police development, and it is a job that falls largely on the shoulders of the immediate supervisor' (Clift 1954: 6).

Should the claimed value added by on-the-job training be the case, and we have no evidence to suggest otherwise, we might want to ask some critical questions. Who trains the coaches and mentors who create the learning environment? How is their work quality assured? What might the selection process be to ensure that coaches and mentors are reflective practitioners? Should they be professionally accredited? How do they help to create a positive frontline learning environment for underrepresented groups in policing, such as minority ethnic officers? These challenges are a significant aspect of professional leadership development and apply across all ranks, roles, and levels of leadership.

An excellent example of a working relationship between leadership, educational development, and academia is to be found in Scotland, where the universities have signed a collaboration agreement with Police Scotland (Fyfe and Wilson 2012). The Scottish Institute for Policing Research (SIPR) was established in 2007 with the strategic aims of high-quality independent research; engagement in knowledge-exchange activities for evidence-based policing; a single focus for policing research in Scotland; fostering development with researchers and policy-makers, and enhancing policing research capacity in Scotland. The SIPR is divided into three departments or 'networks', each with a police and an academic lead (Fyfe and Wilson 2012: 312).

In Australia, a similarly innovative partnership between Charles Stuart University and the New South Wales Police Service has seen the development of a recruit education programme at degree level which combines both practice and knowledge, with academic staff teaching at the police training college (Chambers 2004; Green and Woolston 2009). There exist a number of examples of higher education police programmes; see in particular the review of international literature on the value of such programmes by Paterson (2011), most notably those in place in North America. In the United Kingdom, such developments have been influenced by a range of factors, such as the need to make financial savings and the recognition by police leaders of the benefits to officers from studying at degree level (Lee and Punch 2004).

Learning from the past—when institutions get it wrong

For the purposes of this section, it may be of interest to explore an organization whose relationship with its customer base quickly became problematic. Centrex, charged in 2001 by the Home Office with the mandate of developing policing leadership across the United Kingdom, lasted a mere six years before it was replaced by the NPIA. What are the lessons to be learned?

After its inception, Centrex established a new leadership faculty (the third rebranding of leadership services in five years) and focused on delivering modern and informed leadership products. It had the ambitious goal of not only meeting the complex and competing demands of operational policing leaders (particularly chief inspectors and above), but also helping them to shape their working environments. This was an admirable aim, for as Waddington states, 'the task then is to help the police confront the realities of their work and construct a professional culture that enables them to cope with those realities' (Waddington et al 2013: 6).

Centrex, however, had a difficult start; one from which, it could be argued it never fully recovered. If predictability is a critical aspect of any organizational culture (Foster 2003: 197), at Bramshill, under the guise of a modernization agenda and aligned to a 'new public management' approach (Pollit and Bouckaert 2004), the new chief executive of Centrex took the unusual step of removing much of the policing memorabilia that had been acquired during the College's history. The removal of these 'artefacts and creations' that impacted on the 'feeling and climate' (Schein 1985: 6) at Bramshill had the intention of 'making visible a considered statement about the future direction of the organisation' (Johnson and Scholes 2002). Centrex was theoretically modernizing policing. Intentionally or unintentionally, what quickly emerged from this early cultural purge was a distinct separation of policy-making from delivery: the start of a distancing between the customer, ie the police service, and its educational provider, Centrex.[11]

Over time, this lack of connectivity and poor stakeholder management between the police service and Centrex increased in intensity. As Neyroud notes, 'there was a significant and regrettable disinvestment by senior leaders for quite a number of years in playing their part in the development of police commanders' (Neyroud 2013: 107). Operational demands were cited as the reason for declining attendance on programmes. Centrex, by not effectively negotiating with policing, was simply not delivering products that connected with the workplace. Kleinig states, 'it is critical that intending and practicing officers are appropriately prepared for the situations that will confront them' (Kleinig 2013: 25). Telling the service what *it needed* rather than listening to what the service wanted created an irreparable division between customer and provider.

Recognizing the dysfunctional nature of the professional relationship between policing leadership and its educational provider, two significant steps were taken by the service. First, in 2003[12] Sir Norman Bettison was made Chief Executive of

---

[11] This is not a new phenomenon. See Plumridge 1983 for an earlier account under National Police Training.

[12] Only two years after the inception of Centrex.

Centrex, thus re-aligning policy-makers with ACPO; second, Sir Peter Fahy, a serving Chief Constable, was subsequently appointed director of the symbolic-ally important Strategic Command Course, thus strengthening the direct ties between the SCC and the policing executive.

Why is this important for this discussion? The Centrex experience provides a learning opportunity to explore the complex and at times fractious relationship between senior policing professionals and a learning institution that had a confused, if not conflicting, mandate. It is worth asking, was the primary cus-tomer of Centrex the Home Office, and as part of that relationship was Centrex instructed to change policing culture? Alternatively, was its primary customer the police service, a stakeholder which it simply failed to manage appropriately, most notably through offering poor-quality products that had little impact on the workplace? Or, perhaps it was both of the above?

An unclear purpose, confused mandate, and poor-quality products saw the termination of a professional relationship and the ultimate demise of a learning institution.

Conclusion

We would argue—from knowledge of the literature so far reviewed, our inter-action with policing leaders, and our experiences in designing and delivering learning products for the service—that there is a direct correlation between the qualities of policing, educational and leadership development, and access to current and informed theoretical knowledge and data. There may exist some cultural strains between educational practices and policing, but these are, and should be, minimized in order to bring value to both sides of theory and praxis.

While Stevens would argue that 'Policing programmes should primarily enhance policing, not produce policing academics' (Stevens 2013: 117), there is still some debate regarding the extent to which there is an expectation that policing leaders should be adequately informed by current literature about policing. As Neyroud notes, while the traditional view of the relationship with higher education has been based on accreditation, 'an alternative approach is full partnership in which delivery is either shared or commissioned from a higher education provider'(Neyroud 2013: 93).

Pearson-Goff and Herrington (2013) recently engaged in a comprehensive review of the literature associated with leadership development. Their findings outline the importance of: combining 'education, experience and mentorship' (see also Schafer 2009); the understanding of leadership principles; and exposure to effective coaching and mentoring where experienced leaders could role-model leadership qualities (Pearson-Goff and Herrington 2013: 27). We would support these findings. Indeed, it could be argued that the SCC and the Fast Track HPDS, each with a long history of exploring diverse learning methodologies and with close relationships with academia, have been adopting many of these leadership and educational development practices for some years.

Having explored the literature and further advanced our academic thinking with respect to leadership development, this chapter now reflects on the views of an experienced and informed policing professional—Chief Constable Adrian Lee, who shares his experiences as both a consumer and shaper of leadership programmes within policing in the United Kingdom. We then synthesize and reflect on the learning from both the academic and the professional perspectives.

Practitioner's Perspective

I was promoted to the rank of Sergeant with three years' service and posted to a highly complex operational environment. My early challenges as a leader focused on supervising three high-performing constables. With a law degree and a desire to constantly learn, I believed I had the capacity to be their leader. I could assist by helping them do a good job for the public while at the same time learning from their experiences. My overall learning from this early leadership experience was the need to have professional ability, be a confident leader, and acknowledge the continuing need to learn from others.

On promotion to Inspector, I led a team where I was the youngest in service and age. A sergeant who, though vastly experienced, had lost his sense of vocation for policing tested my skills. I worked hard to establish a relationship of mutual trust and respect with him, making it clear that I wanted to learn from him and that he had to support me in my role. Through mentoring and exploring the dissatisfaction that he felt, we established a professional relationship that enhanced his performance and where leadership was a shared role. I was the senior officer whom he would support and I encouraged him to lead by sharing his experience and knowledge. We established a relationship of trust and focused on sharing power for the benefit of the communities we both served. Managing relationships in such a way that power is minimized and focused on serving communities is a key aspect of leadership and I will return to this issue in relation to the new governance arrangements.

I was promoted to the rank of Chief Inspector on the same day and to the same station as a good friend and colleague. I was the uniform Chief Inspector; he was the Detective Chief Inspector (DCI). On the first weekend a murder occurred and my colleague, as DCI, led the investigation. Working closely with his team, they put in the many additional hours required and within two weeks the murder was detected. As a consequence of this teamwork, he developed a really good understanding of their strengths, their characters, and how they worked. Conversely, we in 'uniform' had no similar operational challenge and my knowledge of the team was less well developed; it took me three months to 'catch up'. I thus learned the importance of investing time in getting to know your people in order to lead appropriately.

On promotion to Chief Superintendent, I was placed in charge of the South Manchester Borough Command Unit (BCU), a post that had never previously been given to a newly promoted chief superintendent. The BCU had over a thousand police officers with responsibility for policing Moss Side, with its unique challenges, diverse communities and cultures, social deprivation, and a lively student population. We also policed Wythenshawe, the largest housing estate in Europe. The BCU had five superintendents and at one of the first meetings it was clear they had come to a common consensus about a particular issue that was different from my own. We discussed the issue for some time and in due course agreed to progress with their preferred option. While my staff officer apologized to me, believing that the meeting had gone badly, I disagreed. My view was that following the discussions at the meeting, I had demonstrated an ability to listen, to compromise, to value their opinion, and to be flexible and prepared to learn. Any future decisions that might go against their thinking would not be perceived as my inflexibility, but rather as a result of a genuinely held belief that the option I was taking was correct. I would expect their support.

As a chief constable, real learning is achieved by focusing on developing people and teams. The strategic leader can only influence the organization through people; investing in individuals and working to ensure the most appropriate people are in the most suitable roles, contributing to high-performing teams. I believe that strong leaders have the confidence to build teams that reflect a different skills base to the leader but connect through vision, values, and vocation. 'The team is greater than the sum of its parts.' This means the leader has to understand their own strengths and any limitations they may have and to build a team of people who cover the whole range of leadership qualities that the organization requires to deliver to communities.

Operational leadership and personal responsibility

Personal responsibility and accountability are key factors in both learning and leadership.[13] A leader has to take personal responsibility to ensure that they have the necessary training, skills, and experience to lead the whole or part of the organization. In Greater Manchester I led many major policing events and firearms incidents, and in each I felt personally responsible for the safety of the public and the staff under my direction. This is a significant responsibility that begins with the leader's preparation, training, and learning. There is a balance between engaging with the organizational provision of leadership development opportunities and, more importantly, the leader's personal responsibility in ensuring they are 'fit for purpose', as suggested by Dr Mark Kilgallon and Dr Martin Wright earlier in this chapter.

---

[13] See Cordner and Shain (2011)—this is an adaptation of the question on individual responsibility.

Ultimately, each of us is responsible for our own development of leadership skills. We need to make the most of the opportunities that are provided, but also to seek out bespoke learning experiences. As a Sergeant on the Special Course, later the High Potential Development Scheme, and now 'Fast Track', I was given the opportunity to visit another organization, and I went to the Boots' Headquarters in Nottingham. The biggest differences I noted between the culture in Boots and the one I had experienced in policing was the approach to training. In policing, significant training opportunities were provided, but were rarely respected by participants, or indeed the organization. At Boots, training was a valued commodity and was *earned* by commitment and performance. It also provided further career opportunities.

I have attended many courses at Bramshill and met too many people who complained about the quality of training provided. However, at Bramshill participants were not on call, and had some time to learn, to gather information, and to reflect on development and learning from others. Anyone unable to benefit from this opportunity was failing themselves, the police service, and the communities they served. Leaders and learners should take personal responsibility for ensuring that courses and other learning opportunities make a positive impact on their performance and the people they lead.

The next generation of leaders

Current leaders should seek to play a part in the development of future leaders and should contribute to their learning agenda. This is partly for the good of the organization, partly as a return on the investment made in them, and partly because it is rewarding to play a part in seeing others flourish.

I led for ACPO on the redesign of the Senior Leadership Development Programme. I shaped the multi-agency approach, the bringing in of syndicate directors from forces, and taking a different approach to finances. There was considerable caution about getting chief officers and senior police staff released to be syndicate directors, but the service demonstrated its willingness to engage in the learning of others, due partly to the quality and practically focused nature of the content. As already stated, it is important for every leader to contribute to the leadership of the future; this needs to be a core part of a new approach to Continual Professional Development by the College of Policing, and I would argue that leaders at any rank/position learn a great deal more when they are involved in training and development. I had the privilege to be a Syndicate Director on the SCC, where I and other directors learned a great deal.

The involvement of current leaders in the development of future leaders is critical in the cultural context of policing. When appointed as Chief Superintendent covering Moss Side, I had already begun to be involved in contributing to courses on police ethics. As well as the operational challenge and experience I obtained from the post, I knew that if I was operationally successful I was more likely to gain credibility and be listened to when speaking about police ethics in a learning environment.

This was exemplified when I worked at Bramshill with Chris Keeble, who was awarded the Distinguished Service Order recognizing his command of the Second Battalion, the Parachute Regiment at a pivotal stage in the Falklands Conflict of 1982. In 1986, Chris established a unique consultancy and lecturing practice that has successfully enabled senior leaders from national and international institutions to balance the concept of people flourishing through a period of business transformation. Chris was too modest about his significant military achievements and I encouraged him to spend more time in his talks establishing his operational credibility prior to asking people to explore a deeper understanding of a person's right to lead, via Greek philosophy. It worked and he was well received by those attending his talks.

Policing will always benefit from those with strong, credible operational backgrounds, who have engaged in an academic journey and can bring the two together. This does not exclude academics from leadership training—far from it—but the need to blend *the academic and the practical* needs to be recognized by police. I believe that strong academic foundations are essential for any profession. The establishing of the College of Policing is part of the journey to greater professionalization; it brings with it the commitment to higher standards, building on the existing links to academia and the commitment of the service to evidence-based policing. These elements will deliver an even better informed and more professional service, which will have greater confidence about its practice and may be less willing for others to apply 'labels' to policing practice and status. Greater professionalization will lead to greater confidence, but we must never become 'too posh to wash'—a phrase used to describe the risk associated with nursing moving towards a requirement that all nurses have degrees. I want all police officers to be more professional, but also to retain their basic commitment to use the office of constable to do good, however complex that is or however simply it can be done.

Direct entry

The police service has nothing to fear from direct entry at any level. I do think there are exceptional people outside policing who can bring a great deal to the leadership of the service. However, as Sir Tom Winsor and the government champion 'direct entry', it is at the same time, and at the time of writing, making those direct entry positions less attractive. The three main ranks of inspector, superintendent, and chief constable are already very demanding roles; we expect these officers to take on significant leadership and management duties, to have high levels of professionalism, to work long hours each day, to be on cover for long periods, to work evenings and weekends in addition to the day job, to make critical life-changing decisions with limited information and time. Yet significant changes are being made to their terms and conditions, and in some cases their contracts, their ability to reach 30 years' pensionable pay, the costs of their pensions, tax on pensions, and their employment benefits. Some of these changes will particularly affect those joining the service under direct entry, who should progress through the ranks quickly, but will be financially penalized for doing so. How is that attractive to the very best from outside the service?

We need leaders to be appointed with a real sense of vision, values, and vocation, people with a real drive to make a difference and to work with their PCC. The relationship between PCCs and their chief constables is important and is covered later in this chapter. We do not want the very best people to be concerned about the financial dis-benefits of promotion and the risk of a fixed-term contract that will expire before they have achieved 30 years' pensionable pay.

Leadership: experience and theory

If each of us is ultimately responsible for our own leadership and development, one of the things we need to understand is how we make the links between our personal experience of leadership, the development of our individual leadership skills, and the alignment with current models and theories of leadership. We develop our leadership style based on a number of inter-related factors—our experiences of family life; other leaders and what works; being a leader and our understanding of what we wanted from those that have led us; organizational leadership demands; and public expectations. If all of these factors influence our personal leadership style, what part do leadership models and learning play? I believe they can provide insight into leadership by articulating clearly our experiences and values in a manner that we may not have fully understood; they can provide structure and comprehension to things we intuitively understand; and they can improve our grasp of concepts we have learned from others. Leadership theories can encourage us to try new things or to do more or less of some aspect of our leadership style. The theory and models are informed by experience and our experience is reinforced by theory.

One particularly helpful theory has been Daniel Goleman's work on emotional intelligence (EI). In the *Harvard Business Review*: 'What Makes a Leader?' (1998a) and in 'Leadership That Gets Results' (2000), Goleman argues that effective leaders are alike in one crucial way—they all have a high degree of EI. Goleman tells us of the five components of EI: self-awareness, self-regulation, motivation, empathy, and social skills. The leadership challenge set by Goleman is to understand our strengths and weaknesses in each of these five areas, to use that information wisely, to engage in a developmental journey that will increase our skills, and to have the humility and courage to know when you need to use the skills of others to achieve the best result. Goleman is part of a long line of people who have argued that the issue that differentiates the most successful leaders is their people skills.

Goleman's analysis is insightful and I have tried to link it to the importance I see in my own understanding of leadership that focuses on the significance of 'vision, values, and vocation'. This thinking builds on Goleman's work by exploring the critical question of why certain people/leaders are more emotionally intelligent than others. My experience informs me that EI is underpinned by a strong sense of values. The reasons people are emotionally intelligent are that they have strong values of honesty, integrity, equality, fairness, and a respect for the dignity of person. In my experience, these values are found in persons that demonstrate strong EI—strong values lead to strong EI. I therefore argue that there is another layer below Goleman's EI model that emphasizes strong values as differentiating the most successful leaders and provide them with the confidence that Dr Mark Kilgallon and Dr Martin Wright seek in their commentary on Goleman earlier in this chapter.

For five years I had the privilege of establishing and chairing the ACPO Professional Ethics Portfolio. The focus of the work we did can be summarized as follows: 'How can the portfolio best support the police officer or member of police staff facing a complex ethical dilemma at 2am in the morning?' We wanted to provide practical tools to enable ethical thinking to influence policing decisions, and for that reason we introduced the National Decision Making Model, which has ethics, now the Code of Ethics, at its centre. Behind the scenes we studied the academic literature that was trying to bridge the gap between pure ethics, applied ethics, and professional decision-making. We were influenced by two key themes within the literature. The first was the contributions that focused on recognizing the importance, scope, and workings of discretion within policing (Skolnick 1975: Ashworth 1998). The second was focused on how theory can be used to address recognized policing dilemmas (Olivet 1976; Pollock-Byrne 1989; Kleinig 1990). The risk we faced was that much of the literature was from the United States, where the cultural setting and issues are not the same as those of the United Kingdom, and that the fact that some of the ethical dilemmas were more about the difficulties associated with implementing the correct course of action, rather than the ethical complexity of the dilemma (see Waddington et al 2013).

Leadership and new governance arrangements

The introduction of PCCs is the biggest constitutional change in policing of our generation, and chief constables and PCC's are learning to establish the precise responsibilities of these two independent corporate roles within the new governance arrangements. The Police Reform and Social Responsibility Act 2011 replaced Police Authorities, which were local committees made up of elected councillors and independent members, with an elected PCC. The 2011 Act sought to make police governance more visible and transparent and was part of a broader police reform agenda. The PCC for an area holds the chief constable to account on behalf of the pubic for the delivery of the Police and Crime Plan. The relationship between the chief constable and the PCC is important to policing in each force area. The 'Policing Protocol' (Home Office 2011) sets out the details of that relationship, and I had the privilege of representing ACPO in the group preparing the draft under the leadership of the Home Office. The group was keen to make a clear statement that the protocol was an important document, but that it could never replace the importance of the relationship between these two individuals. The group was able to protect that clear statement through to the final version; it reads:

> An effective, constructive working relationship is more likely to be achieved where communication and clarity of understanding are at their highest. Mutual understanding of, and respect for, each party's statutory functions will serve to enhance policing for local communities (Home Office 2011: 1).

and:

> The establishment and maintenance of effective working relationships by these parties is fundamental. It is expected that the principles of goodwill, professionalism, openness and trust will underpin the relationship between them and all parties will do their utmost to make the relationship work (Home Office 2011: 2).

With great respect to the Police Authorities and particularly to former chairs of Police Authorities, policing was historically about one clear leader, the chief constable. The constitutional change that was embodied in the Police Reform and Social Responsibility Act 2011 has now given policing two clear leaders, the chief constable and the PCC. Leadership models of the past have focused on organizations that have only one leader. Something different is now required where there are two leaders with different constitutional responsibilities. The situation is made even more complex because of the legislative and practical drivers that ensure that chief constables and PCCs work in collaboration with other forces, other public sector bodies, and the private sector. In these arrangements there are multiple leaders and a new set of leadership models. Learning is required that empowers *all leaders* to flourish from working together, placing the focus not on the success of an individual leader, but rather on the combined success and endeavour of those involved in delivering excellent services to our communities. We need an analysis of leadership learning based on how power is used, distributed, and shared.

Chief constables and PCCs are powerful people, and how they personally view that power can have enormous influence on their leadership and impact. For some, power is a limited resource and in a binary relationship—as one grows, the other diminishes! Power is therefore seen as a finite resource and the struggle can make the relationship difficult and less influential for the good of communities. In other relationships the focus is on *empowerment*, where one partner is seen as strengthening the relationship as a whole and acting as an enabler for others. In these relationships there is a focus on how best everyone can serve the people, that is, *servus servorum populi*[14]—servants of the servants of the people. I believe in

---

[14] *Servus servorum populi*—servants of the servants of the people. This is derived from one of the titles used by the pope, *Servus servorum dei*—servant of the servants of god, and used by the popes at

a style of leadership learning that is confident enough to share power for the greater good—servant-centred leadership.

The leadership challenge has never been greater and the same can be said of the opportunities to do good for our communities. It is right that every person who joins the police service steps forward as a leader because of the unique role in society that the police hold. For those most senior leaders in policing, officers and staff, we have a duty to become the best leader that we can be and that requires a willingness to engage in developing our leadership skills and engaging with academics to ensure we make the best use of their insight and learning.

Shared Reflections

Having addressed the question of policing leadership learning from our two different perspectives—academic and police practitioner—we now wish to consolidate some of the key issues that have emerged in this chapter. Where are the areas within which there is opportunity for leadership theory to better inform policing practice? How can policing practice both benefit from as well as inform the content of leadership provision?

Collaboration

As a result of this discussion, we have identified six areas where we believe academic theory and professional policing practice come together.

The coaching and mentoring leader: developing the next generation

There is clear agreement between academic theory, experience, and policing practice that current leaders need to engage positively in the learning and development of future leaders of the service. If a leader can only influence the service by valuing and developing their staff, then coaching and mentoring are vital aspects in helping the next generation of leaders to flourish. Engagement in the development of future leaders also provides current policing leaders with an opportunity to demonstrate a return on investment—from which they had benefited earlier. It creates a continuous learning environment within which current leaders can compassionately influence the growth in confidence of their future peers.

Chief Constable Adrian Lee argued that quality leadership products attracted experienced operational policing leaders back into the learning environment as syndicate directors, coaching and mentoring future leaders through complex learning materials. At a structural level, we demonstrated how policing Professional Reference Groups, for example, could engage with the design, delivery, and content of learning materials in order to offer programme participants a

---

the beginning of all papal bulls. The reference refers to an important aspect of police leadership; police officers and police staff serve the people and their leaders are there to serve them.

credible quality assurance stamp of approval. This professional role directly connects and informs the learning content with operational need.

A negotiated learning partnership

Policing educators have a reflective, theoretical knowledge base that seeks to push the boundaries of the current leadership paradigm; policing professionals develop an active, operational knowledge that has significant cultural capital. Between reflection and action, there is a negotiated space where learning takes place. There was strong agreement that the credibility of the educator was a significant variable in the acceptance, or otherwise, of the learning being conveyed.

As well, there was a need for theoretical knowledge to recognize the value in policing practice. Therefore, leadership learning and the exploration of knowledge is not conveyed 'one way', educator to practitioner; rather it is a consultative learning partnership where complex and at times competing knowledge is explored.

Emotional intelligence and values-based leadership

There was a difference in emphasis when it came to considering the issue of EI and leadership development. A significant part of the EI literature focuses on developing the professional self-awareness and self-assuredness of leaders. From an academic perspective we asked: are policing leaders sufficiently self-assured to have the confidence to rigorously defend their policing mandate?

However, from the practitioners' perspective it is not just about being emotionally intelligent; rather it was about underpinning the theory with a stronger emphasis on values as an enabler for leadership. From the practitioners' perspective, it is the connection between vision, values, and vocation that provides leaders with the opportunity to learn and further develop an appropriate self-confidence in order to defend their policing mandate.

The credible self-motivated leader

Drawing on the experience of policing learning professionals, there has been an emphasis in this chapter on the importance of the learning environment within which leaders can flourish. From the professional practitioners' perspective, there has been an equal emphasis on the necessity for leaders to constantly learn from operational experiences. It is self-evident, yet worth repeating that the common denominator for learning to take place is the presence of a self-motivated learner who has taken personal responsibility to develop their professionalism. We have demonstrated that a 'learning leader' has the ability to seek out both theoretical and operational knowledge that can help them to develop as a leader and add real value to the organization.

While there is significant debate on whether learning should take place in an educational or workplace environment, the key variable that is missing from this debate is the attitudinal approach of the individual leader and their ability to seek, absorb, and then translate learning from every event with which they interact. Any high-quality leadership programme needs to be matched by the attendance of high-quality leaders possessing an ability to pursue the maximum return from any learning experience through their willingness to impart and embed that knowledge back in force, ultimately by doing things differently and better. This connects directly back to Peel's vision where the quality within policing rests with the people who are picked to lead it.

Direct entry

It was emphasized that policing had nothing to fear and everything to gain from exceptional people entering policing at senior leadership levels. They bring with them their experiences. The current HM Chief Inspector of Constabulary is also convinced (and has convinced the Home Secretary) that leaders need not just come from within the service—thus direct entry to senior levels of the police has been implemented in the United Kingdom. The debate on direct entry is complex and beyond the remit of this chapter. We may, however, offer a word of caution: this chapter has demonstrated that policing leaders award disproportionate cultural capital to operational experiences. Furthermore, they bring these narratives with them as an aid to learning. Policing narratives and value statements are grounded in operational encounters.

By definition, any future direct entry leader does not have this access. Their learning environment therefore needs to acknowledge and then compensate for this lack of access to policing narratives. Development opportunities need to be provided as close to the workplace as possible in order to provide them with a 'virtual' understanding of the context, complexities, and connections that exist within policing. They clearly have their own experiences from other industries and occupations and these should be encouraged, celebrated, and shared in a leadership value exchange relationship, which links their past experience with the new challenges of policing.

Collaborative leadership and the 'what works' agenda

Finally, we turn to the need for a more collaborative leadership model in order to solve cross-sector problems. This would help practitioners to share leadership in an environment where role takes precedence over rank; and where power, influence, and authority need to be negotiated across various government agencies.

This is a relatively new concept in policing leadership[15] and progress in knowledge and understanding would be best served if theory and practice were tightly aligned. This is an ideal opportunity for practice to inform theory (this is very

---

[15] Not to be confused with a partnership approach to problem solving, which historically was heavily influenced by the action-centred culture of policing.

close to the adaptive leadership model outlined by Heifetz et al (2009)) and an opportunity for policing theory to subsequently develop potentially new ways of leading change. Thus the leadership learning cycle is complete.

The learning leader—aligning theory and practice

This chapter started with the statement that *policing demands all staff to be leaders in their own right because they have chosen to be part of a highly demanding and complex occupation.* From an academic perspective, this chapter traced the progress of leadership development and the gradual emergence of the centralized provision of leadership learning services. It explored how difficult professional relationships can emerge when there are unclear terms of reference between the police service as customer, and a learning institute (Centrex) whose terms of reference were unclear. To avoid 'regrettable disinvestment' (Neyroud 2013), strong and significant connectivity with stakeholder requirements becomes critical in order to align leadership products with practitioner requirements.

The authors explored the concept of police leaders bringing their operational cultural norms into the learning environment and the need for educators to recognize this context, to appreciate that their cultural norms have credibility in their own right, and to avoid any attempt at what Cordner and Shain (2011) described as 'one-way learning'. It is therefore vital for policing educators to be 'stewards of complex knowledge' (Sherman 2011). In this way, the appropriate 'pitch' for learning programmes can be achieved and the conflation of knowledge, analytical skills, and wisdom (Grint 2007) is avoided.

Perhaps controversially, we challenged the services' self-belief that their policing leaders are self-confident and professionally self-assured. The significant influence of outside agencies directly impacting on the policing mandate suggested that policing, unlike other professional bodies, was in some cases giving 'undue deference' (PAJ Waddington personal communication) to the views of external bodies. The Service requires 'knowledge of the knowledge' of policing.

The authors explored a number of positive interactions with learning institutions and concluded by suggesting that the correlation between leadership development and exposure to informed theoretical knowledge and data was strong. In this sense, it is vital that police leaders and educators find more appropriate channels to ensure that the bridge between theory and practice is strengthened in order to provide the best possible provision of policing to the communities that the police must serve. In reflecting on these issues from his personal perspective and drawing on his considerable professional experiences, Chief Constable Adrian Lee emphasized the need for those who shape the organization to consistently challenge their current leadership paradigm by making a commitment to continuous learning.

While professional ability, confidence, and creating a flexible environment of trust that invests in people all help to create an excellent team performance—it is the issue of the *learning leader* that is tantamount to continuous professional development. There is a continued need for credible and emotionally intelligent leaders with a strong commitment to values, vision, and vocation to help with the development and learning of those whom they lead. It was emphasized that operational credibility benefited and was informed by engagement with academic theories and challenges.

The Chief Constable addressed the issues of direct entry and the challenges that this faces against a backdrop of changing terms and conditions for leaders; the new governance structures that will require a new multi-faceted approach to leadership development; and finally a challenging insight into the concept of a 'professional body' and the need for this body to be *owned, led, and financed* by the profession that it represents. Together we approached this chapter through our own perspectives and have hopefully demonstrated the increasing requirement for theory to influence practice and for practice to help to shape theoretical constructs.

Recommended Reading

Goleman, D (1998), 'What Makes a Leader', 76(6) *Harvard Business Review* 93

Grint, K (2007), 'Learning to Lead: Can Aristotle Help Us Find the Road to Wisdom? 3(2) *Leadership* 231

Waddington, PAJ (1999), 'Police Canteen Culture: An Appreciation' 39(2) *British Journal of Criminology* 287

References

Adlam, R (2000), 'Culture Change: Attempt to Teach Ethics to Police Leaders and Managers within a Traditional Institution and Changing Social Milieu', unpublished PhD thesis, University of Surrey

Angelou, Maya (1993) *The Inaugural Poem: On the pulse of morning*. New York: Random.

Ashworth, A (1998), 'Should the Police be Allowed to Use Deceptive Practices?' 114 *Law Quarterly Review* 108

Brain, T (2013), *A Future for Policing in England and Wales* (Oxford: OUP)

Chambers, R (2004), 'Collaborative Police Education; A Report', a paper presented at the World Association for Collaborative Education, unpublished, Charles Sturt University, NSW

Chan, J (1996), 'Changing Police Culture' 36(1) *British Journal of Criminology* 109

Clift, RE (1954), 'Police Training' 291 *Annals of the American Academy of Political and Social Science* 113

College of Policing (2013), 'Our Strategic Intent', at <http://library.college.police.uk/docs/college-of-policing/college-strategic-intent.pdf> (accessed 28 April 2015)

Cordner, G and Shain, C (2011), 'The Changing Landscape of Police Education and Training' 12(4) *Police Practice and Research* 281

Foster, J (2003), 'Police Cultures' in Newburn, T (ed), *Handbook of Policing* (Cullompton: Willan) 196

Foucault, M (1972), *Power/Knowledge: Selected Interviews and Other Writings 1972–1977* (New York: Pantheon)

Fyfe, N and Wilson, P (2012), 'Knowledge Exchange and Police Practice: Broadening and Deepening the Debate around Researcher–Practitioner Collaborations' 13(4) *Police Practice and Research* 306

Goffman, E (1959), *The Presentation of Self in Everyday Life* (Harmondsworth: Penguin Books)

Goleman, D (1998a), 'What Makes a Leader' 76(6) *Harvard Business Review* 93

Goleman, D (1998b), *Working with Emotional Intelligence* (London: Bloomsbury)

Goleman, D (2000), 'Leadership that gets results', *Harvard Business Review* March–April 78

Green, T and Woolston, R (2009), 'Police Education for the Profession Through a Collaborative Model: From Recruitment to Retirement—A Case Study' in Higgs, J et al (eds), *Education for Future Practice* (Rotterdam: Sense Publishers) 273

Grint, K (2007), 'Learning to Lead: Can Aristotle Help us Find the Road to Wisdom?' 3(2) *Leadership* 231

Harris, LS and Kuhnert, KW (2008), 'Looking Through the Lens of Leadership: A Constructive Developmental Approach' 29(1) *Leadership and Organization Development Journal* 47

Harris, RE (1949), 'New Police College Opened in Britain' 40(2) *Journal of Criminal Law and Criminology* 217

Hartman, A (1992), Editorial 37(6) *Social Work* 483

Heifetz, R, Grashow, A, and Linsky, M (2009), *The Practice of Adaptive Leadership* (Boston, MA: Harvard Business Review Press)

Herbert, S (1998), 'Police Sub-cultures Reconsidered' 36(2) *Criminology* 343

Holdaway, SL (1983), *Inside the British Police: A Force at Work,* (Oxford: Blackwell)

Hurd, D (2008), *Robert Peel: A Biography* (London: Phoenix)

Home Office (2011), 'The Policing Protocol Order 2011', at <https://www.gov.uk/government/uploads/system/uploads/attachment_data/file/117474/policing-protocol-order.pdf> (accessed 23 April 2015)

Johnson, G and Scholes, K (2002), *Exploring Corporate Strategy* (6th edn, Harrow: Prentice Hall)

Kleinig, J (1990), 'Teaching and Learning Police Ethics: Competing and Complementary Approaches' 18(1) *Journal of Criminal Justice* 1

Kleinig, J (2013) 'Reflections on Teaching Police Ethics with Scenarios' in Waddington, PAJ, Kleinig, W, and Wright, M (eds), *Professional Police Practice: Scenarios and Dilemmas* (Oxford: OUP) 25–42

Kodz, J and Campbell, I (2010), 'What Works In Leadership Development? A Rapid Evidence Review', National Policing Improvement Agency, London

Lee, M and Punch, M (2004), 'Policing by Degrees: Police Officers' Experiences of University Education' 14(3) *Policing and Society* 233

Loftus, B (2009), *Police Culture in a Changing World* (Oxford: OUP)

Manning, PK (1977), *Police Work: The Social Organization of Policing* (Cambridge and London: MIT Press)

Manning, PK (1989), 'Occupational Culture' in Bailey, WG (ed), *The Encyclopedia of Police Science* (London: Garland) 360

Neyroud, P (2013), 'Review of Police Leadership and Training Report', Home Office, London

Office of the Police Ombudsman for Northern Ireland (2007) *Statement by the Police Ombudsman for Northern Ireland on her Investigation into the Circumstances Surrounding the Death of Raymond McCord Junior and Related Matters*, OPONI, Belfast

Olivet, GD (1976), 'Ethical Philosophy in Police Training' 43(8) *The Police Chief* 48

Olsen, B (1959), 'A Centre for Police Planning and Research' 50(3) *The Journal of Criminal Law, Criminology, and Police Science* 296

Parker, General Sir Nick (2013), 'Independent Review of ACPO', at <http://apccs.police.uk/wp-content/uploads/2013/08/Independent-review-of-ACPO.pdf> (accessed 23 April 2015)

Paterson, C (2011), 'Adding Value? A Review of the International Literature on the Role of Higher Education in Police Training and Education' 12(4) *Police Practice and Research* 286

Pearson-Goff, M and Herrington, V (2013), 'Police Leaders and Leadership Development: A Systematic Literature Review', Australian Institute of Police Management, Manly, NSW

Plumridge, M (1983), 'A Study of Police Management and Command Roles' unpublished study, The Police Staff College, Bramshill

Pollit, C and Bouckaert, G (2004), *Public Management Reform: A Comparative Analysis* (Oxford: OUP)

Pollock-Byrne, J (1989), *Ethics in Crime and Justice—Dilemmas and Decisions* (Pacific Grove, CA: Brooks Cole Publishing Company)

Reiner, R (1992), *The Politics of the Police* (2nd edn, London: Wheatsheaf)

Rowson, J and Lindley, E, Foreword by Stanko, B (2012), *Reflexive Coppers: Adaptive Challenges in Policing* (London: Royal Society of Arts)

Schafer, JA (2009), 'Developing Effective Leadership in Policing: Perils, Pitfalls, and Paths Forward' 32(2) *Policing* 238

Schön, DA (1983), *The Reflective Practitioner: How Professionals Think in Action* (London: Temple Smith)

Shein, EH (1985), *Organisational Culture and Leadership* (San Francisco, CA: Jossey-Bass)

Sherman, L (2011), The 2011 Benjamin Franklin Medal Lecture, Royal Society for the Encouragement of Arts, Manufactures and Commerce, London

Skolnick, J (1975), *Justice Without Trial* (2nd edn, London: Collier McMillan)

Stevens, Lord (2013), 'Policing for a Better Britain: Report of the Independent Police Commission', at <http://independentpolicecommission.org.uk/uploads/37d80308-be23-9684-054d-e4958bb9d518.pdf> (accessed 24 April 2015)

Van Maanen, J (1973), 'Observations on the Making of Policemen' 32(4) *Human Organization* 407.

Waddington, PAJ (1999), 'Police Canteen Culture: An Appreciation' 39(2) *British Journal of Criminology* 287

Waddington, PAJ, Kleinig, W, and Wright, M (2013), *Professional Police Practice: Scenarios and Dilemmas* (Oxford: OUP)

Winsor, T (2012), 'HMIC Independent Review of Police Officer and Staff Remuneration and Conditions', Home Office, London

12

Making Connections between Research and Practice

Tackling the Paradox of Policing Research

Jenny Fleming, Nick Fyfe, and Alex Marshall

Introduction

A profession's research base is its foundation. It may not be self-evident that research dating back decades is, in modern times, of great significance, but today's research is based on the inquiry, the empirical data, and the methodologies that have been considered over time and have become the benchmarks by which the profession is perceived. In the context of police, its research base is over 50 years old and today's questions, while mired in the contemporary context, are driven by existing scholarship. For those who wish to understand their profession (and indeed the politics of their profession) should, in the first instance, refer to Reiner (2010) and for those who wish to become leaders in their profession, an understanding of where the profession has come from, and where it might be going, can often be found in its research archives.

This chapter considers the research-based knowledge of, and for, policing. It is not exhaustive and not intended as an authoritative literature review. The police research base is extensive, and space does not allow for more than a cursory consideration of what one might identify as the seminal works of the profession and those that have spearheaded the continuing research efforts of today's academics and practitioners. This work, coupled with the extensive bibliography, provides a strong starting point for those who wish to extend and develop their knowledge. A second caveat concerns the geographical reach of this chapter.

We are concerned here with the early and continuing research in the United States and the United Kingdom. While the chapter acknowledges the work of individual scholars from elsewhere, it does not provide an exhaustive appraisal of the significant work coming out of other Anglo-speaking countries, the burgeoning European literature, nor the considerable research base that is now reflected in the Asian/Australasian countries. Important as this latter work is, it has not had the same long-standing influence on policing in the UK.

This chapter provides a guide for those seeking to expand their knowledge of police research generally and to consider the trajectory through which police research has come to be associated with principles of evidence, experimental methods, and 'what works'. It also highlights something of a paradox in relation to police research. On the one hand, research-based knowledge of, and for, policing has increased significantly in the past 50 years and as Skogan and Frydl (2004: 22) noted over a decade ago, it 'has become a substantial industry...with a dedicated core of scholars, a large body of published work, several specialized journals, many, many accessible data sets, and regular professional meetings'. A decade later, Reiner notes (2015) that, policing research 'has grown to be a formidable intellectual and policy enterprise, including academics and practitioners'. Yet, on the other hand, despite an 'exponential growth over the past four decades in the theoretical and empirical work produced on policing and related issues', police policy and practice has remained relatively uninformed by police research findings, and the demand for evidence to inform policy from within police organizations has been weak (Weisburd and Neyroud 2011; Rojek et al 2012: 332). Somewhat surprising perhaps is that trends in police research demonstrate that at least until 2007, research into 'police strategies'— for example, community policing, patrol, and targeted groups—'dominated the policing literature' (Mazeika et al 2010).

However, if policing is to gain legitimacy and secure investment in an increasingly sceptical world of public services, in which the competition for public finance is growing ever more acute (Ayling et al 2009), the identification of effective and cost-efficient practices and policies is essential. Nowadays, and increasingly, governments and police organizations themselves are commissioning and funding research in their efforts to improve organizational and operational effectiveness. Such investment has encouraged the expansion of an evidence-based policy research tradition (see later) that has been especially evident in the UK and the US.

This section of the chapter provides an overview of the seminal work that has primarily come from the US and the UK. The research forms the body of work that has become established as the canon of policing studies, providing the central source of an understanding of police and policing today and forming the basis of a professional body of work. The section considers the challenges of connecting research and practice with reference to the growing narratives of police–researcher collaboration. The section notes the more recent 'evidence-based' emphasis in police research, focusing on, as Greene notes (2014: 201), 'the connection between means and ends or the impacts of particular police interventions'.

United States

Scientific research in the US was largely stimulated by the President's Commission on Law Enforcement and the Administration of Justice (Black and Reiss 1967), although the work on the internal management and general administration of police by Fuld (1909), Fosdick (1920), Vollmer (1936), Wilson (1950), and Westley (1953; 1970) made significant contributions to an understanding of police administration prior to this and should be acknowledged.

The development of social scientific interest in policing from the 1950s onwards testifies to the political developments that placed institutions of government, with the police serving as the most visible expression of state authority, under increasing scrutiny. A tradition in early police scholarship was shaped by normative concerns and public interest values (Bradley et al 2006), primarily concerned with the 'fairness and lawfulness of police actions' (Skogan and Frydl 2004: 13). In terms of methodology, the participant observer and ethnography was the dominant model, although it was not long before survey data began to feature (Fleming and Wakefield 2009: 269–74). These early studies of the police highlighted the problematic aspects of police discretion, police socialization practices, and corruption within what was shown to be a closed and hidden occupational culture (see Skolnick 1966; Wilson 1968). Interest in police function, style, and practice was also of significant research interest in the 1970s (eg Bittner 1967, 1973; Reiss 1971; Manning 1978).

Further research in the US through the 1970s identified the limited effectiveness of police practice in urban areas, such as beat patrol, calls for service (and service generally), and crime prevention (eg Kelling et al 1974; Brantingham and Faust 1976). Against the background of anti-war protests, civil rights, race relations, and industrial activity, research focused on the complexities of street-corner policing (Muir 1979), police behaviour, its situational influences and determinants, occasionally, its 'tragic perspective' (Black and Reiss 1967; Wilson 1968; Reiss 1971; Muir 1979), and increasingly, public perceptions of police performance (Bayley and Mendelsohn 1969). As Skogan and Frydl (2004: 23) point out, these types of studies shifted the focus from arrest rates and crime statistics as measures of police performance to a more nuanced consideration of notions of legitimacy, fairness, and respect; factors that are now commonplace in police performance indicators and inform the proliferation of research that has developed around police legitimacy and procedural justice in the ensuing years (eg Bradford et al 2009; Jackson et al 2012; Tyler 1990, 2004).

Such research was rarely targeted and few studies were replicated, despite the potential value to police reform agendas, police practitioners, and policy-makers. As Skogan and Frydl (2004: 14) noted, 'many of the most important lessons of research on police effectiveness depend to this day on the conclusions of one or a few now-dated studies'. Goldstein's (1979) work on problem-orientated policing (POP) gave a different slant to the idea of community-orientated policing and the early methodologies and models of both were to become extremely influential in the Anglo-speaking world. Chief Bill Bratton in the US has acknowledged and cited Wilson and Kelling's, 'Broken Windows' thesis (1982), Goldstein's POP work (1979), and JQ Wilson's 'Thinking about Crime' (1983) as major influences on his practice (cited in Rojek et al 2012: 331). As Hoogenboom and Punch (2012: 70) note, despite its apparent problems and 'lack of institutional cohesion', the US was 'a rich source of ideas and innovation'.

United Kingdom

In the UK, early police research had largely been confined to sociological studies—perhaps Michael Banton's, comparative study of Police Forces in Scotland and the US, *Policeman in the Community* (1964), the first book on policing that was based on empirical social science fieldwork (Reiner 2015), and Maureen Cain's, *Society and the Policeman's Role* (1973) being the best known.[1] Robert Mark's work from that period has been a strong influence on police leaders (see Mark 1977; Mark and Charlton 1978), as was Reiner's 1978 sociological study of 'the blue coated worker'. As Hoogenboom and Punch (2012: 69) have pointed out, police research in Britain at this time was 'in its infancy', with most academics looking 'to the US for guidance and inspiration'.

In the 1950s, the UK Home Office established its own research unit in the fields of crime and criminology; consisting then of two researchers and four civil servants (see Butler 1974: 3; Lodge 1974)—the Home Office Research Development and Statistics Directorate provided information to Ministers and policymakers with a view to facilitating 'evidence-based decisions' (see eg Clarke 1972; Clarke and Hough 1984). Thirty-five years later, the Police Research Group (PRG) was established within the Police department of the Home Office with a remit to 'increase the influence of research on police policy and practice' (Davies et al 2000: 236). In 1992, the PRG had an extensive budget, a flexible research programme, and a strong, strategic focus. In 1998, the PGR's remit was extended to include the coordination of a crime reduction programme and changed its name to the Policing and Crime Reduction Programme (Davies et al 2000: 237–40). The research papers and pamphlets that represented the published output of these research units were the basis of many police officers', and indeed academics', introduction to police research in the UK.

---

[1] Although Reiner (2015) notes the historical contributions of Hart (1955) and Radzinowicz (1956).

In the ensuing years, in the US, the UK, and elsewhere there has been a plethora of police researchers addressing police-related issues across a range of disciplines and subjects—tracing the move from the early sociological studies of policing that focused on the public police, to the numerous studies that have addressed the fragmented nature of policing and the growth of private security (Shearing and Stenning 1987; Johnston and Shearing 2009; Johnston 2000); the transformation of policing (Bayley and Shearing 1996; Jones and Newburn 2002) and the move back to 'policing' rather than 'the police', growing 'beyond the capacity of even a dedicated specialist to keep abreast of' (Reiner 2015).

Specific topics include: politics (Reiner 2010); police culture (eg Reuss-Ianni 1983; Chan 1997); partnership policing (Crawford 1999; Fleming 2006); women in policing (Heidensohn 1992; Silvestri 2007); community intelligence (Innes 2006); public order (Waddington 1994, 1999); community policing (Klockars 1988; Skogan 2006); transnational policing (Sheptycki 2000); intelligence-led policing (Ratcliffe 2010); and police corruption (Punch 2009). Important, more general works include Holdaway's *Inside the British Police* (1983), McLaughlin's *New Policing* (2007), Roger Graef's *Talking Blues* (1989), and more recently Jennifer Brown's edited collection, *The Future of Policing* (2013).

The acknowledgement of what Newburn has referred to as the 'core of policing studies' is evident in his *Key Readings*, which brings together the 'canon', the body of work that represents the 'rich history of writing in this area' (Newburn 2005). Extending the range of studies, particularly in terms of context and operational duties, the *Handbook of Policing* (Newburn (2008), with a new edition in 2012) is a comprehensive and authoritative read for those acquainting themselves with the general literature.

Dutch researchers, Hoogenboom and Punch (2012: 81), argue that 'the balance of power in police research has shifted away from North America', making way for a more 'stimulating and wide-ranging' corpus. They contend that 'British academics in this area tend to have a much broader and critical orientation to society, politics and the state than their counterparts in the US' (2012: 81). The extent to which 'the British critical tradition, rich in theoretical diversity' will continue to grow and prosper (Bradley et al 2006: 177–8) will be dependent on a range of issues, including funding and capacity for both researchers and police organizations. Methodological developments in policing research have notably become more quantitative, to the point, as Greene suggests (2014: 206), that 'the orthodoxy of experimentation has now become the "holy grail" for police research and for police problem-solving'. What is happening now is a stronger move towards police practitioners working collaboratively with academics with a renewed focus on evidence-based research. These collaborations are concentrating the minds of police colleges and researchers in the UK and the US with a much stronger consideration of how research can address the significant gaps in police knowledge and drive forward policy and practice.

The Challenges of Connecting Research and Practice

As these brief reviews of the development of police research in the US and UK illustrate, this is a field where there has been considerable expansion in recent years, both in terms of the volume of activity and the breadth of the research agenda. Nevertheless, despite this expansion many would claim that the impact of research evidence on policing policy and practice remains limited. Researchers in the US, for example, have struck a consistently pessimistic note over the past 15 years regarding the integration of research-based knowledge into routine police practice. Bayley (1998), writing in the late 1990s, observed that 'research may not have made as significant, or at least as coherent, an impression on policing as scholars like to think'; five years later Goldstein (2003) noted that 'there is no discernible, sustained and consistent effort within policing to make the basic premise that "knowledge informs practice" a routine part of policing'. More recently, Lum and her colleagues (2012: 72) have acknowledged that 'the notion that science should matter is often trumped by the reality that public opinion, political will, or consensus-based opinions about best practices are what underpin and drive police practices'.

It is important to recognize that even if the impact of research evidence on policing policy and practice has been limited, this does not mean that police research should be viewed as a 'failure'. Police research should not simply be evaluated in narrow instrumental terms, but also by its broader attempts to understand and explain the nature of policing. Those police officers who have engaged with academic study in these areas testify to the usefulness of such research in understanding the complex nature of policing and the importance of environment and context for understanding change and reform. Nevertheless, many of those engaged in research on, for, or with the police are motivated by what Loader and Sparks (2011: 56) term, a 'reformist impulse' and therefore want their research to be taken seriously in the world of policy and practice. The barriers that limit the use of research in policy and practice settings can take a variety of forms. Broadly, those barriers can relate to ideological constraints or even the inherently political nature of evidence-based studies (in the managerial context see Hodgkinson 2012; Hornung 2012). As well, research findings are often messy, ambiguous, and contradictory; there may be a lack of autonomy to implement findings from research, a lack of support for research-based change, and cultural resistance to research and its use (Nutley et al 2007).

All of these barriers are of considerable relevance to understanding the constraints that impact on the integration of research evidence into policing. Bullock and Tilley (2009), for example, highlight how in policing there is often disagreement about what counts as evidence of effective practice, issues about the accessibility of evidence to practitioners, and organizational constraints in terms of a lack of support for practitioners to engage with research that might be seen as a threat to professional expertise. Similarly, Lum et al (2012: 65) highlight a range of issues that hinder receptivity to research in policing. These include an organizational culture and system of promotions that focus on 'rewarding knowledge of procedures and reactivity [and so] help strengthen barriers to using research that promotes proactivity and problem solving'. Other attempts to make sense of the limited impact of research evidence on police policy and practice have pointed to a broader problem of a lack of effective communication between academics and police practitioners.

Constructing an imaginary conversation between a police officer and an academic, MacDonald (1986) characterized the problem as a 'dialogue of the deaf' in which police and academics appear unsympathetic to the different concerns that each have about research:

Academic: Why do the police ignore research findings?

Police: Why don't researchers produce usable knowledge?

Academic: Why do the police always reject any study that is critical of what they do?

Police: Why do researchers always show the police in a bad light?

Academic: Why don't police officers even read research reports?

Police: Why can't researchers write in plain English?

While there may be some substance to these claims and counter-claims, there is also evidence of innovative activity to establish a *dialogue of the listening* between police and research communities, exemplified in the growing range of police–academic collaborations that have emerged in recent years both in the US (Buerger 2010; Engel and Whalen 2010; Rojek et al 2012); the UK (Fyfe and Wilson 2012; Guillaume et al 2012); Europe (Knutsson 2010; Punch 2010); and Australia (eg Wood et al 2008; Bradley and Nixon 2009; Fleming 2010, 2011, 2012; Marks et al 2010). This research and related work have provided detailed narratives of police–academic collaboration, and confirm Cordner and White's (2010) observation that 'the police research/police practice relationship is evolving quite positively'.

Such collaborations can take a variety of forms, from individual researchers or an academic unit within a single university working directly with a police agency, through to larger-scale collaborations of researchers across academic institutions, working directly with several police agencies (see Engel and Henderson 2013). For example, there is The Centre of Excellence in Policing and Security (CEPS 2007–14) in Australia, and the What Works Centre in Crime Reduction (College of Policing 2013) in the UK. In addition, the College of Policing's innovation funding opportunities, designed to bring together practitioners and academics, have gone some way to consolidating more extensive partnerships (College of Policing 2015).

Police Research as Science

In an important intervention in the debate about the limited impact of police research on policy and practice, Weisburd and Neyroud (2011: 2) argue that despite progress in collaborative activity and the production of knowledge about policing, 'there is still a fundamental disconnect between science and policing'. Policing innovations are, they contend, rarely science-based, and research is still viewed by the police as a luxury rather than a necessity. For Weisburd and Neyroud there are important structural reasons why this disconnect between evidence and practice persists:

> The police operate in a reality in which decisions must be made quickly. And issues of finance and efficiency can be as important as effectiveness. But academic policing research generally ignores these aspects of the police world, often delivering results long after they have relevance, and many times focusing on issues that police managers have little interest in (2011: 5).

Sherman has strongly endorsed the arguments of Weisburd and Neyroud, arguing that evidence-based policing is needed not simply to improve public safety but also to enhance police legitimacy. In his 2011, Benjamin Franklin Medal Lecture on 'Professional Policing and Liberal Democracy', Sherman argues that 'police legitimacy may be established, not just on the basis of effectiveness under the rule of law, but on demonstrated police mastery of a complex body of knowledge generated by scientific methods of testing and analysis'.

The contribution by Weisburd and Neyroud (2011) has generated an important debate about the relationship between police research and police practice (see Moore 1995, 2006; Thacher 2008; Sparrow 2011). Sparrow (2011) has argued that the model of police research that has tended to inform the type of evidence-based policing favoured by Weisburd and Neyroud focuses on a narrow range of social research methods, privileging randomized control trials (RCTs) while marginalizing other approaches to advancing knowledge. These are concerns echoed by Moore (2006: 325), who argues that the conception of scientific knowledge needs to be 'more open and flexible' than proponents of evidence-based policing allow. Moore's position is that methods other than RCTs can still produce important knowledge and that for reasons of time, money, and the complexity of the issue, RCTs may simply not be practicable to address many policing problems. Moore also highlights how RCTs risk confining research activities to a small expert elite, frustrating attempts to broaden the community of practitioners involved in applied research. Greene's (2014: 206) reflections on 'meaning in police research' suggest:

> ... while there are clearly benefits to experimentation about what impacts police have in their crime fighting and order maintenance activities, such approaches cannot speak to the wider range of issues, units of analysis, and possible methodologies that can be used to study the complexities of the police ... much of what we do know about the police today is not the result of experimentation.

Perhaps an important point to be made in the context of academic/practitioner partnerships is that police officers themselves feel that they have much to offer the research field by way of experience and their sense of their 'craft'. Willis and

Mastrofski (2014) note the importance of police science engaging with the craft of policing if such scholars want to increase 'the likelihood of a productive alliance between these two partners for the purpose of police reform'.

These debates about police–academic collaborations and the relationship between police research and evidence-based policing are clearly important. In particular, they act as a timely reminder of the challenges involved in forging links between research evidence and police practice and the need to understand some of the barriers that must be overcome if research evidence is to play a more significant role in informing police decision-making.

Engaging with 'what works' to support evidence-based policy

In attempting to overcome some of these barriers, there have been several recent initiatives to develop more effective dissemination strategies between researchers and police practitioners. The work in the US around the Matrix Demonstration Project (Lum et al 2012) centres on an innovative knowledge translation tool, the Evidence-Based Policing Matrix, which brings together a large body of police-related crime prevention research that has been evaluated as meeting high standards of methodological rigour. By mapping these studies using a three-dimensional visualization process,[2] police are in a position to access the key findings from a large body of research and use this knowledge to guide interventions to deal with specific problems. In the UK, there has been a similar initiative to improve the accessibility of the evidence base to police policy-makers and practitioners. This comprises an online toolkit (developed by the What Works consortium in partnership with the College of Policing, see <http://whatworks. college.police.uk/toolkit/Pages/Tolkit.aspx> (accessed 9 June 2015)) that allows the police to access research findings on the effectiveness of interventions to reduce crime. Based on evidence from a series of systematic reviews of the research literature evaluating the impact of different crime reduction strategies in areas such as knife crime, domestic violence, and situational crime prevention, the toolkit provides information on the effect of particular interventions, the mechanisms that brought about any changes, the contexts within which the interventions were located, the implementation conditions, and an economic assessment of their cost-effectiveness (Johnson et al 2015).

Although police research remains a broad field of scholarship, these examples of 'tailored dissemination' exemplify the ways in which much of the recent police research is now increasingly focused not just on 'knowledge creation' but also on 'knowledge exchange' and 'knowledge integration' in order to make research evidence 'part of the conversation' when police practitioners strategize about policy and practice (Lum 2012).

This section has provided an overview of the literature that has formed the basis of policing studies and has contributed significantly to policing's professional

---

[2] See <see http://cebcp.org/evidence-based-policing/the-matrix> (accessed 14 April 2015).

body of work. It has discussed the challenges of bringing together research, policy, and practice and the ways in which researchers have sought to bridge the gap between police practitioners and academics. The Police as Science debate has been explored and the importance of knowledge exchange and tailored dissemination emphasized. In the following section, Alex Marshall, the CEO of the newly formed College of Policing, provides a practitioner's perspective of some of these debates and discusses the relevance of police research to his police practice.

Practitioner's Perspective

Police officers have always known the value of evidence in a legal sense, when investigating potential crimes. Securing witness statements, recovering stolen property, confessions by perpetrators, and constantly evolving scientific methods of identification have always featured in everyday police work. The police are used to providing the courts and prosecuting authorities with evidence upon which guilt may be assessed. However, in setting strategies and making decisions about prioritization and consequent resourcing, police leaders have rarely relied on evidence in the sense of a compelling body of knowledge, created through careful research.

The approach taken by the police has rather been informed by individual past experience, and often by what happens when things go wrong. Murder investigation and public order policing are clear examples where lessons from failure have led to the creation of national guidance or standards. In these examples, the evidence base is formed by inquiries and reviews into incidents that have gone wrong, often with tragic consequences. Learning from past mistakes is understandable but also presents potential limitations. In the broadest terms, it could lead to preparing for the past rather than equipping the workforce of the future.

In some areas, the police service has begun to take a more predictive or preventive approach, working to analyse 'near misses' and identify patterns where changes need to be made. Lessons learnt in police custody about looking after vulnerable people in crisis have led to national guidance and procedures to assess for, and guard against, the consequences of a person at risk being detained in a police cell. There is significant potential to identify patterns in policing and think about how to change them—part of preparing for the future, as part of an evidence-based scientific approach.

When I joined the police in 1980, the influential officers who were nearing the end of their careers had joined at the start of the 1950s. Many were former military personnel and there was a strong culture of hierarchy and adherence to rules. Advice often focused on how to keep out of trouble. One example related to warnings about how you could be sacked. The 'three Ps' were seen as high risk:

1. prisoners—they might escape or die whilst under your care;
2. prostitutes—because you should never be alone with one or they might allege misconduct;
3. property—because it could be lost or stolen whilst you were responsible for it.

That the 'three Ps' 'lesson' has stayed with me for 34 years shows the power of an oral history and that in the culture of policing, compelling anecdotes become widely accepted as evidence.

Street policing is often seen as a craft and much more of an art than a science. In my early years in policing, officers were respected in the police if they were good 'thief takers', particularly brave, or seen as masters of the myriad processes and procedures. There were accepted ways of doing things and in the early 1980s, despite the existence of police-related research and its availability to those who looked for it, I do not recall any reference to academic research in briefings, de-briefings, or as part of my everyday work. The introduction of the Police and Criminal Evidence Act 1984 (PACE) changed the way police operated on the street, with stop and search, and arrest and detention, and with the safety of a detained person on arrival at the police station. The appropriate treatment of suspects throughout the investigative process became a priority. The arrival of PACE coincided with my promotion to sergeant in 1985. PACE not only changed the way we gathered evidence, and how we dealt with suspects, but also corrected many failings of the past by ensuring we, as the police, prioritized evidence as never before. I was completely unaware of the research-based foundation to the changes brought in by the 1984 Act but was very conscious of the new-found belief from the public, legislators, and us—as members of the police—that behaviour and outcomes would change.

In the early 1990s, I was promoted to inspector in Lambeth, and by the mid-1990s had 'responsibility' for an area of Lambeth as the Sector Inspector. For the first time in my career, I was thinking seriously about preventing and reducing crime in a defined geographical area. I would be judged by senior management for my success or failure in bringing an alarmingly high rate of burglary and car crime under control. I realized that there was an emerging library of studies dealing with everyday policing problems and turned to a series of purple (later pink) booklets, produced by the Police Research Group and published by the Home Office. These booklets included, Webb, Brown, and Bennett's (1992) 'Preventing Car Crime in Car Parks' and Tilley and Webb's (1994) 'Burglary Reduction: Findings from Safer Cities Schemes'. The booklets were informative, albeit in my view at the time, lacking in operational application. I looked at some (mainly American) international crime reduction initiatives, but struggled to see the direct relevance to the streets of south London.

On reflection, the crime reduction approaches I tried respected some of the research material I had 'discovered' but leant heavily on what I 'knew' worked. Lots of arrests, hand picking a team of highly motivated officers to concentrate on the problem, better intelligence, and some basic physical crime prevention advice seemed to work. I could show a big fall in crime comparing year on year, and therefore 'success' in police performance terms could be declared.

In the late 1990s, I twice attended programmes at the University of Cambridge. These were my first experiences of working with academics on crime and policing issues and the first time I had looked at policing as if an 'outsider'. In completing a Cropwood Fellowship, I studied the police response to racially motivated hate crime. This was a great opportunity for me, as a practitioner, to observe and report on the police response in my role of temporary academic. As a serving officer, it was relatively easy for me to gain access to any part of policing and to secure permission for using material I had obtained. What I lacked was any detailed knowledge or experience of research methodology. Despite the tireless efforts of my academic supervisor, my ability to describe my findings in an academically sound and authoritative form was also limited. During this period I had access to the University Library and time to read the work of the main writers in this field. Authors such as Reiner, Manning, Skolnick, and Wilson were influential in exposing me to police research. My very limited contribution to police-related research in this period helped me to understand the value of practitioners working with academics and the need for more practitioners to undertake evidence-based research.

By the early 2000s, I was a chief superintendent and area commander for a large swathe of Cambridgeshire Constabulary. This role gave me some opportunity to utilize my increased awareness of police and crime research material and to maintain contact with contemporary researchers. Police performance culture was still strong at this time, with sanction-based detection rates and offences brought to justice being counted, measured, compared, and published in league tables. Judgments on the police were made according to how one area performed by comparison to a list of other police areas assessed to be similar in nature. You were assigned to a 'family' of police areas from all over England and Wales and praised or denigrated depending on where you featured in the 'family' league table. It appeared to be a deeply flawed way of judging success or failure and led to endless and often bizarre disputes about whether or not particular areas were in the 'right' family. Because the actual level of crime became less important than how you compared to others, a change of family could result in one police area suddenly moving from top to bottom or vice versa. I could see no academically sound evidence base for this approach and the unedifying sight of senior police officers arguing about which 'family' they were in, rather than discussing how crime could be prevented, was probably evidence enough of competitive performance culture madness.

As part of the course to qualify as a chief officer, I attended the Institute of Criminology in Cambridge. I completed a diploma in Criminology before embarking on a part-time master's degree from 2004 to 2006. The research element of the masters programme gave me the opportunity to learn much more about methodology and the varying views within academia on the relative value of research approaches. The fact that many senior police officers and staff studied criminology and undertook research during this period was to prove important when they held executive roles, including the position of chief constable, over the following decade. We now have a sizeable cohort of senior people in policing who have combined practitioner experience with academic study. Most importantly, this cohort is in a position to make strategic use of the evidence base, allow their staff to contribute to the evidence through research, and to facilitate academic studies within the force they lead.

As the Chief Constable for Hampshire Constabulary from 2008 to 2013, I was in the privileged position of leading a police force of more than 7,000 people, serving a resident population of nearly two million. This period coincided with the global economic collapse and the requirement to make budget cuts of more than 20%. In making decisions about how to keep people and property safe, whilst cutting the size of the workforce, I made use of the best available evidence on preventing and reducing crime. While accepting the financial reality of being able to employ fewer people, particularly at senior levels, we invested in the education and development of those who remained with us. We supported several senior staff in pursuing academic studies, and this included some of them undertaking policing and crime-related masters' degrees. In return, these 'practitioner academics' carried out research studies in Hampshire to contribute to the evidence base and to establish which police approaches were more likely to succeed. One study, aimed at changing the behaviour of domestic abuse perpetrators (Sherman et al 1992), broke with conventional police thinking in this field and may challenge existing approaches to this endemic and damaging crime type. Similar studies are happening in many forces as the value of using an evidence base is better understood and more people in decision-making roles have experience of conducting research.

As the head of the College of Policing, I now lead the professional body responsible for establishing an authoritative evidence base for the police service. In setting national standards, the College always starts by reviewing the best available evidence. The College promotes the use of an evidence-based approach in police forces and works with practitioners to challenge existing thinking and to test and track new ideas with thorough research and evaluation. While there are many gaps in the police and crime research base, there is a growing body of work and, more importantly, a growing number of people willing and able to contribute to the evidence and knowledge base.

Looking back, I see two main barriers to the use of research evidence in decision-making: culture and inaccessibility. The history of how we do things in policing tends towards more anecdotal than research-based approaches. The key to changing this is less about teaching people during their careers and more about encouraging and recruiting officers to be as curious and questioning of their methods and evidence base as they are curious and questioning in their investigations of crime. My two academic supervisors, Ben Bowling and Anthony Bottoms, both took the time to open my mind and made me more aware of the need to look further and wider for serious research and literature.

For operational officers, to ensure accessibility for those without the luxury of time and vast libraries, the research evidence must be simple to obtain and easy to make sense of, so you can use it to inform decisions in your immediate context. As the What Works Centre for Crime Reduction, working with academics, the College is making the best available research evidence on crime reduction available online via its website. We involve practitioners in deciding how to present that evidence, and how to design new research, to make it more immediately intelligible and applicable, and to make sure it answers the question I had back in the 1990s, 'So what?' or 'So what can I do now?'

Shared Reflections

Towards the end of his contribution, Alex Marshall highlights two key barriers to the use of research evidence in policing: police culture and the inaccessibility of evidence. With respect to the latter, the increasing involvement of academics in making evidence accessible to practitioners via innovative forms of knowledge exchange (such as the Evidence-Based Matrix in the US and the What Works Centre for Crime Reduction online toolkit in the UK) signifies an important shift in the way many academics now approach police (and other policy-relevant) research.

Increasingly, 'knowledge creation' is now seen as a necessary but insufficient condition of research practice, with academics also expected to address how their research can have 'impact' through the development of novel approaches to exchanging this knowledge with practitioners and integrating research findings into discussions about policy and practice. However, innovation and improvements in knowledge exchange cannot, on their own, bring about a fundamental shift toward evidence-based policing. There needs to be, as Marshall also highlights, significant changes at a cultural level. He writes of the need to encourage a 'curious and questioning' attitude among officers towards the evidence base in a way similar to that in which officers would approach the investigation of crime. Such changes at an individual level in terms of how police officers interpret and use research evidence are clearly important and need to be supported at an institutional level—whether this means support for individual academic study or structural support within an institution that provides research resources for libraries, or active research and opportunities for its personnel to develop their own research capacity. As Alex Marshall demonstrates, these things take time, resources (that may be difficult to justify in times of austerity), and the active support of an organization that is determined to change culture and 'the way we do business'.

This support requires addressing the broader question of how engagement with research can be embedded within the police organizational context of systems, practices, and cultures (Davies et al 2000: 233). The key conclusions from existing research from other areas of social policy are that we must look to interactive and social models of the research process, which emphasize the importance of 'receptive contexts and effective facilitation' as crucial for constructive engagement with new forms of knowledge. It is in this realm that the growing range of police–academic collaborations which have emerged in recent years have an important role to play. What such collaborations offer is the opportunity to develop a 'shared academic–practitioner infrastructure' (Weisburd and Neyroud

2011: 15) in which there is regular and routine engagement around the nature and value of the research evidence base for policing. Research 'users', from 'management cops' to 'street cops', are able to interact regularly with research 'providers', helping to secure a *culture of engagement* and a commitment to the *co-production* of research which encourages improved communication between researchers and practitioners (Lunt et al 2010).

These activities are important precisely because they yield the kind of sustained involvement of practitioners in the research process that facilitates a better mutual understanding of the different cultural worlds of police organizations and academia, making a 'dialogue of the deaf', of the kind described by MacDonald (1986), less likely in the future (Nutley et al 2007; Fyfe and Wilson 2012). Nevertheless, while greater police–academic collaboration is to be welcomed in advancing the scope for high quality research evidence to help inform police decision-making, it is also important to acknowledge the point made by Mark Moore, that 'the world of crime and policing is far too important, far too complex, far too urgent to leave entirely in the hands of scientists. We need a great deal of practical wisdom as well as a rigorous and responsive science' (Moore 2006: 336; on this point see also Sparrow 2011). Moore's argument is underlined by recent critical reflections on the achievements of evidence-based medicine.

Although it is more than 20 years since evidence-based medicine was announced as a 'new paradigm' which would revolutionize clinical practice, there are increasing concerns that this approach has devalued clinical experience, leading to a top-down approach to service delivery that is in danger of losing sight of 'real patients' with complex needs that are not captured in clinical trials (Greenhalgh et al 2014). It is important that policing learns these lessons from medicine and other professions that have embraced evidence-based approaches and achieves an appropriate balance between 'craft' and 'science', experience and evidence, in the delivery of fair and effective policing.

Recommended Reading

Newburn, T (ed) (2005), *Policing: Key Readings* (Cullompton: Willan)
Newburn, T (ed) (2012 [2008]), *Handbook of Policing* (London: Routledge)
Reiner, R (2010), *Politics of the Police* (4th edn, Oxford: OUP)
Waddington, PA (1999), *Policing Citizens: Authority and Rights* (Philadelphia, PA: UCL Press)

References

Ayling, J, Grabosky, P, and Shearing, C (2009), *Lengthening the Arm of the Law: Enhancing Police Resources in the Twenty-first Century* (Cambridge: Cambridge University Press)
Banton, M (1964), *The Policeman in the Community* (New York: Basic Books)

Bayley, D (1998), 'Policing in America: Assessment and Prospects' in Police Foundation Series: Ideas in American Policing, Police Foundation, Washington, DC

Bayley, D and Shearing, C (1996), 'The Future of Policing' 30(3) *Law and Society Review* 585

Bayley, DH and Mendelsohn, H (1969), *Minorities and the Police: Confrontation in America* (New York: Free Press)

Bittner, E (1967), 'The Police on Skid-Row: A Study of Peace Keeping' 32(5) *American Sociological Review* 699, at <http://www.jstor.org/stable/2092019> (accessed 2 November 2014)

Bittner, E (1973), 'The Functions of the Police in Modern Society', National Institute of Mental Health, Center for Studies of Crime and Delinquency, Bethesda, MD

Black, D and Reiss, AJ (1967), 'Patterns of Behavior in Police and Citizen Transactions' 2 Studies in Crime and Law Enforcement In Major Metropolitan Areas, US Government Printing Office, Washington, DC

Bradford, B, Jackson, J, and Stanko, EA (2009), 'Contact and Confidence: Revisiting the Impact of Public Encounters with the Police' 19(1) *Policing and Society* 20

Bradley, D and Nixon, C (2009), 'Ending the "Dialogue of the Deaf": Evidence and Policing Policies and Practices: An Australian Case Study' 10(5/6) *Police Practice and Research* 423

Bradley, D, Nixon, C, and Marks, M (2006), 'What Works, What Doesn't Work and What Looks Promising in Police Research Networks' in Fleming, J and Wood, J (eds), *Fighting Crime Together: The Challenges of Policing and Security Networks* (Sydney: University of New South Wales Press) 170

Brantingham, PJ and Faust, FL (1976), 'A Conceptual Model of Crime Prevention' 22(3) *Crime and Delinquency* 284

Brown, JM (ed) (2013), *The Future of Policing* (London: Routledge)

Buerger, M (2010), 'Policing and Research: Two Cultures Separated by an Almost-common Language' 11(2) *Police Practice and Research* 135

Bullock, K and Tilley, N (2009), 'Evidence-based Policing and Crime Reduction' 3(4) *Policing* 381

Butler, Lord (1974), 'The Foundation of the Institute of Criminology in Cambridge' in Hood, R (ed), *Crime, Criminology and Public Policy: Essays in Honour of Sir Leon Radzinowicz* (London: Heinemann) 1

Cain, M (1973), *Society and the Policeman's Role* (London: Routledge and Keegan Paul)

CEPS (2007–2014), Centre of Excellence in Policing and Security, at <http://www.ceps.edu.au/home> (accessed 23 January 2015)

Chan, JB (1997), *Changing Police Culture: Policing in a Multicultural Society* (Cambridge: Cambridge University Press)

Clarke, RGV (1972), 'The Controlled Trial in Institutional Research: Paradigm or Pitfall for Penal Evaluators'?, Home Office Research Study No 15, HMSO, London

Clarke, RGV and Hough, M (1984), 'Crime and Police Effectiveness', Home Office Research Study No 79, HMSO, London

College of Policing (2013), 'About the What Works Centre', at <http://whatworks.college.police.uk/About/Pages/default.aspx> (accessed 14 April 2015)

College of Policing (2015), 'Police Knowledge Fund Open for Bids', at <http://www.college.police.uk/News/College-news/Pages/Police-Knowledge-Fund.aspx> (accessed 14 April 2015)

Cordner, G and White, S (2010), 'The Evolving Relationship between Police Research and Police Practice' 11(2) *Police Practice and Research* 90

Crawford, A (1999), *The Local Governance of Crime: Appeals to Community and Partnerships* (Oxford: OUP)

Davies, H, Laycock, G, Nutley, S, Sebba, J, and Sheldon, T (2000), 'A Strategic Approach to Research and Development' in Davies, H, Nutley, SM, and Smith, PC (eds), *What Works? Evidence-based Policy and Practice in Public Services* (Bristol: Policy Press) 229

Engel, R and Henderson, S (2013), 'Beyond Rhetoric: Establishing Police–Academic Partnerships that Work' in Brown, J (ed), *The Future of Policing* (London: Routledge), 217

Engel, RS and Whalen, JL (2010), 'Police–Academic Partnerships: Ending the Dialogue of the Deaf, the Cincinnati Experience' 11(2) *Police Practice and Research* 105

Fleming, J (2006), 'Working Through Networks: The Challenges of Partnership Policing' in Fleming, J and Wood, J (eds), *Fighting Crime Together: The Challenges of Policing and Security Networks* (Sydney: University of New South Wales Press) 87

Fleming, J (2010), 'Learning to Work Together: Police and Academics' 4(2) *Policing* 139

Fleming, J (2011), 'Qualitative Encounters in Policing Research' in Bartel, L and Richards, K (eds), *Qualitative Criminology: Stories from the Field* (Leichhardt, NSW: Federation Press) 13

Fleming, J (2012), 'Changing the Way We Do Business: Reflecting on Collaborative Practice' 13(3) *Police, Practice and Research* 375

Fleming, J and Wakefield, A (2009), 'Research' in Wakefield, A and Fleming, J (eds), *The Sage International Dictionary of Policing* (London: Sage) 269

Fosdick, RB (1920), *American Police Systems* (New York: The Century Co)

Fuld, LF (1909), *Police Administration* (New York: GP Putnam's Sons)

Fyfe, NR and Wilson, P (2012), 'Knowledge Exchange and Police Practice: Broadening and Deepening the Debate around Researcher-Practitioner Collaborations' 13(4) *Police Practice and Research* 306

Goldstein, H (1979), 'Improving Policing: A Problem-oriented Approach' 25(2) *Crime and Delinquency* 236

Goldstein, J (2003), 'On Further Developing Problem-oriented Policing' in Knuttson, J (ed), *Problem-oriented Policing: From Innovation to Mainstream: Crime Prevention Studies* 15 (London: Sage) 13

Graef, R (1989), *Talking Blues* (London: Collins Harvill)

Greene, JR (2014), 'New Directions in Policing: Balancing Prediction and Meaning in Research' 31(2) *Justice Quarterly* 193

Greenhalgh, T, Howick, J, and Maskrey, N (2014), 'Evidence Based Medicine: A Movement in Crisis?', at <http://www.bmj.com/content/bmj/348/bmj.g3725.full.pdf> (accessed 11 December 2014)

Guillaume, P, Sidebottom, A, and Tilley, N (2012), 'On Police and University Collaborations: A Problem-oriented Policing Case Study' 13(4) *Police Practice and Research* 389

Hart, J (1955), 'Reform of the Borough Police' 70 *English Historical Review* 411

Heidensohn, F (1992), *Women in Control* (Oxford: OUP)

Hodgkinson, GP (2012), 'The Politics of Evidence-based Decision-making' in Rousseau, DM (ed), *The Oxford Handbook of Evidence-Based Management* (Oxford: OUP) 404

Holdaway, S (1983), *Inside the British Police: A Force at Work* (Oxford: Blackwell)

Hoogenboom, B and Punch, M (2012), 'Developments in Police Research' in Newburn, T and Peay, J (eds), *Policing: Politics, Culture and Control* (Oxford and Portland, OR: Hart) 69

Hornung, S (2012), ' "Beyond New Scientific Management?" Critical Reflections on the Epistemology of Evidence-based Management' in Rousseau, DM (ed), *The Oxford Handbook of Evidence-based Management* (Oxford: OUP) 389

Innes, M (2006), 'Policing Uncertainty: Countering Terror through Community Intelligence and Democratic Policing' 605(1) *The Annals of the American Academy of Political and Social Science* 222

Jackson, J, Bradford, B, Hough, M, Myhill, A, Quinton, P, and Tyler, TR (2012), 'Why do People Comply with the Law? Legitimacy and the Influence of Legal Institutions' 52(6) *British Journal of Criminology* 1051

Johnson, J, Tilley, N, and Bowers, KJ (2015), 'Introducing EMMIE: An Evidence Rating Scale to Encourage Mixed-Method Crime Prevention Synthesis Reviews' *Journal of Experimental Criminology* (forthcoming)

Johnston, L (2000), *Policing Britain: Risk, Security and Governance* (Harlow: Longman)

Johnston, L and Shearing, C (2009), 'From a 'Dialogue of the Deaf' to a 'Dialogue of Listening': Towards a New Methodology of Policing Research And Practice' (Special issue: New Possibilities for Policing Research and Practice) 10(6) *Police Practice and Research* 415

Jones, T and Newburn, T (2002), 'The Transformation of Policing? Understanding Current Trends in Policing Systems' 42(1) *British Journal of Criminology* 129

Kelling, GL, Pate, T, Dieckman, D, and Brown, CE (1974), 'The Kansas City Preventive Patrol Experiment: A Summary Report', Police Foundation, Washington, DC

Klockars, CB (1988), 'The Rhetoric of Community Policing' in Greene, JR and Mastrofski, SD (eds), *Community Policing: Rhetoric or Reality* (New York: Praeger) 239

Knutsson, J (2010), 'Nordic Reflections on the Dialogue of the Deaf' 11(2) *Police Practice and Research* 132

Loader, I and Sparks, R (2011), *Public Criminology?* (London: Routledge)

Lodge, TS (1974), 'The Founding of the Home Office Research Unit' in Hood, R (ed), *Crime, Criminology and Public Policy: Essays in Honour of Sir Leon Radzinowicz* (London: Heinemann) 11

Lum, C (2012), 'The Evidence-based Policing Matrix: Translating and Using Research for Strategic and Tactical Interventions', Presentation to the Edinburgh Executive Policing Session, June

Lum, C, Telep, CW, Koper, CS, and Grieco, J (2012), 'Receptivity to Research in Policing' 14(1) *Justice, Research and Policy* 61

Lunt, N, Shaw, I, and Fouché, C (2010), 'Practitioner Research: Collaboration and Knowledge Production' 30(4) *Public Money and Management* 235

Macdonald, B (1986), 'Research and Action in the Context of Policing: An Analysis of the Problem and a Programme Proposal', unpublished, Police Foundation, London

Manning, PK (1978), 'The Police: Mandate, Strategies, and Appearances' in Manning, PK and Van Maanen, J (eds), *Policing: A View From The Street* (Santa Monica, CA: Goodyear) 7

Mark, R (1977), *Policing a Perplexed Society* (London: Allen & Unwin)

Mark, R, and Charlton, E (1978), *In the Office of Constable* (London: Collins)

Marks, M, Wood, J, Ally, F, Walsh, T, and Witbooi, A (2010), 'Worlds Apart? On the Possibilities of Police/Academic Collaborations' 4(2) *Policing* 112

Mazeika, D, Bartholomew, D, Distler, M, Thomas, K, Greenman, S, and Pratt, S (2010), 'Trends in Police Research: A Cross-sectional Analysis of the 2000–2007 Literature' 11(6) *Police Practice and Research* 520

McLaughlin, E (2007), *The New Policing* (London: Sage)

Moore, M (1995), 'Public Health and Criminal Justice Approaches To Prevention', in Tonry, M and Farrington, D (eds), *Building a Safer Society: Strategic Approaches to Crime Prevention* (Chicago IL: University of Chicago Press) 237

Moore, MH (2006), 'Improving Police through Expertise, Experience and Experiments' in Weisburd, D and Braga, AA (eds), *Police Innovation: Contrasting Perspectives* (Cambridge: Cambridge University Press) 322

Muir, WK (1979), *Police: Streetcorner Politicians* (Chicago, IL: University of Chicago Press)

Newburn, T (ed) (2005), *Policing: Key Readings* (Cullompton: Willan)

Newburn, T (ed) (2012 [2008]) *Handbook of Policing* (London and New York, Routledge)

Nutley, S, Walter, I, and Davies, H (2007), *Using Evidence: How Research can Inform Public Services* (Bristol: Policy Press)

Punch, M (2009), *Police Corruption* (Cullompton: Willan)

Punch, M (2010), 'Policing and Police Research in the Age of the Smart Cop' 11(2) *Police Practice and Research* 155

Radzinowicz, L (1956), *A History of the English Criminal Law and its Administration from 1750, Vol III: Cross Currents in the Movement For Reform of the Police* (London: Stevens)

Ratcliffe, JH (2010), 'Intelligence-led Policing: Anticipating Risk and Influencing Action' *Intelligence* 1, at <http://citeseerx.ist.psu.edu/viewdoc/download?doi=10.1.1.364.6795&rep=rep1&type=pdf> (accessed 14 April 2015)

Reiner, R (1978), *The Blue-Coated Worker*, (Cambridge: Cambridge University Press)

Reiner, R (2010), *Politics of the Police* (4th edn, Oxford: OUP)

Reiner, R (2015), 'Revisiting the Classics: Three Seminal Founders of the Study of Policing: Michael Banton, Jerome Skolnick and Egon Bittner' 25(3) *Policing and Society* 308

Reiss, AJ (1971), *The Police and the Public* (New Haven, CT: Yale University Press)

Reuss-Ianni, E (1983), *Street Cops and Management Cops: The Two Cultures of Policing* (New Brunswick, NJ: Transaction Publishers)

Rojek, J, Alpert, G, and Smith, H (2012), 'The Utilization of Research by Police' 13(4) *Police Practice and Research* 329

Shearing, CD, and Stenning, PC (1987), *Private Policing* (Newbury Park, CA: Sage)

Sheptycki, J (2000) (ed), *Issues in Transnational Policing* (London: Routledge)

Sherman, L (2011), 'Professional Policing and Liberal Democracy', The 2011 Benjamin Franklin Medal Lecture, Royal Society of Arts, November, at <http://www.thersa.org/__data/assets/pdf_file/0005/563027/Lawrence-Sherman-Speech-text-01.11.11.pdf> (accessed 11 December 2014)

Sherman, LW, Schmidt, JD, Rogan, DP et al (1992), 'The Variable Effects of Arrest on Criminal Careers: The Milwaukee Domestic Violence Experiment' 83 *Journal of Criminal Law and Criminology* 137

Silvestri, M (2007), '"Doing" Police Leadership: Enter the "New Smart Macho"' 17(1) *Policing and Society* 38

Skogan, W and Frydl, K (2004), *Fairness and Effectiveness in Policing: The Evidence* (Washington, DC: National Academies Press)

Skogan, WG (2006), *Police and Community in Chicago: A Tale of Three Cities* (Oxford: OUP)

Skolnick, JH (1966), *Justice Without Trial: Law Enforcement in Democratic Society* (New York: Wiley)

Sparrow, M (2011), 'Governing Science', New Perspectives in Policing, Harvard Kennedy School and National Institute of Justice, Cambridge, MA, January, at <https://www.ncjrs.gov/pdffiles1/nij/232179.pdf> (accessed 14 April 2015)

Thacher, D (2008), 'Research for the Front Lines' 18(1) *Policing and Society* 46

Tilley, N, and Webb, J (1994), 'Burglary Reduction: Findings from Safer Cities Schemes', Paper 51, Crime Prevention Unit, Home Office, London

Tyler, TR (1990), *Why People Obey the Law: Procedural Justice, Legitimacy, and Compliance* (New Haven, CT: Yale University Press)

Tyler, TR (2004), 'Enhancing Police Legitimacy' 593(1) *Annals of the American Academy of Political and Social Science* 84

Vollmer, A (1936), *The Police and Modern Society* (Berkeley, CA: University of California Press)

Waddington, PA (1994), *Liberty and Order: Public Order Policing in a Capital City* (Abingdon: Taylor & Francis)

Waddington, PA (1999), *Policing Citizens: Authority And Rights* (Abingdon: Psychology Press)

Webb, B, Brown, B, and Bennett, K (1992), 'Preventing Car Crime in Car Parks', Paper 34, Crime Prevention Unit, Home Office, London

Weisburd, D and Neyroud, P (2011), 'Police Science: Toward a New Paradigm', New Perspectives in Policing, Harvard Kennedy School and National Institute of Justice, Cambridge, MA, January, at <https://www.ncjrs.gov/pdffiles1/nij/228922.pdf> (accessed 14 April 2015)

Westley, W (1953), 'Violence and the Police' 59(1) *American Journal of Sociology*, 34

Westley, W (1970), *Violence and the Police* (Cambridge, MA: MIT Press)

Willis, JJ, and Mastrofski, SD (2014), 'Pulling Together: Integrating Craft and Science' 8(4) *Policing* 321

Wilson, JQ (1968) *Varieties of Police Behavior: The Management of Law and Order in Eight Communities* (Cambridge, MA: Harvard University Press)

Wilson, JQ (1983), *Thinking About Crime* (New York: Basic Books)

Wilson, JQ, and Kelling, GL (1982), 'Broken Windows' 249(3) *Atlantic monthly* 29

Wilson, OW (1950), *Police Administration* (New York: McGraw-Hill)

Wood, J, Fleming, J, and Marks, M (2008), 'Building the Capacity of Police Change Agents: The Nexus Policing Project' 18(1) *Policing and Society* 72

13

Change Leadership
The Application of Alternative Models in Structural Policing Changes

Nic Beech, Elizabeth Gulledge, and David Stewart

Introduction

It is commonplace in the current socio-economic climate for organizations to change their goals, structure, and processes in response to both internal and external circumstances. Particularly in the public sector, organizations increasingly face the task of delivering the same or a better level of performance on a significantly lower budget (Fernandez and Rainey 2006). Policing is no exception to some of the general trends in change (Hart 1996; Mastrofski and Willis 2010) and it faces demands for increased performance, accountability, and reduced costs (MacKenzie and Hamilton-Smith 2011). There is considerable debate over what constitutes effective leadership of change in policing (Campbell and Kodz 2011). Equally, the extent to which theories of change leadership developed with commercial or other public sector organizations as the empirical base are applicable to policing leadership is of current interest. In this chapter we identify three key themes in the change leadership literature and discuss insights from an analysis of leadership of the national police reform programme in Scotland. We conclude with a reflection on how the theories might be adapted to fit the demands of the policing context.

Transformational Change Leadership

Transformational change leadership was identified by Bass (1985), drawing on the analysis of questionnaire data produced by leaders. Transformational leadership was contrasted with transactional leadership. The former was initially identified as having three types of behaviour: idealized influence, intellectual stimulation, and individualized consideration. Idealized influence is a set of behaviours through which a leader expresses confidence in a clear vision, and displays a sense of purpose and determination. These behaviours can win respect and confidence on the part of others. Intellectual stimulation seeks to increase the awareness by others of issues and problems, and through the use of imagination and creativity enables them to see issues from a new perspective (Avolio and Bass 1990). Individualized consideration is the adoption of an engaged approach with followers, actively listening, being in close contact and adopting a coaching orientation. The subsequent revision of the theory (Bass and Avolio 1990) added a fourth behaviour: inspirational motivation, through which the leader communicates an attractive vision using symbolic means and role-modelling behaviour. The contrasting transactional leadership adopts a more instrumental approach, offering rewards contingent upon certain behaviours and a management of the exceptions (good and bad) through rewards and sanctions. A considerable amount of empirical research has followed the initial establishment of the theory. Survey research has been the most popular, and most surveys find a correlation between transformative leadership behaviours and effective change in organizations (see Yukl 2002 for an overview). The proponents of the transformative model argued that it was equally applicable in commercial and public organizations and this was reinforced by empirical research by Bennis and Nanus (1985), who conducted a five-year study of 60 leaders in commercial companies and 30 leaders in public sector organizations. Although the contexts were different, the more effective leaders of change displayed transformational behaviours, such as having and communicating a strong vision, stimulating trust from followers, and channelling collective action towards defined goals. Howell and House (1993), however, sound a note of caution. They argue that some change leaders may be 'pseudo-transformational', ie they have the appearance of transformational leadership but encourage an 'us and them' mentality, internal competitiveness, and hierarchical differentiation in the organization.

Rooke and Torbert (2005) argue that transformational change leadership is an umbrella term within which there are various action logics. In their study, the most common were 'experts' who lead change using logic and expertise and 'achievers' who were highly focused on, and enabled others to be focused on, strategic goals. These two groups accounted for 38% and 30%, respectively of their sample. Far less common (less than 5%) were leaders who had brought about identifiable social and personal transformation in their organizations, ie where change is identified as going beyond roles, structures, and tasks and into areas such as emotional engagement and new cultural understandings of internal and external identities, relationships (eg with clients, customers, or partners), and ways of being (eg a service orientation).

In their review of police leadership, Campbell and Kodz (2011) note that several studies have indicated that transformational leadership has had a positive impact on organizational commitment amongst followers. However, they also report that the contrasting transactional leadership approach, where there is a greater reliance on reward/punishment and an 'exchange orientation' to followers, unlike the findings reported in the general literature, shows some positive impacts in police studies. For example, it has been shown that subordinates may respect this style when it is used to deal with poor standards. Campbell and Kodz cite an Australian study (Densten 1999) in which satisfaction with police leaders amongst their officers was higher than levels of satisfaction reported in commercial organizations, even though the leadership style was more transactional than that of the business leaders. This may reflect the structural, 'classical organization theory' perspective taken in some of the police studies literature (Gaines and Worrall 2012), in which change leadership is discussed in terms of behavioural and contingency styles which pre-date transformational theories.

Lewin's (1951) classic force field model is an influential framework for understanding organizational change and this is compatible with both the transformational and transactional change leadership approaches. Lewin argued that it is important to recognize and work with forces for and against change. He proposed a three-step model in which change involves unfreezing current behaviour, moving to the new behaviour, and refreezing the new behaviour. Other similar approaches to change management have followed, identifying 'phases' of change and the 'processes' or methods needed to get to the desired state (eg Cumming and Huse 1989; Bullock and Batten 1985).

In a transformational approach, the change is directed through inspirational leadership towards a clear direction and vision. A change programme is set by senior managers, and followers and stakeholders are communicated with, inspired, and motivated. Change leadership is concentrated in the role and behaviour of either a single individual or possibly a top team. Decision-making happens at the top of the organization and, when effective, it can lead to increased performance of the organization, as followers are clear on what they should be doing and believe that it is a good way of progressing towards the purpose. A Lewin-like phased approach to change may be adopted, with vision setting and communication being followed by implementation and subsequent binding of new practices into the culture (Burnes and By 2012). However, in instances where the followers are unconvinced, especially where there is a perceived inconsistency between the content of communication and the behaviour of leaders, trust can be damaged and performance may be reduced, or be reliant on transactional forms of motivation.

Consultative-Dialogic Change Leadership

Especially in complex situations, it is difficult for a leader to have all the solutions. It may be the case that others are more knowledgeable, are more closely in touch with the perceptions of diverse stakeholders, and can see the situation through different eyes. Hence, leadership may focus not on 'selling' a clear and unifying vision, but instead on seeking to foster and capitalize on diversity. As Heifetz and Laurie (1997) put it: 'the work of the leader is to get conflict out into the open and use it as a source of creativity'. Conflict in this sense is not inter-personal, emotional, or simply political, as those forms of conflict are likely to lead to time being invested in attack and defence, blame and denial. Creative conflict is concerned with ideas, alternative perspectives, and asking new questions of established decision-making routines, principally through dialogue (Beech et al 2010). Hence, the role of the leader is to enable 'voice' to be exercised in dialogue which may enable people to pick up ideas from others, *challenge their own position*, and formulate action as a result. 'Voice' can be enabled in several ways. Open-ended or brainstorming discussions can be used when the issue or problem being addressed is new or unstructured. In situations where an issue is already well understood there may be different opinions on how to solve the problem, and the change leadership role may be to bring out the different opinions and structure them as options so that they can form the basis of a debate. Alternatively, it may be that several people have partial answers to a problem which can be adapted and incorporated into a hybrid solution through dialogue.

The consultative-dialogic view of change leadership sees dialogue not only as a form of interaction, but, much more fundamentally, as the basis for knowledge and social life in general, as people, events, and discourse gain meaning by their relation to others (Barge and Little 2002; Gergen 2009). Especially on important matters, dialogue may not be simply an exchange of ideas—it can be an engagement which substantiates, changes, or challenges people's place in the social structure. Something as apparently task-oriented as agreeing how to divide jobs amongst a team can result in people's professionalism or competence being implicitly lauded or called into question. Giving a person a particularly technical or demanding part of the job may mean that they have more work to do, but symbolically may mean that they are seen as the most competent or professional member of the team. Hence, as people interact about a change there is often an accompanying, unstated subtext in which the social and status hierarchies are being 'worked on' tacitly as claims and counter-claims are made. Such negotiated meanings are relative because a high position in the informal social structure only has meaning if there are other (lower) positions, and if this distinction is recognized by the members of the team. Similarly, visions of the future gain meaning by contrast with the past and with alternative future visions. Perceptions of the best direction of change gain meaning in contrast to different preferences.

Over the course of a dialogue, ideas may converge and diverge. Typically, there is a need for a degree of convergence to move into action, but to seek too much convergence too early is likely to compress the creative potential. Bakhtin's (1981) characterization of dialogue as centripetal (converging) or centrifugal (diverging) has been influential on the literature. Putnam and Fairhurst (2001) and Bebbington et al (2007) argue for a centripetal approach in which dialogue leads to building mutuality and an 'internalizing' perspective. A centripetal approach can be used when bringing together different ideas about how to address an issue. If people see their ideas being incorporated into the collective solution, they can naturally feel included and have ownership of the outcome. Conversely, Kornberger et al (2006) and Deetz (2003) see a centrifugal trajectory in dialogue as sometimes being necessary in order to challenge centralizing tendencies in favour of multiple understandings of events or situations. If a team has become so cohesive that they all think in the same way and adopt well-worn practices, sometimes there is an advantage in deliberately disrupting the normal approach in order to be open to alternatives which might be preferable, but which so far have not been recognized. This might be achieved by looking at examples from other police forces, or other organizations and businesses. It is rare that a practice from another organization could simply be transplanted in, but it is often the case that the 'foreign practice' can be used to stimulate questions, comparisons, and reflections that do not normally arise. Others have argued that genuine dialogical change entails phases of centrifugal and centripetal engagement (Beech et al 2010) as ideas and options open, develop, and then focus. In 'transformative dialogue' new knowledge is co-created by participants and hence action can be taken on a shared basis (Bohm, 1996). So it is not uncommon to start a change process with an initial phase of centrifugal dialogue to scope out the variety of understandings of the issues to be dealt with, a second centripetal phase to agree a definition of the change agenda, a third centrifugal phase to develop and explore options, and a fourth centripetal phase to decide on action.

Raelin (2012) has argued that in certain aspects of policing, particularly building police–community relations, a democratic style of leadership can be most effective in bringing about participatory, dialogical, organizational change. Here the change leadership would build in the overt views of stakeholders and also their 'tacit collective practices'—of which they may not be fully aware. Stimulating dialogue and deliberation are fundamental to enabling stakeholders to express their experiences and views, hence enabling professionals to understand the diverse constructions of their practice. Similarly, Gaines and Worrall (2012) argue that participatory approaches can be helpful, particularly in the areas of community policing and police–community collaboration, although they do not emphasize this approach with reference to other aspects of operational policing.

Critical to consultative-dialogic change leadership is the recognition of power relationships and varied interest groups internally and externally (Burnes 1996). Stakeholder analysis seeks to understand and map the relative power and interest of interest groups (Beech and MacIntosh 2011). In traditional approaches, the aim is to identify those external agents with greatest interest in the change and greatest power to influence its direction and then manage their perception, expectations, and influence (Rasche and Esser 2006). In more consultative approaches, the emphasis is on learning how stakeholders (both internal and external) understand the proposed change, and then taking their views into account as the change is planned. This latter stance assumes less ability to control the views and behaviour of stakeholders. This approach to stakeholder engagement deliberately increases the influence of groups who have 'less voice' and seeks areas of agreed value that could lead to mutual benefit.

Transformational change leadership theory focuses largely on the leader, his/her characteristics, and the impact on followers and the organization. By contrast, the consultative-dialogic approach to change leadership focuses on *process* rather than individuals. Leadership is exercised through establishing and maintaining a dialogical process in which stakeholders can take part in shaping the understanding of the change and defining the actions to be taken. A change programme in this mode may use particular techniques to incorporate 'user needs', employee views, and other stakeholders (eg public consultation) (Morrey et al 2013) or to develop new organizational systems (Hines et al 2004; Davis 2014). Techniques to elicit user or stakeholder views can include the use of questionnaires, interviews, user storytelling, and structured focus groups. The change strategy is regarded as emergent and a result of process rather than being set from the top. This approach is typically applied in pluralistic situations when different views exist in a culture and need to be taken into account (Smollan 2006) and/or when there is benefit to be gained from change leaders having greater insight into the views of staff who are 'closer to the customer' (Edmonds 2011). Such forms of change leadership have been applied increasingly in the public sector (MacIntosh et al 2012) where there are multiple stakeholders and multiple forms of knowledge amongst the workforce.

Dispersed Change Leadership

Dispersed change leadership challenges traditional ideas about leadership. The focus is not on a leader but rather on *activities* of leadership, which may be carried out by a variety of people in different roles. Change is led in a distributed way when staff at a variety of levels can take decisions and enact them (Currie and Lockett 2011) and a corporate activity is needed in order to achieve coordination between the actions (Gronn 2002). This entails a flow of power away from the centre outwards throughout the organization as it changes, and in some cases power is distributed further outside the organizational boundaries (Blackler 2006), as has sometimes been the case in healthcare change when patient groups have taken on the role of devising the desired outcomes of change. Ideas are generated locally and change is typically a process of spreading learning around the organization. This can be done through locally led good-practice exchange workshops, peer-to-peer mentoring, or joint problem-solving activities. Stakeholders (internal and external) are normally involved in analysis and influencing decisions, and change is regarded as continuous. This approach is typically taken in knowledge-based organizations, often in challenging and change-oriented environments, and decisions are taken throughout the organization.

Change leadership, in the sense of framing activity, can also be influenced by the 'material' of the culture (Fenwick and Landri 2012), in which tools, facilities, and systems influence what people can and cannot do. The material of the culture includes things used to do the job such as uniforms, cars, bicycles, horses, radios, and communication devices. These materials influence how the job is done and how changes of leadership can be conducted. For example, a mass communication from the leader to all staff could be made simultaneously if everyone has a communication device capable of receiving it, otherwise it is easy to inadvertently include some and exclude others. Similarly, systems can have a material impact on how jobs are done. An accounting system may enable or disable particular forms of governance and transparency of questioning, or a performance management system may orient behaviour in a particular direction (both positively in engendering certain performances and negatively in encouraging the disguising of other behaviour).

Bolden et al (2011) have traced a considerable growth in the literature on distributed change leadership. Approaches focus either on individual agency or on social systems design which deliberately disperse leadership practices away from the top/centre of organizations. Hence, this offers what is claimed as a new unit of analysis (Gronn 2002), which pays analytic attention to the whole organization or system rather than just the leader. Much of the literature reviewed by Bolden et al (2011) expects distributed change leadership to be effective in knowledge-intensive and professional organizations; however, the majority of empirical studies are in education, with a greater volume in the United States than elsewhere. A question remains, therefore, as to whether or not such an approach may be applicable in policing.

Choices about approach often reflect the culture and assumptions of the senior management. For example, whether perceived speed is significant, how much and how strong opposition might be, to what extent useful knowledge may be distributed around the organization and/or beyond it with other stakeholders, and whether change is understood as a one-off project, or a continuous process. Some research in both public and private sectors indicates that organizations are moving more towards a consultative-dialogic approach, with a dispersed approach being favoured in some knowledge-intensive settings, particularly education. Top-down change leadership has been criticized for leading to high perceived failure rates (eg Burnes and Jackson (2011) claim, on the basis of an extensive literature review, that 70% of such change initiatives fail) and taking a considerable period of time to 'bed in' after initial implementation. However, it still occurs in the private sector, particularly where immediate change is required, for example when downsizing and planning redundancies, and in the public sector where there is a political imperative or public perception that an immediate problem needs to be solved (Higgs and Rowlands 2005). In such cases, change leadership may need to emphasize communication and interaction so that opposing views are understood and engaged in dialogue where possible. Failure to achieve this can lead to longer-term consequences for the morale of the organization and its culture (Woodward and Hendry 2004).

In summary, the alternative theories of change leadership offer choices. Transformational approaches are top-down and, unlike transactional styles, seek to inspire, to be visionary, and to exemplify the behaviours that are needed from followers. A consultative-dialogic approach may see phases of divergent and convergent dialogue in which the leader seeks to expand the pool of opinion or ideas, frame discussions, and converge towards action. The dispersed model takes this a step further, envisaging aspects of the leadership role being undertaken by people at different hierarchical levels and in different jobs in the organization. This can be a very empowering approach but it can also 'give away' some of the leader's ability to direct or set the vision. This may raise particular problems in some cultures of policing (Fyfe et al 2013; Fyfe 2014). In the next section we explore change leadership during a major structural change in policing in Scotland. The timescale of the change, the personal style of the leader, and the cultural setting had a significant influence on the form of change leadership adopted.

Practitioner's Perspective

In 30 years of policing, it is difficult to think of a time when change was not present to some extent. New legislation or practices routinely develop and result in 'tweaks' in processes. Most police forces in the United Kingdom have undergone more significant levels of change, from mergers of Divisions to reductions in officer or support staff numbers and, accordingly, many people in policing circles refer to change as being almost a constant in their organization.

During the course of a full police career, the focus on change alters as, from a police constable 'subject' to change, you become a senior officer and are responsible for the change itself, or at the very least for leading a team of people through the process of change. Police officers are taught at a very early stage that they need to be leaders in a more informal way and deal with incidents, ranging from the routine to the very serious, on a day-to-day basis. Thus, whether they are dealing with a minor crime or policing a football match or demonstration, they need to demonstrate principles of leadership and decision-making, the qualities that separate policing from many other occupations and make it such a rewarding profession. However, arguably the main difference between these routine aspects of leadership in policing and those of leading through periods of change is the need to think long term.

As the police Silver Commander in the immediate aftermath of the terrorist attack on Glasgow Airport in 2007, my immediate focus was on making it through the first hour with a semblance of command and control. Even thereafter the focus was on the next 24 hours and the re-opening of the airport to passengers. As the Programme Manager for the National Police Reform Programme (NPRP) that saw the merger of the ten Scottish policing organizations into the new single Police Service of Scotland, my focus had to be not only on delivering every element of the change but also on 'making it stick'.

In the previous section of this chapter, three main approaches to leadership were considered through change, and some of the more generic models and theories regarding change management were discussed. In this section of the chapter, I consider my experience as a Divisional Commander, although primarily as the Programme Manager for the NPRP in Scotland and my experience of the challenges of leading though periods of significant change.

Change leadership models in the policing context

The change theories addressed earlier all have a similarity in that there is a driver to create the change, followed by some activity to make change happen, and followed by the 'normalizing' of the new way of operating. Lewin's model describes the need to unfreeze, change, and then re-freeze to make the change permanent. In my experience, there is always a keen desire to 'unfreeze' and plenty of willingness to change, but by far and away the most difficult aspect is that of re-freezing.

In the context of the NPRP, a reduction in funding from the UK government to the Scottish government resulted in a need to deliver significant budget savings within the Scottish public sector, and this was the driver to 'unfreeze'. After some work to consider options, the proposal to create a single force was identified as the preferred option and the National Police Reform Team (NPRT) was established to deliver this aspect of the change. Full use was made of traditional programme and project management to ensure that the merger was implemented by the legislative date of 1 April 2013. That element was acknowledged as being the single largest public sector change programme in Scotland and the United Kingdom, and the challenges of delivering the change within the time scales set were considerable. However, on 1 April 2013, the new single service was formally in place. However, making that change 'stick' is something that will take much longer. The project savings targets were significant—£190m in three years and £1.4bn over 15 years—and the changes required to deliver that scale of saving will be significant and ongoing—therefore the final process of the change will be the most challenging aspect. In my experience, there are a number of key themes that are crucial in leading change in policing that will provide the best basis for making the change stick.

Leadership and vision

Although this book is about leadership, there is no doubt that a strong leader with a clear vision for a future state is crucial to delivering change in a policing context.

Within the NPRP, the first Chief Constable of the new Service, Sir Stephen House, was only appointed 6 months before the creation of the legal entity of Police Scotland. For the 12 months prior to that point, the NPRP had been managed through the committee structure of the Association of Chief Police Officers in Scotland (ACPOS). While the formal change programme had been established and teams were working on options for implementation of, for example, the new Divisional structure or the new CID structure, members of the ACPOS Committee of existing Chief Officers of the Legacy Forces were reluctant to make final decisions on the basis that the yet-to-be-appointed first chief constable would have his/her own firm views on how they wanted the organization to be structured. As such, the delivery of the actual change was unable to move forward to the implementation stage for some time.

Within days of the appointment of Chief Constable Sir Stephen House, he had made decisions on a number of options that allowed progress to be made. A further decision was to chair the 'Design Authority', which was the decision-making body on all the internal change proposals. It was initially assumed that the Chief Constable would chair perhaps one or two of these weekly meeting to show his support of the process; however, he subsequently chaired every one of the meetings for the following six months.

At each of these meetings the Chief Constable provided a clear vision to all of those presenting proposals, of what was expected. This in turn provided support for those involved at all levels of delivering the change, in that they were acting with the mandate of the Chief Constable, and the impact of this empowerment cannot be overstated. From a purely personal perspective, the drive, determination, and vision of the Chief Constable was the difference between the NPRP succeeding or failing.

This would suggest that there is merit in the transformational approach to leadership through change, certainly in a policing context where we are used to a command-and-control driven top-down approach. Whilst it would be hoped that in a mature organization, either the consultative or dispersed approach would be taken, the reality from my experience is that in a change programme that is significantly time-bound, and where clear progress needs to be delivered and maintained, a transformational approach through firm leadership will provide the best chance of success.

Stakeholder relations

Within the context of the NPRP, the impact of stakeholder relationships in the delivery of change was significant. Figure 13.1 outlines very simply the stakeholder environment within the NPRP.

While the Chief Constable was the final arbiter of decisions regarding change options internally, the newly created Scottish Police Authority enjoyed an oversight role and, ultimately, the Scottish government also had a significant interest. While the Chief Constable was responsible for building relationships at that

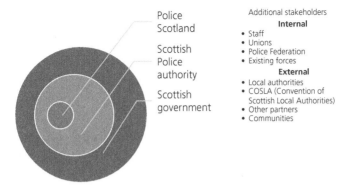

Police
Scotland

Scottish
Police
authority

Scottish
government

Additional stakeholders
Internal
- Staff
- Unions
- Police Federation
- Existing forces

External
- Local authorities
- COSLA (Convention of Scottish Local Authorities)
- Other partners
- Communities

Figure 13.1 Stakeholder Environment within the NPRP

executive level, my own role brought me into regular contact with the officials of the Police Authority and civil servants within the Scottish government. The ability of these individuals to influence their own executive leads was crucial, and it was therefore vital that I ensured that they were fully aware and informed of progress or obstacles. Developing strong links also ensured that my own executive leads were given early warning of nervousness or uncertainty from these stakeholders. The relationship with internal stakeholders was also crucial, and the key to success in this was communication.

Communication

If external stakeholder relations are crucial to the success of any change programme in policing, then internal communications are absolutely critical. In policing, the vast majority of the annual budget is spent on salaries and it is therefore not uncommon to hear senior officers talk about policing being 'about its people'. During a transformational change programme, however, the challenge is to make this rhetoric a reality.

Within the NPRP, relationships had become strained between the central NPRT and the eight legacy forces, each of which, until the legal date of merger, had their own chief constables and internal structures. The perception of the forces was that the change was being driven centrally without sufficient consultation and communication. It was vital that each force was aware of the proposals and, more importantly, what impact these would have on their officers and staff. In addition, even within the NPRP itself, different project teams were not communicating well with each other, resulting in a silo approach. Much of this was the result of the pace of change and the pressure on those involved in each separate project to complete their tasks. This is where programme management becomes vital in supporting the delivery of change, and the role of the programme manager is to ensure that time is taken to bring the various project teams together to ensure they understand that their own areas of work are part of a larger entity.

On my arrival as Programme Manager, I had instigated a review of communications, and within weeks a re-vamped communications strategy had been implemented. This resulted in a number of activities, including:

- daily updates to the NPRP intranet site;
- a fortnightly 'Change' newsletter, with a personal message from the Chief Constable on the front page;
- weekly project manager meetings;
- weekly legacy force transition team meetings that I chaired personally;
- weekly line manager briefings—key messages for all line managers in the legacy forces to deliver to their staff;
- as the new Force Executive took up interim roles, regular visits across the country to brief staff personally on proposed changes; and
- webchat sessions with members of the interim Force Executive.

In order to address the potential problems of silo working within the programme, I held monthly 'dependency workshops' where each project team had time with every other project team to go through the specifics of their own plans and to identify gaps or areas where one team was dependent upon the other or where their plans potentially impacted upon another area. There are elements of the dispersed change leadership model that could be likened to this process; however, the reality during the NPRP was that there were simply things that good management required to be done, as opposed to being driven by academic theory. There is one final area that my experience in leading through the NPRP taught me was crucial, and that goes back to the point about a police organization only being as good as its people.

People

There are two aspects to this area that I think are important. First, change in policing takes place at the same time as continuing to deliver a service to the public and communities. In any significant period of change, morale must be carefully monitored. In the NPRP, police officer jobs were not at risk but those of police staff were. There is a danger of a 'them and us' attitude coming to the fore between sworn officers and the staff who support, and are vital to, policing operations. There is no easy way around this; sometimes it is very hard to deliver unpopular messages, but the mark of a true leader is that he or she can do so in an open, honest, and transparent way to the people upon whom the change will impact.

The second crucial people aspect relates to those who are involved in delivering the change. The NPR Team comprised 14 separate project teams, supported by a central Programme Management Office and Change team. As stated earlier, I assumed the role of Silver Commander in the immediate aftermath of the Glasgow Airport terror attack in 2007, which resulted in a 24-hour period of stress and pressure unlike any I had ever experienced in my police service at that time. However, that stress and pressure paled into insignificance when compared to the last six months of the NPRP, and the pressure continued to grow as the 1 April 2013 merger came closer. There was not a single member of my team who did not feel the same pressure, and it is vital for the person responsible for leading in any change task to appreciate the pressure their team is under.

The important word in that last sentence is 'team' and it is interesting to consider the commentary in the first section of this chapter about the consultative-dialogue method of change leadership. I have always subscribed to the principle that I have never had the franchise on good ideas and that, without the right team around me and supporting me (at all points in my service), progress would stall. This was evident in the Glasgow Airport incident but was even more important in the longer-term NPRP. Again, the consultative dialogue model suggests the benefit of 'process' and there was process a-plenty within a formal programme and project structure, but by far the most important aspect was the people who delivered for me. Without that team and their dedication and resilience, 1 April 2013 would not have come and gone so smoothly.

The result?

At midnight on 31 March, I sat with my team at the 'Day 1 Help Desk' we had created to provide support during the transition to the new single service. Given that there were 25,000 employees, over a 12-day period, the Help Desk received only 73 calls, all of which were about minor issues. By 1 April we had created and implemented a new divisional structure, reducing from the previous 24 to 14. We had delivered a National Major Investigation Team, a National Trunk Roads Patrol Group, and a variety of other national units and departments. We had created a new intranet as well as a new internet site and had merged eight separate email systems into one. Most importantly, the public of Scotland saw no material difference—at 10 past midnight on 1 April, if they called the police, they received the same response as the day before. Day 1 was, however, only that and the change programme in Police Scotland continues apace and is likely to do so for some years still, and it will therefore be some time before, in Lewin's terms, change will stop and become re-frozen as part of the organization.

Reminder of key lessons

- Have a clear vision for what you want to achieve and how you will get there— and if there is someone above you in the rank structure, seek out the vision and the autonomy to implement it.
- Engage with your external stakeholders and identify those who can help to smooth the way for your changes.
- Communicate clearly and effectively within the organization. Morale will undoubtedly suffer, but you can minimize the impact by telling the right people the right things at the right times.

- Develop your team—use their skills, knowledge, and experience and trust in them to support your vision, but always remember the impact that the stress of a challenging change programme can have on that delivery team.

Relevance of academic literature

Writing this section has been an illuminating experience. Within the NPRP we undertook research, supported by the Scottish Institute for Policing Research, to establish good practice elsewhere in the United Kingdom and beyond. However, within the NPRP the focus fell more on the processes that had been adopted elsewhere as opposed to any academic theories surrounding leadership through change.

The theories and models discussed in the first section of this chapter make perfect sense; however, the reality is that time and resource constraints, along with the established culture, may mean that the options for the style of change leadership adopted may not be open-ended. Some of this will simply be as a result of the police 'can do' culture, which is a mix of experience and a determination to deliver. There is no doubt that academic literature can be extremely useful, although much of the academic work around change management will be seen as being overly ethereal and, for experienced police managers used to evidence-based decision-making, a focus on a 'case study' type of academic support may be more valuable, and has worked well before in other policing change programmes. Provision of such firm, evidence-based research providing tangible examples would, at the very least, encourage those involved in significant change in policing, to consider the benefit of academic support to deliver successful and lasting change.

Shared Reflections

Although the current trends in change leadership in commercial organizations may be more towards consultative-dialogic forms, and in some parts of the public sector (eg parts of the health service (Currie and Lockett, 2011)) towards dispersed change leadership, the change experience in Scotland, as discussed, was closest to the transformational approach. This was informed partly by very tight time constraints for the extent of change planned and the resource limitations, but also, and perhaps most importantly, by the extant culture which favoured a more top-down style. In the structural change in Scotland, Sir Stephen House adopted a clear vision and maintained the drive towards it consistently. Similarly, David Stewart adopted the same broad principles in the role he played in leading the Scottish change and in previous examples. However, the examples discussed raise an issue that is less obvious in the current literature on transformational leadership. There are choices about how the leader spends his or her time, and these choices can hold significant symbolic value. In the case just cited, the fact of the leader attending all the design authority meetings, and being hands-on, was crucial. This choice carries opportunity costs, and it is rather different to the ideational leadership which is normally part of transformational change leadership, but here, such choices showed a strong fit with the police culture and enabled a practical orientation for all involved.

In the examples, stakeholder management was significant. There are both formal and informal aspects to this. The formal included consultation and the involvement of statutory and representative bodies. In addition, however, there was a degree of subtlety and nuance which are not normally stressed in the literature. Effective change leaders in this case were able to learn of stakeholders' 'nervousness' and 'uncertainty'. These are things which may not be expressed in stakeholder meetings but might be picked up in the corridors and coffee rooms once there is sufficient trust between the change leader and the stakeholder representatives. In some cases, the change leader was able to learn directly from the stakeholder, but in others the information came through members of the change team. Thus, the challenge for the change leader is to have good enough relations with those people who report to him/her such that they feel able and willing to pass on 'early warnings'.

The model that operated in practice was closest to the transformational form; however, the style of operation included some elements, or flavours, of other models. Communication was central to the change example discussed earlier and it operated by the leader being in close personal touch with the team who were delivering the change. Regular connection is part of the consultative-dialogic model, which seeks to incorporate changes to the direction from the input of team members. Clear leadership, rather than being dogmatic and inflexible, can entail degrees of flexibility and the uncovering of practical steps to the future which may not have been envisaged by the leader. It also involves acknowledging the emotions and stresses of change and being able to support the team as they go through the experience (Asnawi et al 2014).

It is sometimes argued that the alternative models of change leadership are incompatible; for example, a genuinely bottom-up approach cannot incorporate top-down direction without seriously compromising its ethos. However, we have argued elsewhere (Beech and MacIntosh 2012) that hybridity is possible. It can occur at different phases of change—for example, starting in consultative mode and then moving into a transformational phase around an agreed set of object-ives—or it can occur by adopting practices of change leadership to reflect other styles, as in the cases discussed here. Transformational change leadership may fit more naturally with some versions of the police culture; however, the model can benefit from the incorporation of some elements of dialogical orientation during implementation. A key change leadership skill is the ability to judge how much of a blend will work best in any given situation.

Recommended Reading

Beech, N and MacIntosh, R (2012), *Managing Change* (Cambridge: Cambridge University Press)

Fyfe, NR (2014), 'A Different and Divergent Trajectory? Reforming the Structure, Governance and Narrative of Policing in Scotland' in Brown, J (ed), *The Future of Policing: Papers Prepared for the Stevens Independent Commission into the Future of Policing in England and Wales* (London: Routledge) 493

Fyfe, NR, Terpstra, J, And Tops, P (eds) (2013), *Centralizing Forces? Comparative Perspectives on Contemporary Police Reform in Northern and Western Europe* (The Hague: Boom Legal Publishers Eleven)

References

Asnawi, NH, Yunus, NH, and Razak, NA (2014), 'Assessing Emotional Intelligence Factors and Commitment towards Organizational Change' 4(1) *International Journal of Social Science and Humanity* 5

Avolio, BJ and Bass, BM (1990), *Basic Workshop in Full Range Leadership Development* (Binghamton, NY: Bass, Avolio and Associates)

Bakhtin, MM (1981), *The Dialogical Imagination: Four Essays* (Holquist, M (ed)) (Austin, TX: University of Texas Press)

Barge, JK, and Little, M (2002), 'Dialogical Wisdom, Communicative Practice, and Organizational Life' 12 *Communication Theory* 365

Bass, BM (1985), *Leadership and Performance Beyond Expectations* (New York: Free Press)

Bass, BM and Avolio, BJ (1990), 'The Implications of Transactional and Transformational Leadership for Individual, Team, and Organizational Development' in Pasmore, W and Woodman, RW (eds), *Research in Organizational Change and Development*, Vol 4 (Greenwich, CT: JAI Press) 231

Bebbington, KJ, Brown, J, Frame, B, and Thomson, I (2007), 'Theorizing Engagement: the Potential of a Critical Dialogic Approach' 20(3) *Accounting, Auditing and Accountability Journal* 356

Beech, N and MacIntosh, R (2011), 'Practices of Stakeholder Engagement and Identity' in Boje, D, Burnes, B, and Hassard, J (eds), *The Routledge Companion to Organizational Change* (London: Routledge) 456

Beech, N and MacIntosh, R (2012), *Managing Change* (Cambridge: Cambridge University Press)

Beech, N, MacIntosh, R, and MacLean, D (2010), 'Dialogues between Academics and Practitioners: The Role of Generative Dialogic Encounters' 31(9) *Organization Studies* 1341

Bennis, WG and Nanus, B (1985), *Leaders: The Strategies for Taking Charge* (New York: Harper and Row)

Blackler, FHM (2006), Chief Executives and the Modernisation of the English National Health Services 2(1) *Leadership* 5

Bohm, D (1996), *On Dialogue* (NewYork: Routledge)

Bolden, R, Hawkins, B, Gosling, J, and Taylor, S (2011), *Exploring Leadership* (Oxford: OUP)

Bullock, R, and Batten, D (1985), 'It's Just a Phase We Are Going Through: A Review and Synthesis of OD Phase Analysis' 10 *European Group and Organisational Studies* 383

Burnes, B (1996), 'No Such Thing as . . . a "One Best Way" to Manage Organizational Change' 34(10) *Management Decision* 11

Burnes, B and By, RT (2012), 'Leadership and Change: The Case for Greater Ethical Clarity' 108(2) *Journal of Business Ethics* 239

Burnes, B and Jackson, P (2011), 'Success and Failure in Organizational Change' 11(2) *Journal of Change Management* 133

Campbell, I and Kodz, J (2011), 'What Makes Great Police Leadership? What Research Can Tell Us About the Effectiveness of Different Leadership Styles, Competencies and Behaviours. A Rapid Evidence Review', National Policing Improvement Agency, London

Cummings, T and Huse, E (1989), *Organization Development and Change* (St Paul, MN: West Publishing Co)

Currie, G and Lockett, A (2011), 'Distributing Leadership in Health and Social Care: Concertive, Conjoint or Collective?' 13 *International Journal of Management Reviews* 286

Davis, K (2014), 'Different Stakeholder Groups and their Perceptions of Project Success' 32(2) *International Journal of Project Management* 189

Deetz, SA (2003), 'Reclaiming the Legacy of the Linguistic Turn' 10 *Organization* 421

Densten, I (1999), 'Senior Australian Law Enforcement Leadership under Examination' 22(1) *Policing* 47

Edmonds, J (2011), 'Managing Successful Change' 43(6) *Industrial and Commercial Training* 349

Fenwick, T and Landri, P (2012), 'Materialities, Textures and Pedagogies: Sociomaterial Assemblages in Education' 20(1) *Pedagogy, Culture and Society* 1

Fernandez, S and Rainey, HG (2006), 'Managing Successful Organisational Change in the Public Sector' 66(2) *Public Administration Review*, 168

Fyfe, NR, Terpstra, J, and Tops, P (eds) (2013), *Centralizing Forces? Comparative Perspectives on Contemporary Police Reform in Northern and Western Europe* (The Hague: Boom Legal Publishers Eleven)

Fyfe, NR (2014), 'A Different and Divergent Trajectory? Reforming the Structure, Governance and Narrative of Policing in Scotland', in Brown, J (ed), *The Future of Policing: Papers Prepared for the Stevens Independent Commission into the Future of Policing in England and Wales* (London: Routledge) 493

Gaines, LK and Worrall, JL (2012), *Police Administration* (3rd edn, Clifton Park, NY: Delmar)

Gergen, KJ (2009), *Relational Being* (Oxford: OUP)

Gronn, P (2002), 'Distributed Leadership' in Leithwood, K and Hallinger, P (eds), *Second International Handbook of Educational Leadership and Administration* (Dordrecht: Kluwer) 653

Hart, JM (1996), 'The Management of Change in Police Organizations' in Pagon, M (ed), *Policing in Central and Eastern Europe: Comparing Firsthand Knowledge with Experience from the West* (Ljubljana, Slovenia: College of Police and Security Studies) 199

Heifetz, RA and Laurie, DL (1997), 'The Work of Leadership' 75(1) *Harvard Business Review* 124

Higgs, M, and Rowlands, D (2005), 'All Changes Great and Small: Exploring Approaches to Change and Its Leadership' 5(2) *Journal of Change Management* 121

Hines, P, Holweg, M, and Rick, N (2004), 'Learning to Evolve: A Review of Contemporary Lean Thinking' 24(10) *International Journal of Operations and Production Management* 994

Howell, JM and House, RJ (1993), *Socialized and Personalized Charisma* (London, ON: University of Western Ontario Press)

Kornberger, M, Clegg, S, and Carter, C (2006), 'Rethinking the Polyphonic Organization: Managing as Discursive Practice' 22(1) *Scandinavian Journal of Management* 3

Lewin, K (1951), *Field Theory in Social Science* (New York: Harper and Row)

MacIntosh, R, Beech, N, and Martin, G (2012), 'Dialogues and Dialetics: Limits to Clinician–Manager Interaction in Healthcare Organizations' 74(3) *Social Science and Medicine* 332

MacKenzie, S and Hamilton-Smith, N (2011), 'Measuring Police Impact on Organised Crime: Performance Management and Hard Reduction' 34(1) *Policing* 7

Mastrofski, SD and Willis, JT (2010), 'Police Organization Continuity and Change: Into the Twenty-first Century' in Tonry, M (ed), *Crime and Justice: A Review of Research*, Vol 39 (Chicago, IL: University of Chicago Press) 55

Morrey, N, Pasquire, C, and Dainty, A (2013), 'Developing a Strategy to Enact Lean' 3(1) *Journal of Engineering, Project and Production Management* 35

Putnam, LL and Fairhurst, GT (2001), 'Discourse Analysis in Organizations' in Jablinm, FM and Putnam, L (eds), *The New Handbook of Organizational Communication* (London: Sage) 235

Raelin, JA (2012), 'Dialogue and Deliberation as Expressions of Democratic Leadership in Participatory Organizational Change' 25(1) *Journal of Organizational Change Management* 7

Rasche, A and Esser, DE (2006), 'From Stakeholder Management to Stakeholder Accountability' 65(3) *Journal of Business Ethics* 251

Rooke, D and Torbert, WR (2005), 'Seven Transformations of Leadership' 83(4) *Harvard Business Review* 66

Smollan, R (2006), 'Minds, Hearts and Deeds: Cognitive, Affective and Behavioural Responses to Change' 6(2) *Journal of Change Management* 143

Woodward, S and Hendry, C (2004), 'Leading and Coping with Change' 4(2) *Journal of Change Management* 155

Yukl, G (2002), *Leadership in Organizations* (Upper Saddle River, NJ: Prentice Hall)

General Index

n = footnote. *t* = table/diagram.

Names Index

Lightning Source UK Ltd.
Milton Keynes UK
UKOW06f2204040815

256375UK00001B/1/P